Design Driven Testing

Test Smarter, Not Harder

Matt Stephens
Doug Rosenberg

Design Driven Testing: Test Smarter, Not Harder

ISBN 978-1-4302-2943-8

ISBN 978-1-4302-2944-5 (eBook)

President and Publisher: Paul Manning
Lead Editor: Jonathan Gennick
Technical Reviewer: Jeffrey Kantor and David Putnam
Editorial Board: Clay Andres, Steve Anglin, Mark Beckner, Ewan Buckingham, Gary Cornell, Jonathan Gennick, Jonathan Hassell, Michelle Lowman, Matthew Moodie, Duncan Parkes, Jeffrey Pepper, Frank Pohlmann, Douglas Pundick, Ben Renow-Clarke, Dominic Shakeshaft, Matt Wade, Tom Welsh
Coordinating Editor: Anita Castro
Copy Editor: Mary Ann Fugate
Compositor: MacPS, LLC
Indexer: BIM Indexing & Proofreading Services
Artist: April Milne
Cover Designer: Anna Ishchenko

Distributed to the book trade worldwide by Springer Science+Business Media, LLC, 233 Spring Street, 6th Floor, New York, NY 10013. Phone 1-800-SPRINGER, fax (201) 348-4505, e-mail orders-ny@springer-sbm.com, or visit www.springeronline.com.

For information on translations, please e-mail rights@apress.com, or visit www.apress.com.

Apress and friends of ED books may be purchased in bulk for academic, corporate, or promotional use. eBook versions and licenses are also available for most titles. For more information, reference our Special Bulk Sales–eBook Licensing web page at www.apress.com/info/bulksales.

Contents at a Glance

Contents

Foreword

As program manager for ESRI's ArcGIS mapping software product, Jim is responsible for a daily build of 20 million lines of code. He previously managed the transportation and logistics department for ESRI Professional Services, where he brought many multi-million–dollar software projects in on-schedule and on-budget using the design techniques described in this book.

Lots of people have many strong opinions on virtually all aspects of testing software. I've seen or heard of varied methodologies, systems, procedures, processes, patterns, hopes, prayers, and simple dumb luck that some code paths will never get executed. With all this help, we must have figured out how to ship outstanding rock-solid bug-less software, right? Yet, with each new release of the next great, most stable revision of our software products, test engineers still make that wincing face (you know the one), drawing back a little when asked, "Do you have the appropriate tests across the entire software stack?"

The wincing exists because the truthful answer to that question is almost always: "I think so, but I don't really know all the areas I should have had tests for." And the software shipped anyway, didn't it—bummer. This is job security for the technical support team, because the bugs shipped out will be coming right back to your team for the next service pack or emergency hot fix. We can do much better, and this book will show you how.

This book walks you through a proven software development process called ICONIX Process, and focuses on the creation and maintenance of both unit and acceptance tests based on and driven by the software design. This is design-driven testing (DDT). This is leveraging your design to pinpoint where critical tests need to be based on the design and object behavior. This is not test-driven design (TDD), where unit tests are written up front, before design is complete and coding starts. I don't know about you, but I think it's hard to predict the future, and even harder to get a software engineer to code something that "fits" a set of tests.

While lots of folks have opinions about testing, one thing that I think we can all agree upon is that testing is often very hard and complex. As a program manager for a large development team, I know how quickly testing can get out of hand, or just stall out on a development project. Organizations have so much variance in the investment in testing, and, unfortunately, in the return on that investment. It's possible to do way too much testing, thus wasting investment. But it's more likely that you will do too little testing (thinking you did more than enough, of course), in the wrong areas of the software, not investing enough. This can happen because you just don't know where the tests need to be to balance your investments, yielding the right testing coverage.

This book shows how to achieve this balance and optimize the return on your testing investment by designing and building a real web mapping application. Using ICONIX process and DDT makes very clear precisely what tests are needed and where they need to be. Moreover, many of these tests will be automatically generated for you by the tools used (in this case, Enterprise Architect from Sparx Systems), which, in addition to being just super cool, has huge value for your project. So, if you need to build great software using an agile process where your tests are practically generated for free, this book is for you.

Jim McKinney
ArcGIS Program Manager, Esri

About the Authors

 **Matt Stephens** is a software consultant with financial organizations in Central London, and founder of independent book publisher Fingerpress (www.fingerpress.co.uk). He has written for a bunch of magazines and websites including The Register and Application Development Trends. Find him online at Software Reality (http://articles.softwarereality.com).

 **Doug Rosenberg** founded ICONIX (www.iconixsw.com) in his living room in 1984 and, after several years of building CASE tools, began training companies in object-oriented analysis and design around 1990. ICONIX specializes in training for UML and SysML, and offers both on-site and open-enrollment courses. Doug developed a Unified Booch/Rumbaugh/Jacobson approach to modeling in 1993, several years before the advent of UML, and began writing books around 1995.

Design-Driven Testing is his sixth book on software engineering (and the fourth with Matt Stephens). He's also authored numerous multimedia tutorials, including **Enterprise Architect for Power Users**, and several eBooks, including **Embedded Systems Development with SysML**.

When he's not writing or teaching, he enjoys shooting panoramic, virtual reality (VR) photography, which you can see on his travel website, VResorts.com.

About the Technical Reviewers

 **Jeffrey P. Kantor** is project manager of Large Synoptic Survey Telescope (LSST) Data Management. In this capacity, Mr. Kantor is responsible for implementing computing and communications systems to provide calibration, quality assessment, processing, archiving, and end user and external system access of astronomical image and engineering data produced by the LSST.

After four years in the U.S. Army as a Russian Linguist/Signals Intelligence Specialist, starting in 1980, as an entry-level programmer, he has held positions at all levels in IT organizations, in many industry segments, including defense and aerospace, semiconductor manufacturing, geophysics, software engineering consulting, home and building control, consumer durables manufacturing, retail, and e-commerce.

Mr. Kantor has created, tailored, applied, and audited software processes for a wide variety of organizations in industry, government, and academia. He has been responsible for some of these organizations achieving ISO9000 Certification and SEI CMM Level 2 assessments. Mr. Kantor has also consulted with and trained over 30 organizations in object-oriented analysis and design, Unified Modeling Language (UML), use case–driven testing, and software project management.

Mr. Kantor enjoys spending time with his family, soccer (playing, refereeing, and coaching), and mountain biking.

David Putnam has been working in software development for the last 25 years, and since the beginning of this century, he has been one of the UK's most ardent agile proponents.

From his early days producing database systems for the construction industry, he has enjoyed an eclectic career, including positions in the fitness industry and a spell as a university lecturer. During this time, he has published many articles on software development and is a familiar sight at agile software development conferences. David now works as an independent agile software development consultant and has provided invaluable advice to some of the UK's best-known corporations.

Acknowledgments

The authors would like to thank:

The mapplet team at ESRI, including Wolfgang Hall, Prakash Darbhamulla, Jim McKinney, and Witt Mathot for their work on the book's example project.

The folks at Sparx Systems, including Geoff Sparks, Ben Constable, Tom O'Reilly, Aaron Bell, Vimal Kumar, and Estelle Gleeson for the development of the ICONIX add-in and the Structured Scenario Editor.

Alanah Stephens for being the best "Alice" ever, and Michelle Stephens for her patience during yet another book project.

Jeff Kantor and Robyn Allsman from the Large Synoptic Survey Telescope project for their help with the use case thread expander specification.

Mike Farnsworth and the folks at Virginia DMV who participated in the preliminary mapplet modeling workshop. Barbara Rosi-Schwartz for her feedback on DDT, and Jerry Hamby for sharing his Flex expertise, and particularly for his help with reverse engineering MXML.

And last but certainly not least our editors at Apress, Jonathan Gennick, Anita Castro, and Mary Ann Fugate.

Prologue

Beware the agile hype

T'was brillig when the YAGNI'd code
    did build itself ten times a day.
All flimsy were the index cards,
    designs refactored clear away.

Beware the agile hype, my son
    more code that smells, more bugs to catch.
Refactoring seem'd much more fun
    until thy skills were overmatch'd.

With vorpal unit tests in hand
    against the manxome bugs he fought.
Quite dazed was he by TDD,
    some sanity was what he sought.

But, in his timebox made of wood,
    determined by some planning game,
yon tests ran green and all was good
    until the deadline came.

It's half past two, I guess we're through
    it's time to have a tasty snack.
What's that you said, some tests ran red
    all fixed, with one quick hack!

And lo the thought came with a shock,
    design comes first, not tests, O joy!
We found upon this frabjous day
    a simpl'r process to employ.

T'was brillig when the YAGNI'd code
    did build itself ten times a day.
All flimsy were the index cards,
    designs refactored clear away…

## PART 1

DDT vs. TDD

"Let the developers consider a conceptual design," the King said, for about the twentieth time that day.

"No, no!" said the Queen. "Tests first—design afterwards."

"Stuff and nonsense!" said Alice loudly. "The idea of writing the tests first!"

"Hold your tongue!" said the Queen, turning purple. "How much code have you written recently, anyway?" she sneered.

"I won't," said the plucky little Alice. "Tests shouldn't drive design, design should drive testing. Tests should verify that your code works as it was designed, and that it meets the customer's requirements, too," she added, surprised by her own insight. "And when you drive your tests from a conceptual design, you can test smarter instead of harder."

This is a book about testing; not just QA-style visual inspection, but also automated testing—driving unit tests, controller tests, and scenario tests from your design and the customer's requirements. As such, there's bound to be some crossover between the techniques described in this book and what people set out to do with test-driven development (TDD). In some ways the two processes work well together, and we hope that test-driven software developers will gain from combining the best of both worlds. That said, there are also some fundamental differences, both in the practices and the ideas underpinning both disciplines.

Chapter 1 in this book provides a high-level overview of DDT. We also briefly introduce the Mapplet project that we'll be using later in the book to illustrate how to get the best from design-driven testing.

Chapters 2 and 3 go on to compare and contrast DDT and TDD. In Chapter 2 we run through what it's like to approach a project using TDD. By the end of the chapter we hope you're convinced that there must surely be a better way. And there is! We run through the same scenario again in Chapter 3, but this time using DDT. The results are far more satisfying.

■ ■ ■

Somebody Has It Backwards

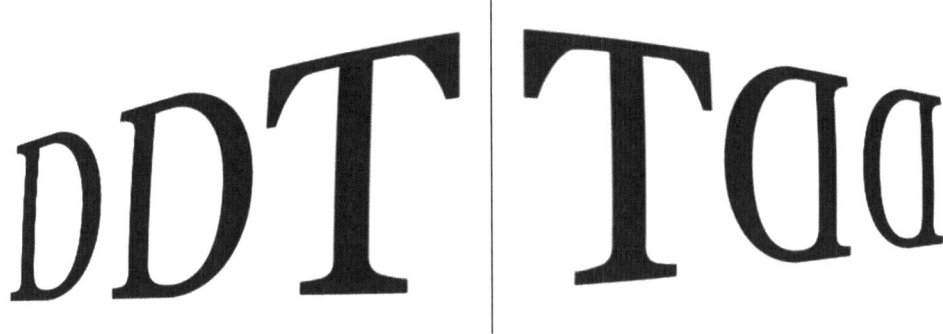

The first time we saw a description of Test-Driven Development (TDD), our immediate thought was: "That's just backwards!" Wanting to give the process the benefit of the doubt, Matt went ahead and put TDD into practice on his own projects, attended seminars, kept up with the latest test-driven trends, and so forth. But the nagging feeling was still there that it just didn't feel right to drive the design from the tests. There was also the feeling that TDD is highly labor-intensive, luring developers into an expensive and ultimately futile chase for the holy grail of 100% test coverage. Not all code is created equal, and some code benefits more from test coverage than other code.[1] There just had to be a better way to benefit from automated testing.

Design-Driven Testing (DDT) was the result: a fusion of up-front analysis and design with an agile, test-driven mindset. In many ways it's a reversal of the thinking behind TDD, which is why we had some fun with the name. But still, somebody obviously has it backwards. We invite you to walk through the next few chapters and decide for yourself who's forwards and who's backwards.

In this chapter we provide a high-level overview of DDT, and we compare the key differences between DDT and TDD. As DDT also covers analysis and acceptance testing, sometimes we compare

---

[1] Think algorithms vs. boilerplate code such as property getters and setters.

DDT with practices that are typically layered on top of TDD (courtesy of XP or newer variants, such as Acceptance TDD).

Then, in Chapters 2 and 3, we walk through a "Hello world!" example, first using TDD and then using DDT.

The rest of the book puts DDT into action, with a full-on example based on a real project, a hotel finder application based in a heterogeneous environment with a Flex front-end and Java back-end, serving up maps from ArcGIS Server and querying an XML-based hotel database. It's a non-trivial project with a mixture of technologies and languages—increasingly common these days—and provides many challenges that put DDT through its paces.

Problems DDT Sets Out to Solve

In some ways DDT is an answer to the problems that become apparent with other testing methodologies, such as TDD; but it's also very much an answer to the much bigger problems that occur when

- no testing is done (or no automated tests are written)
- some testing is done (or some tests are written) but it's all a bit aimless and ad hoc
- *too much* testing is done (or too many low-leverage tests are written)

That last one might seem a bit strange—surely there can be no such thing as too much testing? But if the testing is counter-productive, or repetitive, then the extra time spent on testing could be time wasted (law of diminishing returns and all that). There are only so many ways you can press a doorbell, and how many of those will be done in real life? Is it really necessary to prove that the doorbell still works when submerged in 1000 ft. of water? The idea behind DDT is that the tests you write and perform are closely tied into the customer's requirements, so you spend time testing only what needs to be tested.

Let's look at some of the problems that you should be able to address using DDT.

Knowing When You're Done Is Hard

When writing tests, it's sometimes unclear when you're "done"... you could go on writing tests of all kinds, forever, until your codebase is 100% covered with tests. But why stop there? There are still unexplored permutations to be tested, additional tests to write... and so on, until the customer gives up waiting for something to be delivered, and pulls the plug. With DDT, your tests are driven directly from your use cases and conceptual design; it's all quite systematic, so you'll know precisely when you're done.

■ **Note** At a client Doug visited recently, the project team decided they were done with acceptance testing when their timebox indicated they had better start coding. We suspect this is fairly common.

Code coverage has become synonymous with "good work." Code metrics tools such as Clover provide reports that over-eager managers can print out, roll up, and bash developers over the head with if the developers are not writing enough unit tests. But if 100% code coverage is practically unattainable, you could be forgiven for asking: why bother at all? Why set out knowing in advance that the goal can never be achieved? By contrast, we wanted DDT to provide a clear, achievable goal. "Completeness" in DDT isn't about blanket code coverage, it's about ensuring that key decision points in the code—logical software functions—are adequately tested.

Leaving Testing Until Later Costs More

You still see software processes that put "testing" as a self-contained phase, all the way after requirements, design, and coding phases. It's well established that leaving bug-hunting and fixing until late in a project increases the time and cost involved in eliminating those bugs. While it does make sense intuitively that you can't test something before it exists, DDT (like TDD and other agile processes) gets into the nooks and crannies of development, and provides early feedback on the state of your code and the design.

Testing Badly Designed Code Is Hard

It sounds obvious, but code that is badly designed tends to be rigid, difficult to adapt or re-use in some other context, and full of side effects. By contrast, DDT inherently promotes good design and well-written, easily testable code. This all makes it extremely difficult to write tests for. In the TDD world, the code you create will be inherently testable, because you write the tests first. But you end up with an awful lot of unit tests of questionable value, and it's tempting to skip valuable parts of the analysis and design thought process because "the code is the design." With DDT, we wanted a testing process that inherently promotes good design and well-written, easily testable code.

Note Every project that Matt has joined halfway through, without exception, has been written in such a way as to make the code difficult (or virtually impossible) to test. Coders often try adding tests to their code and quickly give up, having come to the conclusion that unit testing is too hard. It's a widespread problem, so we devote Chapter 9 to the problem of difficult-to-test code, and look at just *why* particular coding styles and design patterns make unit testing difficult.

It's Easy to Forget Customer-Level Tests

TDD is, by its nature, all about testing at the detailed design level. We hate to say it, but in its separation from Extreme Programming, TDD lost a valuable companion: acceptance tests. Books on TDD omit this vital aspect of automated testing entirely, and, instead, talk about picking a user story (aka requirement) and immediately writing a unit test for it.

DDT promotes writing both acceptance tests and unit tests, but at its core are **controller tests**, which are halfway between the two. Controller tests are "developer tests," that look like unit tests, but that operate at the conceptual design level (aka "logical software functions"). They provide a highly beneficial glue between analysis (the problem space) and design (the solution space).

Developers Become Complacent

It's not uncommon for developers to write a few tests, discover that they haven't achieved any tangible results, and go back to cranking out untested code. In our experience, the 100% code coverage "holy grail," in particular, can breed complacency among developers. If 100% is impossible or impractical, is 90% okay? How about 80%? I didn't write tests for these classes over here, but the universe didn't implode (yet)… so why bother at all? If the goal set out by your testing process is easily and obviously achievable, you should find that the developers in your team go at it with a greater sense of purpose. This brings us to the last issue that DDT tackles.

Tests Sometimes Lack Purpose

Aimless testing is sometimes worse than not testing at all, because it provides an illusion of safety. This is true of both manual testing (where a tester follows a test script, or just clicks around the UI and deems the product good to ship), and writing of automated tests (where developers write a bunch of tests in an ad hoc fashion).

Aimless unit testing is also a problem because unit tests mean more code to maintain and can make it difficult to modify existing code without breaking tests that make too many assumptions about the code's internals. Moreover, writing the tests themselves eats up valuable time.

Knowing why you're testing, and knowing why you're writing a particular unit test—being able to state succinctly what the test is proving—ensures that each test must pull its own weight. Its existence, and the time spent writing it, must be justified. The purpose of DDT tests is simple: *to prove systematically that the design fulfills the requirements and the code matches up with the design.*

A Quick, Tools-Agnostic Overview of DDT

In this section we provide a lightning tour of the DDT process, distilled down to the cookbook steps. While DDT can be adapted to the OOAD process of your choice, it was designed originally to be used with the ICONIX Process (an agile OOAD process that uses a core subset of UML).[2] In this section, we show each step in the ICONIX Process matched by a corresponding DDT step. The idea is that DDT provides instant feedback, validating each step in the analysis/design process.

Structure of DDT

Figure 1–1 shows the four principal test artifacts: unit tests, controller tests, scenario tests, and business requirement tests. As you can see, **unit tests** are fundamentally rooted in the design/solution/implementation space. They're written and "owned" by coders. Above these, **controller tests** are sandwiched between the analysis and design spaces, and help to provide a bridge between the two. **Scenario tests** belong in the analysis space, and are manual test specs containing step-by-step instructions for the testers to follow, that expand out all sunny-day/rainy-day permutations of a use case. Once you're comfortable with the process and the organization is more

---

[2] We provide enough information on the ICONIX Process in this book to allow you to get ahead with DDT on your own projects; but if you also want to learn the ICONIX Process in depth, check out our companion book, *Use Case Driven Object Modeling with UML: Theory and Practice.*

amenable to the idea, we also highly recommend basing "end-to-end" integration tests on the scenario test specs. Finally, **business requirement tests** are almost always manual test specs; they facilitate the "human sanity check" before a new version of the product is signed off for release into the wild.

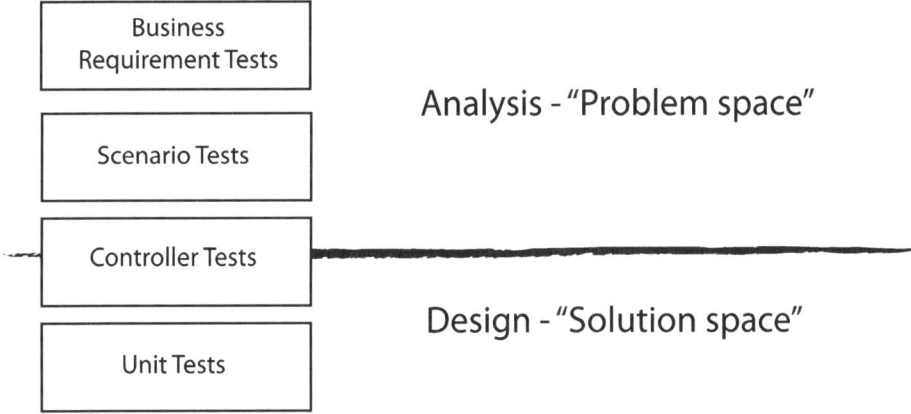

Figure 1–1. The four principal flavors of tests in DDT

The tests vary in granularity (that is, the amount of underlying code that each test is validating), and in the number of automated tests that are actually written. We show this in Figure 1–2.

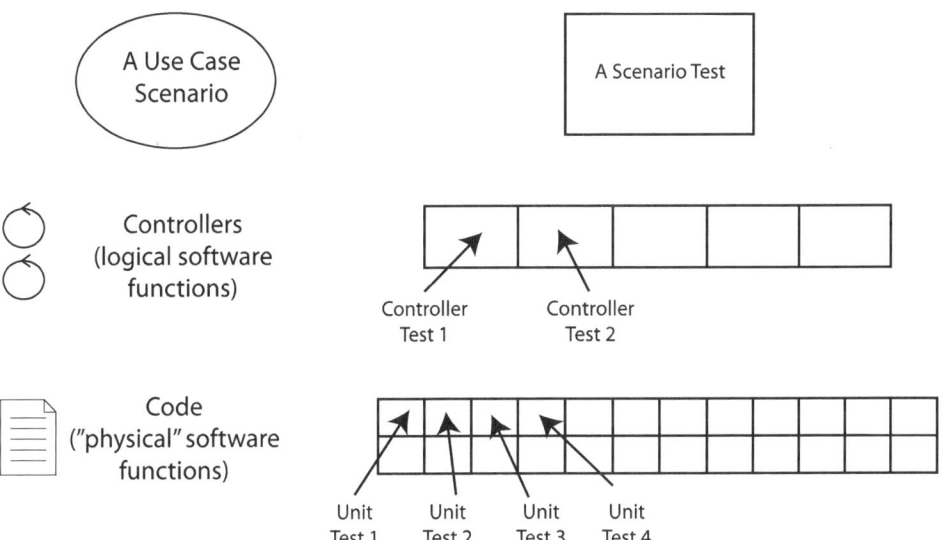

Figure 1–2. Test granularity: the closer you get to the design/code, the more tests are written; but each test is smaller in scope.

Figure 1–2 also shows that—if your scenario test scripts are also implemented as automated integration tests—each use case is covered by exactly one test class (it's actually one test case per use case scenario; but more about that later). Using the ICONIX Process, use cases are divided into controllers, and (as you might expect) each controller test covers exactly one controller. The controllers are then divided into actual code functions/methods, and the more important methods get one or more unit test methods.[3]

You've probably seen the traditional "V" model of software development, with analysis/design/development activities on the left, and testing activities on the right. With a little wrangling, DDT actually fits this model pretty well, as we show in Figure 1–3.

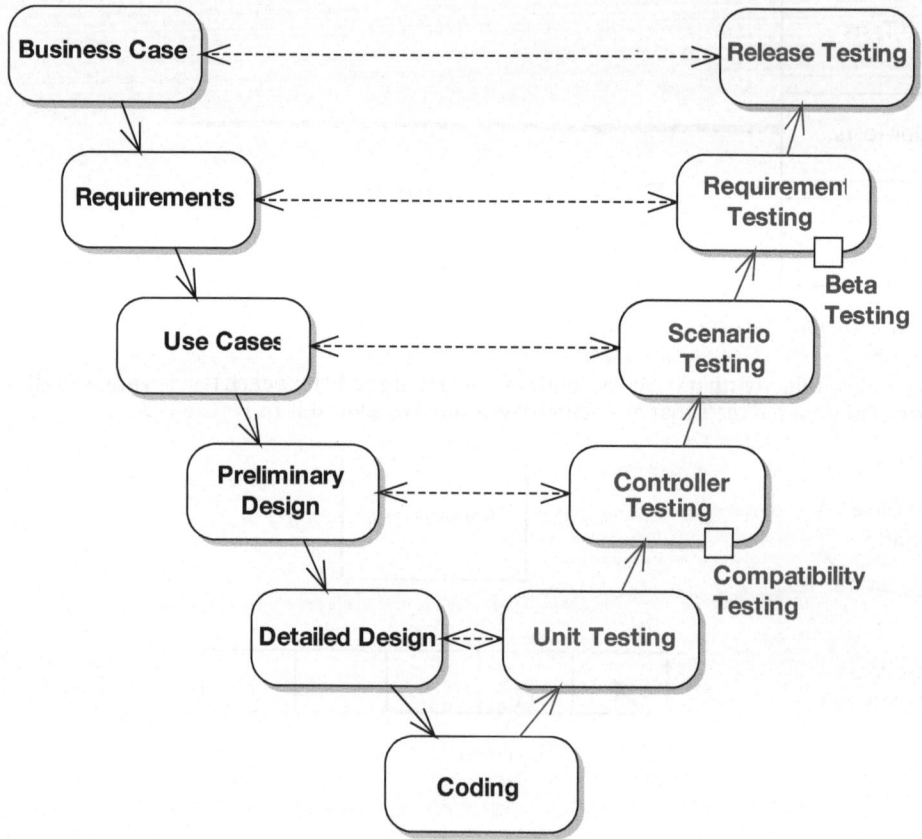

Figure 1–3. V model of development adapted to DDT

---

[3] So (you might well be wondering), how do I decide whether to cover a method with a unit test or a controller test? Simple—implement the controller tests first; if there's any "significant" (non-boilerplate) code left uncovered, consider giving it a unit test. There is more about this decision point in Chapters 5 and 6.

Each step on the left is a step in the ICONIX Process, which DDT is designed to complement; each step on the right is a part of DDT. As you create requirements, you create a requirements test spec to provide feedback—so that, at a broad level, you'll know when the project is done. The real core part of DDT (at least for programmers) centers around controller testing, which provides feedback for the conceptual design step and a systematic method of testing software behavior. The core part of DDT for analysts and QA testers centers around scenario testing.

DDT in Action

With the V diagram in Figure 1–3 as a reference point, let's walk through ICONIX/DDT one step at a time. We're deliberately not stipulating any tools here. However, we encourage you to have a peek at Chapter 3 where we show a "Hello world!" example (actually a Login use case) of DDT in action, using Enterprise Architect (EA). So, with that in mind, let's step through the process.

1. **ICONIX** ➜ Explore the business requirements (that is, functional and non-functional requirements) in detail. Talk to the relevant people—customers, analysts, end-users, and so forth. Draw UI storyboards (wireframes/mockups) and produce a set of high-level requirements or user stories.

   ← *DDT:* Create test cases from the requirements. These should be acceptance criteria that, at a broad level, you can "tick off" one by one to confirm that the project is done.

2. **ICONIX** ➜ Create a domain model, and write some use cases. Think of a use case as a step-by-step description of user/system interaction: "The user presses a button; the system does some stuff and then displays the results. The user does something else… etc." Divide each use case into its Basic Course ("sunny day scenario") and as many Alternate Courses ("rainy day scenarios") as you can think of.

   ← *DDT:* Expand the use case threads into scenario tests. These are test specs that you hand to the testing team, and (if you're heavily "into" the automated testing thing) they can also be automated, end-to-end **integration tests**.[4] Note that the use case descriptions themselves are very useful as test specs, since (written the ICONIX way) they read like step-by-step guides on using the system and exploring the various avenues and success/failure modes.

3. **ICONIX** ➜ For each use case, begin to explore the design at a preliminary level. Using the ICONIX Process, this *conceptual design* is done using **robustness analysis**. This is an effective technique that serves as a "reality check" for your use case descriptions. It also helps you to identify the behavior (verbs, actions, or "controllers") in your design. Think of a controller as a "logical software function"—it may turn into several "real" functions in the code.

---

[4] Integration tests have their own set of problems that, depending on factors such as the culture of your organization and the ready availability of up-to-date, isolated test database schemas, aren't always easily surmounted. There is more about implementing scenario tests as automated integration tests in Part 3.

← *DDT:* Systematically create **controller tests** from the robustness diagrams, as follows:

a. For each controller, create a test case. These test cases validate the critical behavior of your design, as driven by the controllers identified in your use cases during robustness analysis (hence the name "controller test"). Each controller test is created as a method in your chosen unit testing framework (JUnit, FlexUnit, NUnit etc). Because each test covers a "logical" software function (a group of "real" functions with one collective output), you'll end up writing fewer controller tests than you would TDD-style unit tests.

b. For each controller test case, think about the expected acceptance criteria—what constitutes a successful run of this part of the use case? (Refer back to the use case alternate courses for a handy list.)

4. **ICONIX →** For each use case, drill down into the detailed design. It's time to "get real" and think in gritty detail about how this system is going to be implemented. Create a sequence diagram for each use case.

← *DDT:* Systematically create unit tests from the design.

If you're familiar with TDD, you'll notice that this process differs significantly. There are actually many ways in which the two processes are similar (both in mechanics and underlying goals). However, there are also both practical and philosophical differences. We cover the main differences in the next section.

How TDD and DDT Differ

The techniques that we describe in this book are not, for the most part, incompatible with TDD—in fact, we hope TDDers can take these principles and techniques and apply them successfully in their own projects. But there are some fundamental differences between our guiding philosophy and those of the original TDD gurus, as we show in Table 1–1. We explain our comments further in the "top 10" lists at the start of Chapters 2 and 3.

Table 1–1. *Differences Between TDD and ICONIX/DDT*

TDD	ICONIX/DDT
Tests are used to drive the design of the application.	With DDT it's the other way around: the tests are driven from the design, and, therefore, the tests are there primarily to validate the design. That said, there's more common ground between the two processes than you might think. A lot of the "design churn" (aka refactoring) to be found in TDD projects can be calmed down and given some stability by first applying the up-front design and testing techniques described in this book.
The code is the design and the tests are the documentation.	**The design is the design, the code is the code, and the tests are the tests.** With DDT, you'll use modern development tools to keep the documented design model in sync with the code.

TDD	ICONIX/DDT
Following TDD, you may end up with a lot of tests (and we mean a *lot* of tests).	DDT takes a "test smarter, not harder" approach, meaning tests are more focused on code "hot spots."
TDD tests have their own purpose; therefore, on a true test-first project the tests will look subtly different from a "classical" fine-grained unit test. A TDD unit test might test more than a single method at a time.	In DDT, a unit test is usually there to validate a single method. DDT unit tests are closer to "real" unit tests. As you write each test, you'll look at the detailed design, pick the next message being passed between objects, and write a test case for it.
	DDT also has controller tests, which are broader in scope.[5] So TDD tests are somewhere between unit tests and controller tests in terms of scope.
TDD doesn't have acceptance tests unless you mix in part of another process. The emphasis (e.g., with XP) tends to be on automated acceptance tests: if your "executable specification" (aka acceptance tests) can't be automated, then the process falls down. As we explore in Part 3, writing and maintaining automated acceptance tests can be very difficult.	DDT "acceptance tests" (which encompass both scenario tests and business requirement tests) are "manual" test specs for consumption by a human. Scenario tests can be automated (and we recommend doing this if at all possible), but the process doesn't depend on it.
TDD is much finer-grained when it comes to design.[6] With the test-first approach, you pick a story card from the wall, discuss the success criteria on the back of the card with the tester and/or customer representative, write the first (failing) test, write some code to make the test pass, write the next test, and so on, until the story card is implemented. You then review the design and refactor if needed, i.e., "after-the-event" design.	We actually view DDT as pretty fine-grained: you might base your initial design effort on, say, a package of use cases. From the resulting design model you identify your tests and classes, and go ahead and code them up. Run the tests as you write the code.
A green bar in TDD means "all the tests I've written so far are not failing."	A green bar in DDT means "all the critical design junctures, logical software functions, and user/system interactions I've implemented so far are passing as designed." We know which result gives us more confidence in our code...

---

[5] If some code is already covered by a controller test, you don't need to write duplicate unit tests to cover the same code, unless the code is algorithmic or mission-critical—in which case, it's an area of code that will benefit from additional tests. We cover design-driven algorithm testing in Chapter 12.

[6] Kent Beck's description of this was "a waterfall run through a blender."

TDD	ICONIX/DDT
After making a test pass, review the design and refactor the code if you think it's needed.	With DDT, "design churn" is minimized because the design is thought through with a broader set of functionality in mind. We don't pretend that there'll be no design changes when you start coding, or that the requirements will never change, but the process helps keep these changes to a minimum. The process also allows for changes—see Chapter 4.
TDD: An essential part of the process is to first write the test and then write the code.	With DDT we don't stipulate: if you feel more comfortable writing the test before the accompanying code, absolutely go ahead. You can be doing this and still be "true" to DDT.
With TDD, if you feel more comfortable doing more up-front design than your peers consider to be cool… go ahead. You can be doing this and still be "true" to TDD. (That said, doing a lot of up-front design and writing all those billions of tests would represent a lot of duplicated effort).	With DDT, an essential part of the process is to first create a design, and then write the tests and the code. However, you'll end up writing fewer tests than in TDD, because the tests you'll most benefit from writing are pinpointed during the analysis and design process.

So, with DDT you don't drive the design from the unit tests. This is not to say that the design in a DDT project isn't affected by the tests. Inevitably you'll end up basing the design around testability. As we'll explore in Chapter 3, code that hasn't been written with testability in mind is an absolute pig to test. Therefore, it's important to build testability into your designs from as early a stage as possible. It's no coincidence that code that is easily tested also generally happens to be well-designed code. To put it another way, the qualities of a code design that result in it being easy to unit-test are also the same qualities that make the code clear, maintainable, flexible, malleable, well factored, and highly modular. It's also no coincidence that the ICONIX Process and DDT place their primary emphasis on creating designs that have these exact qualities.

Example Project: Introducing the Mapplet 2.0

The main example that we'll use throughout this book is known as Mapplet 2.0, a real-world hotel-finder street map that is hosted on vresorts.com (a travel web site owned by one of the co-authors). We invite you to compare the use cases in this book with the finished product on the web site.

Mapplet 2.0 is a next-generation version of the example generated for our earlier book, *Agile Development with ICONIX Process*, which has been used successfully as a teaching example in open enrollment training classes by ICONIX over the past few years. The original "Mapplet 1.0" was a thin-client application written using HTML and JavaScript with server-side C#, whereas the groovy new version has a Flex rich-client front-end with server-side components written in Java. In today's world of heterogeneous enterprise technologies, a mix of languages and technologies is a common situation, so we won't shy away from the prospect of testing an application that is collectively written in more than one language. As a result, you'll see some tests written in Flex and some in Java. We'll demonstrate how to write tests that clearly validate the design and the requirements, walking across boundaries between architectural layers to test individual business concerns.

Figures 1–4 and 1–5 show the original, HTML-based Mapplet 1.0 in action.

Figure 1–4. *The HTML/Ajax-based Mapplet 1.0 following the "US Map" use case: starting with the US map, zoom in to your region of interest.*

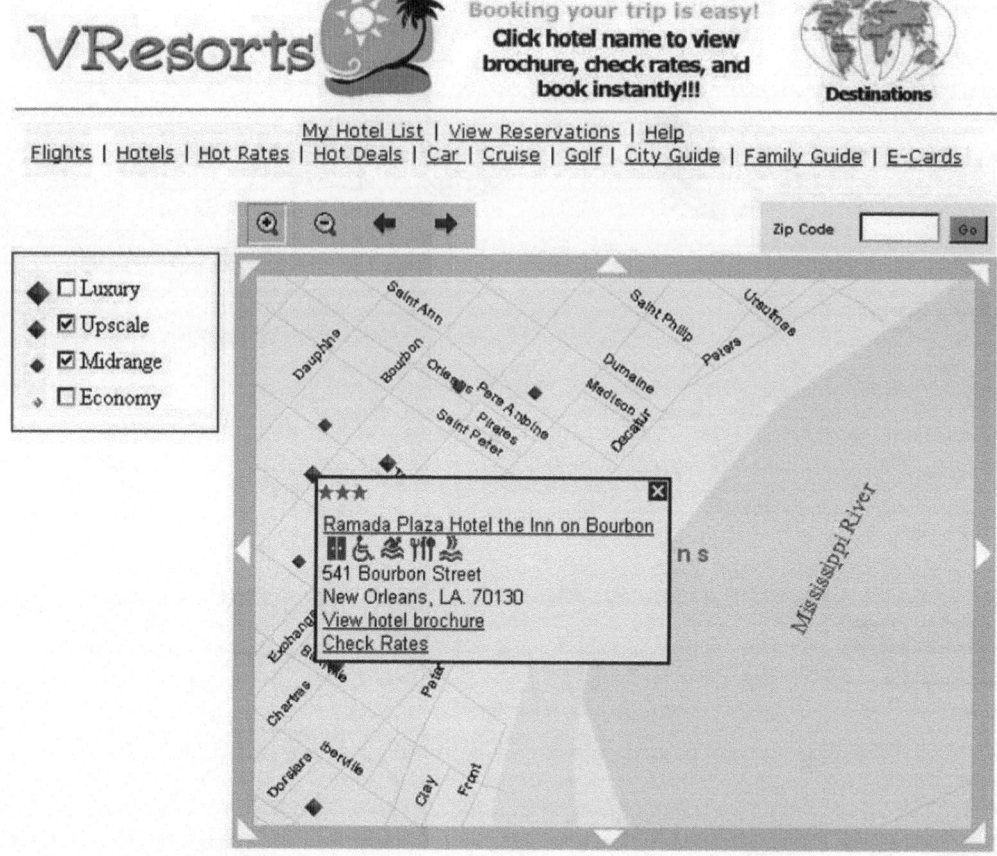

Figure 1–5. Using Mapplet 1.0 to find a suitable hotel

By contrast, Figure 1–6 leaps ahead to the finished product, the Flash-based Mapplet 2.0.

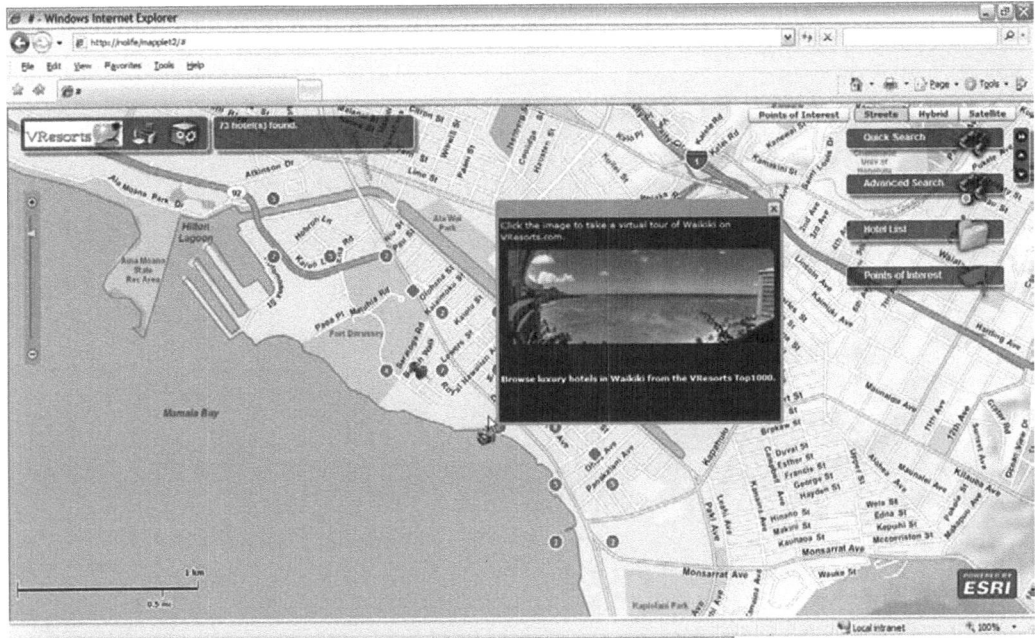

Figure 1–6. Son of Mapplet, complete with location-based photography and virtual tours

Summary

In this chapter we introduced the key concepts that we'll be exploring in this book. We gave a 40,000-ft. overview of DDT and compared it with Test-Driven Development, which in many organizations is becoming increasingly synonymous with "writing some unit tests." We also introduced the main project that we'll be following, a real-life GIS/hotel-search application for a travel web site.

Although this book isn't specifically about Test-Driven Development, it does help to make comparisons with it, as TDD is very much in the developer consciousness. So in the next chapter, we'll walk through a "Hello world!" example—actually a "Login" use case—developed first using TDD, and then (in Chapter 3) using DDT.

In Part 2, we'll begin to explore the Mapplet 2.0 development—backwards. In other words, we'll start with the finished product in Chapter 4, and work our way back in time, through detailed design, conceptual design, use cases, and finally (or firstly, depending which way you look at it) the initial set of business requirements in Chapters 5-8.

We'll finish this first chapter by introducing the DDT process diagram (see Figure 1–7). Each chapter in Part 2 begins with this diagram, along with a sort of "you are here" circle to indicate what's covered in that chapter. As you can see, DDT distinguishes between a "developer's zone" of automated tests that provide feedback into the design, and a "customer zone" of test scripts (the customer tests can also be automated, but that's advanced stuff—see Chapter 11).

Acceptance Testing

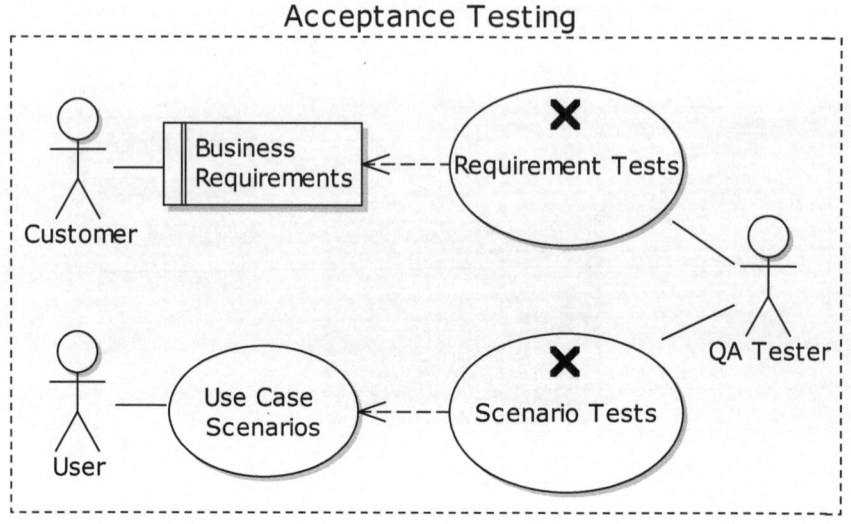

Developer Testing

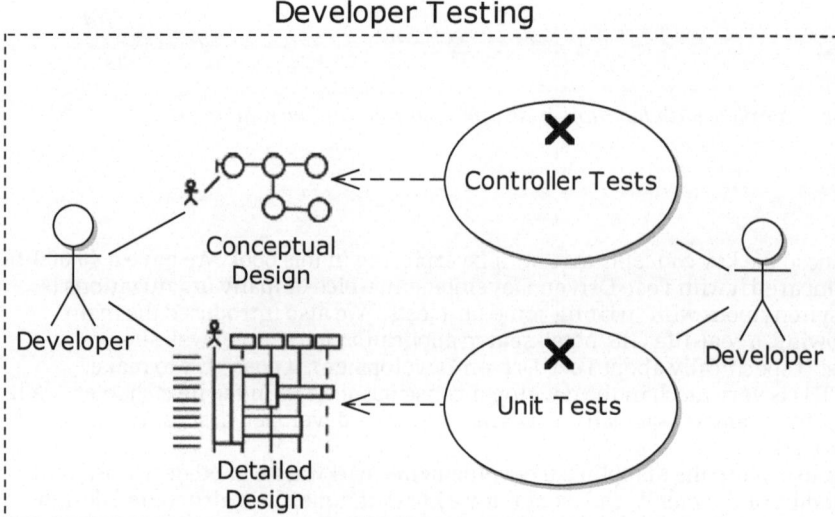

Figure 1–7. *Anatomy of DDT: the four test types, what drives each one, and who "owns" which tests*

If your team is debating whether to use DDT in place of TDD, we would suggest that you point out that controller tests are essentially a "drop-in" replacement for TDD-style unit tests—and you don't have to write as many!

## CHAPTER 2

TDD Using Hello World

We continue our comparison of TDD and DDT techniques in this chapter, with a straightforward "Hello world!" example (actually a system login) performed using the TDD approach. Logging in seems strangely apt for a "Hello world!" example, as (a) it's a simple concept and exists in virtually every serious IT application, and (b) it's the system saying "Hello" to the user (and the user saying "Hello" back).

Note For non-TDDers: You may want to have a casual flip through this chapter just to see what's going on in the coding room down the hall at the TDD shop, and then get engaged in the DDT way of doing things, in Chapter 3.

For TDDers: We understand your pain, and try to make clear in this chapter just how hard your job is. Then, in the next chapter, we're going to show you what we believe is an easier way.

Before we dive down the TDD rabbit hole and get started on the example, let's look at the top ten characteristics of TDD (from, we admit, an ICONIX/DDT perspective).

Top Ten Characteristics of TDD

This section expands on the left column in Table 1-1 from the previous chapter, which lists the main differences between TDD and DDT.

10. Tests drive the design.

With TDD, tests have essentially three purposes:

- Drive the design
- Document the design
- Act as regression tests

The first item, that of tests driving the design during coding, rather than an up-front process of thinking and modeling driving the design, is the defining characteristic of TDD. It's what made TDD such a revolutionary (not the same as "good") approach. TDD drives designs at a short-range, tactical level, leaving more strategic decisions to be handled elsewhere. Think of a blind man with a cane being able to detect what's immediately in front of him, as opposed to being able to see a truck heading straight at you, a bit further down the road.

9. There is a Total Dearth of Documentation.

Documentation isn't an inherent part of the TDD process. Result: no documentation.

The mantra that "the code is the design" means that very little design documentation may be written, making it difficult for newcomers to learn the details of the project. If they ask for a system overview, or which class is the main one for a particular screen or business function, being told to go and trawl through the unit tests (as "the tests are the design") isn't going to be too helpful. Enterprising individuals might well think to set up a project wiki and put some pages on there covering different aspects of the design… or they might not. Creation of design documentation isn't an inherent part of the process, so it's not likely to happen.

8. *Everything* is a unit test.

If it's not in JUnit, it doesn't exist…

The mindset of a test-first methodology is, as you'd expect, to write a test first. Then add something new to make the test pass, so you can "prove" that it's done (fans of Gödel's incompleteness theorems should look away now). Unfortunately, this can mean that just the "sunny day scenario" is proven to be implemented. All the "unexpected" stuff—different ways the user may traverse the UI, partial system failures, or out-of-bounds inputs and responses—remain unexpected because no one took the time to think about them in any structured, systematic kind of way.

BUT …

7. TDD tests are not quite unit tests (or are they?).

There's been some discussion in the TDD world about the true nature of TDD tests,[1] mainly centering around the question: "Are TDD tests true unit tests?" The quick and simple answer is: "Yes. No. Not really." TDD tests (also sometimes called *programmer tests*, usually to pair them up with *customer tests*, aka acceptance tests) have their own purpose; therefore, on a true test-first project the tests will look subtly different from a "classical" fine-grained unit test. A TDD unit test might test more than a single unit of code at a time. TDDer and Extremo Martin Fowler writes the following:

> *Unit testing in XP is often unlike classical unit testing, because in XP you're usually not testing each unit in isolation. You're testing each class and its immediate connections to its neighbors.[2]*

This actually puts TDD tests roughly halfway between classical unit tests (which DDT uses) and DDT's own *controller tests* (see Chapter 6). In this book, however, we'll keep on calling TDD tests "unit tests," as it's what the rest of the world generally calls them.

6. Acceptance tests provide feedback against the requirements.

Acceptance tests also form part of the specification… or they would if we had acceptance tests (and if we had a specification). Unless you've layered another process on top of TDD (such as XP or Acceptance TDD), you'll be driving unit tests directly from the requirements/stories.

5. TDD lends confidence to make changes.

Confidence to make the continual stream of changes that is "design by refactoring". But is that confidence misplaced?

To rephrase the heading, a green bar means "all the tests I've written so far are not failing." When running unit tests through a test-runner such as that built into Eclipse, Flash Builder, IntelliJ, etc., if all your tests pass you'll see a green bar across the window: a sort of minor reward (like a cookie but not as tasty) that may produce an endorphin kick and the feeling that all's well with the world, or at least with the project.

Having covered your code with a thick layer of unit tests, the idea is that this notion of "all being well" should give you the confidence needed to be able to continuously refactor your code without accidentally introducing bugs. However, do take a read through Matt's "Green Bar of Shangri-La" article.[3] (Hint: how do you know if you missed some unit tests?)

---

[1] See http://stephenwalther.com/blog/archive/2009/04/11/tdd-tests-are-not-unit-tests.aspx.

[2] See www.artima.com/intv/testdriven4.html.

[3] See www.theregister.co.uk/2007/04/25/unit_test_code_coverage/

4. Design emerges incrementally.

First you write a test, and then you write some code to make the test pass. Then you refactor the code to improve the design, without breaking any tests that have been written so far. Thus, the design emerges as you grow the code base incrementally through the test/code/refactor cycle. For non-TDDers, this is roughly analogous to banging your forehead against a wall to make sure that you're able to feel pain, before you start building the wall, whose existence you will then verify by banging your forehead against it. Of course you need a "mock wall" to bang your forehead against, since the real wall doesn't exist yet...we like to call this "Constant Refactoring After Programming" since it has such a descriptive acronym.

3. Some up-front design is OK.

It's absolutely within the TDD "doctrine" to spend time up-front thinking through the design, even sketching out UML diagrams—though ideally this should be in a collaborative environment, e.g., a group of developers standing at a whiteboard. (That said, doing a lot of up-front design and writing all those billions of tests and refactoring the design as you go would represent a lot of duplicated effort.)

In theory, this means upfront design will get done, but in practice TDDers (who often do TDD in conjunction with SCRUM) find that upfront design is not on the deliverable list for the current sprint.

2. TDD produces a lot of tests.

The test-first philosophy underlying TDD is that before you write any code, you first write a test that fails. Then you write the code to make the test pass. The net result is that aggressive refactoring—which will be needed by the bucket-load if you take this incremental approach to design—is made safer by the massive number of tests blanketing the code base. So the tests double as a design tool and as heavily leaned-upon regression tests.

TDD also doesn't really distinguish between "design level" (or solution space) tests and "analysis level" (or problem space) tests.[4]

1. TDD is Too Damn Difficult.

From the Department of Redundancy Department, TDD is Too Damn Difficult. The net effect of following TDD is that everything and its hamster gets a unit test of its own. This sounds great in theory, but in practice you end up with an awful lot of redundant tests.[5] TDD has an image of a "lightweight" or agile practice because it eschews the notion of a "big design up-front," encouraging you to get coding sooner. But that quick illusion of success is soon offset by the sheer hard work of refactoring your way to a finished product, rewriting both code and tests as you go.

---

[4] That is except for XP-style customer acceptance tests, although these aren't officially part of TDD. If you want to add acceptance tests to TDD, you need to look outside the core process, to some other method such as BDD, Acceptance Test-Driven Development (ATDD), or XP itself. Or ICONIX/DDT, of course.

[5] Our idea of a "redundant test" may be different from a TDDer's—more about factoring out redundant unit tests (by writing coarser-grained **controller tests** instead) in Chapter 6.

Login Implemented Using TDD

We thought it was important to show a full-blown example of TDD early in the book, so that's precisely what this chapter is about. The general idea behind TDD is that you tackle a list of requirements (or user stories) one at a time, and for each one implement just enough to fulfill the requirement. Beginning with a good understanding of the requirement, you first give some thought to the design. Then you write a test. Initially the test should fail—in fact, it shouldn't even compile—because you haven't yet written the code to make it pass. You then write just enough code to make the test pass, and revisit the design to make sure it's "tight."[6] Re-run the tests, add another test for the next element of code, and so on. Repeat until the requirement is implemented. Eat a cookie.

Understand the Requirement

Let's consider a simple Login user story:

> *As an end-user, I want to be able to log into the web site.*

It feels like there's some missing detail here, so you and your pair-programming pal Loretta go in search of Tim, the on-site customer.

"Ah, that's slightly more involved," Tim explains. "There's more to it than simply logging the user in. You need to see it from both the end-user's perspective and the web site owner's perspective. So, as a web site owner, I'm interested in making sure freeloading users can't get access to paid-for functionality, that they're channeled through a revenue-maximizing path, and that the site isn't susceptible to brute-force attempts to crack users' passwords."

"And you'd want users to feel secure, too," you add, and Tim nods.

You and Loretta head back to the programmer's palace and expand the user story into a more detailed set:

1. a. As a website owner, I want to provide a secure login capability so I can gain revenue by charging for premium content.

   a. As a website user, I want to be able to log in securely so I can access the premium content.

2. As a website owner, I want the system to lock a user account after 3 failed login attempts.

3. As a website user, I want my password entry to be masked to prevent casual shoulder-surfers from seeing it.

You argue briefly about whether this is really just one user story with added detail, or two—or three—separate stories. Then you agree to simply move on and start coding.

---

[6] In other words, the design should cover just what's been written so far, in as efficient a way as possible—with no code wasted on "possible future requirements" that may never happen.

A PEEK AT THE ANSWER

Figure 2–1 shows how we'd normally design something like a web site login using a sequence diagram (an ICONIX Process design would be more "domain driven" as we'll see in the next chapter):

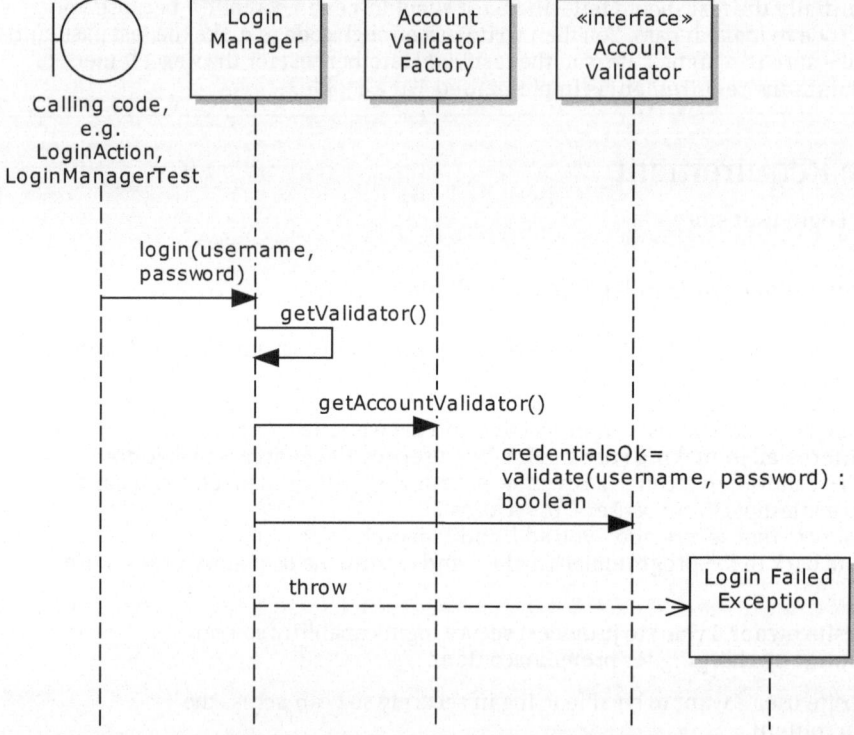

Figure 2–1. Sequence diagram for a web site login process

The design in Figure 2–1 is pretty simple stuff, really. You'd think designing a system like this wouldn't be very difficult to accomplish, especially with as popular a method as TDD. But, as you'll see in the remainder of this chapter, if we actually follow TDD (instead of drawing the simple sequence diagram that you see in Figure 2–1) it takes a whole chapter's worth of refactoring and tail-chasing to get to the final code shown in Figure 2–2.

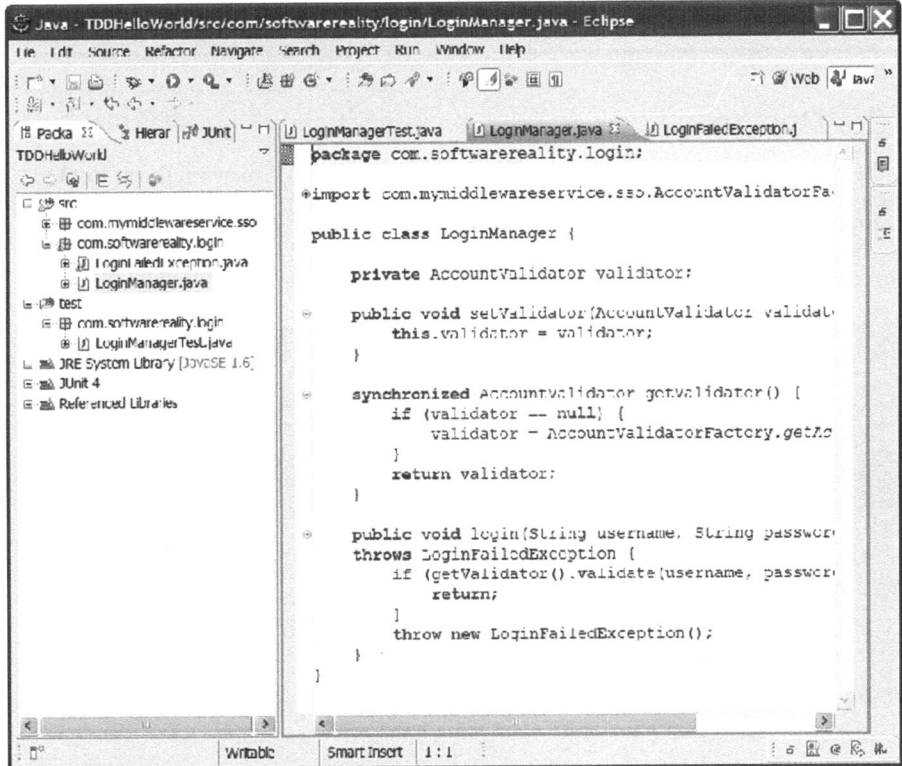

Figure 2–2. Final code for a web site login solution

In other words, we're about to spend a ton of work getting to not much more than 20 lines of code in the remainder of this chapter. It all "feels" somehow correct as you're coding it, as the focus is on detecting poor design and improving it incrementally, and the green bar continually lights up, like a reward given to a hamster for drinking from the correct Kool-Aid dispenser. The endorphins are rollin' and the project is tricklin' along… except… at the end of the day, after all that effort, only 20 lines of code have been written.

If you're familiar with the ICONIX Process, or use cases in general, we suspect you'll already have equated these stories with high-level requirements. A natural next step would be to expand these into use cases, as the stories by themselves really don't address a number of questions that will spring up while the system is being implemented: what should happen if a wrong password is entered? (Is a different page displayed with "forgot password" and "create new account" links?) What page is the user taken to upon being logged in? What happens if the user attempts to view a page without being logged in? (Presumably he should be redirected to the login page, but is this definitely what the customer wants?) And so on. These are the sorts of questions that the ICONIX Process (and therefore DDT) encourage you to think about early on, and thus to factor into the design.

But more about that later. For now, fasten your seatbelt, as this chapter is about to dive down the rabbit-hole into "unit test wonderland." Let's get back to our intrepid pair of TDDers, who are now ready to code.

Think About the Design

Before leaping into the code, it's normal to give a little thought to the design. You want the system to accept a login request—presumably this means that the user will enter a username and password. You may need to send Loretta back to extract more details from the on-site customer. But then what? How will the password be checked?

Some collaborative white-boarding produces the sketch shown in Figure 2–3.

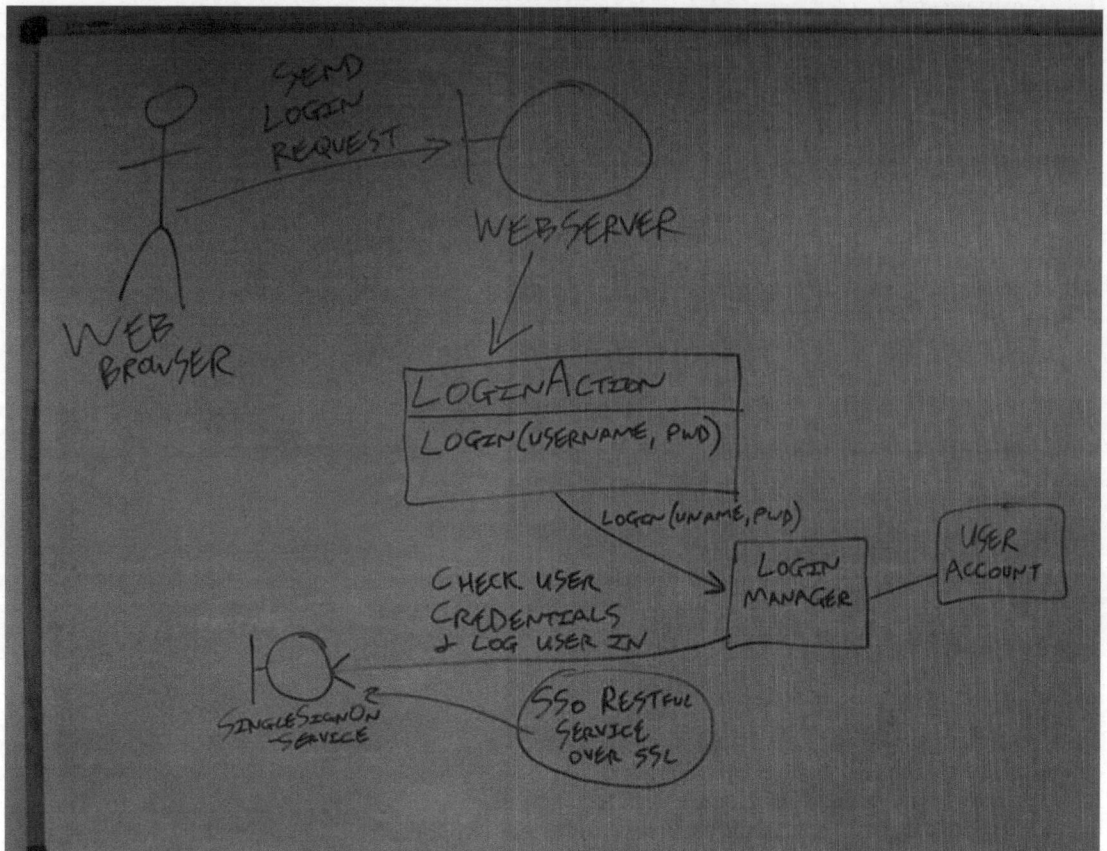

Figure 2–3. Initial design sketch for the Login story

> ■ **Note** Figure 2–3 shows a mix of notation styles; but this diagram isn't about UML correctness, it's about thinking through the design and conveying an overview of the developers' plan of attack.

LoginAction is a generic, Spring Framework-esque UI action class to handle incoming web requests—in this case, a login request. It accepts two input values, the username and password, and simply hands the parameters on to a class better suited to handle the login request.

LoginManager accepts the username and password, and will need to make an external call to a RESTful service in order to validate the username and password. If validation fails, a ValidationException is thrown, and caught by the LoginAction, which sends a "FAIL" response back to the user. We also suspect that UserAccount will be needed at some point, but we hope to find out for sure when we begin coding.

Write the First Test-First Test First

Let's take a quick look at the project structure. Using Eclipse we've created a project called "LoginExample-TDD," which gives us the following folders:

```
LoginExample-TDD
    |__ src
    |__ test
    |__ bin
```

All the production code will go in packages beneath "src," all the unit tests will go into "test," and the compiled code will go into "bin."

Given the white-boarded design sketch in Figure 2–1, it makes sense to focus on LoginManager first. So we'll start by creating a LoginManager test class:

```
import static junit.framework.TestCase.*;
import org.junit.Test;

public class LoginManagerTest extends TestCase {

    @Test
    public void login() throws Exception {
    }

}
```

So far, so good. We've created a test skeleton for the login() method on LoginManager, which we identified during the brief design white-boarding session. We'll now add some code into this test, to create a LoginManager instance and attempt a login:

```
    @Test
    public void login() throws Exception {
        LoginManager manager = new LoginManager();
        try {
            manager.login("robert", "password1");
        } catch (LoginFailedException e) {
            fail("Login should have succeeded.");
        }
    }
```

At this stage, Eclipse's editor has become smothered with wavy red lines, and compilation certainly fails (see Figure 2–4).

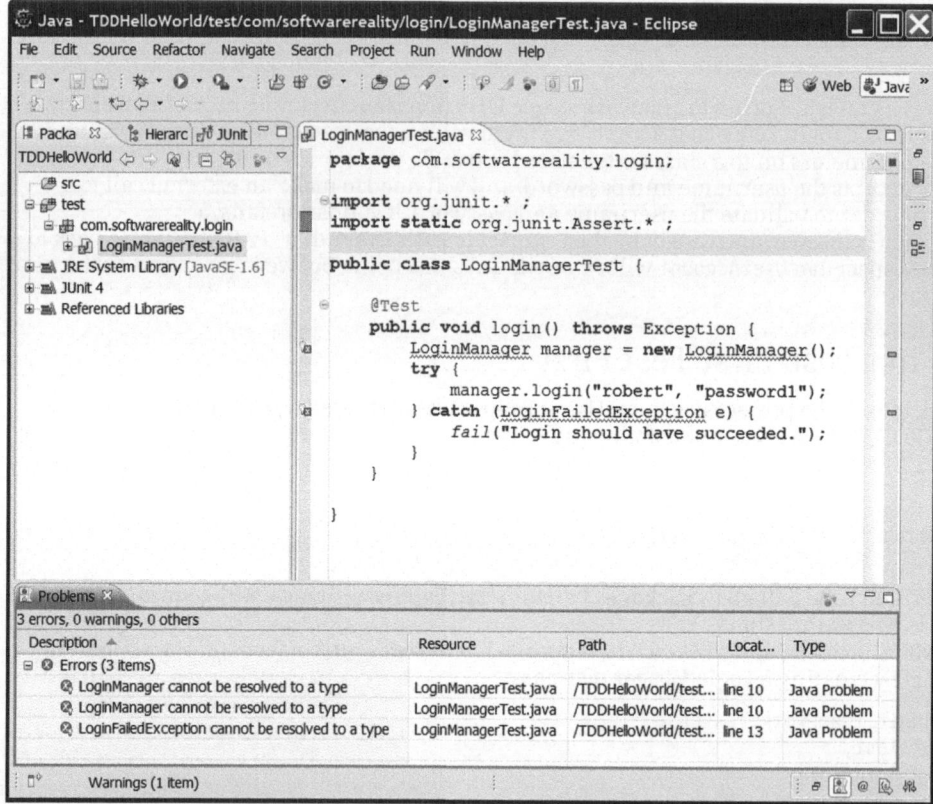

Figure 2–4. *All dressed up with nowhere to go . . . this test needs some code to run against.*

This compilation failure is a valid stage in the TDD process: the test compilation errors tell us that some code must be written in order to make the test pass. So let's do that next, with two new classes:

```
public class LoginManager {
    public void login(String username, String password)
    throws LoginFailedException {
    }
}

public class LoginFailedException extends Exception {
}
```

A NOTE FROM OUR EDITOR

Our editor Jonathan Gennick sent us this comment, which we thought we would share with you as it sums up our own feelings about TDD pretty well:

Last summer, I had someone replace the windows in my dining and living rooms. I should have insisted that the builder attempt to close a window (running the "close window" test on the empty openings before placing any windows into the wall). Only after running the close window test and having it fail should he have actually inserted the new windows into the opening.

Next would come the "see if the window falls out and crashes to the ground and breaks" test. That would fail, indicating the need for screws to secure the windows to my walls. Of course, by then, we'd have broken several hundred dollars' worth of double-paned windows with krypton gas (or whatever) inside.

The builder would think I was an idiot to suggest such an approach. It's amazing that so many developers have been led down essentially that same path.

The code now compiles, so—being eager-beaver TDDers—we rush to run our new unit test straightaway, fully expecting (and hoping for) a red bar, indicating that the test failed. But surprise! Look at Figure 2–5. Our test did not successfully fail. Instead, it failingly succeeded.

Oops, the test passed when it was meant to fail! Sometimes a passing test should be just as disconcerting as a failing test. This is an example of the product code providing feedback into the tests, just as the tests provide feedback on the product code. It's a symbiotic relationship, and it answers the question, what tests the tests? (A variant of the question, who watches the watchers?)

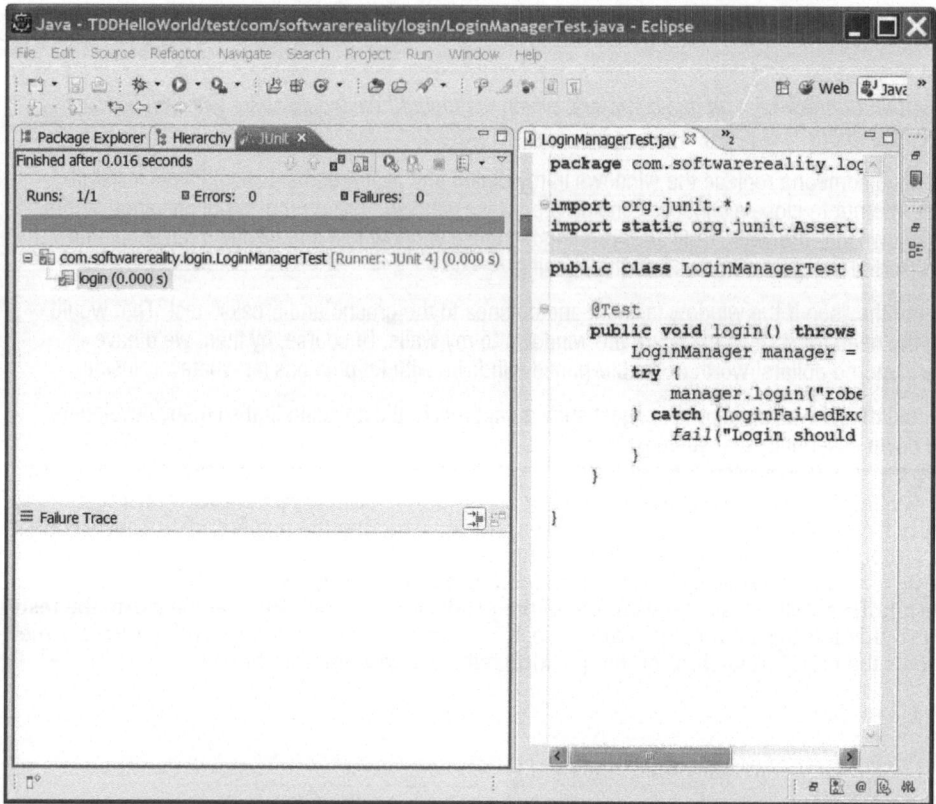

Figure 2–5. Green bar—life is good. Except… what's that nagging feeling?

Following the process strictly, we now add a line into the code to make the test fail:

```
public void login(String username, String password)
throws LoginFailedException {
    throw new LoginFailedException();
}
```

The login() method simply throws a LoginFailedException, indicating that all login attempts currently will fail. The system is now pretty much entirely locked down: no one can login until we write the code to allow it. We could alternatively have changed the first test to be "@Test loginFails()" and pass in an invalid username/password. But then we wouldn't have been implementing the basic pass through the user story first—to enable a user to log in successfully. At any rate, we've now verified that we can indeed feel pain in our forehead when we bang it against a wall!

Next, let's add some code to make the test pass:

```
public void login(String username, String password)
throws LoginFailedException {
    if ("robert".equals(username)
     && "password1".equals(password)) {
```

```
        return;
    }
    throw new LoginFailedException();
}
```

If we re-run the test now, we get a green bar, indicating that the test passed. Does it seem like we're cheating? Well, it's the simplest code that makes the test pass, so it's valid—at least until we add another test to make the requirements more stringent:

```
@Test
public void anotherLogin() throws Exception {
    LoginManager manager = new LoginManager();
    try {
        manager.login("mary", "password2");
    } catch (LoginFailedException e) {
        fail("Login should have succeeded.");
    }
}
```

We now have two test cases: one in which valid user Robert tries to log in, and another in which valid user Mary tries to log in. However, if we re-run the test class, we get a failure:

```
junit.framework.AssertionFailedError: Login should have succeeded.
        at com.softwarereality.login.LoginManagerTest.anotherLogin(LoginManagerTest.java:24)
```

Now, clearly it's time to get real and put in some code that actually does a login check.

Write the Login Check Code to Make the Test Pass

The real code will need to make a call to a RESTful service, passing in the username and password, and get a "login passed" or "login failed" message back. A quick instant-message to the relevant middleware/single-sign-on (SSO) team produces a handy "jar" file that encapsulates the details of making a REST call, and instead exposes this handy interface:

```
package com.mymiddlewareservice.sso;

public interface AccountValidator {

    public boolean validate(String username, String password);
    public void startSession(String username);
    public void endSession(String username);
}
```

The library also contains a "black-box" class, AccountValidatorFactory, which we can use to get at a concrete instance of AccountValidator:

```
public class AccountValidatorFactory {
    public static AccountValidator getAccountValidator() {…}
}
```

We can simply drop this jar file into our project, and call the middleware service in order to validate the user and establish an SSO session for him or her. Utilizing this convenient library, LoginManager now looks like this:

```
public class LoginManager {
    public void login(String username, String password)
```

```
        throws LoginFailedException {
            AccountValidator validator =
                AccountValidatorFactory.getAccountValidator();
            if (validator.validate(username, password)) {
                return;
            }
            throw new LoginFailedException();
        }
}
```

If we were to re-run the tests now, the call to AccountValidator would make a network call to the remote SSO service and validate the username and password... so the test should pass quite happily.

But wait, is that the screeching halt of tires that you can hear?

This raises an important issue with unit testing in general: you really don't want your tested code to be making external calls during testing. Your unit test suite will be executed during the build process, so relying on external calls makes the build more fragile: suddenly it's dependent on network availability, servers being up and working, and so forth. "Service not available" shouldn't count as a build error.

For this reason, we generally go to great lengths to keep the unit-tested code insular. Figure 2–6 shows one way this could be done. In the sequence diagram, LoginManager checks whether it's running in the "live" environment or a unit-test/mock environment. If the former, it calls the real SSO service; if the latter, it calls a mock version.

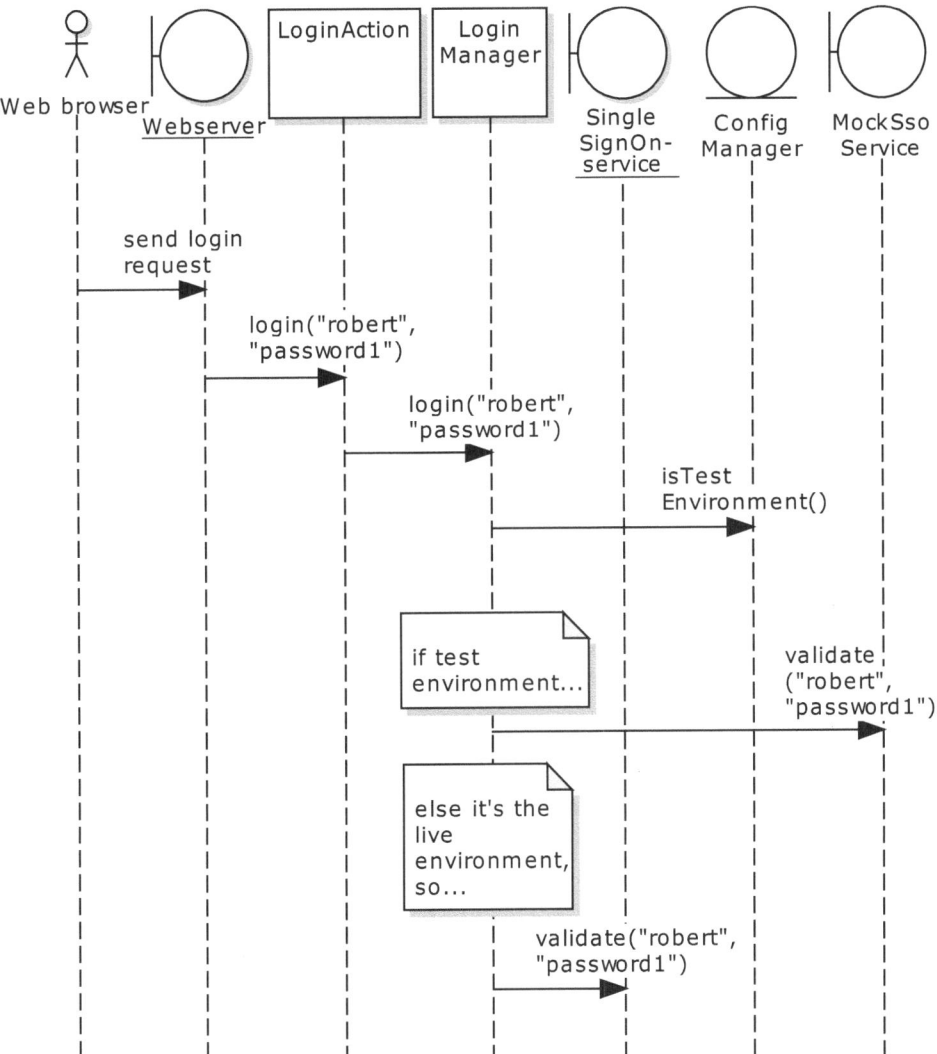

Figure 2–6. *A common anti-pattern: the code branches depending on which environment it's in.*

Yikes. This would quickly become a nightmare of "if-else if" statements that check whether this is a live or test environment. Production code would become more complex as it becomes littered with these checks every time it needs to make an external call, not to mention special-handling code to return "dummy" objects for the tests' purposes. You really want to place as few restrictions and stipulations (aka hacks, workarounds) on the production code as possible—and you definitely don't want the design to degrade in order to allow for unit testing.

Create a Mock Object

Luckily, there's another way that also happens to promote good design. So-called mock object frameworks such as JMock, EasyMock, and Mockito[7] use special magic (okay, Java reflection and dynamic proxies behind the scenes) to create convenient, blank/non-functioning versions of classes and interfaces. For this example, we'll use JMock (we also use Mockito later in the book).

Going back to our `LoginManagerTest` class, we make it "JMock-ready" using an annotation and a context:

```
@RunWith(JMock.class)
public class LoginManagerTest  {
    Mockery context = new JUnit4Mockery();
```

Re-running the test now—and getting the same error as earlier—you can verify that the test is now going through JMock by scanning through the stack trace for the `AssertionFailedError`:

```
junit.framework.AssertionFailedError: Login should have succeeded.
        at com.softwarereality.login.LoginManagerTest.anotherLogin(LoginManagerTest.java:32)
        at sun.reflect.NativeMethodAccessorImpl.invoke0(Native Method)
        at sun.reflect.NativeMethodAccessorImpl.invoke(NativeMethodAccessorImpl.java:39)
        at
sun.reflect.DelegatingMethodAccessorImpl.invoke(DelegatingMethodAccessorImpl.java:25)
        at org.junit.internal.runners.TestMethod.invoke(TestMethod.java:66)
        at org.jmock.integration.junit4.JMock$1.invoke(JMock.java:37)
```

Creating a mock instance of AccountValidator is pretty straightforward:

```
validator = context.mock(AccountValidator.class);
```

The next problem is how to get `LoginManager` to use this mock instance instead of the production version of `AccountValidator` returned by `AccountValidatorFactory`. In the `LoginManager` code we just wrote, the `login()` method directly calls `AccountValidatorFactory.getAccountValidator()`. We have no "hook" with which to tell it to use our version instead. So let's add a hook:

```
public class LoginManager {

    private AccountValidator validator;

    public void setValidator(AccountValidator validator) {
        this.validator = validator;
    }

    synchronized AccountValidator getValidator() {
        if (validator == null) {
            validator = AccountValidatorFactory.getAccountValidator();
        }
        return validator;
    }
```

------

[7] See www.jmock.org, http://mockito.org, and http://easymock.org. Mock object frameworks are available for other languages, e.g., Mock4AS for use with FlexUnit. NUnit (for .Net) supports dynamic mock objects out of the box.

```
    public void login(String username, String password)
    throws LoginFailedException {
        if (getValidator().validate(username, password)) {
            return;
        }
        throw new LoginFailedException();
    }
}
```

This version uses a little bit of dependency injection (DI) to allow us to inject our own flavor of AccountValidator. Before the login() method is called, we can now set an alternative, mocked-out version of AccountValidator. The only change inside login() is that instead of using the validator member directly, it calls getValidator(), which will create the "real" version of AccountValidator if we haven't already injected a different version.

The complete login() test method now looks like this:

```
@Test
public void login() throws Exception {
    final AccountValidator validator = context.mock(AccountValidator.class);
    LoginManager manager = new LoginManager();
    manager.setValidator(validator);

    try {
        manager.login("robert", "password1");
    } catch (LoginFailedException e) {
        fail("Login should have succeeded.");
    }
}
```

Running the test still causes a red bar, however. This is because the new, mocked-out AccountValidator.validate() method returns false by default. To make it return true instead, you need to tell JMock what you're expecting to happen. You do this by passing in one of its appropriately named Expectations objects into the context:

```
    context.checking(new Expectations() {{
        oneOf(validator).validate("robert", "password1"); will(returnValue(true));
    }});
```

■ **Note** At first glance, this probably doesn't look much like valid Java code. The designers of JMock are actually going for a "natural language" approach to the syntax, giving it a so-called *fluent interface*[8] so that the code reads more like plain English. Whether they've achieved a clearer, human-readable API or something far more obtuse is open to debate![9]

This code snippet is saying: "During the test, I'm expecting one call to validate() with the arguments "robert" and "password1", and for this one call I want the value true to be returned. In fact, this is one of JMock's great strengths—it allows you to specify exactly how many times you're expecting a method to be called, and to make the test fail automatically if the method isn't called at all, is called the wrong number of times, or is called with the wrong set of values.

For our immediate purposes, however, this is just a pleasant bonus: at this stage we're interested only in getting our mock object to return the value we're expecting.

Re-running the code with the new Expectations in place results in a green bar. We'll now need to do the same for the other test case—where we're passing in "mary" and "password2". However, simply repeating this technique will result in quite a bit of duplicated code—and it's "plumbing" code at that, very little to do with the actual test case. It's time to refactor the test class into something leaner.

Refactor the Code to See the Design Emerge

We'll start by refactoring the test code, as that's our immediate concern. However, the real point of this exercise is to see the product code's design emerge as you add more tests and write the code to make the tests pass.

Here's the refactored test code:

```java
@RunWith(JMock.class)
public class LoginManagerTest {

    Mockery context = new JUnit4Mockery();
    LoginManager manager;
    AccountValidator validator;

    @Before
    public void setUp() throws Exception {
        validator = context.mock(AccountValidator.class);
        manager = new LoginManager();
        manager.setValidator(validator);
    }
```

---

[8] See www.martinfowler.com/bliki/FluentInterface.html.

[9] This white paper by the creators of JMock describes the evolution of an embedded domain-specific language (EDSL), using JMock as their example. It's well worth checking out if you're interested in DSLs/fluent interfaces: www.mockobjects.com/files/evolving_an_edsl.ooplsa2006.pdf.

```
@After
public void tearDown() throws Exception {
    manager.setValidator(null);
    manager = null;
    validator = null;
}

@Test
public void login() throws Exception {
    context.checking(new Expectations() {{
        oneOf(validator).validate("robert", "password1"); will(returnValue(true));
    }});

    try {
        manager.login("robert", "password1");
    } catch (LoginFailedException e) {
        fail("Login should have succeeded.");
    }
}

@Test
public void anotherLogin() throws Exception {
    context.checking(new Expectations() {{
        oneOf(validator).validate("mary", "password2"); will(returnValue(true));
    }});

    try {
        manager.login("mary", "password2");
    } catch (LoginFailedException e) {
        fail("Login should have succeeded.");
    }
}
}
```

We've created @Before and @After fixtures, which are run before and after each test case to set up the mock validator and the LoginManager, which is the class under test. This saves having to repeat this setup code each time. There's still some work that can be done to improve the design of this test class, but we'll come back to that in a moment. Another quick run through the test runner produces a green bar—looking good. But so far, all we've been testing for is login success. We should also pass in some invalid login credentials, and ensure that those are handled correctly. Let's add a new test case:

```
@Test( expected = LoginFailedException.class )
public void invalidLogin() throws Exception {
    context.checking(new Expectations() {{
        oneOf(validator).validate("wideboy", "blagger1"); will(returnValue(false));
    }});

    manager.login("wideboy", "blagger1");
}
```

This time, that old trickster Wideboy is trying to gain access to the system. But he won't get very far—not because we have a tightly designed SSO remote service running encrypted over SSL, but because our mock object has been set to return false. That'll show 'im! Stepping through the code, the first line uses a JUnit 4 annotation as with the other test methods; however, this time we've also specified that we're expecting the LoginFailedException to be thrown. We're expecting this exception to be triggered because the mock object will return false, indicating a login failure from the mocked-out SSO service. The code that's actually under test is the login() method in LoginManager. This test demonstrates that it's doing what's expected.

THE MAD HATTER'S REFACTORING PARTY[10]

"How can designs figure themselves out from code?" asked Alice

Alice, not knowing what else to do, and feeling somewhat shaky again after hearing about designs figuring themselves out from code, decided to follow the rabbit for a while. On they went, the rabbit pausing every few feet to iterate around in a circle a few times. Eventually, the rabbit, rushing ahead at top speed, pulled far enough ahead that Alice couldn't see him anymore.

Alice kept walking, and after a time she came to a clearing where she saw the rabbit, along with a large mouse and a little man wearing a big hat, all working furiously over a table and some chairs. When Alice walked up, all the legs from the table and chairs were sitting in a big pile on the ground. Alice watched as the Hatter, the rabbit, and the dormouse each grabbed four legs from the pile and screwed them into a chair. The problem was that the legs were of different lengths, and Alice watched in fascination as they each finished assembling their chair, turned it over, and sat down. The chairs often tipped over, what with the legs being of different lengths and all, and when this happened they all yelled out in unison, "Failed the unit test," flipped the chairs back over, and began unscrewing the legs and tossing them back onto the pile.

---

[10] An excerpt from Doug's talk, "Alice in Use Case Land," given as the keynote speech at the UML World conference way back in 2001. See the full transcript here: www.iconixsw.com/aliceinusecaseland.html and also in Appendix "A for Alice".

"What kind of game are you playing?" asked Alice.

"It's not a game, we're refactoring the furniture," replied the Hatter.

"Why don't you read the documentation for assembling the chairs?" asked Alice. "It's sure to specify which legs should go on which chairs."

"It's oral documentation," said the Hatter.

"Oh. You mean you don't have any."

"No," said the Hatter. "Written documentation is for cowards. We can refactor very quickly, so we can be brave enough to let the design figure itself out," he added.

"Oh, yes. The rabbit said I should ask you about that," said Alice. "How can designs figure themselves out from code?"

"You poor, ignorant child," said the Hatter, in quite a condescending tone. "The code *is* the design, don't you see? Perhaps you'd better let the Duchess explain it to you."

He resumed refactoring the chairs.

Looking at the last three test methods, you should see that there's something of a pattern of repeated code emerging, despite our recent refactoring. It would make sense to create a "workhorse" method and move the hairy plumbing code—setting the test case's expectations and calling LoginManager—into there. This is really just a case of moving code around, but, as you'll see, it makes a big difference to the test class's readability. Actually, we end up with two new methods: expectLoginSuccess() and expectLoginFailure().

Here are our two new methods:

```
void expectLoginSuccess(final String username, final String password) {
    context.checking(new Expectations() {{
        oneOf(validator).validate(username, password); will(returnValue(true));
    }});
    try {
        manager.login(username, password);
    } catch (LoginFailedException e) {
        fail("Login should have succeeded.");
    }
}

void expectLoginFailure(final String username, final String password) throws
LoginFailedException {
    context.checking(new Expectations() {{
        oneOf(validator).validate(username, password); will(returnValue(false));
    }});
    manager.login(username, password);
}
```

Here's what the three refactored test methods now look like:

```
@Test
public void login() throws Exception {
    expectLoginSuccess("robert", "password1");
}
```

```
@Test
public void anotherLogin() throws Exception {
    expectLoginSuccess("mary", "password2");
}

@Test( expected = LoginFailedException.class )
public void invalidLogin() throws Exception {
    expectLoginFailure("wideboy", "blagger1");
}
```

All of a sudden, each test case looks very focused on purely the test values, without any of the plumbing code hiding the purpose or expectations of the test case. Another quick re-run of the tests produces a green bar (see Figure 2–7) so the change doesn't appear to have broken anything.

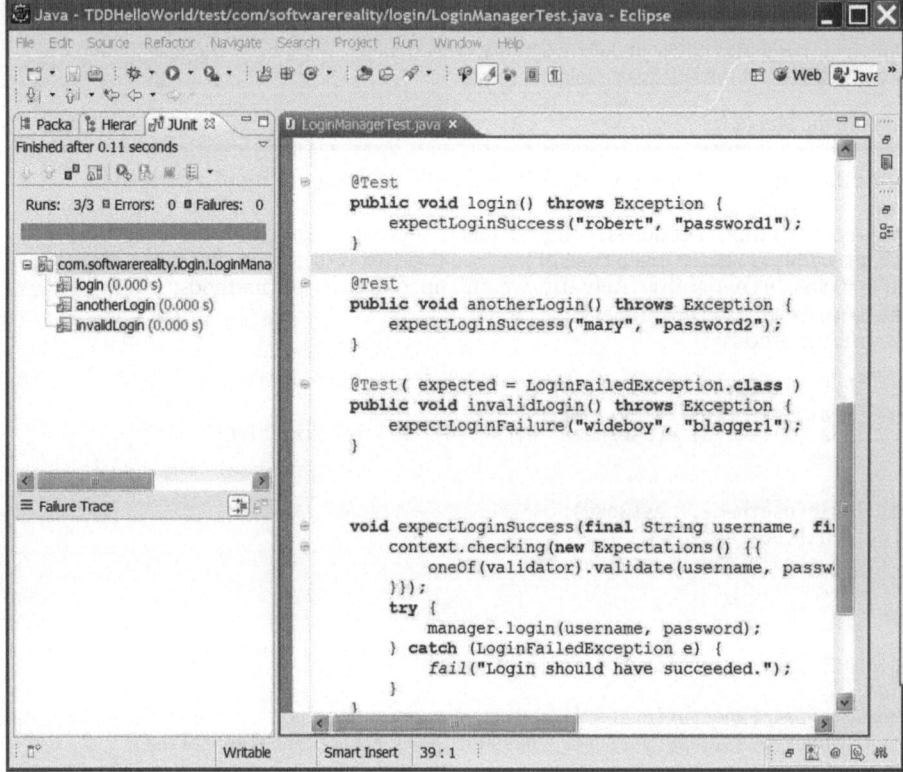

Figure 2–7. We refactored the code (again), so we re-run the tests to make sure nothing's broken.

Although UML modeling is sometimes seen as anathema to TDD (though by a shrinking minority, we hope), we took advantage of Enterprise Architect (EA)'s reverse engineering capability to vacuum up the new source code into a class model—see Figure 2–8. We also put together a quick sequence diagram to show how the code interacts—see Figure 2–9. Note that these diagrams might or might not be created on a real TDD project. We'd guess probably not, especially the sequence diagram. After all, who needs documentation when there's JUnit code?

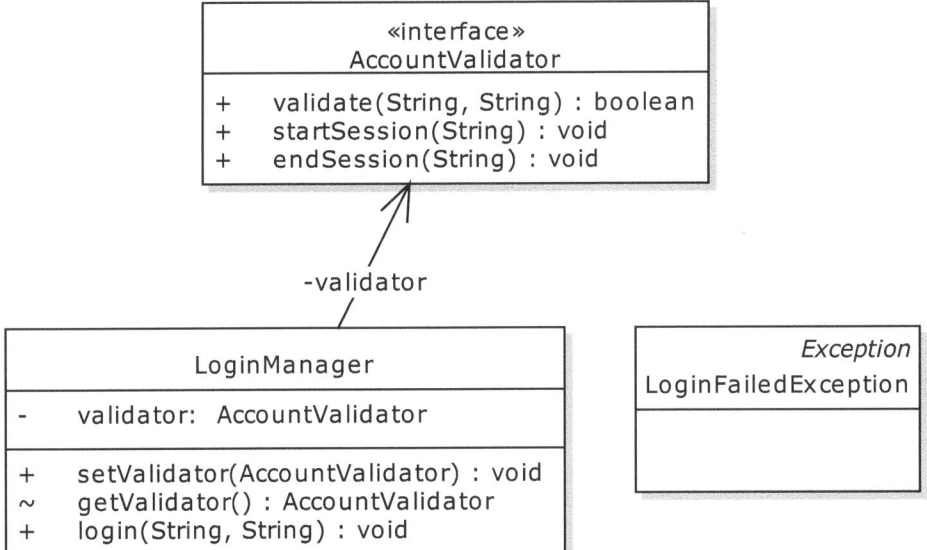

Figure 2–8. The product code, reverse-engineered into EA

Notice that throughout this coding session, we haven't even attempted to write any tests for the remote SSO service that our code will call at production time. This is because—at this stage, at least— the SSO service isn't what we are developing. If it turns out that there's a problem in the SSO code, we'll have enough confidence in our own code—as it's covered with unit tests—to safely say that the problem must be inside the "black box" service. This isn't so much "it's their problem, not ours," as that's distinctly territorial, but rather it helps to track down the problem and get the issue resolved as quickly as possible. We can do this because we've produced well-factored code with good unit-test code coverage.

Having said that, at some stage we *do* want to prove that our code works along with the SSO service. In addition to good old-fashioned manual testing, we'll also write an acceptance test case that tests the system end-to-end.

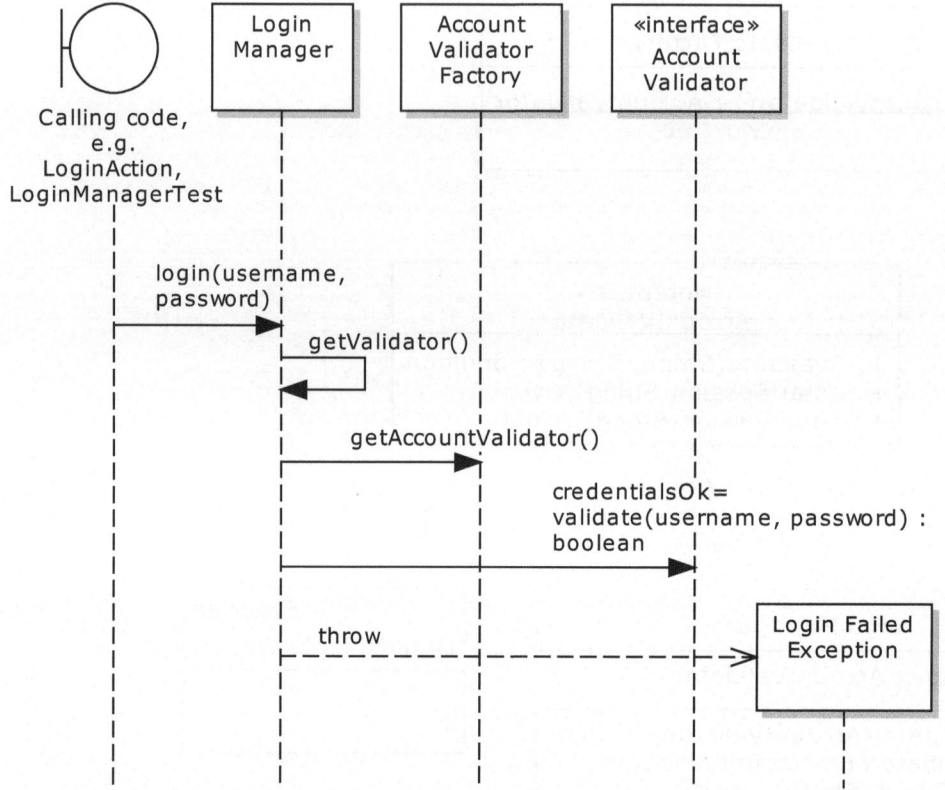

Figure 2–9. *A sequence diagram showing the product behavior that's under test*

Acceptance Testing with TDD

The TDD story pretty much starts and ends with unit testing. Given a user story, you create test fixtures and unit test code, and drive the product code from the tests. However, there's a major aspect of testing that is often overlooked by teams who adopt TDD: customer tests (aka acceptance tests).

With acceptance tests you're writing tests that "cover" the requirements; with unit tests you're writing tests that "cover" the design and the code. Another way to look at it is that acceptance tests make sure you're coding the right thing; unit tests make sure you're coding it right.

While unit testing principles are crisp, clear, well understood, and generally easy to grasp, guidance on acceptance testing is rare, vague, and woolly. Acceptance testing frameworks such as Fitnesse provide little more than holding pages for tables of values, while leaving the difficult part—plumbing the tests into your code base—as an exercise for the reader. In fact, we've noticed that many TDDers just don't think about acceptance tests. It seems that when TDD was unshackled from XP and allowed to float away over the horizon, a vitally important part of it—customer acceptance tests—was left behind. This almost blinkered focus on the code isn't surprising, as it tends to be programmers who introduce TDD into organizations.

Conclusion: TDD = Too Damn Difficult

Now that we've been through the exhausting exercise of driving the design from the unit tests, let's reflect again on the anemic amount of code that was produced by this herculean effort. Figure 2–10 shows the sum total of the code that we've tested (on the right, a grand total of 28 lines in LoginManager), and the unit test code that got us there (65 lines in LoginManagerTest, on the left).

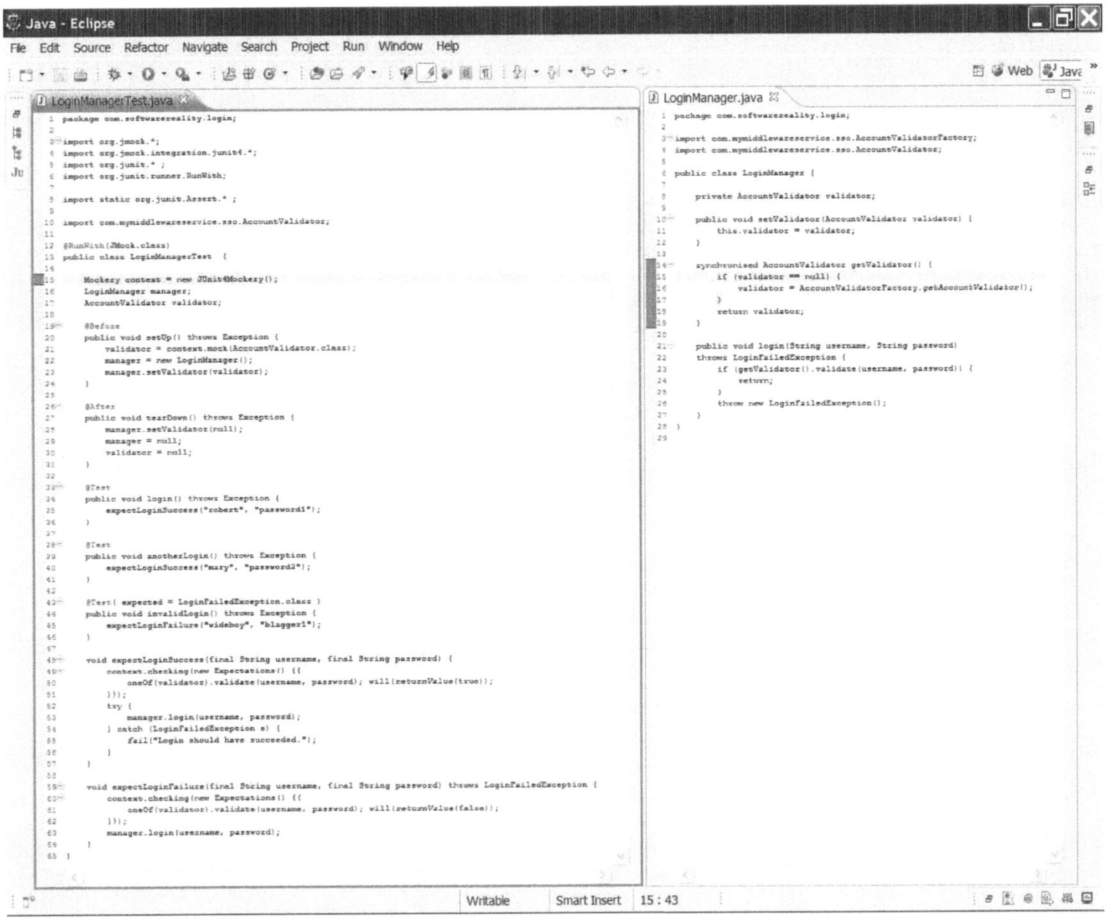

Figure 2–10. *It took this amount of test code (on the left),* ***not counting refactoring****, to produce this amount of product code (on the right).*

At first glance, this really doesn't appear all that unreasonable. Sixty-five lines of unit test code to produce 25 lines of production code—a bit more than 2:1—isn't that unreasonable a price to pay for having a good suite of regression tests. The real issue is how much work it took us to get to those 65 lines of JUnit code.

When you consider that our 65 lines of final test code took somewhere around eight refactorings to develop, you can come up with an approximate level of effort on the order of writing *500 lines of test code to produce 25 lines of product code*. So we're looking at an "effort multiplier" of something on the order of 20 lines of test code for every line of product code.

For all this churning of wheels, gnashing of teeth, and object mockery, we've actually tested only the "check password" code. All of the other requirements (locking the account after three failed login attempts, username not found in the account master list, etc.) haven't even begun to be addressed. So the TDD version of Login (all requirements) would be a 60- or 70-page chapter.

If this seems Too Damn Difficult to you, we think you'll enjoy the next chapter, where we'll show you an easier way.

Summary

In this chapter, we continued our comparison of TDD and DDT by following along with a "Hello world!" (aka Login) requirement using TDD. It became obvious how the design begins to emerge from the code and the tests. However, you may have noticed that we were spending more time refactoring the test code than the "real" product code (though this was in large part exaggerated by the simplicity of the example—there will be lots more refactoring of product code in a more complex example). The process is also very low-level, we might even say myopic, focusing on individual lines of code from quite an early stage. While one of the primary goals of TDD is improved code quality, it's definitely not a "big picture" methodology. To gain the picture of your overall system design, especially on larger projects, you would need some other design process in addition to TDD.

In the next chapter we restart the "Hello world!" example and, this time, use it to illustrate how Design-Driven Testing works.

CHAPTER 3

■ ■ ■

"Hello World!" Using DDT

In this chapter, Alice wakes up and wonders if her adventures through the TDD looking glass were all just a disturbing dream. Meanwhile we'll hit Reboot on the *Login* example and start over, this time following DDT. We hope this will help to illustrate some of the key differences between the two approaches. In particular, DDT provides a systematic method of identifying, up-front, the critical areas of a design that will benefit the most from automated testing.

■ **Note** As this chapter provides an "end-to-end" run of DDT (from requirements to tests and product code), we'll breeze through a number of concepts that we'll return to later, and spend the rest of the book exploring at a more sedate pace. So don't panic if things aren't entirely clear at first; this chapter is more about providing a taste of what DDT is all about.

Top Ten Features of ICONIX/DDT

Before we get started, let's look at the top ten features of ICONIX/DDT. This section expands on the right column in Table 1-1 (see Chapter 1), which lists the main differences between TDD and DDT.

10. DDT Includes Business Requirement Tests

When you design software following the ICONIX Process, you will typically create "requirement" elements in your UML model, and allocate those requirements to use cases. Since you've taken the trouble to do this, it seems only reasonable that any automated support for DDT should create tests to verify that each requirement has been satisfied. So that's what we do.

9. DDT Includes Scenario Tests

A key feature of DDT is that you create scenario tests by expanding use cases into "threads." ICONIX Process is a use case–driven approach to development. Following this approach, your use cases will be modeled to identify both *sunny day* and *rainy day* scenarios. As it turns out, this is very convenient for defining scenario tests... these tests typically involve a *script* of user actions and expected system responses. Each "script" or "thread" might involve part of the sunny day scenario combined with one of the "rainy day" branches. DDT includes a **thread expansion** algorithm that helps us to create these acceptance tests automatically from the use cases. We'll talk more about scenario testing and "use case thread expansion" in Chapter 7.

8. Tests Are Driven from Design

With DDT, the tests have two purposes:

- Validate your implementation of the design (primary task)
- Act as regression tests (secondary task)

The tests are driven from the design, and, therefore, the tests are there primarily to validate the design. That said, there's more common ground between this and TDD than you might think. A lot of the "design churn" (aka refactoring) to be found in TDD projects can be calmed down and given some stability by first applying the up-front design and testing techniques described in this book.

With DDT the tests also document the intent of the code to an extent, but that's a nice side effect rather than the main purpose, as the process also generates "real" documentation for you along the way.

So the tests are not the design, and the design is not driven from the tests, but rather the tests are identified systematically from the design. *With DDT the design is the design, the code is the code, and the tests are the tests.* (Pretty radical, hey?) You'll use modern development tools to keep the documented design model in sync with the code. You'll also distinguish between the design level—unit tests—and the analysis level—acceptance tests—and clearly understand when it's time to write each one.

7. DDT Includes Controller Tests

What's a "controller test," you ask? Simply put, it's similar to a unit test, but it tests a small group of closely related methods that together perform a useful function. You can do controller testing with DDT because the ICONIX Process supports a "conceptual design" stage, which uses robustness diagrams as an intermediate representation of a use case at the conceptual level. If you think of unit tests as "atomic," you can think of controller tests as "molecular."

6. DDT Tests Smarter, Not Harder

DDT takes a "test smarter, not harder" philosophy, meaning tests are more focused on code "hot spots." With true DDT, you don't take an incremental approach to design; therefore, you don't need to refactor nearly as much, and you don't need eleventy billion tests poking into every nook and armpit of the deepest recesses of your code. Instead, the tests are targeted precisely at the critical junctures of the code that you've highlighted in the course of the design and requirements modeling as being the most cost-effective areas to test.

5. DDT Unit Tests Are "Classical" Unit Tests

DDT unit tests are driven directly from the detailed design. You'll write one or more unit tests for each method you've drawn on a sequence diagram (unless it's already covered by a controller test—but more about that in Chapters 5 and 6).

This contrasts with TDD unit tests (sometimes also called programmer tests), which, as you saw in Chapter 2, are somewhere between classical, atom-sized unit tests and DDT-style controller tests.

4. DDT Test Cases Can Be Transformed into Test Code

As you saw in the overview in Chapter 1, there are a few steps involved in DDT. But at the high level, we first identify test cases from the design, and then we transform the tests into UML classes, from which actual test code can be generated. We've worked with Sparx Systems to build automated test transformations for JUnit, NUnit, and FlexUnit.

3. DDT Test Cases Lead to Test Plans

As you'll see later in the chapter (and especially in Part 2), once you identify a test you can populate it with things like inputs, outputs, descriptions, and expected results. You can essentially generate test plans from your cases. These will get forward-generated into xUnit test code, and you can also generate test plan reports.

2. DDT Tests Are Useful to Developers and QA Teams

DDT test cases are useful to both developers and QA teams—and the customer and business analysts, too. Since the scope of DDT includes identifying requirements tests and acceptance tests, it's quite naturally relevant to quality assurance folks. So, while still serving the "green bar" needs of comprehensive unit testing by the development team, it's also going to be useful for independent QA teams. As you'll see in Chapter 7, use case scenario descriptions transform rather nicely into QA-style test specs.

1. DDT Can Eliminate Redundant Effort

One of the big benefits of doing a model-based design that includes identifying requirements and allocating those requirements to use cases, as opposed to refactoring a system into existence, is that you can eliminate a lot of redundant work. A little later in this chapter you'll see an example of a requirement (Validate Password syntax) that is germane to both a Create Password use case and to Login. It's easy to see how someone could assign one of these "stories" to one team and the other to a different team, each of whom could come up with a separate (and, we hope, similar) definition for the requirement and two redundant sets of tests. This sort of duplicate effort is guarded against with DDT, as the requirement (and associated tests) would be defined once, and the tests would be re-used.

Login Implemented Using DDT

In Chapter 1, you saw a "bare bones" description of the steps in DDT. In the real world, of course, even the most agile teams rely heavily on software tools to support their development efforts. So for this walkthrough we'll show you how DDT can be made to sing when it has the right tools support.

ICONIX/DDT AND ENTERPRISE ARCHITECT

While you don't have to use vendor-specific tools to follow DDT, we'd recommend that you take a look at Sparx Systems' Agile/ICONIX add-in for their UML modeling tool, Enterprise Architect (EA). We use EA extensively in this book. The Agile/ICONIX add-in requires at least EA 7.5, available from www.sparxsystems.com. EA itself is reasonably priced; there's also a 30-day trial version if you want to give it a go.

You can find more information about both EA and the Agile/ICONIX add-in at www.iconixsw.com. Simply follow the links, and then download and run the add-in installer to install the add-in into your copy of EA.

As you saw in the previous chapter, TDD is generally used in conjunction with XP-style user stories rather than functional requirements and use cases. TDD and use cases are not incompatible: in fact, TDDers should be able to use a lot from this book, which follows a use case–driven process.

One big differentiator between the two approaches is that ICONIX/DDT separates user stories into "active voice" use cases, which describe user interactions with the system, and "passive voice" requirements, which specify what the customer wants the system to do. There's quite a significant benefit from treating these two kinds of "stories" differently, as you'll see shortly.

Let's consider a simple Login use case, which satisfies the three requirements shown in Figure 3–1.

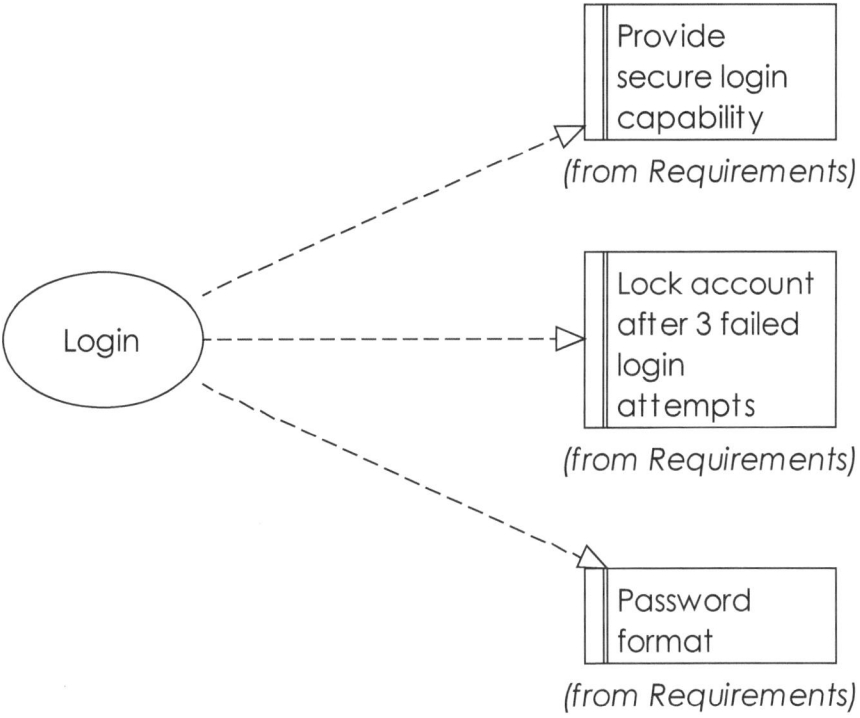

Figure 3–1. *Login use case that satisfies three requirements*

You'll notice a striking similarity between the three requirements and the three user stories from Chapter 2. The Login use case itself consists of the following active voice, user-focused Basic Course (sometimes known as the "sunny day scenario"), and a number of Alternate Courses (the "rainy day scenarios"):

BASIC COURSE:
The system displays the Login page. The user enters the username and password, and then clicks Login. The system checks the syntax of the password, finds the user's account in the master account list, verifies that the password is correct, and starts a session.

ALTERNATE COURSES:
Improperly formatted password: *System displays "Invalid login credentials" message to user.*
Account not found, or password incorrect: *System displays "Invalid login credentials" message.*
User clicks Cancel: *System closes the Login page.*

The process for writing a use case of this form is a simple one. First, to identify the Basic Course, ask, *what happens? (and then what happens, and then what happens…)* Second, to identify the first Alternate Course, ask, *what else happens? (and how do we deal with that when it happens)* And then keep on asking, *what else happens?* until you can't think of any more Alternate Courses. The key here is to think of as many "rainy day scenarios," or even just different ways the user might want to interact with the system, and make sure they're all recorded. This way, they won't be forgotten about when you move on to the design.[1]

■ **Note** We explore how to write concrete, complete, design-ready use case scenarios in Chapter 7.

Let's move on to the DDT-specific steps to get from our use case to the code and a comprehensive, targeted set of tests. The steps that we'll follow in this chapter are the following:

Step 1: Create a robustness diagram (conceptual design).

Step 2: Create the controller test cases from your robustness diagram.

Step 3: Add scenarios to each test case.

Step 4: Transform your controller test cases into test classes.

Step 5: Generate the controller test code.

Step 6: Detailed design: create a sequence diagram for the use case.

Step 7: Create unit test cases from your sequence diagram, and cherry-pick the non-redundant ones.

Step 8: Fill in the test code using the generated comments as guidance, and write the code to make the tests pass.

Step 1: Create a Robustness Diagram

Using the ICONIX Process, you create a use case for each robustness diagram… whoops, we're still in TDD mode there—let's flip it around! You create a robustness diagram for each use case. You can think of this as the conceptual design phase.

---

[1] Actually, just to see if you're awake (and to show you why we put requirements onto robustness diagrams), we forgot one, as you'll see in a few pages. You win a pork pie if you caught it. If you missed it, time for a cup of coffee.

Note A robustness diagram is a picture version of your use case: it's a form of preliminary, or conceptual, design, in which you start to link your use case scenarios to objects and actions. The robustness diagram also provides a "sanity check" for your requirements: if it's proving difficult to create a loosely modeled conceptual design from your requirements, then it would be virtually impossible to drive code and tests from them. So robustness analysis provides a tighter feedback loop than "requirements then tests+code" to get the requirements right from the start.

If you're following along with EA, here's the neat thing (the first of many): you can generate the robustness diagram using the Agile/ICONIX add-in. To do this, select the use case and choose "Create New Robustness Diagram" from the Add-Ins/ICONIX Agile Process menu (see Figure 3–2).

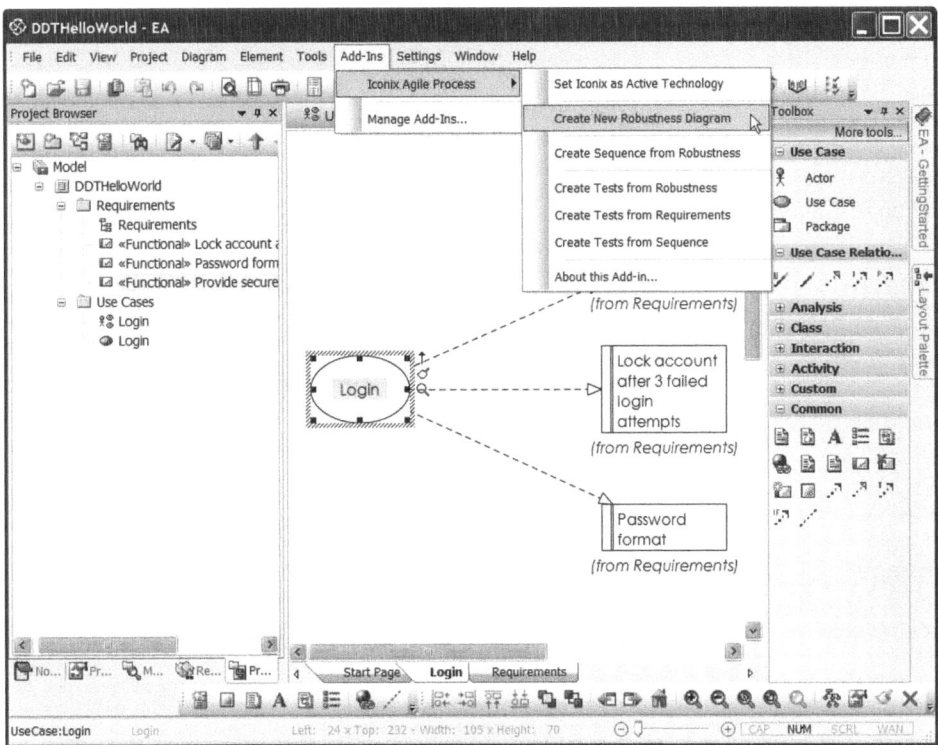

Figure 3–2. Generating a robustness diagram for the Login use case

The add-in creates a new robustness diagram under the use case in the Project Browser, and propagates the requirements (if desired) onto the new diagram—see Figure 3–3.

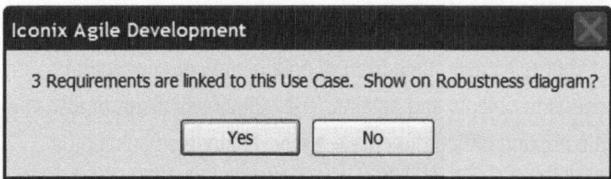

Figure 3–3. Click Yes to add the requirements to the new robustness diagram.

The add-in also creates a new note that is hot-linked to the use case text—see Figure 3–4.

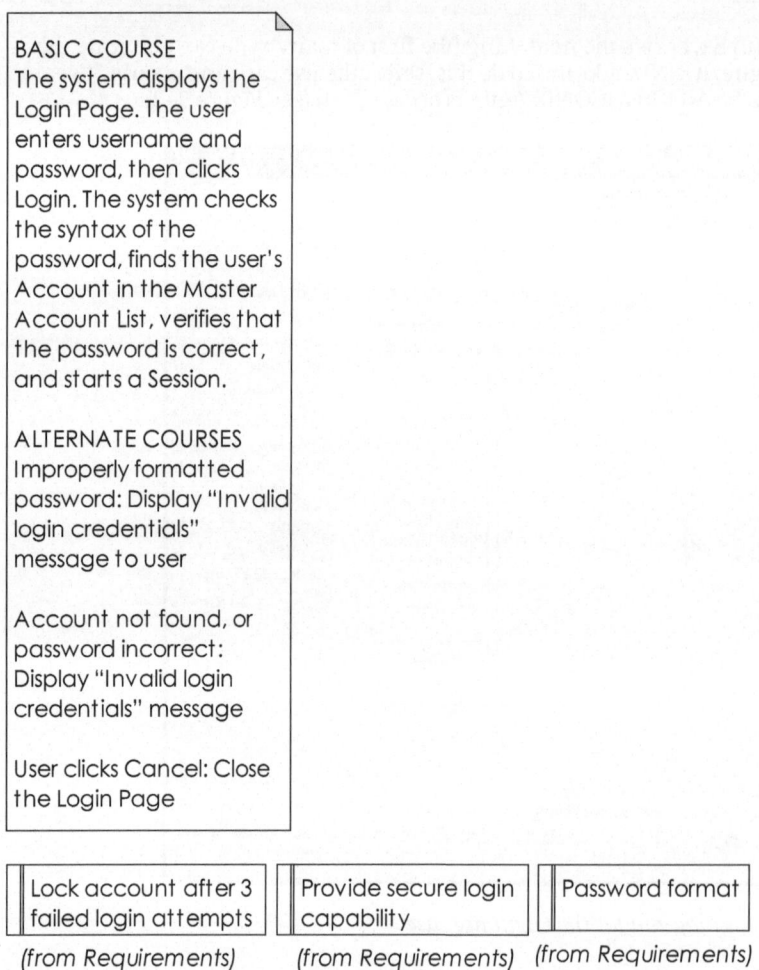

Figure 3–4. The blank robustness diagram, with the use case text and requirements automatically added

Having the requirements on the robustness diagram helps to make sure you haven't forgotten any requirements as you analyze the use case.

Next you'll want to draw the robustness diagram (see Figure 3–5). This is essentially a picture of the use case. Starting from the top left of the diagram, you should be able to trace the use case text along the diagram. Creating the robustness diagram is known as conceptual design—it's an early "sanity check" to ensure that the use case is fit to drive a detailed design, and tests, of course. Don't worry about the details for now. We'll cover robustness analysis in Chapter 6, but for a really detailed illustration of the technique, we can recommend our other book, *Use Case Driven Object Modeling with UML: Theory and Practice.*

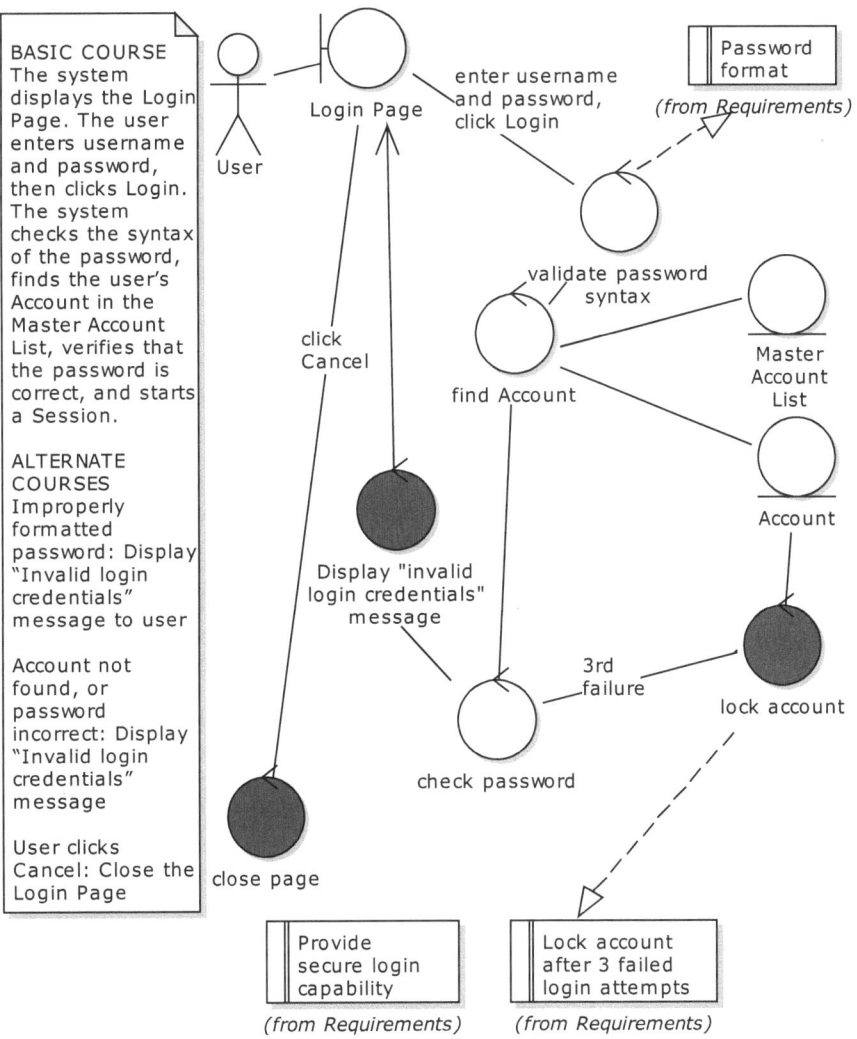

Figure 3–5. The completed robustness diagram. Whoops, why isn't that "lock account" requirement discussed in the use case?

A couple of questions arose during robustness analysis:

- Isn't the first alternate course, "Improperly formatted password," better suited to a *Create New Account* use case, where checks would be made on the new password for such things as minimum size and mix of upper/lower case letters? The idea is that if the same initial check is made when the user is logging in, then it saves a database lookup if the password is obviously invalid—as long as we generate the same "invalid login credentials" message as opposed to a different one.

- There's a requirement "Lock account after 3 failed login attempts," but why isn't this also in the use case text? (It should be an alternate course.) That one's easy: we forgot to add it in, but on drawing the robustness diagram, because the requirement is right there on the diagram, it stood out like Che Guevara at a Canary Wharf wine bar.

These kinds of "reality checks"—questions arising about the requirements, prompting a chat with the customer/project stakeholders, or gaps highlighted in the use case text—happen time and time again during robustness analysis. The added benefit for DDTers is that we won't redundantly generate unit tests for the password format requirement in the "Create a New Password" story, as might have happened if two pairs of TDDers were each given one of the stories.

By analyzing your use case using robustness analysis, you've added a lot of information to the model that can be used to drive the testing of the application. To begin with, the add-in can automatically generate test cases for each "controller" on the robustness diagram… which brings us to the next step.

Step 2: Create Controller Test Cases

On the robustness diagram (see Figure 3–5), the circles with an arrow at the top are *controllers*. These represent the verbs, or actions—something that the system does in response to a user's impetus. For example, "Lock account," "Validate password syntax," etc. are all actions, so they are represented as controllers. If you think about it, these are the real processing points in the system being designed, so… these are the hot spots in the system that you'll want to cover with automated tests.

It's worth emphasizing that, because if you understand this point then you're easily within reach of fully appreciating and understanding the "test smarter" philosophy that underpins DDT:

> *The controllers represent the system behavior organized into convenient bite-size pieces that usually represent a small group of methods working together to perform a logical function. They're the moving parts in the machine, so they are the critical areas that most need to be tested. As it turns out, robustness analysis is a straightforward, efficient method of discovering these critical areas.*

Controllers are also known as logical software functions: when you identify controllers, you're specifying the system behavior. If you think of unit tests as "atomic," you can think of controller tests as "molecular," as in Figure 3–6. [2]

---

[2] Regarding the molecule picture, for you chemists, that's dichlorodiphenyltrichloroethane, of course.

Figure 3–6. A bug-killing molecular controller test composed of "atomic" unit tests

So, to generate the controller test cases, again go to the Add-ins menu, and this time choose "Create Tests from Robustness." For the result, see Figure 3–7. The add-in has generated one test case for each controller on the robustness diagram.

With Figure 3–7, it's not too early to start noticing the increased scope of test coverage compared with Chapter 2. We're immediately getting *test coverage across the entire use case*, not myopically focused in on password validation. In Figure 3–8 you can see that we're also automatically generating test cases against the requirements.

So the benefits of DDT vs. TDD are beginning to emerge, which, we hope, will benefit you on your own project:

- The tools support will help make sure you don't forget any requirements.

- You'll get broader test coverage, focusing in on all the "behavior points" of the use case.

- You'll be validating functional requirements in addition to testing the design.

- You'll be able to do all of the preceding very quickly.

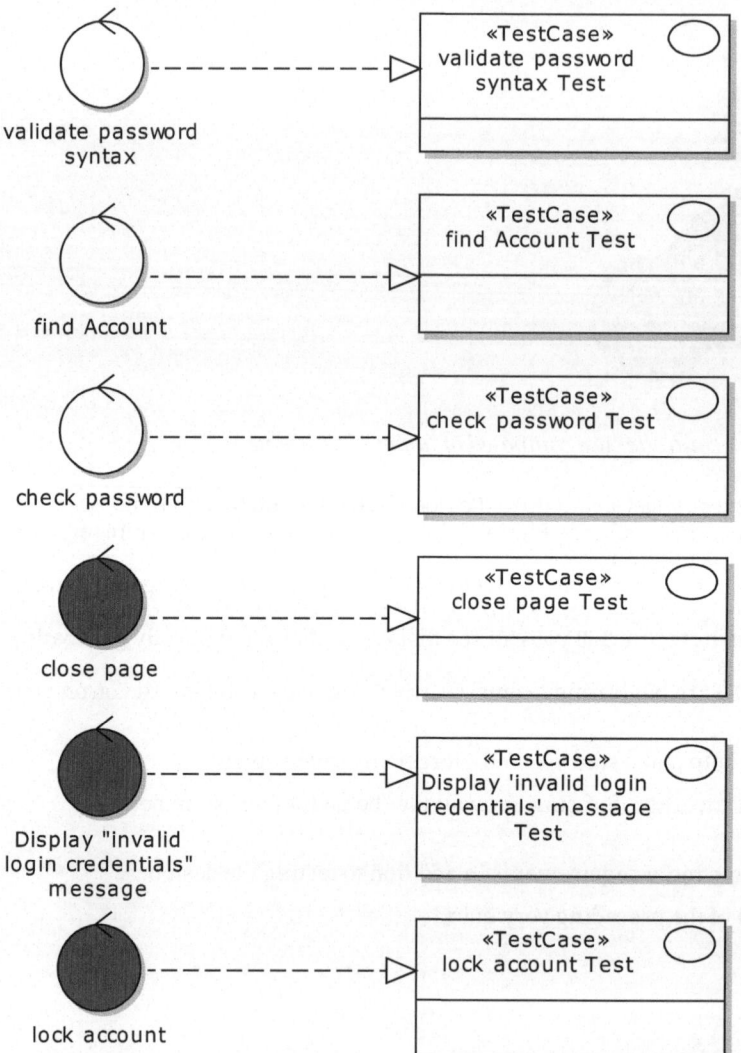

Figure 3–7. *A test case generated for each controller on the robustness diagram*

You can also choose to generate test cases for your requirements—see Figure 3–8.

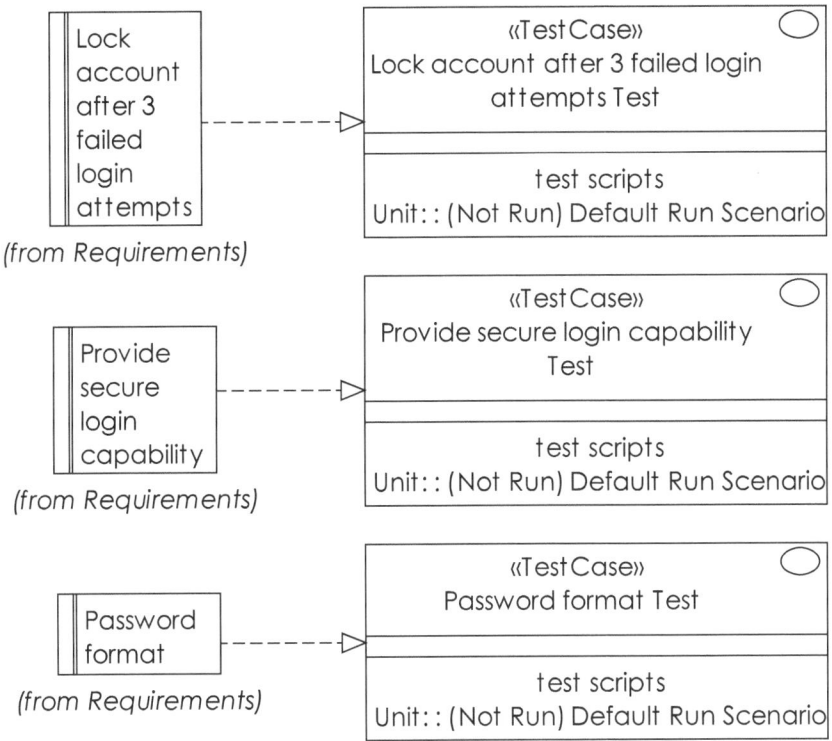

Figure 3–8. An acceptance test case generated for each requirement

The development team should own the controller tests (the test cases generated from the controllers), while an independent QA team might own the acceptance tests (the test cases and scripts generated from the customer requirements and use cases). We'll discuss acceptance testing further in Chapters 7 and 8.

As you'll see later in this chapter, you can also generate *unit test cases* for messages on sequence diagrams. The sequence diagrams represent the detailed design, so the tests you generate here are pretty close to the sorts of unit tests you would see in TDD (though they're not an exact match, as we discussed in Chapter 2).

Step 3: Add Scenarios

Once you've generated the test cases, you can add *test scenarios* using EA's "Testing View" (see Figure 3–9). This view is switched on from EA's View menu, or by pressing Alt+3 or most easily by simply double-clicking on the default scenario within the test case. For example, let's take the test case that validates the format of a password. You need to check that the password is of the required length, contains a mix of alpha and numeric characters, and is a mix of upper and lower case. Each of these is a scenario.

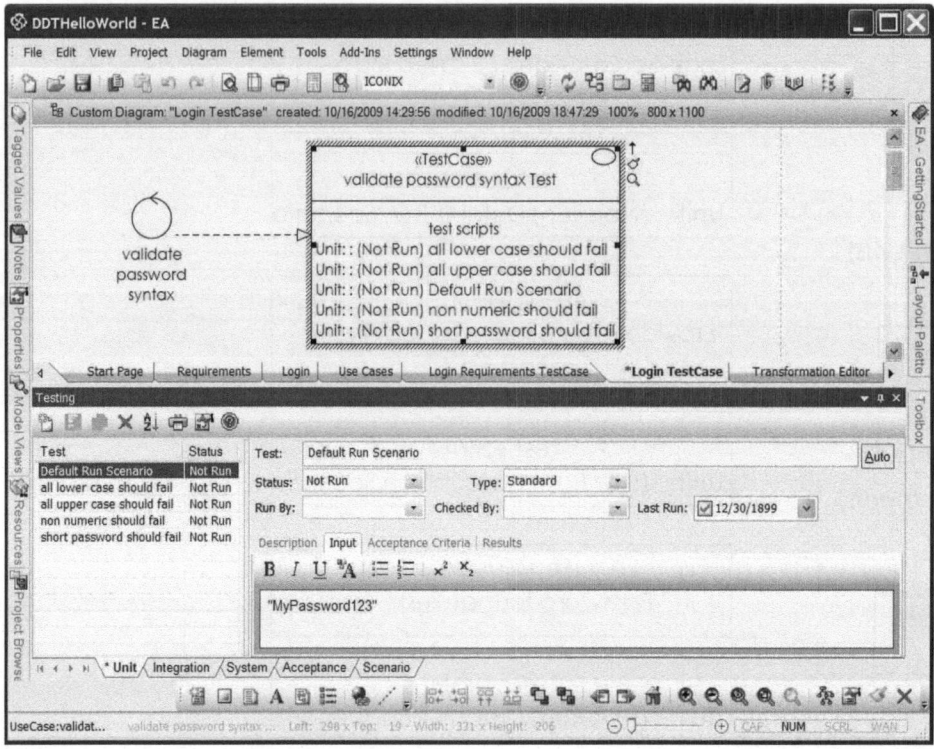

Figure 3–9. Adding scenarios to the Validate Password test case

The "Default Run Scenario" was added to all the test cases by EA, and represents a step in the "basic course" (success, or sunny day scenario) through the use case. In Figure 3–9, note the tabs available for each test scenario in the Testing View: Description, Input, Acceptance Criteria, and Results. The two we're particularly interested in are Input and Acceptance Criteria, as they let you define precisely the input values for each test scenario, and what constitutes a pass or fail given the input values.

Table 3–1 shows all of the test scenarios for the Validate Password Syntax test case, and their Input/Acceptance Criteria values; Table 3–2 shows the same done for the Lock Account test case. For the other test cases we'll just use the default run scenario, and won't add any additional test scenarios.

For "short password should fail," this raises the question, what's the minimum password length? This is the right time to be thinking about this and chasing down the answer, when project stakeholders are present—not later, when the programmer is cutting the code and likely to just make a snap decision himself.

Table 3–1. Test Scenarios for the Validate Password Syntax Test Case

Test Scenario	Description	Input	Acceptance Criteria
Default Run Scenario	The "sunny day" scenario	"MyPassword123"	Validation passes.
all lower case should fail		"mylowercasepassword"	Validation fails.
all upper case should fail		"MYUPPERCASEPASSWORD123"	Validation fails.
non-numeric should fail		"no-numbers"	Validation fails.
short password should fail	Minimum 6 characters	"Ab123"	Validation fails.

Table 3–2. Test Scenarios for the Lock Account Test Case

Test Scenario	Description	Input	Acceptance Criteria
account active after 2 attempts		2 invalid passwords are submitted	The account should still be active.
account locked after 3 attempts		3 invalid passwords are submitted	The account should be locked.

In Table 3–2, we haven't included a default run scenario (EA creates it by default, but we removed it from the Lock Account test case), since—checking back to the robustness diagram in Figure 3–5—this test is for an alternate course ("rainy day"); therefore, there is no sunny day scenario.

These values make it through to the generated test code: you'll see them later in the test method "Javadoc" comments, so they're right there for the programmer to refer to. Notice that we haven't filled in all of the descriptions. Where there's redundancy, err on the side of brevity. It beats "filling out the long form," and gets you to the finished product that much sooner.

Even if the add-in did nothing more than what's been shown so far, it would still be extremely useful. But there's significantly more capability ahead.

Step 4: Transform Controller Test Cases into Classes

Sparx Systems has developed automatic transforms between test cases and test classes. At the time of writing, transforms exist for widely used unit testing frameworks JUnit 3 and JUnit 4 (for Java), NUnit (for .Net), and (as we go to press) FlexUnit (for Adobe Flex/ActionScript). We're also hoping to see others soon.

In this example, as there are six test cases for this use case, we're going to multi-select all of them and transform the whole lot in one go.

To transform test cases, right-click the selected ones and choose "Transform…" The Model Transformation dialog appears (see Figure 3–10). Choose the target transformation. For this example, choose ICONIX_JUnit4. A dialog appears, asking for a root package where the new classes should be created. As these are test classes, create a new view called Test, and select the new view (see Figure 3–11). It's important to keep these test classes in a separate view, as EA replicates the entire package structure beneath the root package that you select.

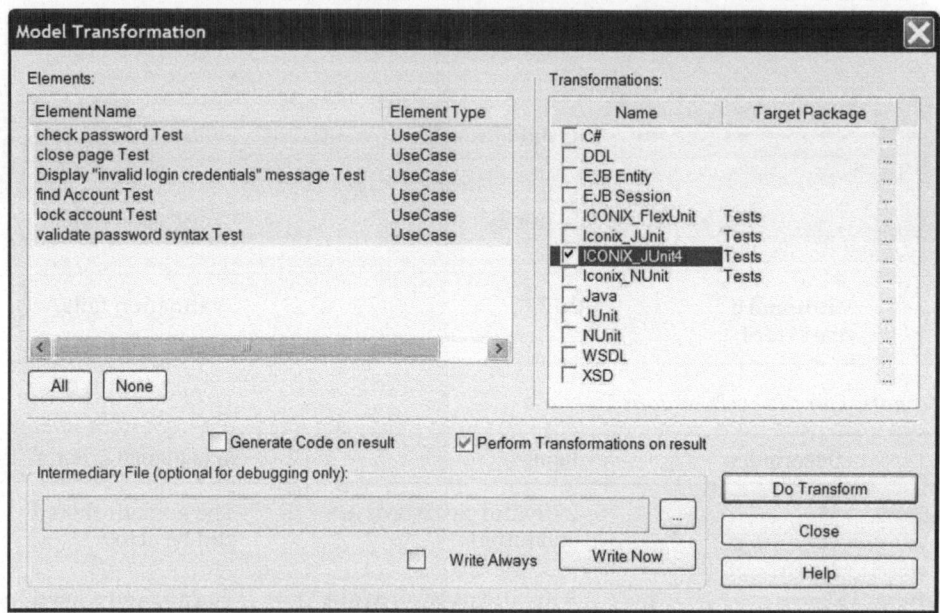

Figure 3–10. Transforming your test cases into controller test classes

■ **Tip** In Figure 3–10 there's a "Generate Code on result" check box. If you tick this, the next step (Step 5: Generate Controller Test Code) will be performed straightaway. We've separated the steps for the purpose of this tutorial, but in practice there's no reason you wouldn't merge these two steps and save a few seconds…

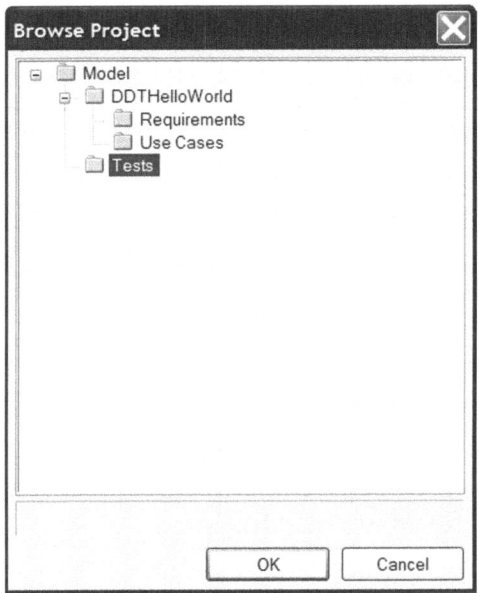

Figure 3–11. *Choosing the root package/view to generate the new test classes*

When you transform your test case using the ICONIX JUnit transform, setup() and tearDown() methods are added automatically, and a test method is created for each scenario (see Figure 3–12). This transformation captures the essence of the Design Driven Testing approach. So, for example, the "all lower case should fail" scenario has a test method generated called allLowerCaseShouldFail(), adorned with a @Test annotation to mark it as a test case.[3]

---

[3] For those interested in the "behind-the-scenes" details, EA marks each method with a *tagged value* to represent the @Test annotation. A tagged value is simply a name/value pair that you can associate with pretty much anything in your UML model. You can see the tagged values for each operation by activating the Tagged Values view from the View menu (or press Ctrl+Shift+6).

CheckPasswordTest
+ setUp() : void
+ tearDown() : void
+ defaultRunScenario()

ClosePageTest
+ setUp() : void
+ tearDown() : void
+ defaultRunScenario()

DisplayInvalidLoginCredentialsMessageTest
+ setUp() : void
+ tearDown() : void
+ defaultRunScenario()

FindAccountTest
+ setUp() : void
+ tearDown() : void
+ defaultRunScenario()

LockAccountTest
+ setUp() : void
+ tearDown() : void
+ accountActiveAfter2Attempts()
+ accountLockedAfter3Attempts()

ValidatePasswordSyntaxTest
+ setUp() : void
+ tearDown() : void
+ defaultRunScenario()
+ allLowerCaseShouldFail()
+ allUpperCaseShouldFail()
+ nonNumericShouldFail()
+ shortPasswordShouldFail()

Figure 3–12. The transformed controller test classes, ready to be code-generated. Note the increased scope of test coverage vs. the TDD Login example in Chapter 2.

Step 5: Generate Controller Test Code

Once the controller test cases have been transformed to test classes, they can be code-generated, using EA's normal code-generation techniques (see Figure 3–13). Right-click the transformed test class, and choose "Generate Code…" from the pop-up menu (or alternatively just select the test class and hit F11). Figure 3–14 shows the generated code loaded up into Eclipse.

■ **Tip** You can generate several classes at once by multi-selecting them; alternatively, select a package and choose "Generate Source Code…" (or press Shift+F11) to generate a whole package of classes in one go.

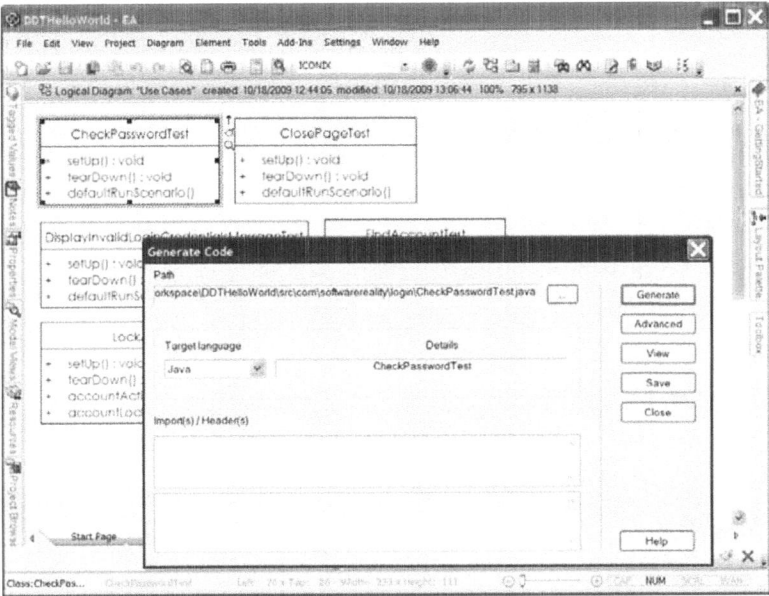

Figure 3–13. Generating the test code from the transformed UML test classes

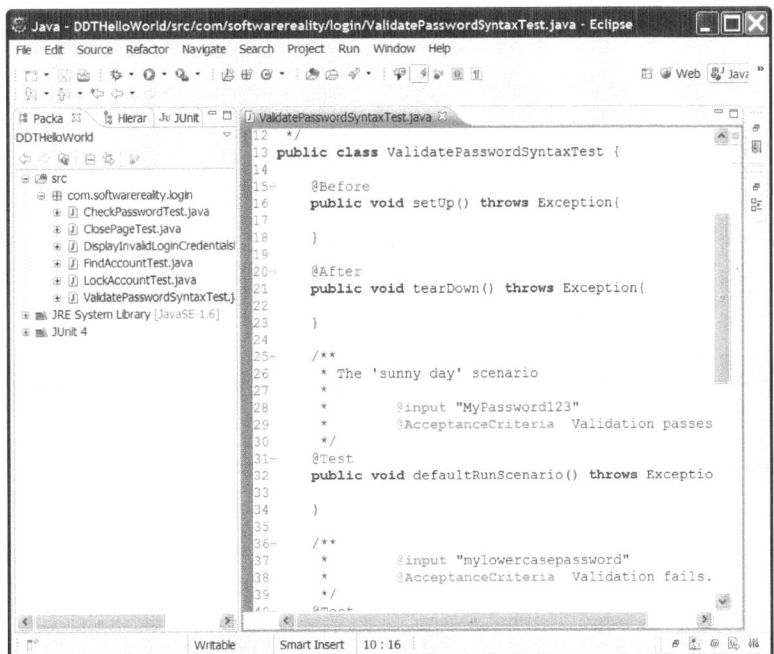

Figure 3–14. The six new controller test classes in Eclipse

Here's the complete generated controller test code for ValidatePasswordSyntaxTest.

```java
package com.softwarereality.login;

import org.junit.*;
import static org.junit.Assert.*;

public class ValidatePasswordSyntaxTest {

        @Before
        public void setUp() throws Exception{

        }

        @After
        public void tearDown() throws Exception{

        }

        /**
         * The 'sunny day' scenario
         *
         *          @input "MyPassword123"
         *          @AcceptanceCriteria  Validation passes.
         */
        @Test
        public void defaultRunScenario() throws Exception{

        }

        /**
         *          @input "mylowercasepassword"
         *          @AcceptanceCriteria  Validation fails.
         */
        @Test
        public void allLowerCaseShouldFail() throws Exception{

        }

        /**
         *          @input "MYUPPERCASEPASSWORD123"
         *          @AcceptanceCriteria  Validation fails.
         */
        @Test
        public void allUpperCaseShouldFail() throws Exception{

        }

        /**
         *          @input "no-numbers"
         *          @AcceptanceCriteria  Validation fails.
         */
        @Test
        public void nonNumericShouldFail() throws Exception{
```

```
        }

        /**
         * Minimum 6 characters.
         *
         *          @input "Ab123"
         *          @AcceptanceCriteria  Validation fails.
         */
        @Test
        public void shortPasswordShouldFail() throws Exception{

        }

}
```

Obviously there are gaps in the generated code where a programmer needs to hook up the tests with the code under test; but each test method is annotated with the input (values required when setting up the text fixtures); the acceptance criteria can go straight into the assert... statements. We'll return to the test code later in this chapter; first, we need to complete the design and identify unit tests to cover any code not already covered by the controller tests.

Step 6: Draw a Sequence Diagram

By this stage our *Login* use case is in pretty good shape. You have a set of requirements tests that QA can own, a set of controller test cases and the generated code that just needs the "blanks" filled in, and you have a conceptual design (the robustness diagram in Figure 3–5) from which to drive the detailed design and the code. The next step is to create a detailed design: the point of this step is to really start thinking hard about the implementation details, and to identify any further tests that can be created, which aren't already covered by the controller tests.

To do the detailed design, create a sequence diagram based on the robustness diagram in Figure 3–5. The initial step for the sequence diagram is quite formulaic, so with the help of our Agile/ICONIX add-in, EA can do this bit for you. (If you're using a different UML modeling tool, it doesn't take long to quickly draw this bit, though it's a fairly "robotic" process: put the use case text in a note, and copy the actor(s) and all the "nouns"—entity and boundary objects—onto the new diagram.) Within EA, simply right-click the robustness diagram and choose "Create Sequence from Robustness." The result—a new diagram with the use case note, actor, and all the entity and boundary objects copied over from the robustness diagram—is shown in Figure 3–15.

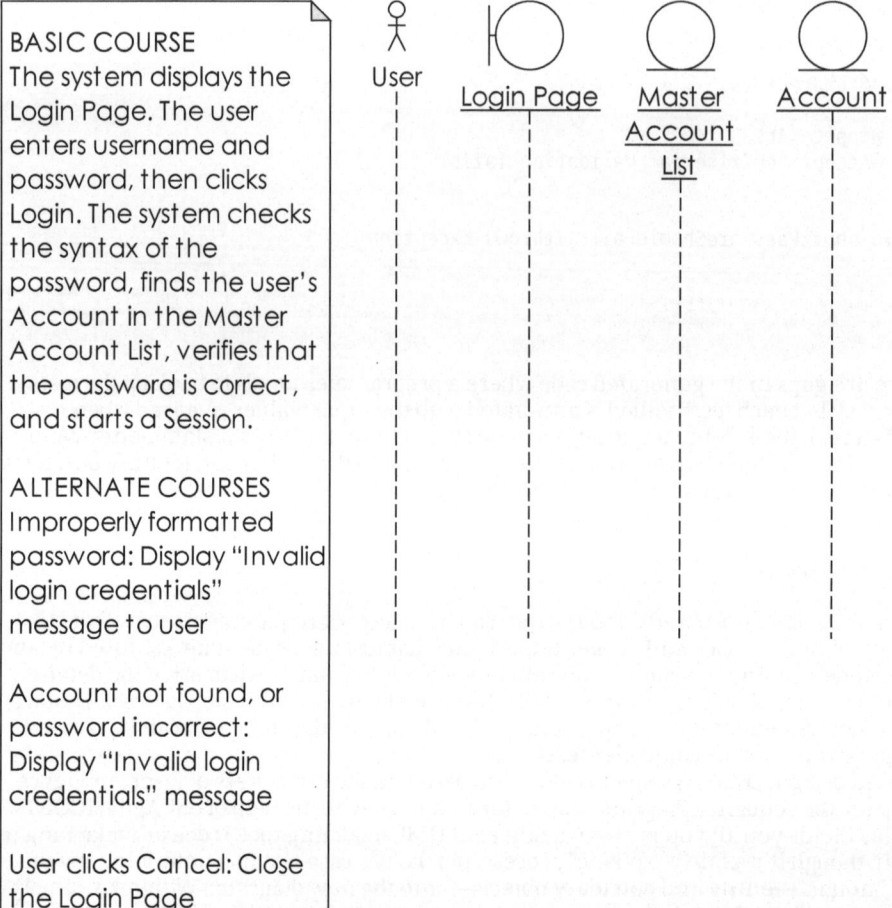

BASIC COURSE
The system displays the Login Page. The user enters username and password, then clicks Login. The system checks the syntax of the password, finds the user's Account in the Master Account List, verifies that the password is correct, and starts a Session.

ALTERNATE COURSES
Improperly formatted password: Display "Invalid login credentials" message to user

Account not found, or password incorrect: Display "Invalid login credentials" message

User clicks Cancel: Close the Login Page

Figure 3–15. The (not-so-blank) sequence diagram that EA creates as a starting point from your robustness diagram

---

■ **Note** If you've noticed that we're still forgetting to lock the account in Figures 3-15 and 3-16, you've won a pork pie for catching our mistake... and incidentally demonstrated why a careful review of the conceptual design is so important before proceeding with detailed design. These sorts of mistakes are incredibly easy to make, and even authors aren't immune to them. It's worth noting that writing a unit test for all the methods in the detailed design and getting a green bar would completely miss this sort of 'error by omission'. We've got a whole chapter on conceptual design reviews in *Use Case Driven Object Modeling With UML - Theory and Practice*.

The design session itself must be led by the programmers. The final design should be thoroughly grounded in reality, with all the "nitty-gritty" implementation details discussed and factored into the sequence diagram. The basic guideline is to draw the controllers onto the sequence diagrams as operations/methods; however, this is only a guideline to get you started—while you're allocating behavior to the objects on the sequence diagram, the main thing is to "keep it real." If there are classes and operations involved that weren't in the conceptual design, make sure they're added in now.

■ **Note** There will be more about the detailed design stage—and writing unit tests based on the design—in Chapter 5.

Figure 3–16 shows the result (we've omitted the use case note from the diagram to fit it on the page). To keep the example consistent with the TDD example from Chapter 2, this version also delegates the user credentials checking to an SSO service over encrypted HTTP.

Notice how the method names in the sequence diagram mostly match up with the controller names from the robustness diagram. This is useful, as it means you can check the methods identified on the sequence diagram with the controller names to identify which methods on the sequence diagram are already covered by tests, and which ones are shockingly exposed. That brings us to the next stage… now that you have your detailed design, it's time to add the unit tests.

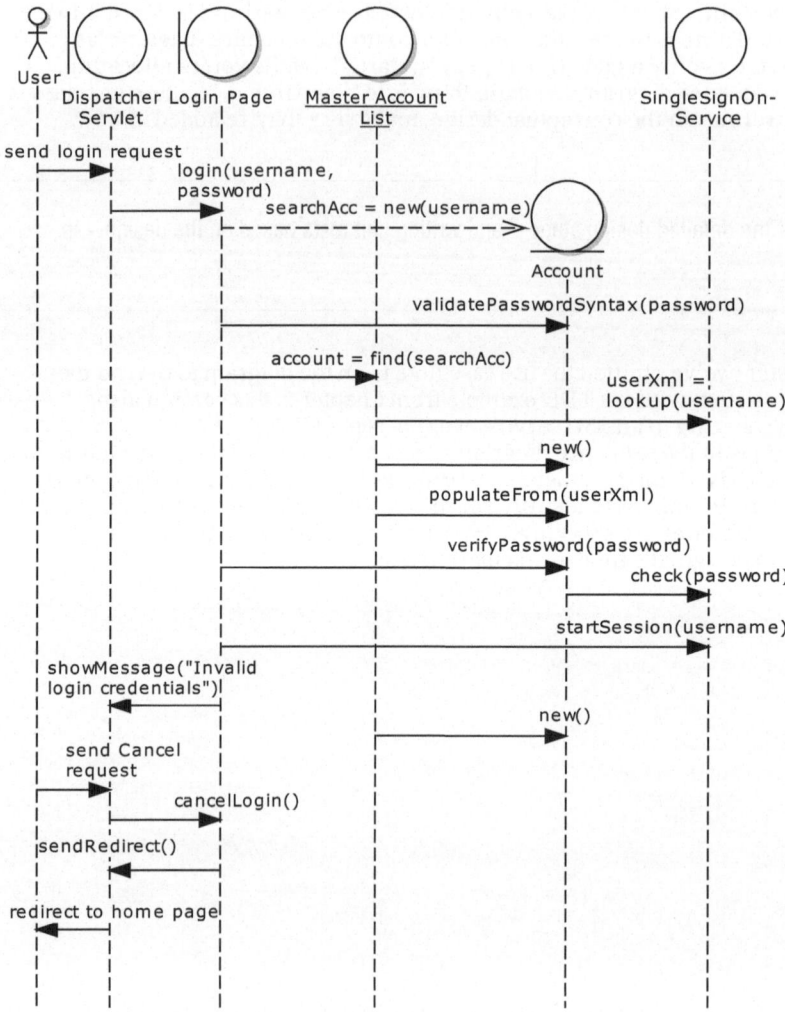

Figure 3–16. *The completed sequence diagram*

Step 7: Create Unit Test Cases

The idea here is to fill in any "important" gaps left by the controller tests; so you wouldn't want to create unit tests for every single operation on the sequence diagram. Instead, cherry-pick the non-redundant ones and write tests for those.

As you'd expect by now, EA can auto-create test cases from your sequence diagram, just as it can from your robustness diagram. Simply right-click the sequence diagram and choose "Create Tests from Sequence." The result can be seen in Figure 3–17.

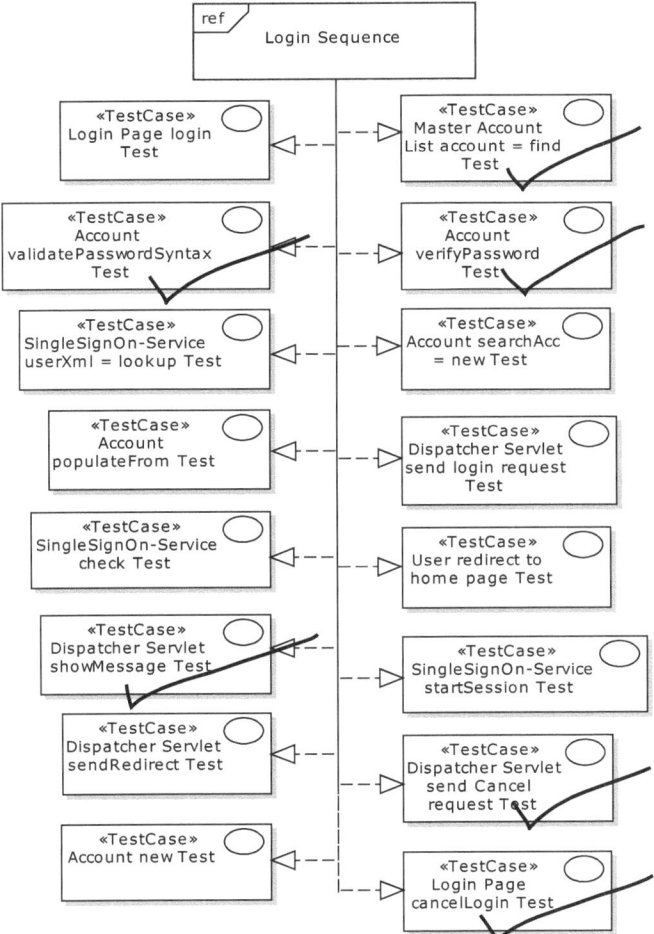

Figure 3–17. *All the operations from each class on the sequence diagram, turned into unit test cases*

The generated test case diagram in Figure 3–17 is comprehensive, to say the least. Every operation on each object has been turned into a test case, including the object constructors, any property "getters," and so forth. This could be a TDDer's dream come true: complete, fully mappable test coverage at his or her fingertips! However, since we don't care much for the Department of Redundancy Department, this is of less interest to us—remember that we're following the "test smarter" route. So, what we want to achieve from this diagram is to compare it with the controller tests, and figure out which operations are already covered. When we've done that, we'll create unit tests only for the few operations that don't already have controller tests. The easiest way to do this is literally to print out the test case diagram and then go through it with a colored marker pen, ticking each test case that's already covered by a controller test. You can see the result of this process in Figure 3–17.

This leaves the following potential candidates for unit tests—working through Figure 3–17:

- Account new (the Account constructor)

- DispatcherServlet.sendLogin()
- SingleSignOn-Service.lookup()
- Account.populateFrom()
- SingleSignOn-Service.check()
- Redirect user to the home page

- DispatcherServlet.sendRedirect()
- SingleSignOn-Service.startSession()
- Account new (another Account constructor call)

- LoginPage.login()

Some of these we can discard immediately. "Redirect user to the home page" isn't a method call, so it doesn't need a unit test; SingleSignOn-Service is an external service, and, therefore, outside the scope of the unit tests (however, we would definitely cover it using the requirements and acceptance tests, which are "end-to-end" integration tests).

As we'll explore further in Chapters 5 and 6, it's possible to cover several methods in one test by identifying a point "higher up" in the method chain where the results are returned, and testing just that point—in other words, one "molecular" test instead of several "atomic" tests. (If this sounds to you like exactly what controller tests are about, you win another pork pie.) Looking at Figure 3–16, you identify these points by looking at the boundary object (Login Page) and following its method calls. Login Page makes several calls:

```
searchAcc = new Account();
searchAcc.validatePasswordSyntax(password)
account = MasterAccountList.find(searchAcc)
account.verifyPassword(password)
SingleSignOn-Service.startSession(username)
DispatcherServlet.sendRedirect()
```

You can then step through this list, deciding in each case whether the call warrants a unit test. Figure 3–18 illustrates.

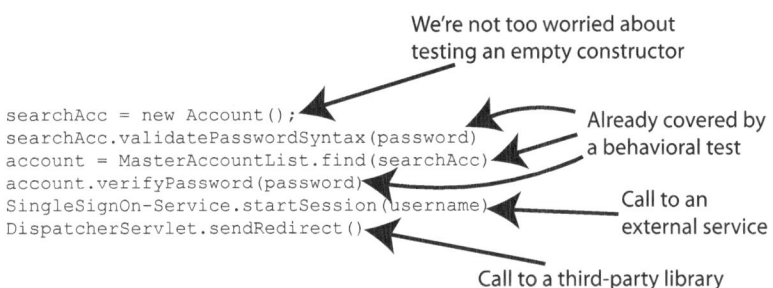

Figure 3–18. Stepping through a list of method calls

As you can see, that apparently leaves no methods whatsoever that require a unit test. The controller tests already have it covered, which is just as you'd hope. However, it's always worth a quick scan through the sequence diagram just in case there are any complex operations buried deep in the method chain. The one method that stands out is Account.populateFrom(xml). The XML document is returned from the SingleSignOn-Service, and could contain any number of oddities and caveats, which we must ensure are covered by this single innocuous populateFrom(xml) method. So let's create a unit test class for that one.

This process should be familiar now from working with the controller test cases. Within the Test Case diagram (see Figure 3–19), first hit Alt+3 to switch on EA's Testing View. Now click the *Account populateFrom* test case, and add some test scenarios. As with the controller test scenarios, this is where you put on your tester's hat and think about what could possibly go wrong, as well as "normal usage" scenarios that must also be tested. Every possible eventuality (short of external events such as meteors striking the Earth) should get its own test scenario. For this example, we came up with the scenarios in Table 3–3—however, in a real-life project, you'd expect this to be quite a lengthy list.

Table 3–3. Test Scenarios for the Account.populateFrom() Test Case

Test Scenario	Description	Input	Acceptance Criteria
Default Run Scenario	A normal, expected XML document is passed in.	see separate file: tests/resources/NormalAccount.xml	Each field in Account is populated from the expected XML element.
Quotation marks in each element		see separate file: tests/resources/AccountWithQuotes.xml	Correctly parsed.
Throw error if expected fields are missing.	The Username, First Name, and Last Name elements must be present.	see separate file: tests/resources/AccountWithMissingElements.xml	A parse exception should be thrown.

Next, let's turn this into a test class: right-click the test case and choose "Transform…" In the Model Transformation dialog that pops up, choose ICONIX_JUnit4, make sure the target package is Tests, and click "Transform." The result is the UML test class shown in Figure 3–19.

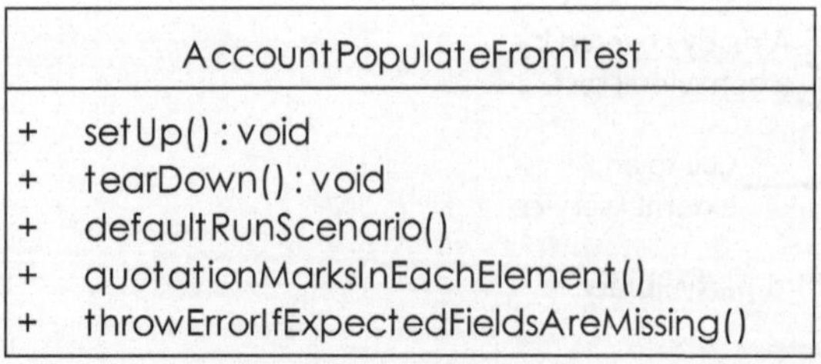

AccountPopulateFromTest
+ setUp() : void
+ tearDown() : void
+ defaultRunScenario()
+ quotationMarksInEachElement()
+ throwErrorIfExpectedFieldsAreMissing()

Figure 3–19. Our new unit test class, ready to be generated

Our main thought here is that the name of the test class is a bit odd. The name was derived from the populateFrom(xml) operation on the Account object. There's no reason not to rename it here to make it clearer, so we'll rename the test class PopulateAccountFromXmlTest.

Next, right-click the new test class and choose "Generate Code." (Again, as with the controller tests, simply ticking "Generate Code on result" in the Model Transformation Dialog performs this step as part of the previous step.) Here's the result:

```java
public class PopulateAccountFromXmlTest {

    @Before
    public void setUp() throws Exception{

    }

    @After
    public void tearDown() throws Exception{

    }

    /**
     * A normal, expected XML document is passed in.
     *
     * @input see separate file - tests/resources/NormalAccount.xml
     * @AcceptanceCriteria  Each field in Account is populated from the expected XML element.
     */
    @Test
    public void defaultRunScenario() throws Exception{

    }

    /**
     * @input see separate file - tests/resources/AccountWithQuotes.xml
     * @AcceptanceCriteria  Correctly parsed.
     */
    @Test
    public void quotationMarksInEachElement() throws Exception{
```

```
    }

    /**
     * The Username, First Name and Last Name elements must be present.
     *
     * @input see separate file - tests/resources/AccountWithMissingElements.xml
     * @AcceptanceCriteria  A parse exception should be thrown.
     */
    @Test
    public void throwErrorIfExpectedFieldsAreMissing() throws Exception{

    }
}
```

While we're here, let's also generate the Account class, which this unit test will be operating on:

```
public class Account {

    private String username;
    private String firstName;
    private String lastName;

    public Account() {
    }

    public Account(String username) {
        this.username = username;
    }

    public void validatePasswordSyntax(String password) {

    }

    public void populateFrom(String userXml) throws XPathParseException {

    }

    public void verifyPassword(String password) {

    }

    // getters and setters for username, firstName and lastName omitted for brevity…

}
```

Now we're ready to move into the code and implement it, along with the tests. Perhaps not surprisingly, given the preparation, this is the easy part. If you prefer to write the tests before the code, do feel free… but note that one of the goals of TDD (interface discovery) is somewhat redundant here, as you'll have already done that bit with the design step.

Step 8: Fill in the Test Code

Now it's time to fill in the test code, using the generated comments as guidance. Of course, this is where TDD pretty much begins; however, it's the last step in DDT, the "slam-dunk" having spent sufficient time lining up the shot. As you'll see in a moment, this step is the easy part because all of the "hard design thinking" has already been done (and the design modeling is most effective when done as a collaborative effort by the team). Let's start with the PopulateAccountFromXmlTest unit test class, as it's fresh in our minds. We'll start with the default run scenario (aka basic course):

```java
public class PopulateAccountFromXmlTest {

    private Account account;

    @Before
    public void setUp() throws Exception{
        account = new Account();
    }

    @After
    public void tearDown() throws Exception{
        account = null;
    }

    /**
     * A normal, expected XML document is passed in.
     *
     * @input see separate file - tests/resources/NormalAccount.xml
     * @AcceptanceCriteria  Each field in Account is populated from the expected XML element.
     */
    @Test
    public void defaultRunScenario() throws Exception{
        String userXml = loadFile("tests/resources/NormalAccount.xml");
        account.populateFrom(userXml);
        assertEquals("jsmith", account.getUsername());
        assertEquals("John", account.getFirstName());
        assertEquals("Smith", account.getLastName());
    }

    //  . . .
```

As you can see from the code, we first set up an Account text fixture. In the defaultRunScenario() test, we load our sample XML file containing "normal" user data. Then we call the Account.populateFrom(userXml) method (i.e., the method under test). And finally we assert that the fields within Account have been populated as expected. The generated method comments served as a handy reminder of the inputs and expected output (Acceptance Criteria) while writing the test.

Now, of course, we need to write the code to make this test pass. Here's the Account.populateFrom() method:

```java
public void populateFrom(String userXml) throws XPathParseException {
    XPathHelper helper = new XPathHelper(userXml);
    helper.populate(this, "setUserName", "//username");
    helper.populate(this, "setFirstName", "//firstname");
    helper.populate(this, "setLastName", "//lastname");
```

XPathHelper is a general-purpose helper class that we cobbled together (we haven't shown it here as it doesn't lend much to the discussion). It initially parses an XML document (the Account XML in this case). Then with each populate() method call, it populates the target object (Account) using the given setter method name ("setUserName"), and an XPath expression to dig the element out of the XML ("//username").

PopulateAccountFromXmlTest contains another two scenarios, which we'll implement next:

```
/**
 * @input see separate file - tests/resources/AccountWithQuotes.xml
 * @AcceptanceCriteria  Correctly parsed.
 */
@Test
public void quotationMarksInEachElement() {
    String userXml = loadFile("tests/resources/AccountWithQuotes.xml");
    try {
        account.populateFrom(userXml);
    } catch (XPathParseException e) {
        fail("Parsing should have succeeded: " + e.getMessage());
    }
}
```

This one simply loads an XML file in which the data contains quotation marks. If a parse exception is thrown, the test fails. The third test scenario is the flipside of this one: we want to see the parsing trip up over some invalid data (missing elements):

```
/**
 * The Username, First Name and Last Name elements must be present.
 *
 * @input see separate file - tests/resources/AccountWithMissingElements.xml
 * @AcceptanceCriteria  A parse exception should be thrown.
 */
@Test(expected=XPathParseException.class)
public void throwErrorIfExpectedFieldsAreMissing() throws Exception{
    String userXml = loadFile("tests/resources/AccountWithQuotes.xml");
    account.populateFrom(userXml);
}
```

This one's easy: it uses a nice feature of JUnit to specify that we're expecting an XPathParseException to be thrown. If the exception is thrown, the test passes; otherwise, it fails. Referring back to the populateFrom(userXml) method that we added a few moments ago, there's no specific code there to check for the mandatory fields; however, the helper class, XPathHelper, throws an exception if the element it's looking for is absent.

Let's move on to one of the controller test classes, ValidatePasswordSyntaxTest. First, here is the fixture setup:

```
public class ValidatePasswordSyntaxTest {

    private Account account;

    @Before
    public void setUp() throws Exception{
        account = new Account();
```

```
    }

    @After
    public void tearDown() throws Exception{
        account = null;
    }
```

The "sunny day scenario" passes in a valid password. No assertXX statement is needed: we simply declare AccountValidationException in the throws clause. If the validation exception is thrown, the test basically fails:

```
    /**
     * The 'sunny day' scenario
     *
     *          @input "MyPassword123"
     *          @AcceptanceCriteria  Validation passes.
     */
    @Test
    public void defaultRunScenario() throws AccountValidationException {
        account.validatePasswordSyntax("MyPassword123");
    }
```

The remaining test scenarios are easy: each one passes in an invalid password, and expects an AccountValidationException to be thrown:

```
    /**
     *          @input "mylowercasepassword"
     *          @AcceptanceCriteria  Validation fails.
     */
    @Test(expected=AccountValidationException.class)
    public void allLowerCaseShouldFail() throws Exception{
        account.validatePasswordSyntax("mylowercasepassword");
    }
```

■ **Note** It's not unknown in test-driven teams to include an empty assert statement so that the test "shows up" and is counted in the code metrics. However, this would be relevant only if you're looking at code coverage as a measure of project success—and, as we hope you'll agree after reading this book, such metrics are entirely spurious (and at worst misleading). It's rather like measuring productivity by the number of lines of code written—rather than something more meaningful, like the number of use cases/user stories completed, or whether the customer is smiling or frowning.

We've omitted the other three scenarios (allUpperCaseShouldFail(), nonNumericShouldFail(), and shortPasswordShouldFail()) as they each follow exactly the same pattern.

The code to make these test scenarios pass is also pretty straightforward. Let's implement the required method on the Account class:

```
    public void validatePasswordSyntax(String password) throws AccountValidationException {
        if (password.toLowerCase().equals(password)
            || password.toUpperCase().equals(password))
```

```
    {
        throw new AccountValidationException(
                "Password must be a mixture of upper and lower case");
    }
    if (password.length() < 6) {
        throw new AccountValidationException(
                "Password must be at least 6 characters long");
    }
    if (!containsAtLeastOneDigit(password)) {
        throw new AccountValidationException(
                "Password must contain at least 1 numeric digit");
    }
}

static boolean containsAtLeastOneDigit(String password) {
    for (char ch : password.toCharArray()) {
        if (Character.isDigit(ch)) return true;
    }
    return false;
}
```

We could go on, but we hope you get the general idea. Filling in the test methods is a breeze, as the design work has been done so the required fixtures are obvious, and the inputs/acceptance criteria are right there above each test method. Similarly, the coding is pretty much a slam-dunk because the hard thinking went into the detailed design, and all the "rainy day scenarios" were thought through in detail. The result is nicely factored code that's easily unit-tested, with tests in all the right places, and in which "design churn" (where supposedly finished code is rewritten to make way for new functionality) is kept to a minimum.

Summary

This brings us to the end of Part 1, in which we've compared and contrasted DDT with its inverse counterpart, TDD. Chapter 2 took us through the looking glass to implement the *Login* use case using TDD. In this chapter, we've applied up-front design principles along with DDT to the problem, and we've delivered a tested and documented login function. Figure 3–20 contrasts the difference between what we've achieved in Chapter 2 and in this chapter.

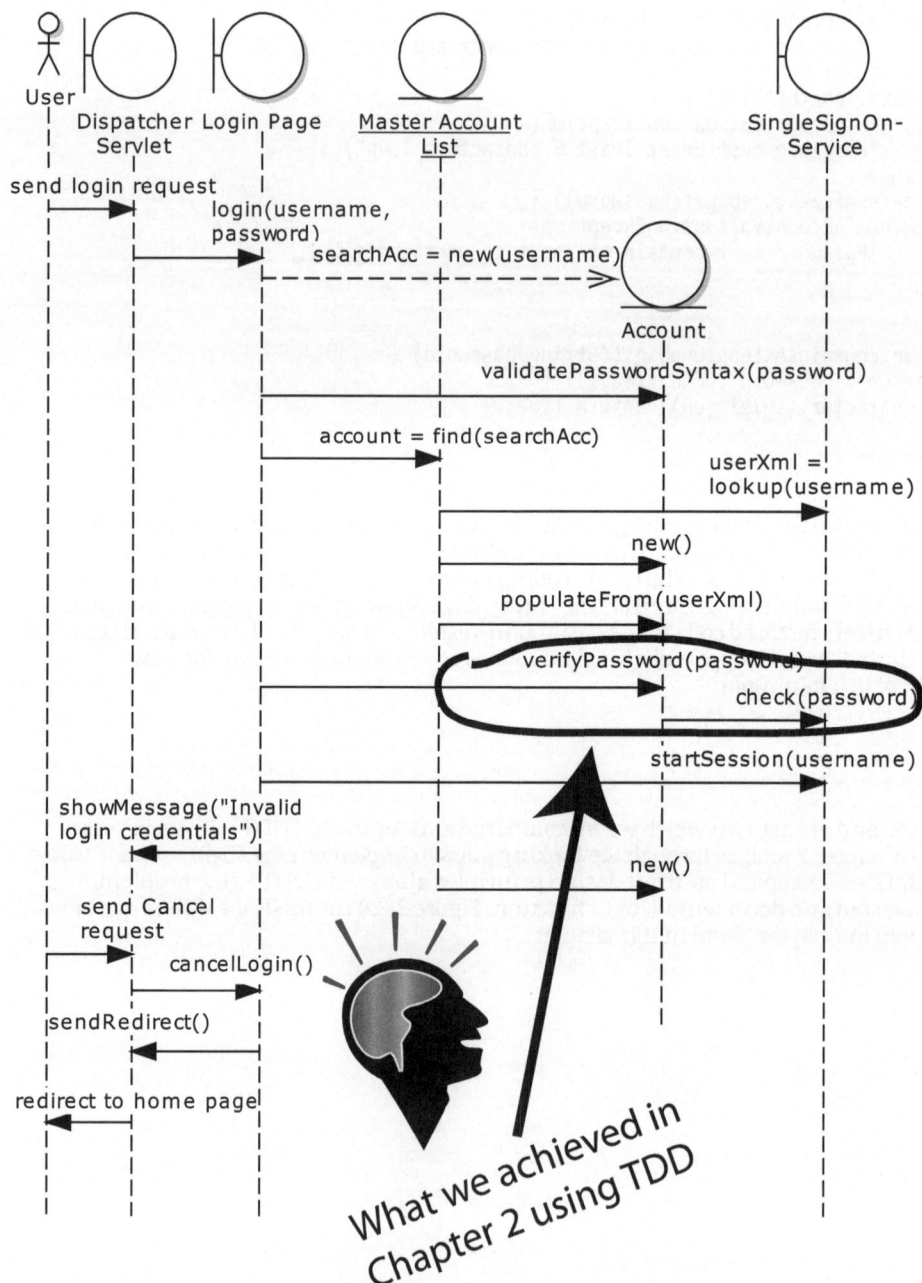

Figure 3–20. Designed, documented, and test-driven, vs. simply test-driven

Let's sum up a few key points:

- DDT gives you much more "bang for the buck" than TDD does. Figure 3–20 makes this pretty obvious: you can get more accomplished when your process isn't Too Damn Difficult. We spent most of Chapter 2 refactoring our unit tests, with the end result being that we developed the checkPassword method. By contrast, with considerably *less* effort following the DDT approach, we've designed the entire Login use case in this chapter.

- We haven't covered **customer requirement tests** or **scenario tests** (collectively known as **acceptance tests**) in this chapter, but we'll have a chapter on each topic in Part 2. But it's worth noting here that we've already identified requirement test cases (Figure 3–8), and we'll be driving the acceptance testing from the text of the use case.

- In Chapter 2, the TDD design led to an interface called AccountValidator, while the "behavior allocation" techniques using ICONIX/DDT put a validate method on the Account class. You'll find that this approach results in a more **domain-driven design**.[4]

- We've actually realized more of the intent behind TDD following this approach than we realized by applying TDD in Chapter 2. With the DDT approach, we found ourselves thinking much more along the lines of "What could possibly go wrong?" and "What else could go wrong?" and creating test scenarios to cover each of these possibilities. The result is a much more rigorously designed system, where "rainy day scenarios" are accounted for and tested right from the get-go, rather than refactored into the design later.

---

[4] We suspect that we're preaching to the converted in this instance, but it's worth checking out Eric Evans's book *Domain Driven Design: Tackling Complexity in the Heart of Software*, for an in-depth treatment of the subject.

## PART 2

DDT in the Real World: Mapplet 2.0 Travel Web Site

Alice continued walking for a time, and was just in the midst of wondering whether she could use her Palm Pilot to get a map home from this curious place that she was lost in (or at least find a nice hotel

room), when two soldiers, who looked strangely like index cards, approached her.

"Excuse me, Miss" said the first soldier, "but the Queen of Hearts demands to see how much code you have written."

Over the next few chapters, we'll illustrate how to use DDT, using the real-life example of a hotel search application for travel web site *VResorts.com*. Because testing tends to be a "backwards-looking" activity, providing feedback on something just created, we'll step backwards through the project. So Chapters 4, 5, and 6 cover the coding and design activities, or "developer's space," while Chapters 7 and 8 cover the analysis activities, or "customer's space."

- **Chapter 4** introduces the Mapplet project, and explores the ICONIX/DDT "best practices" that we recommend in order to give your project the best possible start. We discuss what to do on delivery of a staged release, to keep the project on track.

- **Chapter 5** shows how to write fine-grained, "white box" unit tests against the detailed design.

- **Chapter 6** explores broader-grained, "gray box" controller tests, which are based on a conceptual design.

- **Chapter 7** explores one half of acceptance testing, covering scenario tests that are based on the system's behavioral specification (use cases).

- **Chapter 8** walks through the other half of acceptance testing, business requirement tests—i.e., test scripts that are the corollary of the customer's requirements. As with scenario tests, these test scripts can be signed off by the customer and used by a team of testers.

## CHAPTER 4

Introducing the Mapplet Project

Acceptance Testing

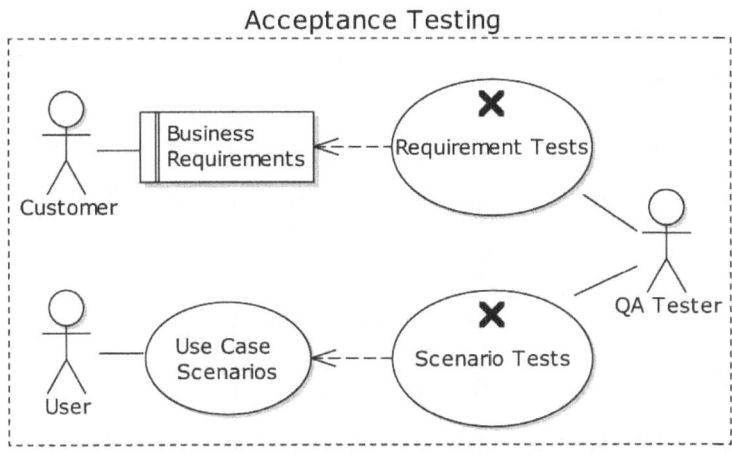

Developer Testing

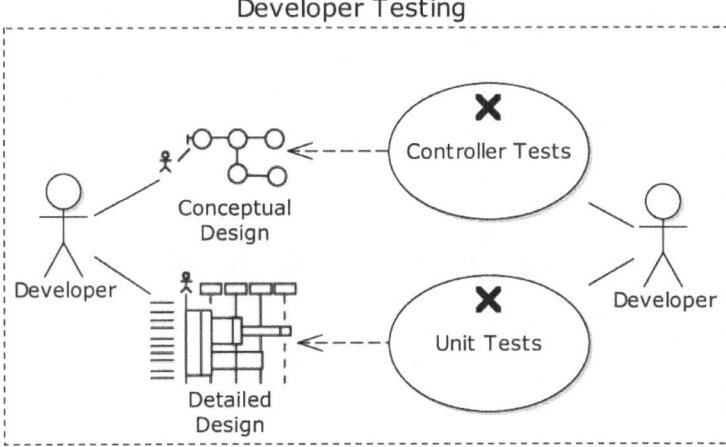

It's more difficult (and more time consuming) to base a book around a real software project than it is to write one with a toy example. For this book, though, we thought it was important to show how DDT works on the real thing, as we expect a bit of skepticism from test-driven developers. This chapter introduces you to our example project, which we call the Mapplet 2.0, and Chapters 5–8 will show how we've unit tested it (at two levels of abstraction) and how we've done acceptance testing against use-case scenarios and against the requirements. As you can see in the chapter-opener diagram, these two levels of developer testing and two levels of independent QA testing form the core of DDT.

The Mapplet project itself is a next-generation version of the map-based hotel finder that we presented in *Agile Development with ICONIX Process*. That book was an experiment in minimalist modeling—we were pushing the boundaries of how little modeling we could get away with and still come up with an application that satisfied the use cases and met the requirements. In this book, we employed the full arsenal of ICONIX Process techniques, augmented with their design-driven testing counterparts. This book focuses on testing and leaves out most of the design process; however, we're documenting the forward-thinking design process in a companion book from ESRI Press called *Best Practices for ArcGIS Server Development*.

As for the Mapplet project itself, we wanted Mapplet version 2 to work "more or less like Mapplet 1" (i.e., show me a map with hotels on it), with a few notable extensions, including the following:

- Worldwide coverage (Mapplet 1 was restricted to the US)

- A better, more modern user interface (we decided to use Flex)

- Real-time rate and availability checking (using an XML interface to the hotel database)

- Integration with a "photography overlay" (and an ability to see satellite imagery of a destination)

We think that, in addition to providing a good example for a couple of book projects, we've actually managed to break some new ground in the travel industry in terms of improving the "hotel shopping experience" for travelers, and we invite you to try out the Mapplet on www.vresorts.com.

We'll present the Mapplet 2.0 architecture and design in this chapter, which will serve to establish context for the testing chapters that follow. We'll focus on two use cases: *Quick Search* (which shows all the hotels in a particular area of interest) and *Advanced Search* (which lets you quickly zero-in on exactly the sort of hotel you're looking for, and makes sure it's available on your travel dates).

Top Ten ICONIX Process/DDT Best Practices

When embarking on a new project, or maintaining an ongoing project through successive iterations, be sure to follow our top-ten "to-do" list. We divide our list into two categories.

First, we begin with "starting the project right."

10. Create an architecture.

9. Agree on the business requirements, and test against them.

8. Drive your design from the problem domain.

7. Write use cases against UI storyboards.

6. Write scenario tests to verify that the use cases work.

5. Create conceptual and detailed designs, and test against them.

Then we move on to "keeping the project on track."

4. Update the model regularly to keep it in-sync with the code.

3. Keep the acceptance test scripts in-sync with the requirements.

2. Keep the automated tests up-to-date.

1. Compare the release candidate with the original use cases.

As you can see, this list forms something of a high-level roadmap of "best practices" for your software project. Steps 5, 6 and 9 are the main focus of Part 2, so we won't cover them in this chapter. The remaining steps (which aren't specifically to do with testing) are discussed in this chapter, using the Mapplet project as the example. We cover these remaining steps in more detail in the book's companion volume, *Use Case Driven Object Modeling with UML: Theory and Practice*. If you're interested in the forward-looking design of the Mapplet, you might also like to check out our upcoming book, *Best Practices for ArcGIS Server Development*, from ESRI Press.

■ **Note** ICONIX Process can be thought of as a fusion between **rapid application development** (RAD) (because the code is driven from the storyboarded UI prototypes, which are put together directly in Flash Builder, Visual Studio, etc.), **domain-driven design** (because the entity classes are driven directly from the domain model, keeping the developers from going down the path of creating one big MXML file with at least 50,000 functions in it), **use-case–driven development** (because the use cases hold it all together and keep development focused on the customer's requirements), and **responsibility-driven design** (allocating behavior to classes using sequence diagrams).

---

10. Create an Architecture

The architecture represents a high-level overview of the system you're about to analyze and design. Architectural diagrams are usually topological—i.e., they show server nodes with their conceptual locations (whether local or remote, or the name of a particular site if known), and the proposed comms protocols to link the server nodes together. For example, Figure 4–1 shows a high-level architecture diagram for the VResorts Mapplet.

Sometimes the protocols may be a foregone conclusion (as in the case of the Mapplet, which was partly intended to showcase the ESRI technology, and had some decisions made up-front based on its predecessor, the Mapplet 1.0). One such decision was that the new Mapplet would use a Flex-based client UI to create a "rich client" user experience; this, in turn, suggested that Adobe's BlazeDS would be used for client<-->server communication. These sorts of decisions are never completely set in stone, but they tend to end up on architecture diagrams as a sort of hint to the designers.

Another way to look at this is that the requirements drive the architecture (as you'd expect); but occasionally, as we intimated earlier in this chapter, the architecture can also drive the requirements. For example, with the Mapplet, a big prerequisite was that the XML Service (an external hotel search system) would be used, as VResorts wanted the ability to check pricing and availability in real-time. It was also known that ESRI would be providing the development team, who, in turn, would be targeting ArcGIS Server for the hotel mapping functions. While there was a lot of input from VResorts into the requirements and the UI, many of the requirements were driven by the capabilities known to be available in ArcGIS Server.

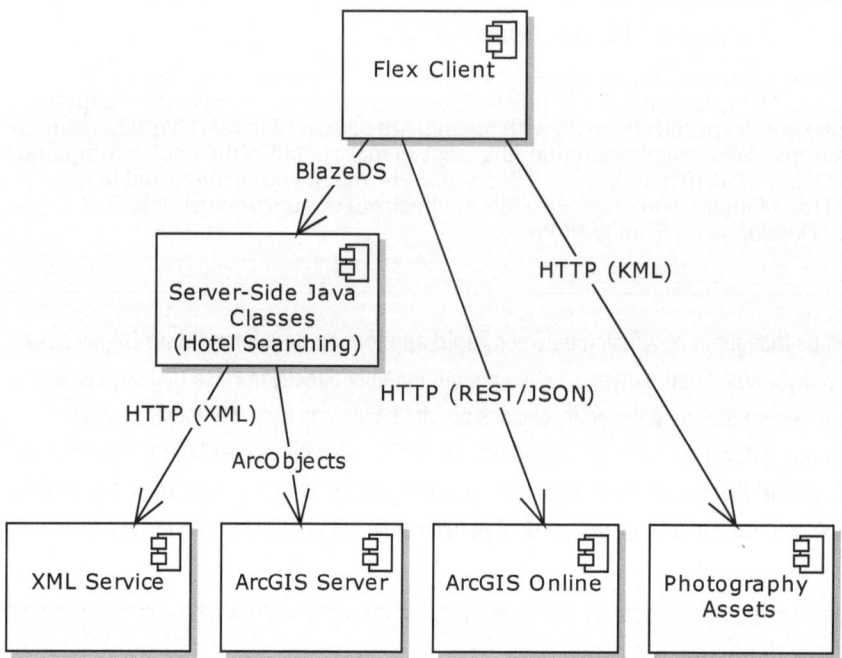

Figure 4–1. *Mapplet architecture*

In Figure 4–1, the idea is that the user wants to search for hotels in the vicinity of a particular address or point of interest. So he or she browses a map (served up by ArcGIS Server), which is combined with a list of matching hotels from the XML Service. The Java-based Hotel Search Service returns these details to the Flex client.

The XML search is for "live" hotel data access, whereas the ArcGIS Server search is against a static copy of the hotel data that has been imported into its geodatabase. The geodatabase also contains landmark or "Point of Interest" (POI) data.

9. Agree on Requirements, and Test Against Them

Next, you should agree on business requirements, and then write tests in support of those requirements. As you'll see in the next section, the business requirements are sometimes driven (to an extent) by the already-known architectural constraints. However, for the most part, requirements tend to start out as an unstructured stream-of-consciousness from the customer: a long list of "what I want is" statements. It's the job of a business analyst to push back on these requirements and extract the real reason for them from the customer: to establish "why" as well as "what" (which customers tend to start off with). Often this pushing-back process can result in a different set of requirements, or a brand-new set being discovered. The business analyst then structures these business requirements into logically grouped areas, though they tend to remain throughout the project as a long list of "wants." As you'll see later in this chapter, it's worth doing further modeling on the business requirements to create behavioral requirements (i.e., use cases).

We cover requirements modeling and testing in Chapter 8; but, for now, here's a brief overview of the Mapplet requirements. The requirements were entered into Enterprise Architect (EA) and grouped into the following areas, or packages:

```
Functional Requirements
     |__ User Interface
     |__ Hotel Filter
     |__ Map
```

Figure 4–2 shows the Hotel Filter requirements, which led to the Advanced Search use case. The idea behind hotel filtering is to be able to declutter a map that shows a large number of hotels, in order to quickly and easily "zero-in" on a specific set of "filter" criteria. Mapplet 1.0 supported filtering against a set of amenities (pool, room service, etc.) and a few other categories. Mapplet 2.0's use of a live XML data feed allows us to include availability during a given time period, and filtering by price (which is not a static property of a hotel, but varies by date and availability and is continuously updated in something called the Global Distribution System).

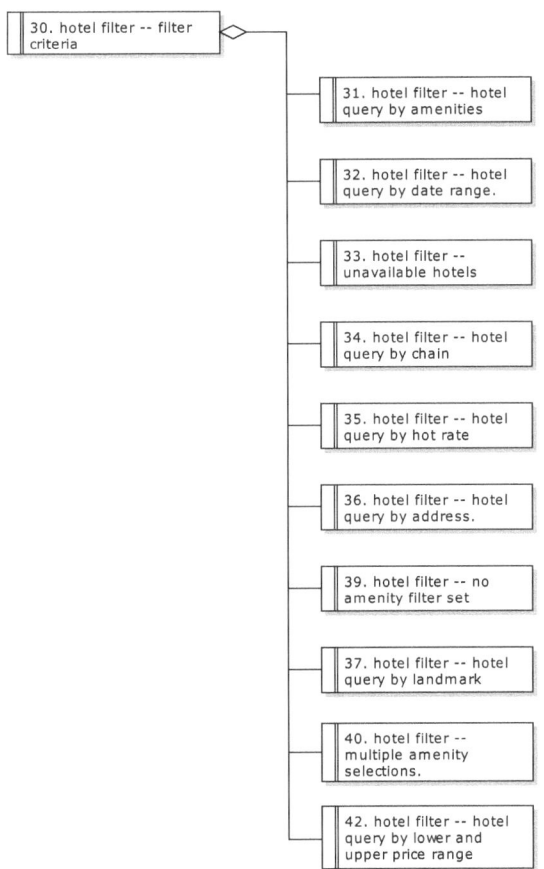

Figure 4–2. Mapplet 2.0 Hotel Filter requirements

> ■ **Note** We'll return to the Mapplet requirements in Chapter 8, where we'll illustrate how to drive "customer-oriented" acceptance tests from them.

8. Drive Your Design from the Problem Domain

The "problem domain" is the area of knowledge that describes the business problem that an IT system will attempt to solve. Most commonly, the problem domain is captured in a **domain model**: a collection of names for things. The domain model can be shared between the customer, business analysts, and developers, and understood by all. It's created during a collaborative brainstorming session between the project stakeholders. The domain model's usefulness can't be underestimated: the requirements and architecture are written/drawn up using the names defined in the domain model; the developers will design and code the system using class names based on the domain object names; the tests will be based on the domain model, and so on. It's a common vocabulary that ties everything in the project together, and helps to eliminate ambiguity.[1]

Figure 4–3 shows the domain model created for the Mapplet project. This was a collaborative effort between the ESRI Professional Services team, and the VResorts customer.

During the OOAD process, your domain model will evolve into a detailed design: the domain objects become **entity classes**, with attributes (the data) and operations (the behavior) allocated to each entity (we recommend allocating behavior to classes according to a "responsibility-driven" thought process).[2] As we're focusing on Quick Search and Advanced Search, let's take a closer look at the detailed design for those two use cases.

---

[1] We demonstrate domain-driven design in the context of use cases in *Use Case Driven Object Modeling with UML: Theory and Practice*. Eric Evans's book *Domain Driven Design: Tackling Complexity in the Heart of Software* is also well worth reading. It's a pretty big book, though, so if you're in a hurry, check out the much shorter *Domain Driven Design Quickly*, by Abel Avram and Floyd Marinescu, available in print or as a free PDF: www.infoq.com/minibooks/domain-driven-design-quickly.

[2] For an excellent introduction to responsibility-driven design, see Rebecca Wirfs-Brock's book *Designing Object Oriented Software* and the more recent *Object Design: Roles, Responsibilities and Collaborations*.

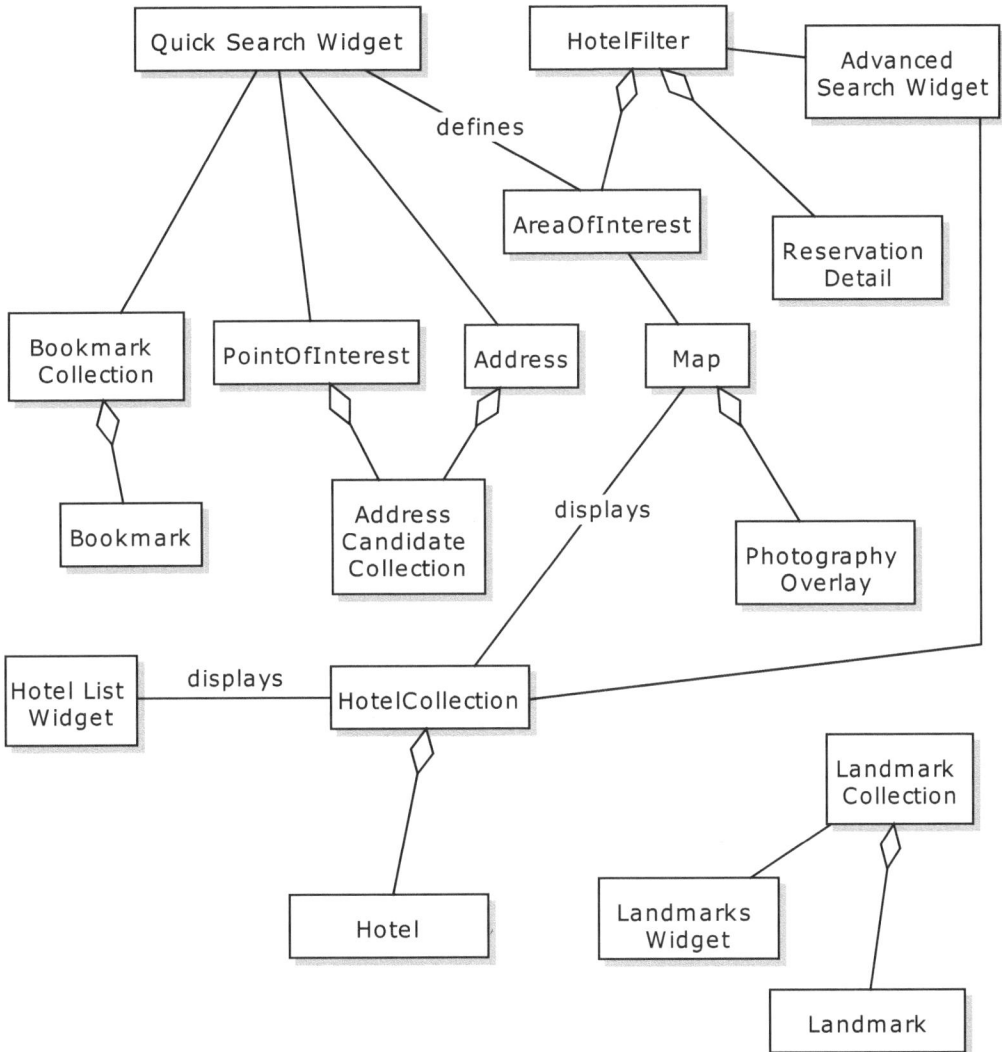

Figure 4–3. Mapplet domain model

Figure 4–4 shows an overview of the classes that together implement the *Quick Search* use case; Figure 4–5 shows an overview of the classes that implement *Advanced Search*. To shoehorn these two diagrams onto the page, we've hidden the attributes and operations, so they show just the relationships between classes. (We show the complete classes near the end of this chapter.) We're driving the design from the domain model by systematically and vigorously analyzing the use cases. The result is inherently domain-driven. As you can see from these two class diagrams, the entity classes evolved directly from the domain model.

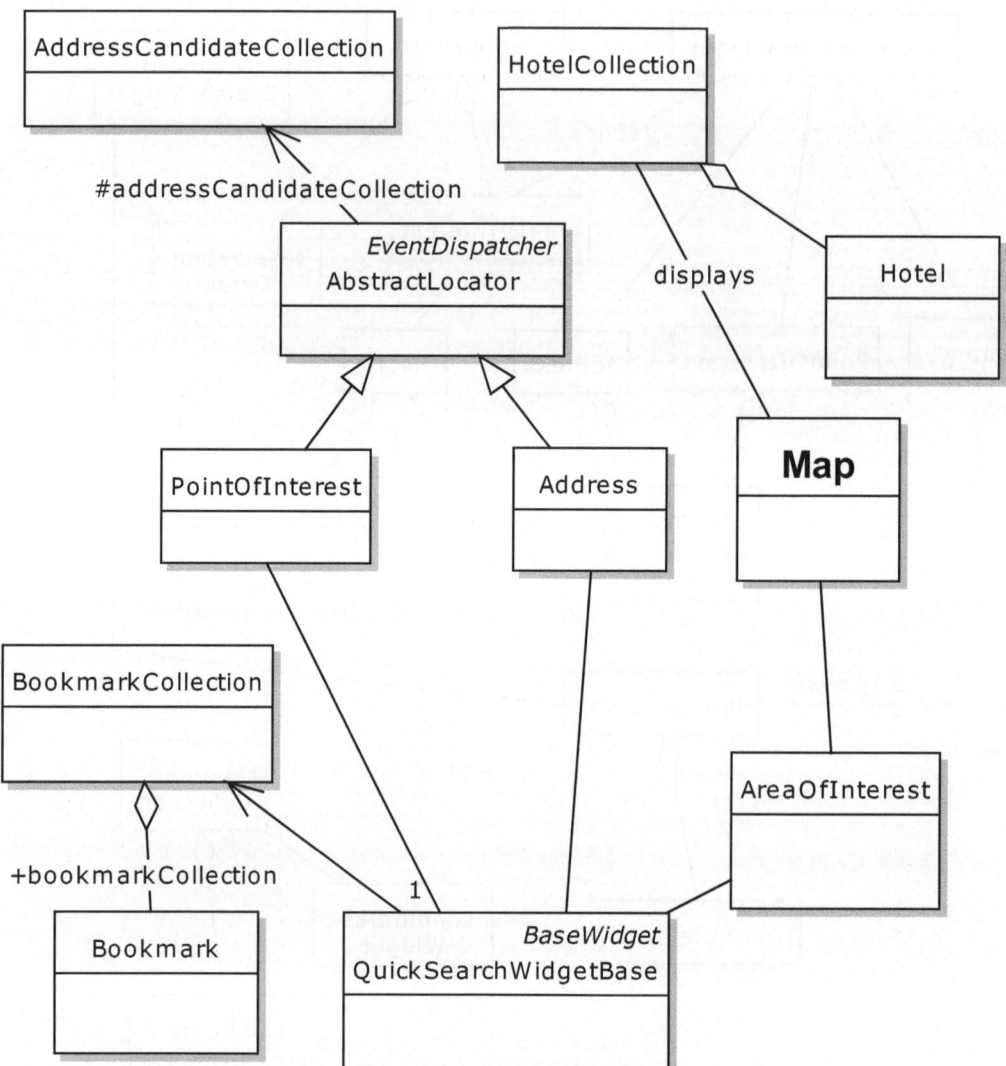

Figure 4–4. Quick Search detailed design (attributes and operations hidden)

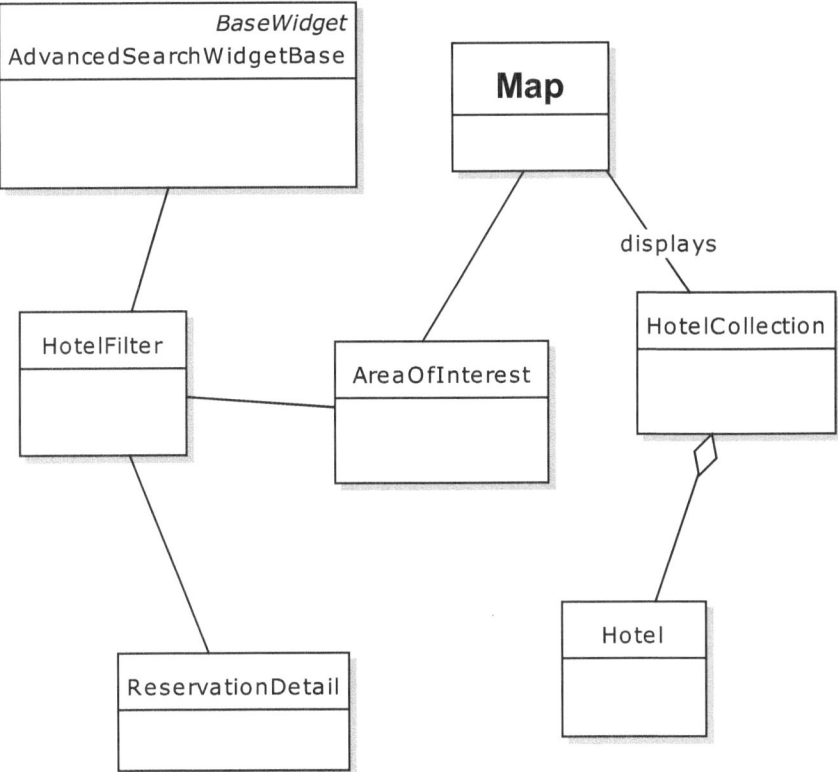

Figure 4–5. Advanced Search detailed design (attributes and operations hidden)

7. Write Use Cases Against UI Storyboards

Over the next few chapters we'll focus on the hotel search part of the Mapplet, as this is really the core functionality. People use the Mapplet chiefly to search for hotels, by first zooming in to a particular location (or a "Point of Interest" such as a famous landmark, conference center, beach, or whatever they want to be close to), and then search for hotels in and around that location that match a more detailed set of filter criteria (e.g., star rating, amenities, price, and room availability).

One of the first steps during the requirements-gathering stage was to storyboard the new Mapplet, creating candidate screenshots of how the finished product could look. From this storyboarding session, it quickly became clear that searching would need to be split across two functions: a basic search and a more detailed step to further refine the search results. These two steps quickly evolved into two separate use cases, Quick Search and Advanced Search. Quick Search is used to pull up all the hotels in a desired location, and Advanced Search is used to "declutter" (filter) this display while checking availability, price, amenities, etc.

Figure 4–6 shows the storyboarded Quick Search created in Flash Builder and then imported into EA, linked directly to the Quick Search use case; Figure 4–7 shows the storyboarded Advanced Search. Near the end of this chapter we show the finished product: not far off the original storyboards!

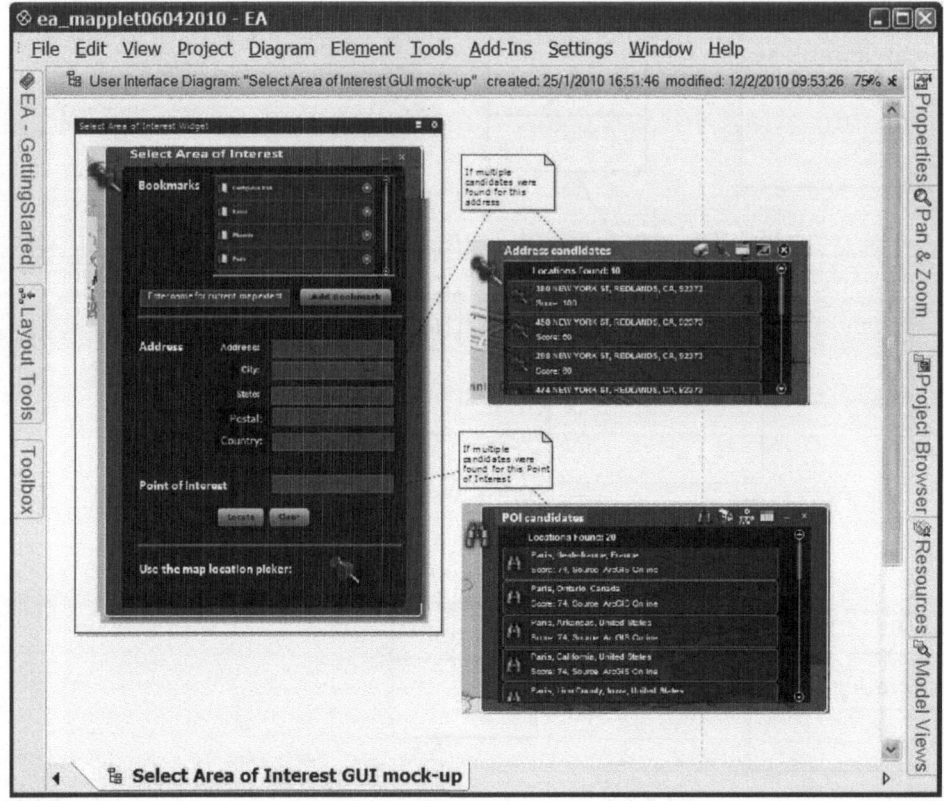

Figure 4–6. Quick Search storyboard screenshot

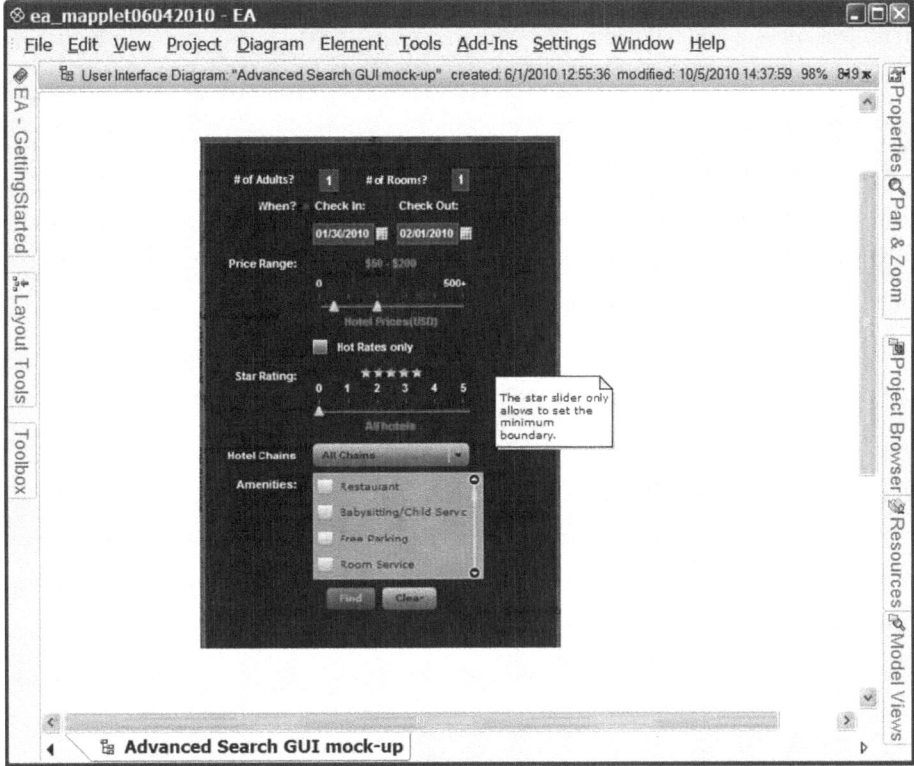

Figure 4–7. *Advanced Search soryboard screenshot*

6. Write Scenario Tests to Verify That the Use Cases Work

Use cases are behavioral requirements. While the business requirements can contain both high- and low-level, functional and non-functional requirements, the behavioral requirements are exactly that: a specification of the system behavior. Behavioral requirements are detailed descriptions of how the user and the system interact; because they are much more detailed, writing them helps to uncover holes in the business requirements.

The term "use case" has become rather nebulous, encompassing, as it can, a range of descriptions from the sketchy to the insanely detailed, including (or not) descriptions of the UI and target platform, pre-conditions and post-conditions, and templates several pages long. ICONIX-style use cases are, simply, an active-voice description of a user clicking and typing his way through a UI, and the system's responses.

Each use case is divided into "sunny day" and "rainy day" sections. There's always one basic course, or "sunny day" scenario: this is the user's default course through the use case, the "path most travelled." You should also expect to see plenty of alternate courses, or "rainy day" scenarios: these are the "paths less travelled"—things that can go wrong, or just alternative choices made by the user—which are often breezed over in many projects, but which can easily account for 80% or so of the system's functionality. *If the rainy day scenarios aren't explored in sufficient depth before coding begins, all sorts of nasty surprises can leap up during coding, often resulting in a need to rethink the design.* As a result, we regard modeling of the rainy day scenarios to be an extremely important activity, one that can mean the difference between project success and failure.

■ **Note** There will be more about use-case scenarios (and their corollary, scenario testing) in Chapter 7.

For the Mapplet project, we divided the use cases into two packages: **Displaying** and **Searching**. Let's take a look at the Searching use cases (see Figure 4–8), as this package contains the *Quick Search* and *Advanced Search* use cases that we'll be focusing on. (In Chapter 6 we also look at *Use Address*, which is really part of *Quick Search*—as you can see in Figure 4–8, *Quick Search* invokes *Use Address*.)

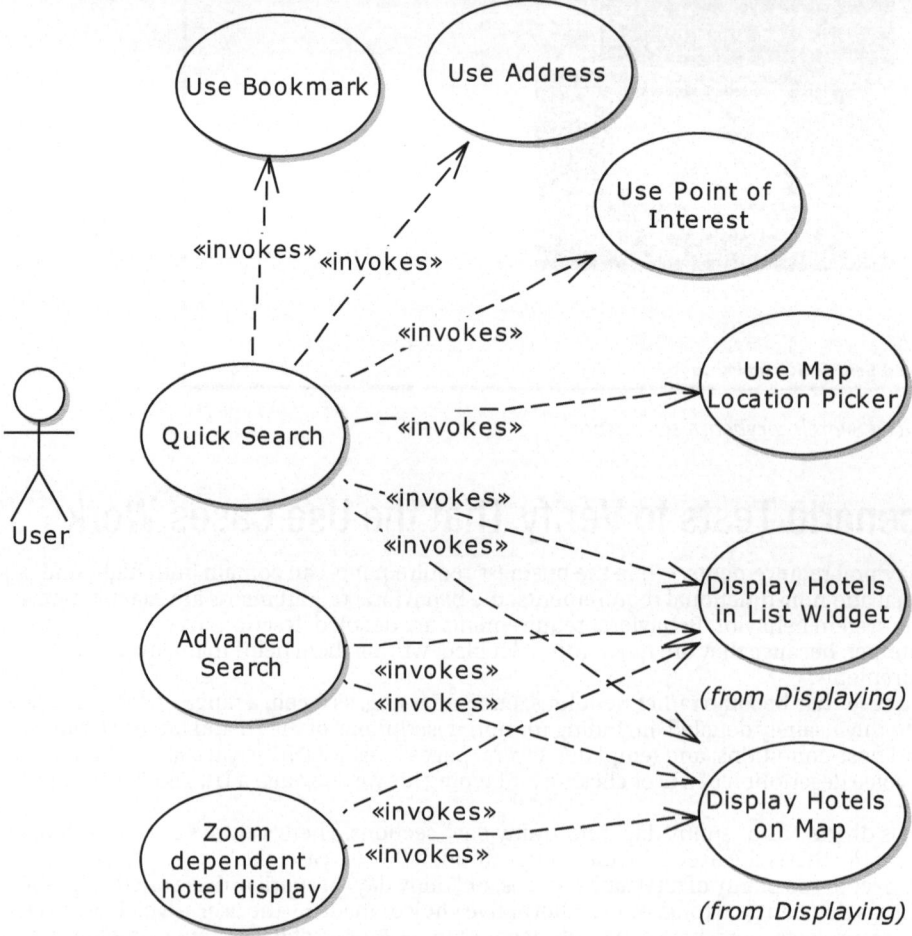

Figure 4–8. The Mapplet use cases: "Searching" package

Here's the complete narrative text for the *Quick Search* use case:

BASIC COURSE:
The system displays the Quick Search Widget, which contains several options for specifying an Area of Interest (AOI).
User double clicks on a Bookmark: Invoke Use Bookmark
User clicks Locate button on Address panel: Invoke Use Address
User clicks Locate button on POI Panel: Invoke Use Point of Interest
User clicks push-pin icon on Location Panel: Invoke Use Map Location Picker
The system updates the map extent and AOI based on the location. AOI is smaller than "Local View" limit.
System searches the static geodatabase for hotels within the specified AOI.
Invoke Display Hotels on Map
Invoke Display Hotels in List View

ALTERNATE COURSE:
AOI greater than "Local View" limit: *System displays message: "Please zoom in further to display hotels."*
No Hotels Found (and AOI within Local View limit): *System displays message: "No hotels found."*
"Show Landmarks" button is enabled: *System searches the geodatabase for Landmarks within the specified AOI and displays them on the map.*
User selects Pan/Zoom tools: *Invoke Zoom-Pan on Map*

And here's the complete narrative text for *Advanced Search*:

BASIC COURSE:
The system enables the Advanced Search widget when an AOI exists of "local" size. The user clicks the Advanced Search icon; the system expands the Advanced Search widget and populates Check-in/Check-out fields with defaults. The user specifies the the Reservation Detail including Check-in and Check-out dates; the system checks that the dates are valid. The user selects the number of adults from the drop-down menu (range: 1–6), and then enters the number of rooms from the drop-down menu (range: 1-number of adults). Optionally, the user selects desired amenities, price range, star rating, hotel chain, and the "hot rates only" check box. The user clicks FIND. The system searches for hotels within the current AOI, producing a Hotel Collection.
Then invoke Display Hotels on Map and Display Hotels on List Widget.

ALTERNATE COURSES:
Check-out date prior to Check-in date: *The system displays a user-error dialog: "Check-out date prior to Check-in date."*
Check-in date prior to today: *The system displays a user-error dialog: "Check-in date is in the past."*
System did not return any matching hotels: *The system displays a message: "No hotels found."*
"Show Landmarks" button is enabled: *The system displays Landmarks on the map.*

User clicks the Clear button: Refine Hotel Search clears all entries and populates check-in/check-out fields automatically with defaults.

■ **Note** The "Check-in date prior to today" scenario raises the question, shouldn't the UI prevent the user selecting an invalid date in the first place? Absolutely! But a big criterion of defensive coding is to ensure that each "tier" in the system guards against invalid data being passed through it. There will be more about this aspect of integration testing in Chapter 11.

To help make sure that the use cases satisfy all of the customer's requirements, EA includes a Relationship Matrix screen, which shows each use case in the selected package (down the left side) linked to its "parent" requirement (along the top). Figure 4–9 shows this screen for the Searching package (use cases) and the Hotel Filter package (the requirements).

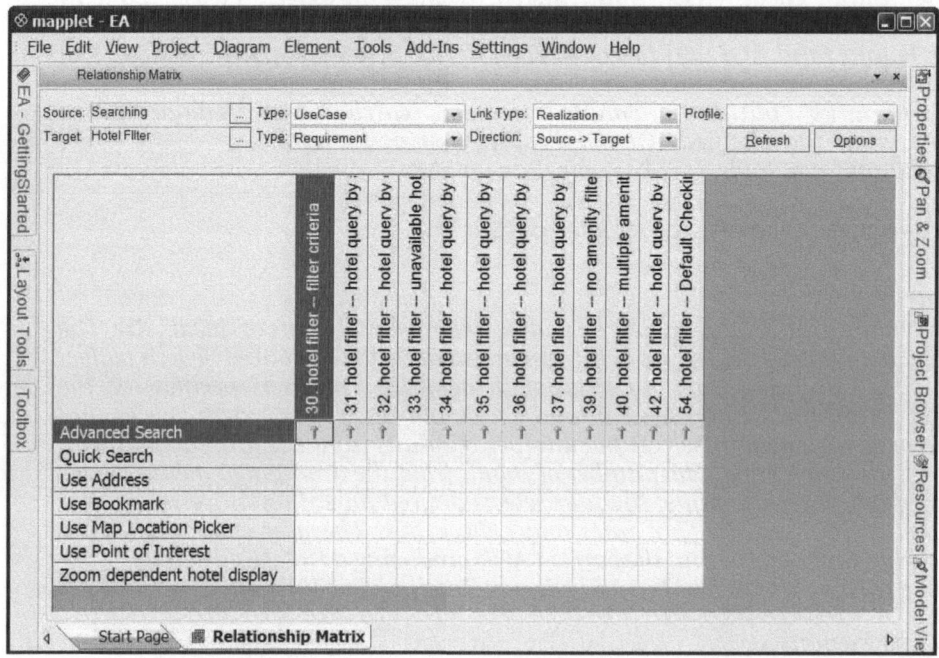

Figure 4–9. Use cases linked back to their "parent" business requirements

You'd be forgiven for looking at the use-case scenarios and thinking, "Great! Now how on earth do I turn these into a design, ready to create unit tests and source code?" The **conceptual design** is the first next step: a brief exploration into an object-oriented representation of the use-case text. When you get good at doing conceptual designs, you'll be surprised how quickly you can create them—and they have the added benefit of identifying the key behavioral parts of the system that you'll want to write JUnit/FlexUnit/NUnit (etc.) tests for.

■ **Note** There will be more about conceptual design in Chapter 6.

---

5. Test Against Conceptual and Detailed Designs

A "conceptual design" is a halfway house between the use cases and the detailed, code-level design that you're aiming for. The benefit of creating a conceptual design is that you get an early indication of whether the use cases have been thought through sufficiently: whether they're realistic and can be mapped to a design without too much kerfuffle. If it's difficult to map use cases to a conceptual design, then mapping them to a "real" detailed design would be even more difficult.

Another benefit is that a conceptual design helps to break the use-case scenarios down into logical software functions. These eventually map to one or more "actual" code functions; but by identifying the broader-grained logical/conceptual functions, you'll have created the ideal set of tests with which to provide just enough coverage of your codebase. These "controller tests" are like acupuncture points: they're strategically placed to test the flow of system state without having to test all the transitional stuff in between.

There will be more about conceptual designs and controller tests—in some ways the core of DDT (at least for programmers!)—in Chapter 6.

Having created a conceptual design and fed this back into your use case, possibly discovering new domain objects in the process and generally bolstering the behavioral requirements, it's time to evolve the conceptual design into a detailed design. There will be more about detailed designs and unit tests in Chapter 5.

Using the ICONIX Process, detailed designs are mapped out using class diagrams to show the static class structure, and sequence diagrams to show the event/response flow through the objects at runtime. The sequence diagrams are also used as a tool to allocate behavior to classes. In Chapter 5, Figure 5-1 shows the sequence diagram for *Advanced Search*.

So far we've been looking at things to do at the start of a project (or at the start of a new iteration with fresh new features to add to an existing system). The remaining sections in this chapter are about keeping the project on track once it's fully underway.

4. Update the Model Regularly

So the use cases are written, the design is done, the code and tests implemented, and the first development iteration is signed off, with software that's either released or (for an ongoing project) could be released now if the customer wants it. But what happens next? All too often, the next step is that the developers abandon all the work put into the model, and continue to write new code. The result is that the design becomes more and more out-of-date. We're sure you've worked on projects where this has happened. The moment one class is refactored and the design model isn't updated, there's a disparity between the model and the code. So the model, having become less useful, is used less, and so more code is written without updating the model; the model becomes even more out-of-date, making it less useful again. And so on. It's a feedback loop of the nastiest order.

Thankfully, modern tools support makes it actually pretty easy to avoid this trap, allowing you to get the full ongoing benefit of an up-to-date model, without slowing the team down on new developments. If you're using Enterprise Architect (EA), you'll be pleased to hear that EA has an add-in that goes by the rather unassuming name **MDG Integration**,[3] with versions available to integrate EA directly into Visual Studio and Eclipse (and, therefore, Flex/FlashBuilder). This enables round-trip engineering so that changes in the code are automatically reflected in the model.

■ **Note** There is an article on the ICONIX web site that shows how to integrate your EA model with Visual Studio and sync up the model and code.[4] The steps involved for Eclipse/Flash Builder are pretty similar.

Figure 4–10 shows the Mapplet UML model (on the right) integrated into Flash Builder, with the Flex classes in the Package Explorer on the left. As you can see, there's the added benefit of having the original domain model (which should also include a definition of each domain object), requirements, use cases, and UI prototypes right there in the coding environment. Last but not least, the test cases are also right there.

If you double-click on a diagram in the Project Explorer, you'll get the "true" UML diagram showing all the class relationships, etc., within Flash Builder (see Figure 4–11).

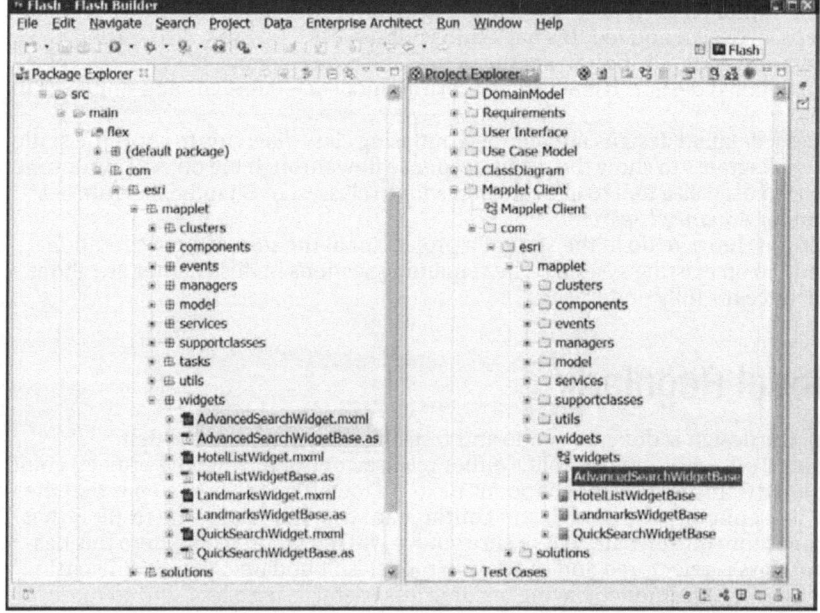

Figure 4–10. The model and code doing a harmonious singsong

---

[3] There is more information about MDG Integration at www.sparxsystems.com/products/#integration.

[4] See www.iconixsw.com/Articles/UML_visual_studio.html.

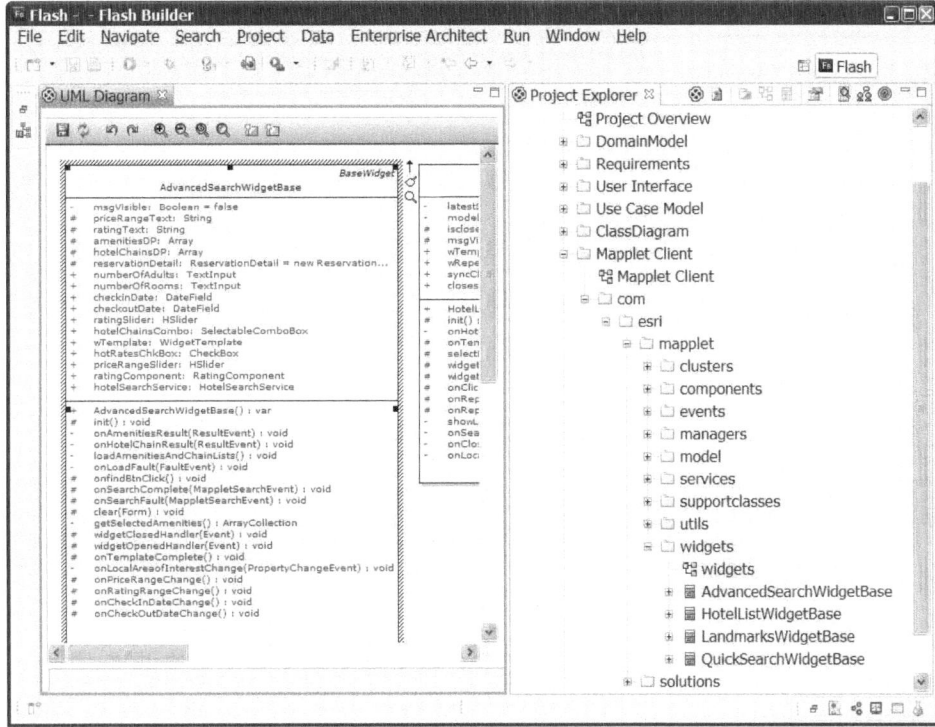

Figure 4–11. The Mapplet Client UML model in Flash Builder

If you prefer not to use tools support to keep the model and code in-sync, it's still worth allocating a small amount of time (say, at the end of a one- or two-week sprint) to revisit the model and update it in line with the code.

Figures 4–12 through 4–16 show some of the Mapplet classes reverse-engineered directly from the Flex code. If you compare them with the domain model in Figure 4–3, you'll see there's a pretty direct mapping.

```
                                                         BaseWidget
                    widgets::QuickSearchWidgetBase
─────────────────────────────────────────────────────────────────
-    ICON_URL: String = "com/esri/solut... {readOnly}
-    hitimer: uint
-    graphicsLayer: GraphicsLayer
-    deleteBookmarkId: int
#    addressCandidates: ArrayCollection
#    msgVisible: Boolean = false
#    isLocationPickerActive: Boolean = false
#    imageManager: ImageManager = ImageManager.ge...
+    wTemplate: WidgetTemplate
+    pointOfInterestTxt: PromptingTextInput
+    streetTxt: TextInput
+    cityTxt: TextInput
+    stateTxt: TextInput
+    postalTxt: TextInput
+    countryTxt: TextInput
+    bookMarkInput: PromptingTextInput
+    viewStack: ViewStack
+    resultTxtMessage: Text
+    swfMessage: SWFLoader
+    hotelSearchService: HotelSearchService
+    pointOfInterest: PointOfInterest
+    address: Address
+    bookmarkCollection: BookmarkCollection
─────────────────────────────────────────────────────────────────
+    QuickSearchWidgetBase() : var
#    init() : void
#    onCreationComplete() : void
#    onTemplateComplete() : void
-    showResultsHandler(MouseEvent) : void
-    showQuickSearchHandler(MouseEvent) : void
#    onAddBookmark() : void
#    removeBookmark(Event) : void
-    onBookmarkDeleteConfirmation(CloseEvent) : void
#    zoomtoBookmark(MouseEvent) : void
#    mouseOverRecord(MouseEvent) : void
#    mouseOutRecord() : void
#    selectLocation(MouseEvent) : void
#    clearAddressFrm() : void
#    clearPOI() : void
#    onLocateAddress() : void
#    onLocatePOI() : void
#    onLocateComplete(MappletLocatorEvent) : void
#    onLocateFault(MappletLocatorEvent) : void
#    toggleLocationPicker() : void
-    showLocation(Object) : void
-    showHighlight(Array) : void
-    zoomToLocation(Array) : void
-    onMarkerPlacingMouseOver(MouseEvent) : void
-    onMarkerPlacingMouseOut(MouseEvent) : void
-    onMarkerPlaced(MapMouseEvent) : void
-    mouseOverGraphic(MouseEvent) : void
#    widgetOpenedHandler(Event) : void
-    showMessage(String, Boolean) : void
-    onMapExtentChange(Event) : void
#    onSearchComplete(MappletSearchEvent) : void
#    onSearchFault(MappletSearchEvent) : void
```

Figure 4–12. Quick Search widget with all its attributes and operations allocated

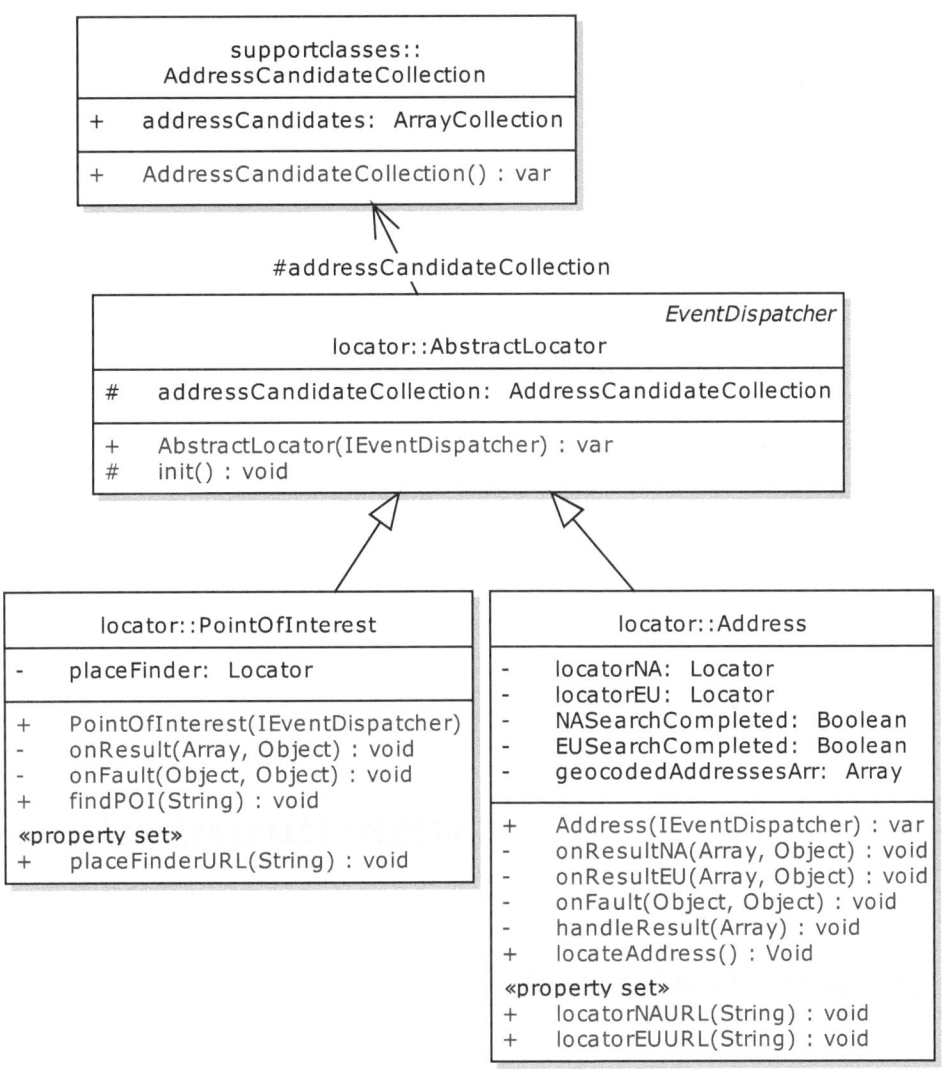

Figure 4–13. Quick Search: classes for locating address candidates

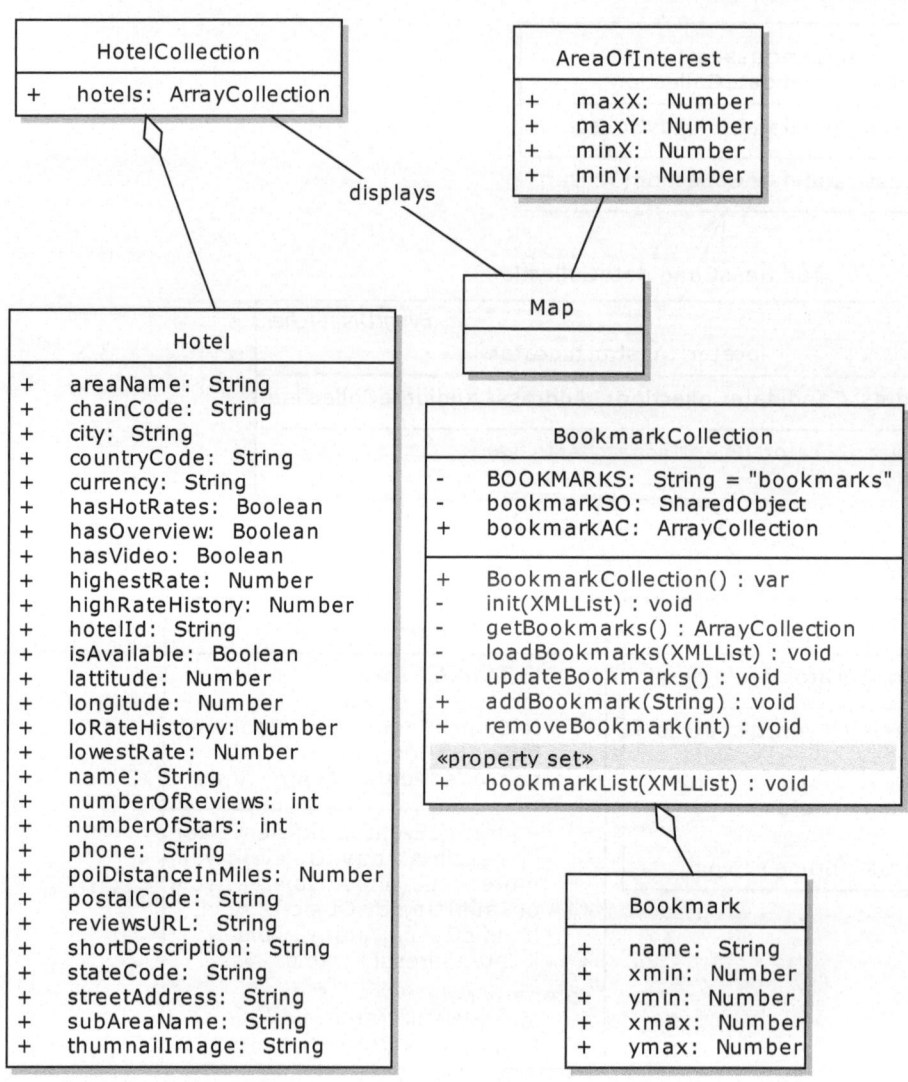

Figure 4–14. *The remaining Flex classes for Quick Search*

```
                                          BaseWidget
              widgets::AdvancedSearchWidgetBase
─────────────────────────────────────────────────────
 -      msgVisible:  Boolean = false
 #      priceRangeText:  String
 #      ratingText:  String
 #      amenitiesDP:  Array
 #      hotelChainsDP:  Array
 #      reservationDetail:  ReservationDetail
 +      numberOfAdults:  TextInput
 +      numberOfRooms:  TextInput
 +      checkinDate:  DateField
 +      checkoutDate:  DateField
 +      ratingSlider:  HSlider
 +      hotelChainsCombo:  SelectableComboBox
 +      wTemplate:  WidgetTemplate
 +      hotRatesChkBox:  CheckBox
 +      priceRangeSlider:  HSlider
 +      ratingComponent:  RatingComponent
 +      hotelSearchService:  HotelSearchService
─────────────────────────────────────────────────────
 +      AdvancedSearchWidgetBase() : var
 #      init() : void
 -      onAmenitiesResult(ResultEvent) : void
 -      onHotelChainResult(ResultEvent) : void
 -      loadAmenitiesAndChainLists() : void
 -      onLoadFault(FaultEvent) : void
 #      onfindBtnClick() : void
 #      onSearchComplete(MappletSearchEvent) : void
 #      onSearchFault(MappletSearchEvent) : void
 #      clear(Form) : void
 -      getSelectedAmenities() : ArrayCollection
 #      widgetClosedHandler(Event) : void
 #      widgetOpenedHandler(Event) : void
 #      onTemplateComplete() : void
 -      onLocalAreaofInterestChange() : Void
 #      onPriceRangeChange() : void
 #      onRatingRangeChange() : void
 #      onCheckInDateChange() : void
 #      onCheckOutDateChange() : void
```

Figure 4–15. Advanced Search widget

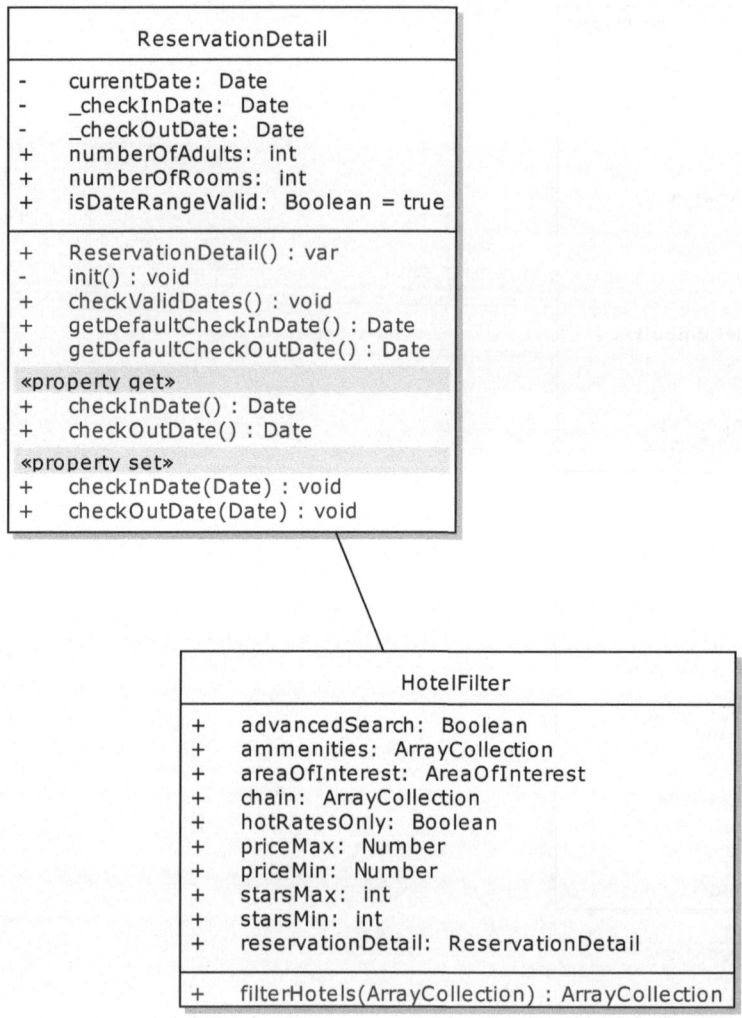

Figure 4–16. *Advanced Search: the ReservationDetail and HotelFilter classes*

3. Keep Test Scripts In-Sync with Requirements

It's a fact of life that the business requirements can change over the course of a project. The original customer representative might be replaced by someone who has a different perspective on what's needed; the economic conditions might change, leading to a shift in priorities; the BAs might realize that they misunderstood what was needed; the developers might realize that they misunderstood the BAs (although the process described in this book should help to minimize such misunderstandings), and so on.

When requirements do change, it's important to update the acceptance tests so that they always reflect the true, up-to-date requirements. A good set of acceptance tests is like a barometer of the project's overall health. If a lot of tests are failing, they're telling you that part of the system isn't being developed to the customer's specification. But if the tests don't actually match up with the requirements, then all you've got is a faulty barometer.

2. Keep Automated Tests Up to Date

As you'll see later in Part 2, it's important to make the unit tests and controller tests part of your automated build, so that when some code is committed, a complete build is triggered, including running the tests. If compilation fails because of the code just committed, the team is notified straightaway. Similarly, if the tests fail, the team finds out straightaway, and they're obliged to fix the tests (i.e., bring them up to date) in order to have a working build again.

Why such a draconian approach? It's simple: if the tests aren't run regularly and automatically, no one will ever bother running the whole test suite. As soon as a test fails, the team will become even less likely to want to run it, and it may even end up being removed altogether. So it's preferable to keep the tests up to date by making them run automatically.

That said, there are some tests that you may not want to run every single time a piece of code is committed to source control. Integration tests (which call external systems and thus tend to be quite fragile, dependent as they are on other teams, shared test data, etc.) and long-running tests would just make the build take all day, assuming it doesn't break on a regular basis (which it would, if it included integration tests), and they should be strictly kept out of the main build. They can still be run automatically, of course, but it's better to keep them on a separate run schedule: e.g., set them up to run overnight, or once per hour… as long as they're not connected with the main build.

We would also suggest that if you follow the ICONIX Process and DDT, with a design mapped out up-front based on a set of use cases signed-off by the customer, then you should find that code that has already been written and "finished" shouldn't need to be refactored over and over, as part of an "evolving design." Of course, you'd expect the design to change a *bit*: no design is ever set in stone, so you do need to be prepared to change things around if necessary. But the level of "design churn" should at least be greatly reduced.

1. Compare the Release Candidate with Original Use Cases

As seasoned software developers will tell you, "job done" doesn't just mean "have the release party." Actually, we hope it *does* mean that—an event of some kind gives a good sense of closure on a project or release. But first, before the project manager grabs the karaoke mic and does his best/worst impression of Tina Turner singing "You're Simply the Best," it's important to get some sense out of him—and the customer, the developers, BAs, and testers. Take one moment of sobriety and introspection before the desks are pushed to one side and the *Dance Dance Revolution* mat is unrolled. During this quiet moment, walk through the original use cases and compare them with the release candidate.

If there are significant differences, the customer might even feel that the project isn't so complete after all, and there's still work to be done before it can be released. That's a worst-case scenario, of course. A less drastic scenario is that the requirements shifted during development for one of the following reasons: (as we noted in "to-do" item #3) a shift in business priorities genuinely changed the requirements—in which case there's not a lot your team could do except modify the use cases and re-estimate the delivery date as the changes ripple through the design to the code and tests; the team didn't have a thorough understanding of the requirements or of the business itself when the project began; the requirements simply weren't analyzed in sufficient detail to create realistic use cases; the BAs didn't walk through the use cases and prototype UIs with the customer; there weren't any prototype UIs at all; the customer wasn't given the opportunity to review the business requirement tests and scenario test specs. In these cases, it's important to review the process and discuss what may have gone wrong, so that the same mistakes aren't repeated in the next bout of development or on the next project.

Importantly, the project review isn't a finger-pointing (or finger-wagging) exercise, and mustn't be approached as such. But it's a vital opportunity to improve your team's ability to create great software to spec.

Let's do a little release/use case comparison for the Mapplet. The *Quick Search* use case, if you'll recall from the start of this chapter, allows the user to jump to a particular place of interest on a map, and see hotels in that area. Figure 4–17 shows the finished product doing exactly that—in this case, searching for hotels in Waikiki. Figure 4–18 shows the results of the quick search.

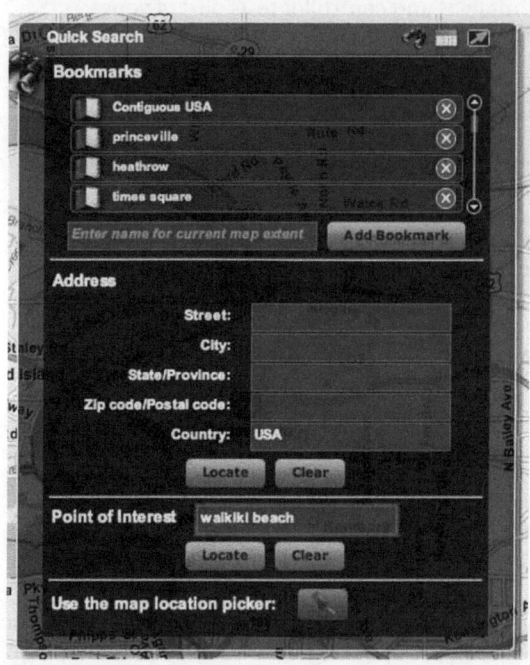

Figure 4–17. The finished Quick Search use case: the user enters some basic search criteria.

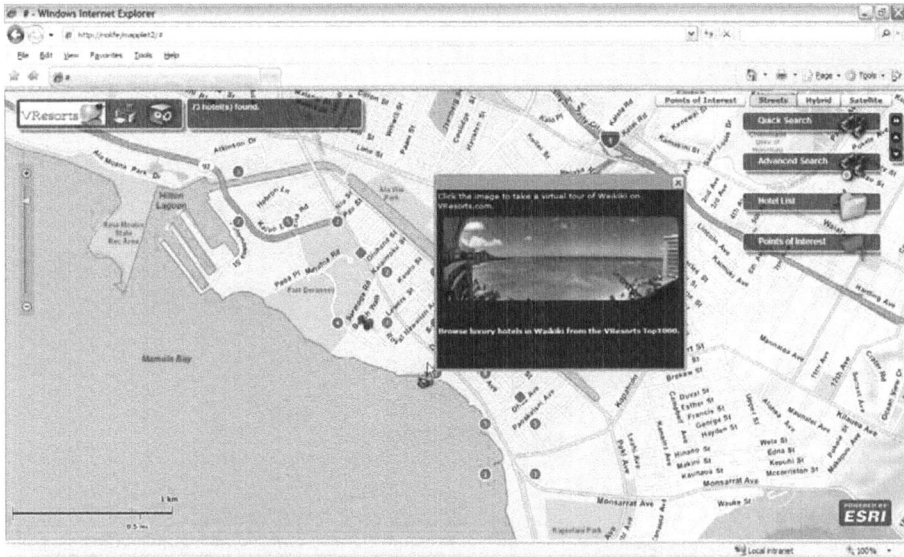

Figure 4–18. Results of a Quick Search: that's a lot of hotels to choose from…

Obviously that's a lot of matching hotels, so it's reasonable for the user to want to eliminate some of these. Enter the *Advanced Search* use case, which allows the user to declutter the map using price/amenity filtering. Figure 4–19 shows the user refining the search criteria; Figures 4–20 and 4–21 show the search results.

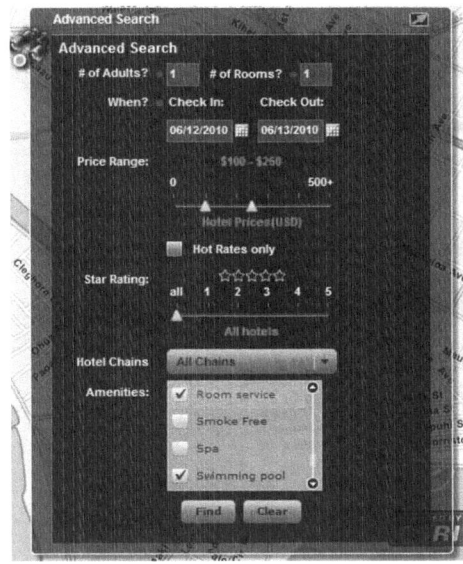

Figure 4–19. Advanced Search in action: the user refines the search criteria.

Figure 4–20. *Advanced Search in action: we've decluttered the map, making it easy to choose a hotel.*

Figure 4–21. *Advanced Search in action: the release matches the use cases, so we can take a vacation!*

Of course, screenshots can convey only so much: we invite you to head over to www.VResorts.com and walk through the steps in the use case using the actual completed product.

If you compare these screenshots with the use cases from the start of this chapter, we hope you'll agree that they match up pretty much exactly—so exactly, in fact, that they look pretty much identical. There's a good reason for this: they *are* identical! But before you fill out a complaint card and mail it to our publisher, we would hastily point out that the reason they're identical is that the UI was storyboarded in Flash Builder, resulting in "non-functioning" MXML (in the sense that the event handlers were empty, and the application was bereft of code). Development then consisted of filling in the event handlers and writing ActionScript classes using a domain-driven approach, with unit and controller tests keeping the code well-behaved.

Summary

In this chapter we introduced the Mapplet 2.0 project and focused on two of its use cases, *Quick Search* and *Advanced Search*—really the core of the Mapplet functionality. We walked through our top-ten list of "project best practices." If you kickstart your project using these practices, it's a sure way to match up the team's understanding of what's required with the customer's real business requirements, and to ensure that the project starts off in the right direction.

We also compared the finished Mapplet with the original use cases—an important review step that should be carried out with the customer actively involved.

For the rest of Part 2, we'll walk backwards through the development process, starting with the finished code and design, to show how you write tests that validate and provide feedback on each stage.

CHAPTER 5

■ ■ ■

Detailed Design and Unit Testing

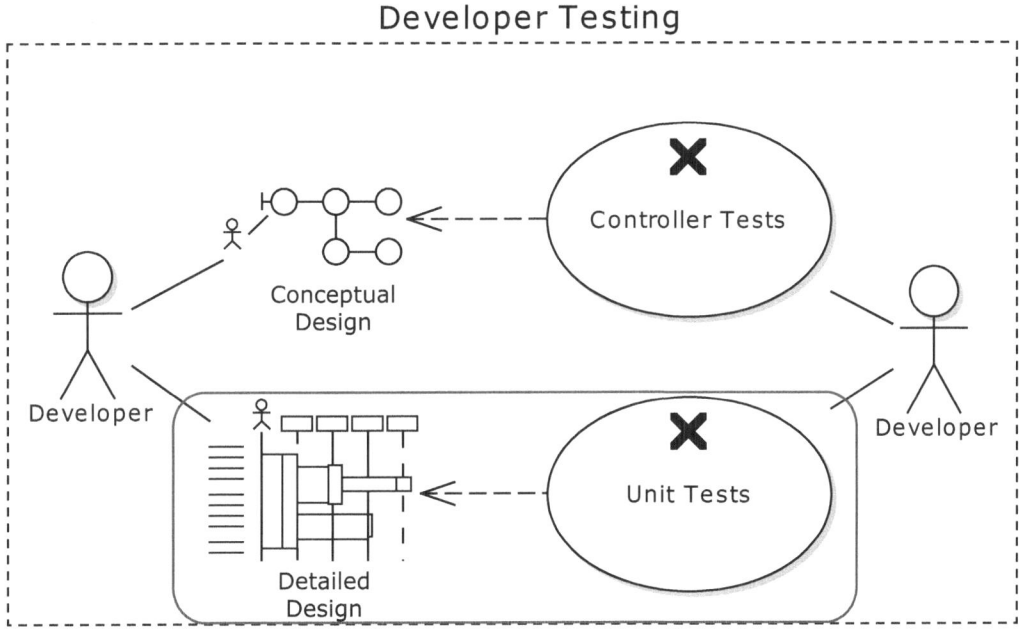

"Detailed design" is when the team really starts to make the hard decisions about how the system will be implemented. The team may also be creating prototypes to explore various facets of the design and to help produce more realistic time/effort estimates; but, ultimately, they need to gain common consensus on how the system will be put together, with a clear design agreed upon and understood by all the members of the development team.

As you can see from the chapter-opening diagram, unit tests have a close symbiotic relationship with the detailed design. A unit test "knows" about the internals of the method under test, e.g., specific variables and the other objects and methods that the code depends on. A unit test is also very fine-grained, being concerned as it is with an individual method and the results of a single call into that method.

■ **Geek Alert** In the movie *Avatar*, if you think of the way that the N'avi connect to other creatures using their funny wiggly connector things, unit tests have a similar connection to the code: the unit test "gets inside" the code and controls it, telling it what to do and sensing both the before and after of each instruction; finally, the unit test readily disconnects from the code as soon as it's done.

By contrast, in Chapter 6 you'll learn about *controller tests* that manipulate and read the code from the outside. Controller tests are also broader-grained than unit tests, and are a sort of halfway house between detailed design and the requirements—in other worse, they test against the *conceptual design*. In that chapter we'll compare the two types of tests, and contrast the advantages and disadvantages of each. You'll find that each approach does have its place.

You'll most likely want to use unit tests for complex algorithmic logic (more about this in Chapter 12), where you want the test to have an intimate knowledge and control over each miniscule state change that takes place in the code. Such code still benefits from being designed; so in this chapter we'll show how to drive unit tests from a detailed UML design.

There are essentially two classes of unit tests: isolated tests (that is, where the code being tested is kept within a "walled garden" to keep it relevant to the particular test), and integration tests (where there are no walls, and the code is allowed to make calls to remote systems, or just to other parts of the same system). This chapter is chiefly about isolated unit tests, as these are the easier of the two to write and maintain. But integration unit tests, while they face more issues (due to the nature of what they're testing), are no less important. There will be more about these in Chapter 11.

The chapter is structured around our "top ten" unit testing "to do" list.

Top Ten Unit Testing "To Do"s

When you're exploring your project's detailed design, writing the corresponding unit tests, and thinking about refactoring and code maintenance, be sure to follow our top ten "to do" items.

10. Start with a sequence diagram that shows how the code satisfies the behavior requirements from a use case.

9. Identify test cases from your design.

8. Write test scenarios for each test case.

7. Test smarter: avoid writing overlapping tests.

6. Transform your test cases into UML test classes (and the test scenarios into unit test methods).

5. Start to write the unit tests and the accompanying code.

4. Write "white box" unit tests.

3. Use a mock object framework to make life easier.

2. Test algorithmic logic with unit tests.

1. Write a separate suite of unit-level integration tests.

10. Start with a Sequence Diagram

Different UML diagrams are intended for different stages of analysis and design. Sequence diagrams, for example, are best used to think through a detailed design, and, in particular, to *allocate behavior* (functions/methods) to classes. With "proper" object-oriented design, you start by defining domain classes—which generally contain data—and then you allocate behavior to these data classes, so that the classes encapsulate both data and functions.[1] So, for example, when creating a ReservationDetail class with check-in and check-out dates, ReservationDetail would have at least two fields, checkInDate and checkOutDate, and during detailed design you might add the function checkDatesAreValid(), which performs a series of validation checks on the fields. To put it another way, if you want to track down some behavior related to a reservation, the first place in the code you'd go to would be the ReservationDetail class. It's just good OO design to allocate behavior to the relevant domain class.

As you might expect, allocating behavior is what sequence diagrams help you to do. And the added bonus is that this "responsibility-driven" approach to design also makes your code easier to unit test.

Let's use the approach we've just described to implement part of the Mapplet, complete with unit tests. The Mapplet requires an Advanced Search widget, which will allow the user to search for hotels using search fields such as city, check-in/check-out date, and so on. The user enters a search value and then clicks "Find." The Flex client contacts the Java-based search service, which, in turn, calls out to an external, XML-based search system. The Java code then compiles the XML results into a HotelCollection, which it returns to the Flex client.

■ **Note** We will walk through the Flex-based ReservationDetail example in Chapter 6, so for this chapter we'll look at server-side code, a Java class called SearchHotelService.

Figure 5–1 shows the sequence diagram for the search request that we've just described (this is, in fact, for the *Advanced Search* use case, which we will show more of in Chapter 6). It's pretty clear from the sequence diagram that SearchHotelService (our server-side Java class) needs a public method called getHotels() and a private method (called on itself) called getHotelsFromSearchService(). This second method is the one that makes an HTTP call to an external hotel search service, which returns its results in a big XML stream. But it's the public method, getHotels(), that we want to unit-test. We want to test how the Java code handles some hotels being returned, and also whether it copes with no hotels being returned.

---

[1] When we learned object-oriented design, this was actually the definition of a class... a programmatic unit that encapsulated data and functions, with said encapsulation having benefits like controlling the means of accessing a set of data. Nowadays it seems fashionable to have "data classes" (which have no behavior) and "single-method classes" (aka functions wearing "class" clothing). This seems like a giant step backwards to us, which obliterates all the (very real) benefits of doing an object-oriented design.

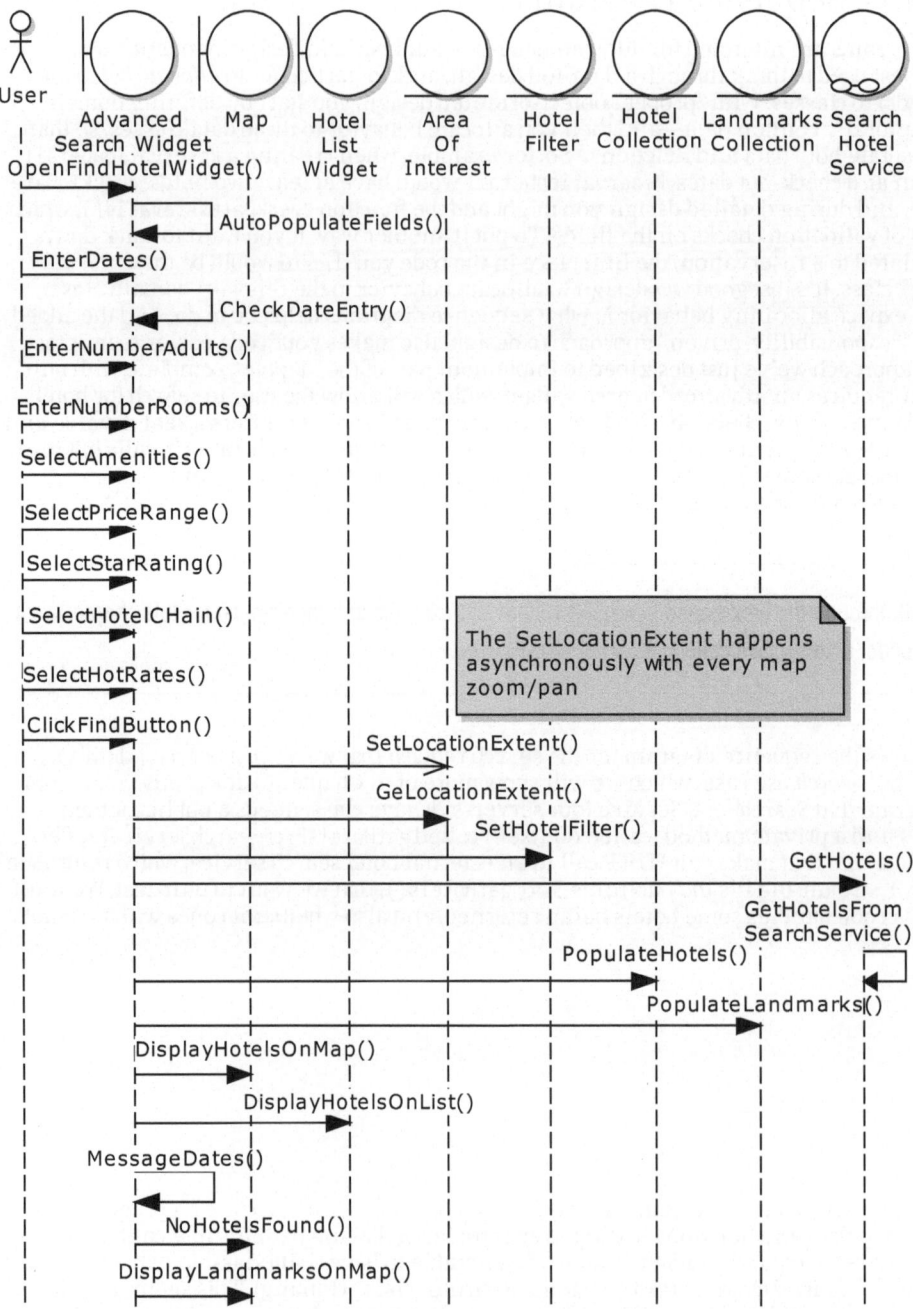

Figure 5–1. *Sequence diagram for the Advanced Search use case*

9. Identify Test Cases from Your Design

Let design diagrams drive your creation of test cases. If you're using EA, first make sure that you have the ICONIX add-in installed (it's a free download[2]). Then in your sequence diagram, right-click and choose Add-Ins… Agile ICONIX Process… Create Tests from Sequence (see Figure 5–2). This creates a test case diagram with one test case on it for each operation on the sequence diagram (see Figure 5–3).

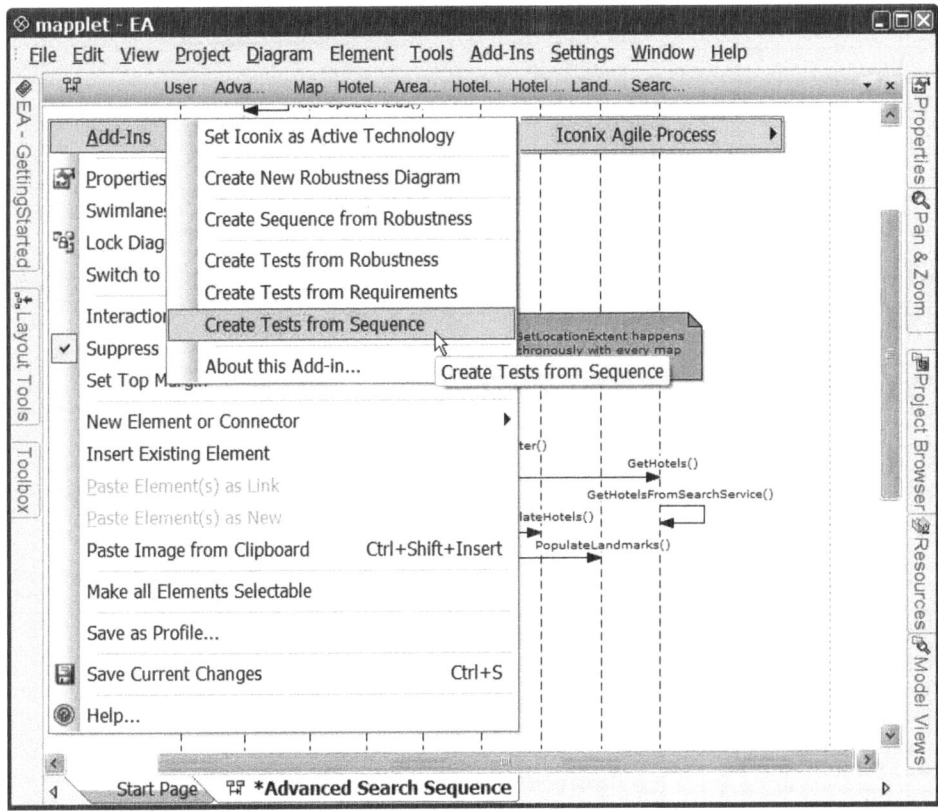

Figure 5–2. *Using the Agile ICONIX add-in to create test cases based on your design*

As you can imagine, a test case for each operation means a lot of test cases—in Figure 5–3 we've deleted most of them to fit the diagram onto the page. But, in fact, you'll find that you won't need unit tests for some of the generated test cases, as many of them will already have been covered by controller tests, which we will talk about in Chapter 6. But we're getting ahead of ourselves…

---

[2] There's a link to the download page here: http://iconixsw.com/EA/PowerUsers.html

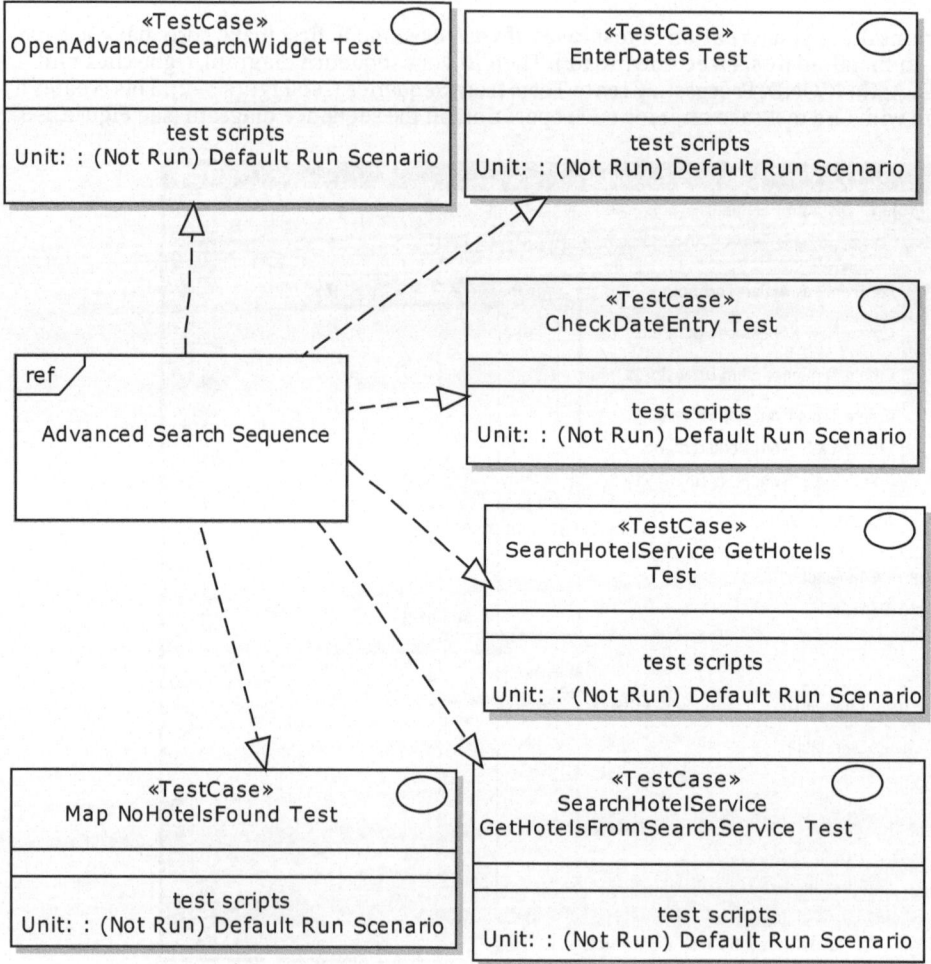

Figure 5–3. Test cases generated from the operations on the sequence diagram

The test case that we're interested in is the one for the getHotels method—the third one down on the right in Figure 5–3. But simply creating a test called "Get Hotels" doesn't say very much: "Let's test getting hotels!" With DDT we're much more interested in "testing with a purpose," identifying specific scenarios for each test case—e.g., "Let's confirm that when the Search Service returns no hotels, the code survives it." We'll look at how to create specific test scenarios next.

8. Write Scenarios for Each Test Case

Be sure to write scenarios for each test case. A test case with one default scenario is only part of the story. Additional test scenarios allow for things like alternative inputs (and, therefore, different expected outputs), creating a more comprehensive test case.

In Figure 5–3, notice that each test case has the following line on it:

```
Unit:  : (Not Run) Default Run Scenario
```

"Default Run Scenario" is the name of—you guessed it—a default scenario. Each test case gets one of these by default. But we want to get more specific than that. For getHotels(), we'll replace the default scenario with two new ones.

To add these new scenarios, first zap EA into Testing Mode: either press Alt+3, or choose View… Testing, or double-click on the Default Run Scenario. You should see a Testing window appear. If you click the GetHotels test case, then you can now start adding individual test scenarios (see Figure 5–4).

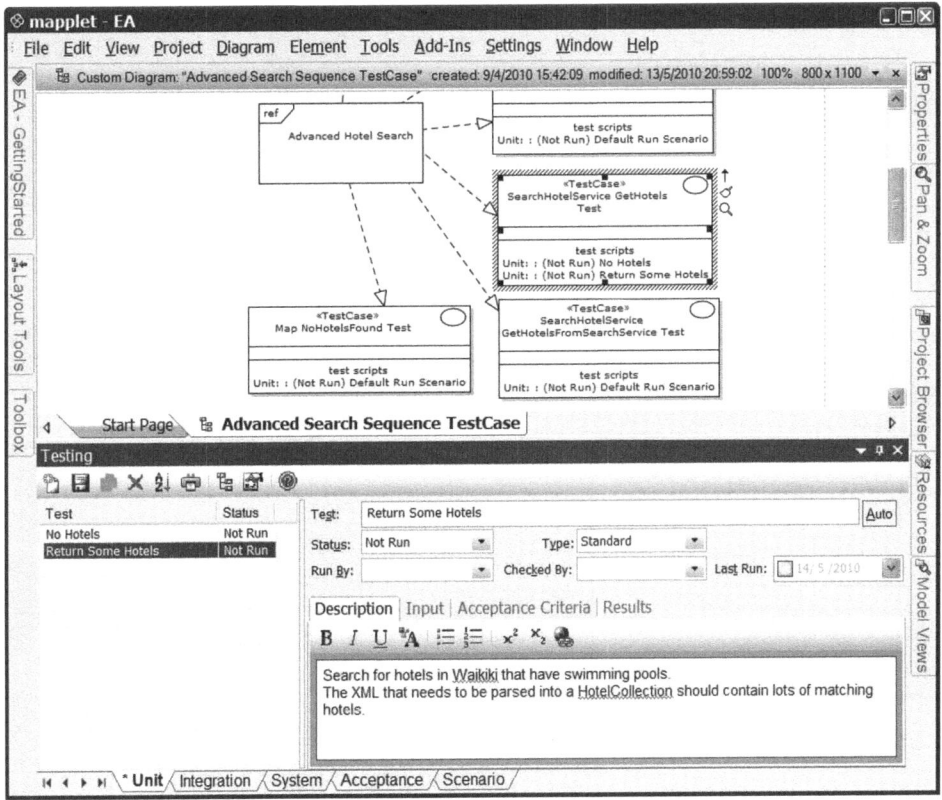

Figure 5–4. *Adding test scenarios for the GetHotels test case*

Along the bottom of the screen you should see some tabs: Unit, Integration, System, Acceptance, and Scenario. Make sure you're adding the tests onto the Unit tab.

Halfway up the window, there are tabs for the current test scenario: Description, Input, Acceptance Criteria, and Results. The information you put in these will be written into comments on the unit test class, so be sure to write something good, meaningful, and unambiguous. And specific.

Table 5–1 shows the test data we've added for GetHotels.

Table 5–1. *Test Scenario Details for the "Get Hotels" Test Case*

Description	Input	Acceptance Criteria
Specify a 5–star hotel in NY City for $50. Should result in an XML response containing zero hotels.	Hotel Filter with: starsMin: 5 starsMax: 5 location: New York priceMin: $50 priceMax: $50	Should survive parsing the zero-hotel XML result and return an empty HotelCollection.
Search for hotels in Waikiki that have swimming pools. Should result in an XML response containing *lots* of matching hotels.	Hotel Filter with: Location: Waikiki Amenities: Swimming Pool	The HotelCollection returned should contain as many hotels as are in the XML result.

Notice how "up-close" these test scenarios are: we're not looking at the overall interaction, but instead a single point, one link in the chain. So, for example, this particular test isn't about whether the UI displays the result correctly; it's about whether one method successfully parses the search result.

The GetHotels test case now looks like the illustration in Figure 5–5.

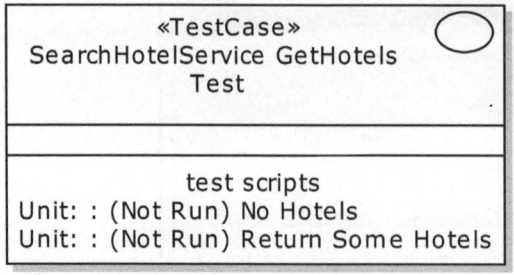

Figure 5–5. *The GetHotels test case*

If you want to get as close as possible to 100% code coverage (*Fly, Icarus! Fly!*), then creating test scenarios for every test case generated from each operation will pretty much get you there. Of course, you'll be a hairy old man (or woman) by the time they're all done, so it pays to be more selective about which tests you want to focus your efforts (and the customer's time, aka money) on. In Chapter 6 we will show an effective method of being selective—but we're getting ahead of ourselves again. For now, you should find that it's quite an intuitive process to look at each generated test case on the diagram and decide whether the project will benefit from turning it into a unit test class. As soon as you've determined that a particular test case isn't needed, just delete it from the model.

Let's take a closer look at why you can afford to leave some tests out.

7. Test Smarter: Avoid Overlapping Tests

One of the issues we have with "100% code coverage" is that you potentially end up with duplicate tests: ones that are already covered by another test. Overlapping tests represent wasted effort. One way to "test smarter, not harder," is to avoid writing two or more tests covering the same ground. It isn't always obvious that two tests overlap. To illustrate, Figure 5–6 shows a sequence diagram for a prototype version of the Hotel Search Service.

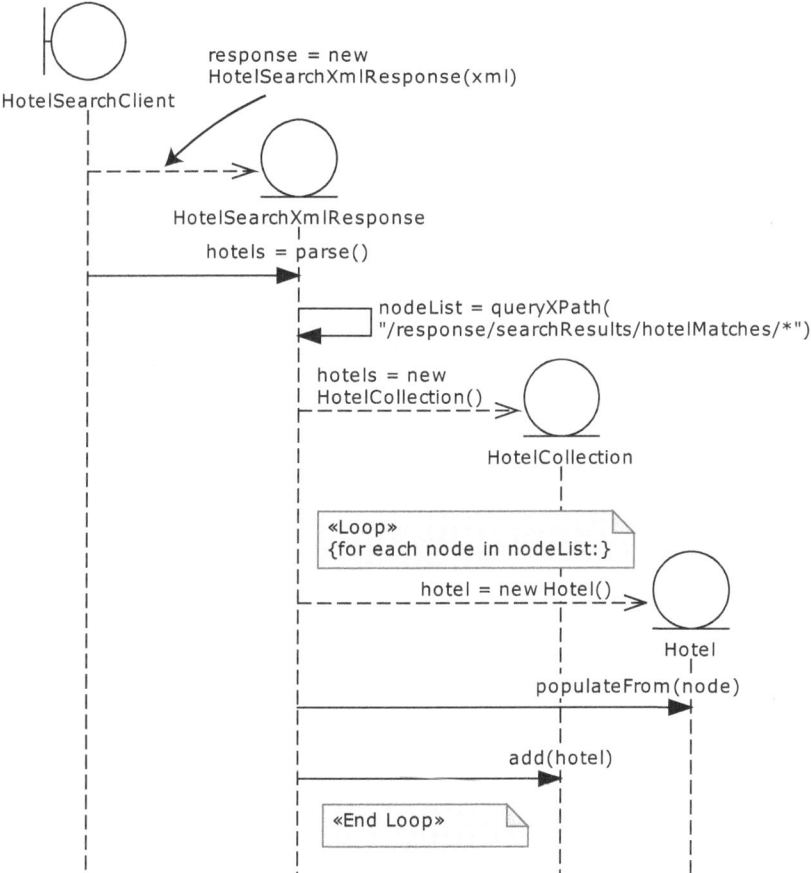

Figure 5–6. Part of the design for an earlier prototype Hotel Search Service

Following TDD, you would write tests for the three constructors (Hotel, HotelCollection, and HotelSearchXmlResponse) to ensure that each object was created properly. You would also write tests for the methods Hotel.populateFrom(node), HotelCollection.add(node),

HotelSearchXmlResponse.queryXPath(..), and HotelSearchXmlResponse.parse(). Each of these might end up with more than one test case, to cover all the permutations and ins and outs. That's rather a lot of test code, but, ultimately, what does all of that actually buy you (aside from rather a lot of test code)?

The sequence diagram provides an important visual clue that all of those tests may not be needed. The boundary object, HotelSearchClient, is really in charge of this particular sequence: it's the orchestrator, the entry and exit point for the XML parsing and creation of a HotelCollection. It initially creates a HotelSearchXmlResponse object, then kick-starts the sequence by calling the parse() method.

If you think of the best Rube Goldberg-esque machine you've ever seen,[3] most likely the sequence is begun in quite a humble way: a toy truck being pushed into some dominos, triggering a marble rolling down a chute. The marble disappears into a more complex mechanism, and a whole sequence of events is kicked off. The final result, several buckets of multicolored paint sprayed across some musicians, is consistently the desired outcome. Each time the machine is run, the only variant might be the speed and direction at which the toy truck knocks over the dominos, right at the start. Everything in between there and the paint spray/dour musicians result is a constant: so one unit test could feasibly cover it. Inputs=toy truck velocity; acceptance criteria=grumpy paint-spattered musicians.

The principle is exactly the same for the sequence shown in Figure 5–6. HotelSearchXmlResponse.parse() is called, and everything after that is constant and predictive, right up to the point where the HotelCollection is returned. The only variations are to do with the XML passed in (e.g., different number of hotels, or the XML itself may be invalid), and the number of Hotel objects returned in the HotelCollection.

So, in theory, you could get away with just the one unit test, right at the top level of the sequence. If anything within the encapsulated code doesn't work, the HotelCollection won't return the correct result.

This is "black box testing" at its most opaque, of course. You may well find that you don't want to stretch one unit test across too big an expanse of complex or algorithmic code. Even if the measurable outcome is already covered, you might find it beneficial to add more tests within the code. Sometimes this helps to create cleaner code, and may also help the developer to understand the code more as he's writing it. There will be more about "white box testing" later in this chapter.

Sometimes finding the "sweet spot" between black box and white box tests is obvious, and other times it's subjective. In Chapter 6 we present a technique (using controller tests that are essentially "gray box") to help identify the key software functions to test.

6. Transform Your Test Cases into UML Classes

At this stage you can quite readily take the test scenarios you've created and use them as a guide to write the unit test code. To that end, you should transform your test cases into unit test classes. Also transform your scenarios into unit test methods.

For each test case, create a unit test class, e.g., for "Get Hotels Test" you'd have a class called GetHotelsTest. For each test scenario, create a test method; for "No Hotels" you'd write a method called noHotels() and for "Return Some Hotels" you'd write a method called returnSomeHotels(). (For JUnit 3 users these would be prefixed with "test", e.g., testReturnSomeHotels().) With the test method signatures in place, you can then start to write the test code itself, writing the target/product code as you go along.

---

[3] And if you haven't seen it, here it is: http://www.youtube.com/watch?v=qybUFnY7Y8w (or search for "This Too Shall Pass").

Converting the test cases into test classes and the test scenarios into test methods is almost a menial process, though: it's the sort of thing you'd think a computer could do for you. Luckily, EA has another trick up its sleeve, and can transform the test cases first into UML test classes, and from there into "real" source code.

Bring up your test case diagram. Then right-click the test case and choose *Transform...* (see Figure 5–7).

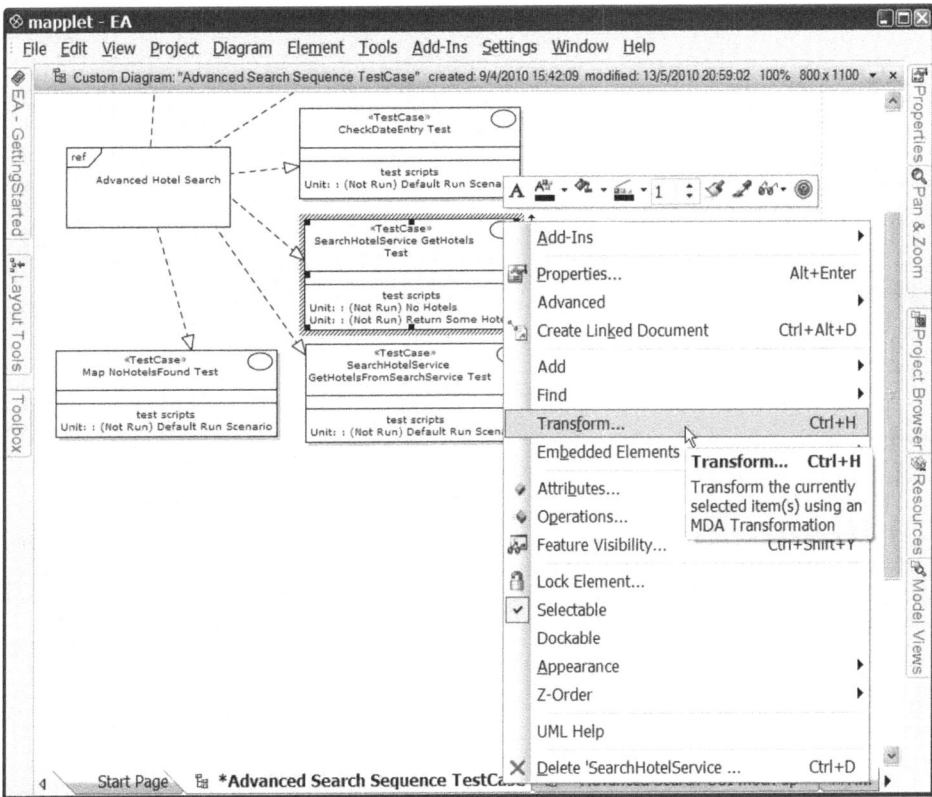

Figure 5–7. Time to transform the test cases into actual test classes

This brings up the Model Transformation dialog (see Figure 5–8). Choose one of the ICONIX transformations—this example is for Java code targeting JUnit 4, so we've selected "Iconix_JUnit4." Also make sure the Target Package points to a top level/root package separate from the main model.

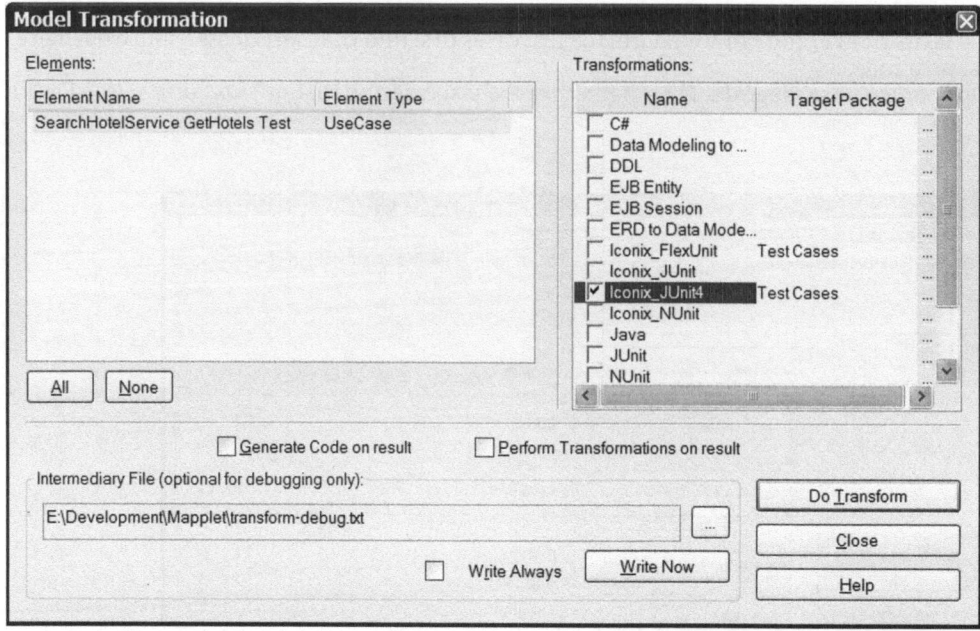

Figure 5–8. Transforming the test scenarios

Finally, click "Do Transform." You should see your model's package structure replicated beneath the Test Cases package, along with a new class diagram containing the test classes, and, of course, a new test class matching the test case you selected. (You can also select multiple test cases at a time, or a package full of them.) The new test class looks like that in Figure 5–9.

SearchHotelServiceGetHotelsTest
+   setUp() : void
+   tearDown() : void
+   noHotels() : void
+   returnSomeHotels() : void

Figure 5–9. Our new test class

The class name follows this pattern:

"Name of Target Class Being Tested" + "Test Case Name"

In this case the Java class being tested is SearchHotelService, and the test case is "Get Hotels Test." The test methods themselves are simply the test scenario names, camel-cased into the Java method-naming convention.

To generate the actual Java code, right-click the UML class and choose *Generate Code...* (see Figure 5–10). Note that if you ticked the "Generate Code on result" check box shown in Figure 5–7, this step takes place automatically.

■ **Tip** If you've generated the code previously and want to merge in some changes either to or from the existing code, choose *Synchronize with Code...* instead.

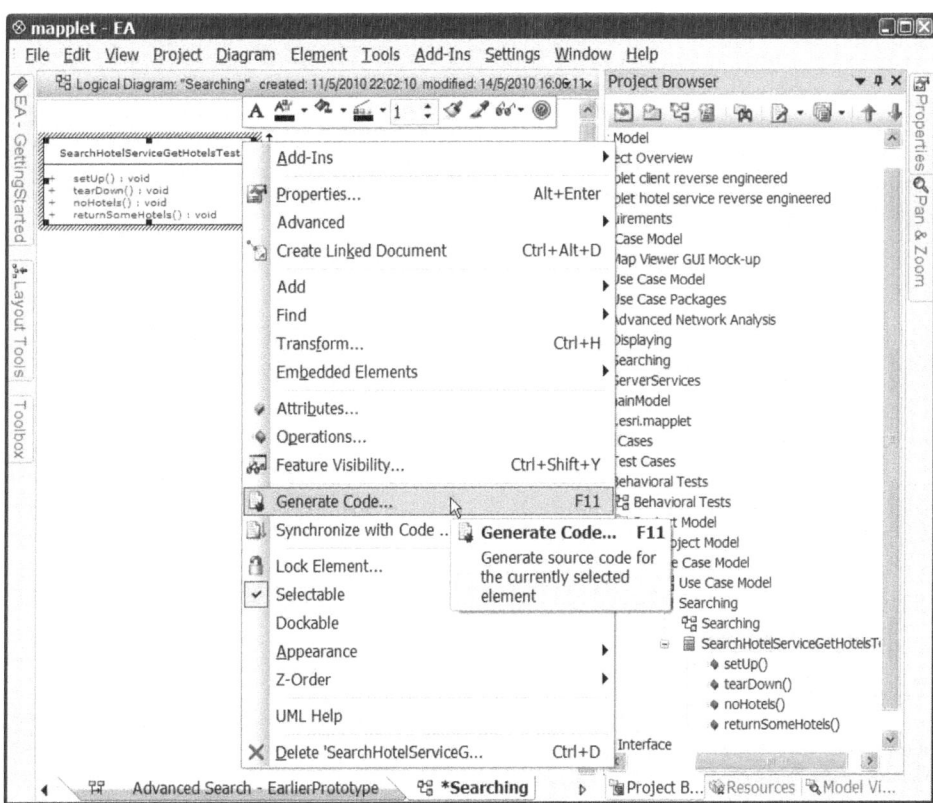

Figure 5–10. Generating the unit test code

Here's the JUnit 4 test class that gets generated. As you can see, the test methods tie back precisely to what was specified in the test scenarios:

```
package Searching;
import org.junit.*;
import static org.junit.Assert.*;

public class SearchHotelServiceGetHotelsTest {
```

```java
@Before
public void setUp() throws Exception {
    // set up test fixtures here...

}

@After
public void tearDown() throws Exception {
    // destroy test fixtures here...

}

/**
 * Specify a 5 star hotel in NY City for $50.
 * Should result in an XML response containing zero hotels.
 *
 * Input: Hotel Filter with:
 *          starsMin: 5
 *          starsMax: 5
 *          location: New York
 *          priceMin: $50
 *          priceMax: $50
 *
 * Acceptance Criteria: Should survive parsing the zero-hotel
 *    XML result and return an empty HotelCollection.
 */
@Test
public final void noHotels() throws Exception {

}

/**
 * Search for hotels in Waikiki that have swimming pools.
 * Should result in an XML response containing LOTS of matching hotels.
 *
 * Input: Hotel Filter with:
 *          Location: Waikiki
 *          Amenities: Swimming Pool
 *
 * Acceptance Criteria: The HotelCollection returned should
 *    contain as many hotels as are in the XML result.
 */
@Test
public final void returnSomeHotels() throws Exception {

}
}
```

■ **Tip** Don't forget to substitute "Searching" with the real package where you want the test class to go.

Above each method, @Test is the JUnit 4 annotation that tags it as a unit test method. Notice also that each test method includes JavaDoc comments to remind the programmer exactly what the test needs to achieve: a summary, the inputs into the code under test, and the final acceptance criteria.

Now all that's left is to write the test code itself, along with the code that we actually want to test, and then, of course, to run the tests.

5. Write Unit Tests and Accompanying Code

It's now time to step through the generated unit test methods, fill them in with actual test code, and write the accompanying product code, referring to the design as you go along. This is an area where DDT and TDD can be nicely complementary (yes, you read that right!). The code can be filled in by writing the tests first, and re-running the tests as you add further code to make sure you haven't broken anything that's already been written. Strictly speaking, this isn't test-first design, but it's certainly test-first coding (though it's certainly not mandatory to take a "test-first" approach to the coding at all).

Let's write the noHotels() test first.

Writing the "No Hotels" Test

As you can see in the sequence diagram in Figure 5–1, the method we want to test, getHotels(), is on the SearchHotelService. So we'll need to create an instance of that, call it, and assert that the result is as expected:

```
/**
 * Specify a 5 star hotel in NY City for $50.
 * Should result in an XML response containing zero hotels.
 *
 * Input: Hotel Filter with:
 *         starsMin: 5
 *         starsMax: 5
 *         location: New York
 *         priceMin: $50
 *         priceMax: $50
 *
 * Acceptance Criteria: Should survive parsing the zero-hotel
 *    XML result and return an empty HotelCollection.
 */
@Test
public final void noHotels() throws Exception {
    SearchHotelService searchService = new SearchHotelService();
    HotelFilter filter = new HotelFilter();
    filter.setStarsMin(5);
    filter.setStarsMax(5);
    filter.setLocation("40.7590,73.9845"⁴);
    filter.setPriceMin(50.0);
    filter.setPriceMax(50.0);
```

---

[4] 40.7590,73.9845 is lat/long position of Times Square in New York.

```
    HotelCollection hotels = searchService.getHotels(filter);
    assertEquals(0, hotels.getHotels().size());
}
```

The first part of this test sets up the test fixtures: we create SearchHotelService, and then a HotelFilter that we populate with the search parameters specified in the test method comments above it. The second part of the test invokes the search service, gets the result, and checks that it's zero, as expected. If some kind of error occurred on the way, either an exception would be thrown or a different value would be returned; either way the test would fail. If zero is returned, then essentially (for the purposes of this particular test) the service is working.

Notice the first line in the test method:

```
SearchHotelService searchService = new SearchHotelService();
```

As you add more test methods, you may find this line being replicated each time, as each test method needs to create its own instance of the SearchHotelService. So it would make sense to create an object-level test fixture, and move this line into the setUp() method that is called before each test method, like so:

```
SearchHotelService searchService;

@Before
public void setUp() throws Exception {
    searchService = new SearchHotelService();
}
```

Most books on TDD or unit testing would tell you to refactor the test code as you go along, rewriting previously "finished" test methods when new ones are added. But the benefit you get from following DDT is that you already know exactly which tests you're going to write, and they're already right there in the generated test class. So you would know in advance to set up searchService so that it can be shared among tests, and this code would need to be written only once. It's almost like being clairvoyant... wonderfully powerful feeling, isn't it?

Of course, the test code as it currently stands would fail compilation, as we haven't yet written the product code that it calls. So next, we'll implement the code needed to make the test pass.

Implementing SearchHotelService

Here's the implementation of SearchHotelService:

```
public class SearchHotelService {

    public HotelCollection getHotels(HotelFilter filter) {
        String xml = getHotelsFromSearchService(filter);
        HotelCollection hotels = parse(xml);
        return hotels;
    }

    private String getHotelsFromSearchService(HotelFilter filter) {
        XmlServiceClient client = new XmlServiceClient();
        return client.callSearchService(filter);
    }

    private HotelCollection parse(String xml) {
```

```
        // bunch of code to parse the XML response and
        // turn it into a HotelCollection

        return new HotelCollection();
    }
}
```

We've omitted the nitty-gritty XML parsing code, as it could take up a chapter's worth of explanation in its own right, and doesn't really have anything to do with what we're discussing here. But just to illustrate, it consists of lots of this sort of stuff:

```
/**
 *  Construct a predicate from each name/value and include them
 *  all in the XPath expression to be evaluated on the hotels document.
 */
private String buildXPathExpression(NodeList queryNodes) {
    StringBuilder predicates = new StringBuilder();
    predicates.append("//generalInfo[");
    String and = "";
    // e.g.  //generalInfo[city='New York' and countryCode='US']
    // ("hotels" is our own root node that we've added so that all the
    // hotel details can be contained in one XML document)
    for (int idx=0, len=queryNodes.getLength(); idx<len; idx++) {
        Node node = queryNodes.item(idx);
        String name = node.getNodeName();
        if (NON_SEARCH_ELEMENTS.contains(name)) {
            continue; // ignore flags etc as they would prevent a match being made
        }
        String value = node.getFirstChild().getNodeValue();
        predicates.append(and);
        predicates.append(name).append("='").append(value).append("'");
        and = " and ";
    }
    predicates.append("]");
    return predicates.toString();
}
```

In other words, it's definitely something that you'd want to cover with unit tests.

Returning to the test itself, have a look at the last two lines:

```
HotelCollection hotels = searchService.getHotels(filter);
assertEquals(0, hotels.getHotels().size());
```

Calling getHotels() actually triggers an external call to a remote HTTP service. This is fine if you don't want the unit tests to be run automatically with every build. If you're planning to write a unit-level integration test (see Chapter 11), then your work on this test is pretty much done (aside from dealing with any integration issues that may arise, of course).

The rest of this chapter is mostly about how to isolate your unit tests—effectively put a walled garden around them—so that they can be run automatically without relying on external systems being available and correctly configured.

SERVICES CALLING SERVICES

In multi-tiered software systems, it's not at all unusual for one service to be calling another service. In the Mapplet design shown in this chapter, for example, we have a Flex client that makes a call to a Java-based Search Hotel Service, which sits on the VResorts server. This service, in turn, makes an HTTP call to an XML Search Service, to return an XML document containing the hotel search results. The "middle layer," Search Hotel Service, parses the XML and relays the result back to the Flex client. (See the architecture diagram in Chapter 4 for an explanation for this design.)

The unit tests in this chapter are testing the Java-based Search Hotel Service. So when we talk about "mocking" the XML Search Service, or writing a "stunt service" replacement for the XML Search Service, remember we're not talking about replacing the Search Hotel Service—as that's the code being tested.

4. Write White Box Unit Tests

To illustrate where the code under test is making an external call (and what we can do to isolate the unit of code from the external service), we'll refer back to the design. Figure 5–11 shows a "zoomed-in" detail from the sequence diagram, with additional details added.

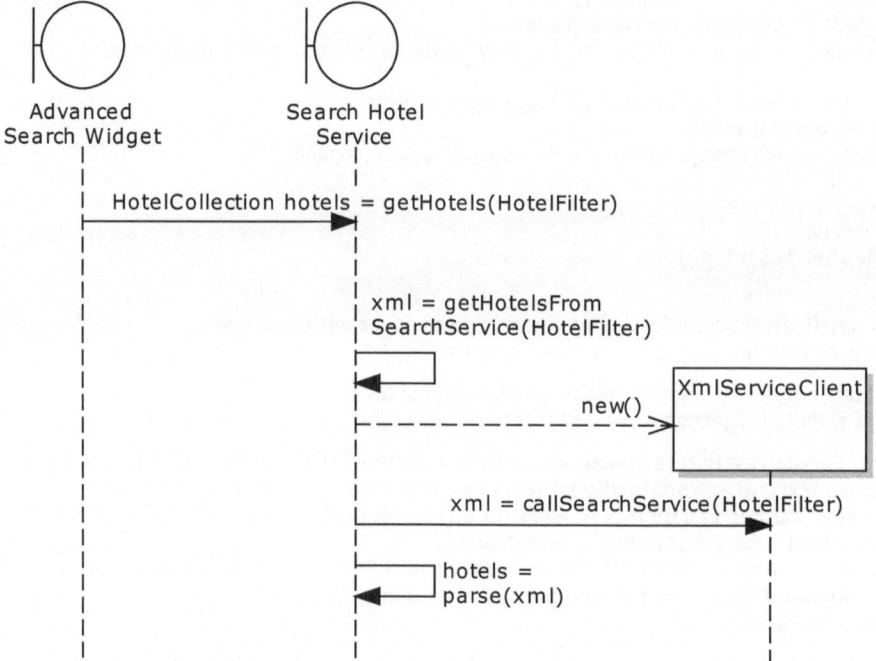

Figure 5–11. Back to the design, with additional details relevant to the hotel search

Hotel and HotelCollection (both shown back in Figure 5–1) are quick and easy to create: Hotel is, for now at least, a big bag of data (though that will change later as Hotel-specific behavior gets added in), and HotelCollection is really a big bag of Hotels, rather like the start of a game of Monopoly.

SearchHotelService is more interesting, however. Remember this contains the public getHotels() method that we want to unit-test. As you can see from Figure 5–11, getHotels() is handed a HotelFilter, a value object that specifies the user's search criteria (city, country code, amenities, nearby landmarks, etc.). getHotels() quickly calls a private method, getHotelsFromSearchService(), passing the HotelFilter along. This method then creates an XmlServiceClient, which, in turn, does some remote invocation magic over HTTP to call the Search Service. Back in SearchHotelService, a method is then called to parse the returned XML and turn it into a HotelCollection.

The problem with this picture is that you generally don't want unit tests to call out to external services. For one thing it'll make your automated build more fragile and potentially very slow (as we discuss later in this chapter); for another, it means that the test is stepping way outside the scope of the single, self-contained unit that it's meant to be testing. Unfortunately for us, calling getHotels() is always going to result in XmlServiceClient being told to call out to the external search service.

There's more than one possible solution to this problem, the two primary ones being the following:

1. Walk further down the sequence diagram and just test the parse(xml) method instead.

2. Replace the XmlServiceClient with a "mock" version that pretends to make an external call.

The first option seems perfectly reasonable, but it would mean exposing the private parse(xml) method so that the unit test can call it, breaking encapsulation—this is to be avoided if at all possible. The other drawback is that this option leaves the "outer" code uncovered by tests. The "test smarter" idea introduced at the start of this chapter isn't about leaving code uncovered by tests; it's about writing fewer tests that cover more code, with the same amount of "test leverage." Moving the tests solely to the "inner code" doesn't achieve this.

So that points us to the second option, passing in a mock object (or "stunt service" in this example)[5] to isolate the code under test and avoid external dependencies.

Implement a Stunt Service

One way to avoid external dependences is to implement a stunt service. The XmlServiceClient contains the code that calls outside the company firewall to a third-party HTTP service. So it would make sense, purely while the tests are running, to replace this class with a stand-in, or "stunt service" (the term "mock objects" is just *so* passé…).

We'll call the mock version StuntServiceClient. Figure 5–12 shows the UML diagram for the service.

---

[5] We'll outline the differences between mock objects and stunt services later in this chapter.

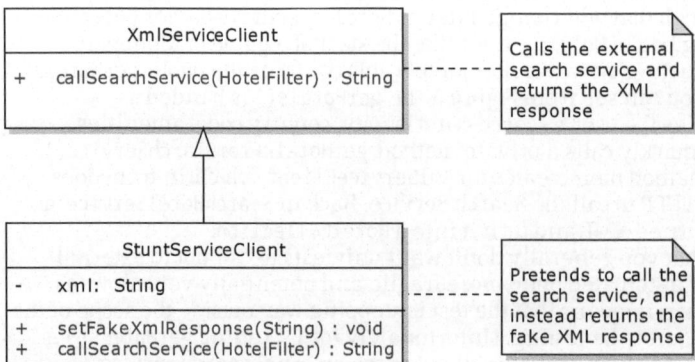

Figure 5–12. A stunt service to stand in for an external service while testing

---

■ **Tip** Remember, the StuntServiceClient is replacing the third-party XML/HTTP-based search service, and not our Java-based SearchHotelService. The SearchHotelService is the code being tested, so we definitely don't want to swap this out with "stunt" or mock code during the test. Live by this mantra: *The stunt/mock objects are part of the test, not part of the code being tested.*

Here's the new StuntServiceClient in code form:

```java
public class StuntServiceClient extends XmlServiceClient {

    private String xml;

    public void setFakeXmlResponse(String xml) {
        this.xml = xml;
    }

    @Override
    public String callSearchService(HotelFilter filter) {
        return xml;
    }
}
```

If we were writing this service only for the "No Hotels" test scenario, then we could simply make callSearchService(HotelFilter) return an empty XML document. But—it's that precognitive dissonance kicking in again[6]—we know from the design that there's also going to be a "Return Some

---

[6] It's almost as if developers were capable of **forethought and planning**...

Hotels" test. So we've added a slightly sneaky method, setFakeXmlResponse(xml), which the unit tests can call before the service is invoked. This might seem like cheating, but the area of the code that the design tells us these unit tests are covering is still fully operational and gets the full test treatment. The actual fetching and returning of the XML from the external service is outside the scope of these tests.

■ **Note** That's not to say the XML-fetching won't ever get tested, but that would be the job of an **integration test**—more about those in Chapter 11.

We also need to add two new methods to SearchHotelService, to allow the unit tests to swap in their stunt version of the XmlServiceClient:

```
public class SearchHotelService {

    private XmlServiceClient serviceClient = null;

    public void setServiceClient(XmlServiceClient serviceClient) {
        this.serviceClient = serviceClient;
    }

    private XmlServiceClient getServiceClient() {
        if (serviceClient==null) {
            serviceClient = new XmlServiceClient();
        }
        return serviceClient;
    }
}
```

The first new method allows the unit tests to set their own stunt service client. The second method will be used inside the class: any time the code wants to create or use an XmlServiceClient, it just calls this method. If no service client was set, a new one is created and returned (this will be the normal usage pattern at run-time); but if a unit test passed its own client in, that'll be returned instead.[7]

And, still in SearchHotelService, the private method getHotelsFromSearchService(), which used to look like this,

```
    private String getHotelsFromSearchService(HotelFilter filter) {
        XmlServiceClient client = new XmlServiceClient();
        return client.callSearchService(filter);
    }
```

… now looks like this:

```
    private String getHotelsFromSearchService(HotelFilter filter) {
        XmlServiceClient client = getServiceClient();
```

---

[7] Note that getServiceClient() isn't synchronized, so there's a huge assumption here that it will only ever be called on a single thread. But if in doubt, synchronize it…

```
        return client.callSearchService(filter);
    }
```

In other words, instead of simply creating its own XmlServiceClient and running with it, the code now calls the new method, which will return either the "real" XmlServiceClient, or the stunt version.

■ **Note** If you're using an Inversion-of-Control (IoC) framework such as Spring Framework, injection of service objects is that much easier, as Spring can be configured to inject stunt services for tests, while injecting the real service objects in the live environment. However, a potential downside of such frameworks (not picking on Spring in particular) is that it's easy to fall into the "framework is king" trap, where short-term convenience is gained at the expense of a more maintainable OO design (e.g., IoC frameworks tend to encourage a functional decomposition approach to design, with one-method "action" classes and the like. So if you're already using an IoC framework, it makes sense to utilize it for stunt service/mock object injection; but we wouldn't advise adopting such a framework solely for this purpose.

Update the Test Code to Use the Stunt Service

We need to update the unit test to pass in the new stunt service client. We'll do this in the setUp() code:

```
StuntServiceClient stuntClient;
SearchHotelService searchService;

@Before
public void setUp() throws Exception {
    stuntClient = new StuntServiceClient();
    searchService = new SearchHotelService();
    searchService.setServiceClient(stuntClient);
}
```

To mitigate possible memory leakage, we'll also un-set the fixtures when the test has finished:

```
@After
public void tearDown() throws Exception {
    searchService.setServiceClient(null);
    searchService = null;
    stuntClient = null;
}
```

And of course, the test method itself just needs to tell the stuntClient to return the "prop" XML document when requested. The new code is shown in bold:

```
@Test
public final void noHotels() throws Exception {
    SearchHotelService searchService = new SearchHotelService();
    HotelFilter filter = new HotelFilter();
    filter.setStarsMin(5);
    filter.setStarsMax(5);
    filter.setLocation("40.7950,73.9845");
```

```
        filter.setPriceMin(50.0);
        filter.setPriceMax(50.0);

        String xml = load("NoHotels.xml");
        stuntClient.setFakeXmlResponse(xml);

        HotelCollection hotels = searchService.getHotels(filter);
        assertEquals(0, hotels.getHotels().size());
    }

    private String load(String name) throws Exception {
        InputStream in = SearchHotelServiceGetHotelsTest.class.
                                        getResourceAsStream(name);
        StringWriter writer = new StringWriter();
        IOUtils.copy(in, writer);
        return writer.toString();
    }
```

The load(name) method loads up an XML file that will reside locally with the unit test classes.[8]

So that leaves us with just the second unit test method, returnSomeHotels(). Implementing this one is easy, because we've done all the setting up already for noHotels(). But in the next section we'll explore a way to make the Stunt Service implementation even easier, using returnSomeHotels() as the example.

3. Use a Mock Object Framework

The StuntServiceClient is a valid way of swapping in a "pretend" version of a service, in order to isolate the code being tested from the rest of the system. However, there's an easier way to do it: using a mock object framework. For a while, two Java mock object frameworks (JMock and EasyMock) battled over which of the two had the bulkiest boxing gloves. But virtually from nowhere, Mockito[9] marched in and KO'd them both with its simplicity.

Like its two predecessors, Mockito uses Java's dynamic proxy capability to swap in "virtual" implementations of classes and interfaces at runtime. It hides the complexity behind a notably simple interface.

The Stunt Service Approach

Before we do a mocked-up version of @Test returnSomeHotels(), here's how it would look using our old, faithful StuntClientService:

```
/**
 * Search for hotels in Waikiki that have swimming pools.
 * Should result in an XML response containing LOTS of matching hotels.
```

---

[8] This code uses Apache Commons' IOUtils to read the InputStream into a String. Apache Commons does wonders for eliminating boilerplate code. See http://commons.apache.org/io/.

[9] http://mockito.org/

```
 *
 * Input: Hotel Filter with:
 *            Location: Waikiki
 *            Amenities: Swimming Pool
 *
 * Acceptance Criteria: The HotelCollection returned should
 *    contain as many hotels as are in the XML result.
 */
@Test
public final void returnSomeHotels() throws Exception {
    SearchHotelService searchService = new SearchHotelService();
    HotelFilter filter = new HotelFilter();
    filter.setLocation("21.2766,157.8284"[10]);

    List<String> amenities = new ArrayList<String>(1);
    amenities.add("Swimming Pool");
    filter.setAmenities(amenities);

    String xml = load("SomeHotels.xml");
    stuntClient.setFakeXmlResponse(xml);

    HotelCollection hotels = searchService.getHotels(filter);
    assertEquals(10, hotels.getHotels().size());
}
```

Very simply, it creates a SearchHotelService (the class we want to test), specifies the search filter (hotels must be in Waikiki; amenities must include a swimming pool), and tells the stunt service to return the "prop" XML response ("SomeHotels.xml") when prompted. We know in advance that the XML response will contain ten hotels, because that's what is in the local SomeHotels.xml; so the check at the end can safely assert that the XML was correctly parsed and the HotelCollection does contain ten hotels, as expected.

The Mock Object Framework Approach

We'll now look at a solution that uses Mockito to create a mock client instead of StuntServiceClient. We'll need to make some changes to SearchHotelServiceGetHotelsTest. First, add this static import to the top of the unit test class:

```
import static org.mockito.Mockito.*;
```

With this version, the main point is that we no longer need to create a subclass of the real service class—so no more StuntServiceClient. Instead we just declare it as a good old XmlServiceClient:

```
XmlServiceClient stuntClient;
```

In setUp(), instead of creating a StuntServiceClient, we instead ask Mockito for a "mock version" of XmlServiceClient:

```
stuntClient = mock(XmlServiceClient.class);
```

----

[10] 21.2766,157.8284 is the lat/long position of Waikiki.

And then in the test method itself, instead of doing

```
String xml = load("SomeHotels.xml");
stuntClient.setFakeXmlResponse(xml);
```

… do this:

```
String xml = load("SomeHotels.xml");
when(stuntClient.callSearchService(filter)).thenReturn(xml);
```

The test contains virtually the same amount of code, but we don't need the additional StuntServiceClient class.

Figure 5–13 shows the result of running our two unit tests in Eclipse.

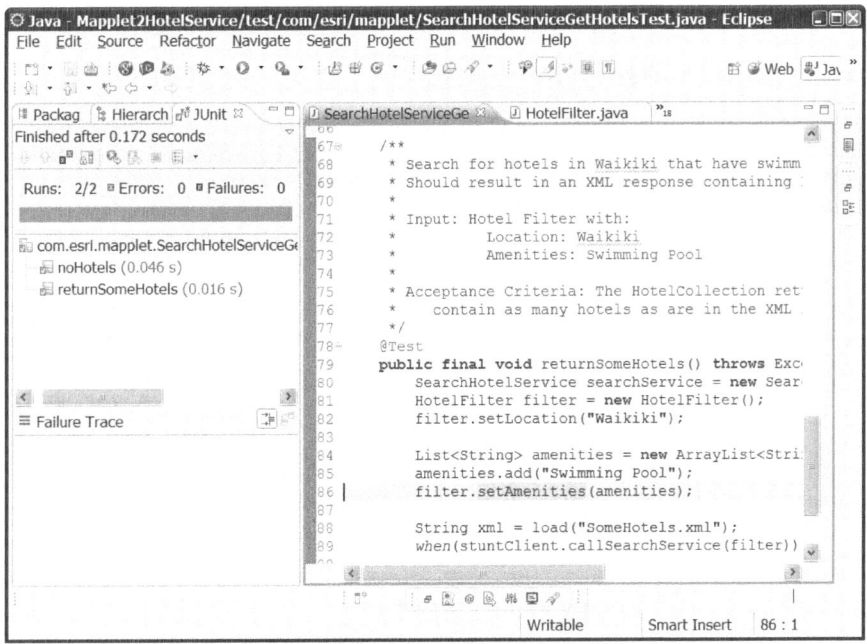

Figure 5–13. Green bar, indicating that the XML parsing unit is working as expected

WHEN SHOULD I USE A STUNT SERVICE INSTEAD OF A MOCK OBJECT FRAMEWORK?

Mock objects are great for straightforward cases where you just want to say, "If this method is called, always return this value." They take a second to add, and mean that your unit testing effort can focus on the unit under test. However, your needs may be more complex. For example, you might want to create a system-wide message queue (MQ) client that pretends to listen to a topic/queue.

Your test could call a method on your StuntMQ, such as the following:

```
simulateReceivingAMessage(String msg)
```

The StuntMQ would then broadcast this to any listening code, just as if it had received a real message. The code using the StuntMQ would be none the wiser that it's receiving events from a simulated service. This sort of setup makes potentially troublesome scenarios (listening to message queues) surprisingly easy to test.

Between noHotels(), which ensures that a zero-result search will indeed produce an empty HotelCollection, and returnSomeHotels(), which ensures that a 10-result search will produce a HotelCollection with 10 hotels, the XML parsing is pretty much covered. Of course, this doesn't cover more detailed XML parsing ephemera, or certain edge cases that may only become evident while designing the XML parsing code. For example, you might want to assert that our results parser accounts for all types of amenities. In this case, something more detailed and even finer-grained is needed: a set of algorithmic tests.

2. Test Algorithmic Logic with Unit Tests

Some code is definitely more "equal" than other code: in other words, some code cries out to be unit-tested, whereas with other code there would be very little point adding tests. For example, you would probably find no gain whatsoever in covering boilerplate code (e.g., property getters/setters) with unit tests; all this does is create additional code to maintain. Other code may benefit from being covered, at least at the "top level," by a test (as we discussed earlier in this chapter). Further along the scale, some code can be very intensive, where almost every character is highly significant in some way to the function's eventual output.

With this sort of code, it isn't sufficient to simply have a test that gives it an input and an expected output, with a virtual sea of significant computation taking place between the two. The tests need to get beneath the surface of the code much more, to prove that each part of the algorithm is sound. The tests can (and should) still be driven from the design, but the design needs to delve into more detail, e.g., you could use activity diagrams or state chart diagrams to map out the algorithmic logic, then base the unit tests on these diagrams.

This level of design-driven unit testing takes us somewhat beyond the scope of this chapter, though; in fact, we'd be inclined to call it advanced DDT. So we'll return to the subject in Chapter 12. See you there!

1. Write a Separate Suite of Integration Tests

Integrating separate components is probably the most problematic aspect of development (especially when the components are remote, and developed by separate teams). What works today might not work tomorrow, because another team has published a new interface to their component. It's out of your team's control, but an automated end-to-end test running overnight would catch the problem.

So far in this chapter we've advised you to isolate the code that each unit test covers: so the code doesn't call out to remote services, or even just to an adjacent class that's outside the scope of the unit test. The benefit you get from doing this is that the test results are entirely predictive: run the tests today and they'll pass. Run the same tests tomorrow, and (assuming the code under test hasn't changed) the tests will still pass. The benefit of this benefit (if you will) is that the test suite can reliably be made a part of your automated build. So any time someone commits a code change into the source control system, a build is triggered and the tests are run as well (see the sidebar).

However, integration tests—ones that call out to systems outside your team's direct control—don't have this same predictive property. "Chaotic" might be a better description, because you can never predict when or why an integration test will fail. But the interfaces between remote systems do need to be tested (precisely because they *are* so chaotic and prone to breakage). When another team has made a change to their published remote interface, breaking your own project, you'll want to know about it sooner rather than later. So it makes sense to write automated integration tests, but keep them in a separate test suite that isn't tied to the automated build. (In other words, "the database is down" shouldn't count as a type of build failure, or otherwise prevent your project from building.)

Integration tests are difficult to write and maintain, though, and you'll find that the issues you encounter while writing them are fiddly and time-consuming. So we've put the details in Chapter 11, as it's really an advanced topic; however, we'd suggest that you don't view integration tests as "optional," because *they might just turn out to be the most important tests that you write*: they help you to tame the chaos of integrating disparate systems.

MAKE YOUR UNIT TESTS PART OF THE BUILD, TO HELP KEEP THE TESTS UP-TO-DATE

One of the goals of unit testing is to provide a comprehensive suite of regression tests. The idea behind regression tests is that they catch errors introduced by new or modified code entering the code base. Nowadays it's pretty commonplace for the complete unit test suite to be run automatically whenever code is checked into a project's version control system. So if your team is asking "Why should we be doing this?" the answer is "Why aren't we doing this already?"

Before triggering the tests automatically, you would also need to make sure the whole code base is built each time anyone commits some new code. There's a huge range of build server software out there to do this: Cruise Control, Bamboo, TeamCity, Hudson, Apache Continuum, to name a few.[11] If compilation fails, then whoever just committed a change must have broken the build. An email is circulated to the team, and (you hope) whoever broke the build scrambles to fix it.

To be able to trigger a server-side build, you'll also need to make sure your product builds automatically, using a build tool such as Apache Ant or Maven. Maven is generally preferred these days, as it also simplifies traditionally problematic areas such as library dependencies.

Once you have a build server and automated build script in place, it's a simple next step to configure the build to also run the unit tests. This effectively makes the tests part of the build: if the tests fail, the whole build fails. The desired effect is then that whoever caused a test to fail will scramble to fix it, so that the build works for everyone again. It's an effective method of ensuring that the tests are not allowed to grow stale or out-of-date. Without this impetus, it would be too tempting to leave failing tests, thinking "I'll come back to that later…"

---

[11] There are a lot more examples listed here: http://en.wikipedia.org/wiki/Continuous_integration.

Summary

In this chapter we illustrated how to drive unit tests from a software design, identifying test scenarios in a systematic way that ensures the code is covered in all the right places. We also illustrated the use of "stunt services" and mock objects to isolate the code being tested; finally, we discussed driving unit tests deeper into algorithmic code that may benefit from finer-grained testing.

Is there a way to get 95% of the benefit of the comprehensive unit testing we did in this chapter with significantly fewer tests? In the next chapter, we'll show how to do exactly that with **controller tests**. As you'll see, unit tests do have their place, but controller tests can often represent a smarter, more structured approach to application testing.

CHAPTER 6

Conceptual Design and Controller Testing

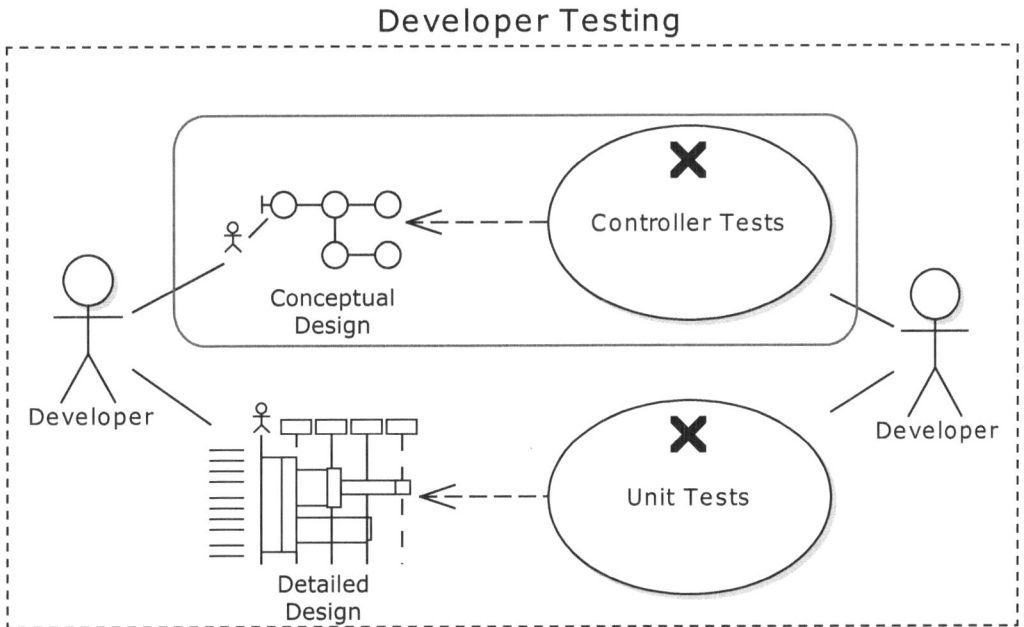

Developer Testing

As you saw in Chapter 5, unit testing doesn't have to involve exhaustively covering every single line of code, or even every single method, with tests. There's a law of diminishing returns—and increasing difficulty—as you push the code coverage percentile ever higher. By taking a step back and looking at the design on a broader scale, it's possible to pick out the key areas of code that act as input/output junctures, and focus the tests on those areas.

But what if you could take an even smarter approach? What if, rather than manually picking out the "input/output junctures" by sight, you could identify these areas systematically, using a conceptual design of the system? This would give your tests more leverage: proportionately fewer tests covering greater ground, but with less chance of missing key logic.

DDT provides *controller tests* for exactly this purpose. Controller tests are just like unit tests, but broader-grained: the controller tests are based on "logical software functions" (we'll describe that term in just a moment).

Meanwhile, the more traditional, finer-grained unit tests do still have a place: they're still perfect for testing algorithmic code and business logic, which is usually at the core of some systems and should be covered with tests from all angles, like soldiers surrounding a particularly dangerous alien rabbit.[1] *But you should find that you need to write far fewer unit tests if you write the controller tests first.*

Whereas a unit test may be "concerned" with one software method, a controller test operates on a small group of closely related methods that together perform a useful function. You can do controller testing with DDT because the ICONIX Process supports a "conceptual design" stage, which uses robustness diagrams as an intermediate representation of a use case at the conceptual level. The robustness diagram is a pictorial version of a use case, with individual software behaviors ("controllers") linked up and represented on the diagram.

■ **Note** Developers indoctrinated with the TDD mindset are certainly welcome to pursue full and rigorous comprehensive unit testing until they've passed out at the keyboard. But those developers who would like to get 95% of the benefits for 25% of the work should find this chapter to be quite useful! If you've opened this book looking for the ***"test smarter, not harder"*** part, you'll want to pay close attention to this chapter.

As with unit tests in Chapter 5, this chapter is chiefly about controller tests that "isolate" the code being tested: that is, they substitute external system calls with "pretend" versions, so as to keep the tests focused on the software functions they're meant to be focused on. Integration tests—where the code is allowed to call out to external systems—are still incredibly important, as they test a fragile and inherently error-prone part of any system, but they're also harder to write and maintain. So—without lessening their importance—we see integration tests as an advanced topic, so they're covered in Chapter 11.

■ **Note** Traditionally, "integration tests" involve testing groups of units that are all part of the system under test, as well as testing external interfaces—i.e., not just tests involving external systems. With DDT, the former is covered by controller tests, so we've reserved the term "integration test" to mean purely tests that involve code calling out to external systems.

Let's now start with our top ten controller testing "to-do" list, which we'll base the whole chapter around, following the Mapplet *Use Address* use case for the examples.

---

[1] One of the authors may have been watching too much Dr. Who recently.

Top Ten Controller Testing "To-Do" List

When you're exploring your project's conceptual design and writing the corresponding controller tests, be sure to follow these ten "to-do" items.

10. Start with a robustness diagram that shows the conceptual design of your use case.

9. Create a separate test case for each controller.

8. For each test case, define one or more test scenarios.

7. Fill in the Description, Input, and Acceptance Criteria fields for each test scenario. These will be copied right into the test code as comments, making the perfect "test recipe" to code the tests from.

6. Generate Junit, FlexUnit, and NUnit test classes from your test scenarios.

5. Implement the tests, using the test comments to stay on course.

4. Write code that's easy to test.

3. Write "gray box" controller tests.

2. String controller tests together, just like molecular chains, and verify the results at each step in the chain.

1. Write a separate suite of controller-level integration tests.

10. Start with a Robustness Diagram

Begin your journey into controller testing by creating a robustness diagram showing the conceptual design of your use case. In this chapter we'll follow along with the *Advanced Search* use case from the Mapplet project. In Chapter 5 we covered the server-side part of this interaction with unit tests. In this chapter we'll cover the client-side, focusing on the "Dates are correct?" controller.

The Use Case

To recap, here's the use case that we'll be working from in our example:

BASIC COURSE:
The system enables the Advanced Search widget when an AOI exists of "local" size. The user clicks the Advanced Search icon; the system expands the Advanced Search widget and populates Check-in/Check-out fields with defaults.
The user specifies their Reservation Detail including check-in and check-out dates, number of adults, and number of rooms; the system checks that the dates are valid.

The user selects additional Hotel Filter criteria including desired amenities, price range, star rating, hotel chain, and the "hot rates only" check box.
The user clicks "Find." The system searches for hotels within the current AOI, and filters the results according to the Hotel Filter Criteria, producing a Hotel Collection. Invoke Display Hotels on Map and Display Hotels on List Widget.

ALTERNATE COURSES:
Check-out date prior to check-in date: *The system displays the user-error dialog "Check-out date prior to Check-in date."*
Check-in date prior to today: *The system displays the user-error dialog: "Check-in date is in the past."*
System did not return any matching hotels: *The system displays the message "No hotels found."*
"Show Landmarks" button is enabled: *The system displays landmarks on the map.*
User clicks the Clear button: *Refine Hotel Search clears all entries and populates check-in/check-out fields automatically with defaults*

If you're wondering how to get from this kind of behavioral description to working source code, that's what the ICONIX Process is all about. DDT provides the corollary to this process: as you analyze the use case and turn it into a conceptual design, you create controller tests based on the design. The controller tests provide a duality: they're like yin to the conceptual design's yang. But what is a conceptual design, and how do you create controller tests from it? Let's look at that next.

Conceptual Design from Which to Drive Controller Tests

The ICONIX Process supports a "conceptual design" stage, which uses robustness diagrams as an intermediate representation of a use case at the conceptual level. *The robustness diagram is a pictorial version of a use case*, with individual software behaviors ("controllers") linked up and represented on the diagram.[2] Figure 6–1 shows an example robustness diagram created for the *Advanced Search* use case. Notice that each step in the use case's description (on the left) can be traced along the diagram on the right.

A robustness diagram is made up of some key pictorial elements: boundary objects (the screens or web pages), entities (classes that represent data, and, we hope, some behavior too), and controllers (the actions, or verbs, or software behavior). Figure 6–1 shows what each of these looks like:

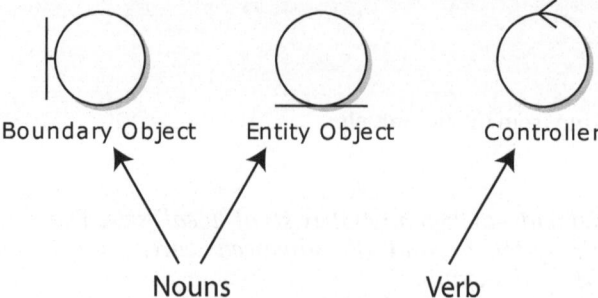

Figure 6–1. Elements of conceptual design

---

[2] For more about conceptual design and drawing robustness diagrams to "disambiguate" your use case scenarios, see Chapter 5 of *Use Case Driven Object Modeling with UML: Theory and Practice*.

■ **Note** In Flex, MXML files are the boundary objects. The Advanced Search widget will be mapped out in `AdvancedSearchWidget.mxml`. It's good OO design to keep business logic (e.g., validation) out of the boundary objects, and instead place the behavior code where the data lives—on the entity objects. In practical terms, this means creating a separate ActionScript class for each entity, and mapping controllers to ActionScript functions.[3]

So in Figure 6–2, which follows, the user interacts with the Advanced Search widget (boundary object, i.e., MXML). Clicking the "Find" button triggers the "Search for hotels and filter results" controller. Similarly, selecting check-in and check-out dates triggers the creation of a Reservation Detail object (entity) and validation of the reservation dates that the user entered. You should be able to read the use-case scenario text while following along the robustness diagram. Because all the behavior in the scenario text is also represented in the controllers on the diagram, it is an excellent idea to write a test for each controller… *done consistently, this will provide complete test coverage of all the system behavior specified in your use cases!*

■ **Tip** When drawing robustness diagrams, don't forget to also map out the alternate courses, or "rainy day scenarios." These represent all the things that could go wrong, or tasks that the user might perform differently; often the bulk of a system's code is written to cover alternate courses.

Robustness diagrams can seem a little alien at first (we've heard them referred to as "Martian"), but as soon as you realize exactly what they represent (and what their purpose is), you should find that they suddenly click into place. And then you'll find that they're a really useful tool for turning a use case into an object-oriented design and accompanying set of controller tests. It's sometimes useful to think of them like an object-oriented "stenographer's shorthand" that helps you to construct an object model from a use case.

It's easiest to view a robustness diagram as somewhere between an activity diagram (aka flowchart) and a class diagram. Its main purpose is to help you create use cases that can be designed from, and to take the first step in creating an OO design—"objectifying" your use case. Not by coincidence, the same process that turns your use case into a concrete, unambiguous, object-oriented description of software behavior is also remarkably effective at identifying the "control points" in your design that want to be tested the most.

To learn about robustness diagrams in the context of the ICONIX Process and DDT, we suggest you read this book's companion volume, *Use Case Driven Object Modeling with UML: Theory and Practice.*

---

[3] An example Flex design pattern that helps you achieve this is "Code Behind": `www.insideria.com/2010/05/code-behind-vs-template-compon.html`.

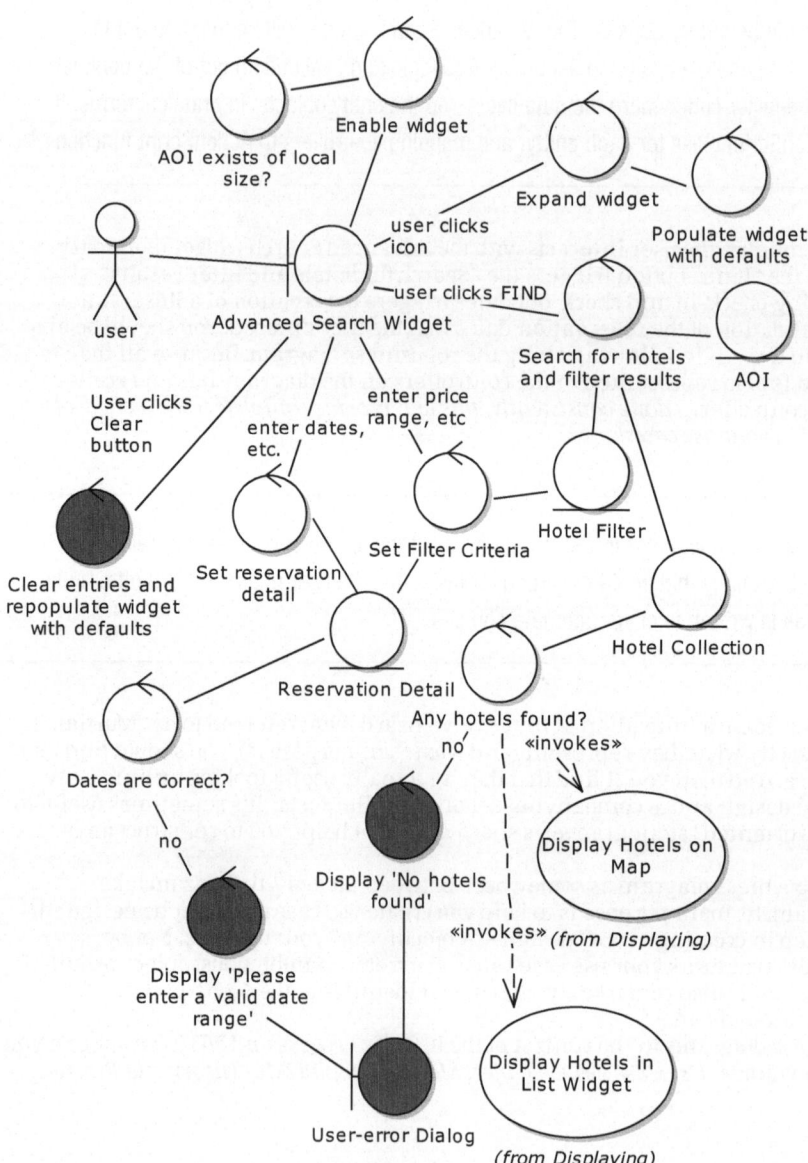

Figure 6–2. *Robustness diagram for the Advanced Search use case (shading indicates alternate course-driven controllers)*

Notice that the use case Basic Course starts with the system displaying the Advanced Search widget; this is reflected in the diagram with the Display widget controller pointing to the Advanced

Search widget boundary object. Display code tends to be non-trivial, so it's important for it to be accounted for. *This way you'll also end up with a controller test for displaying the window.*

One of the major benefits of robustness analysis is disambiguation of your use-case scenario text. This will not only make the design stage easier, it'll also make the controller tests easier to write. Note that the acceptance tests (which we cover in Chapters 7 and 8) shouldn't be affected by these changes, as we haven't changed the *intent* of the use case, or the sequence of events described in the scenarios from an end-user or business perspective. All we've really done is tighten up the description from a technical, or design, perspective.

9. Identify Test Cases from Your Controllers

For each controller, create a single test case.

Take another look at the controllers that we created in the previous step (see Figure 6–2). Remember from Figure 6–1 that the controllers are the circles with an arrow at the top: they represent the logical functions, or system behavior (the verbs/actions). When you create the detailed design (as you did in Chapter 5), each of these "logical functions" is implemented as one or more real or "physical" software functions (see Figure 6–3). For testing purposes, the logical function is close enough to the business to be a useful "customer-level" test, and close enough to the real code to be a useful design-level test—sort of an über unit test.

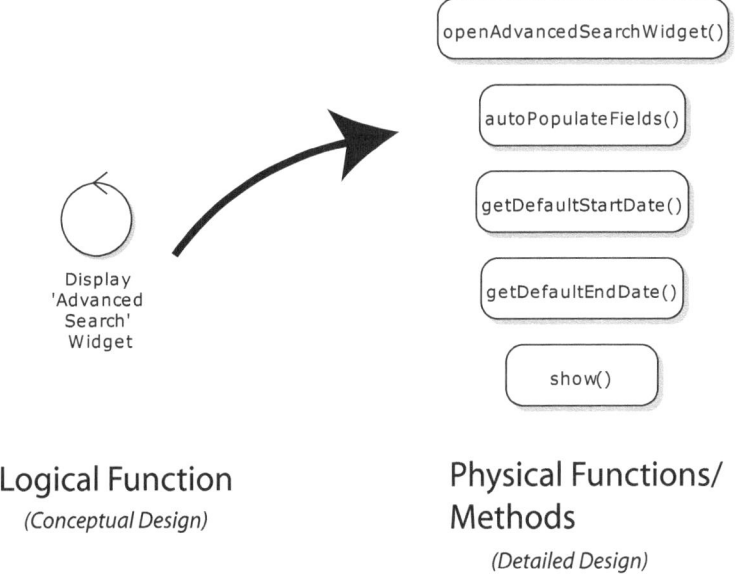

Logical Function
(Conceptual Design)

Physical Functions/ Methods
(Detailed Design)

Figure 6–3. During detailed design, the logical functions are mapped to "real" implemented functions or methods. They're also allocated to classes. In the conceptual design we simply give the function a name.

■ **Note** Figure 6–3 illustrates why controller testing gives you more "bang for your buck" than unit testing: it takes less test code to cover one controller than to individually cover all the associated fine-grained (or "atomic") software methods. But the pass/fail criteria are essentially the same. You do, however, always have the option to test at the atomic level. We're not saying "don't test at the atomic level"; it's always the programmer's choice whether to test at the physical or logical levels. If you're running out of time with your unit testing[4], it's good to know that you do at least have all the logical functions covered with controller tests.

When each controller begins executing, you can reasonably expect the system to be in a specific state. And when the controller finishes executing, you can expect the system to have moved on, and for its outputs to be in a predictable state given those initial values. *The controller tests verify that the system does indeed end up in that predicted state after each controller has run (given the specific inputs, or initial state).*

Let's now create some test cases for the controllers in our robustness diagram. To do this in EA, use the Agile/ICONIX add-in (as in Chapter 5). Right-click the diagram and choose Create Tests from Robustness (see Figure 6–4).

---

[4] *In theory* you might not worry about running out of time while unit testing, but *in practice* it often becomes an issue, especially if you're using a SCRUM approach with sprints and timeboxes. So, in practice it's a great idea to get breadth of test coverage first, and then dive down deeper when testing the trickier parts of your code.

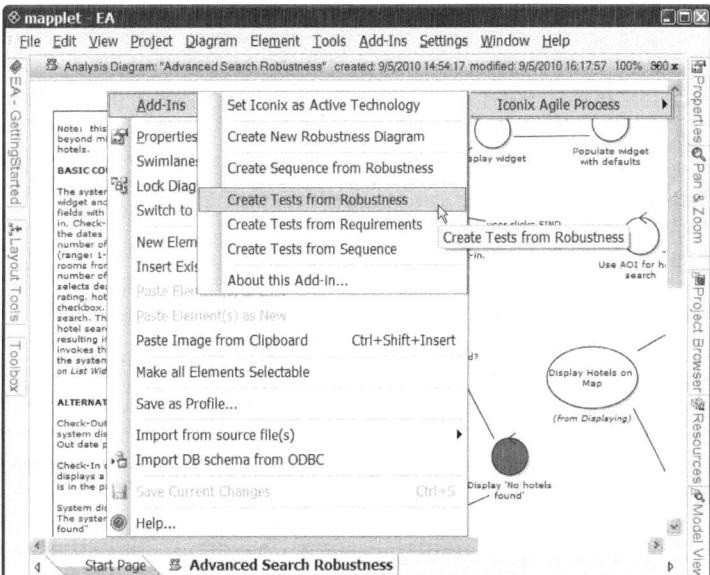

Figure 6–4. Creating test cases from your robustness diagram

The new test cases are shown in Figure 6–5. The original controllers (from the robustness diagram) are shown on the left; each one now has its own test case (shown on the right).

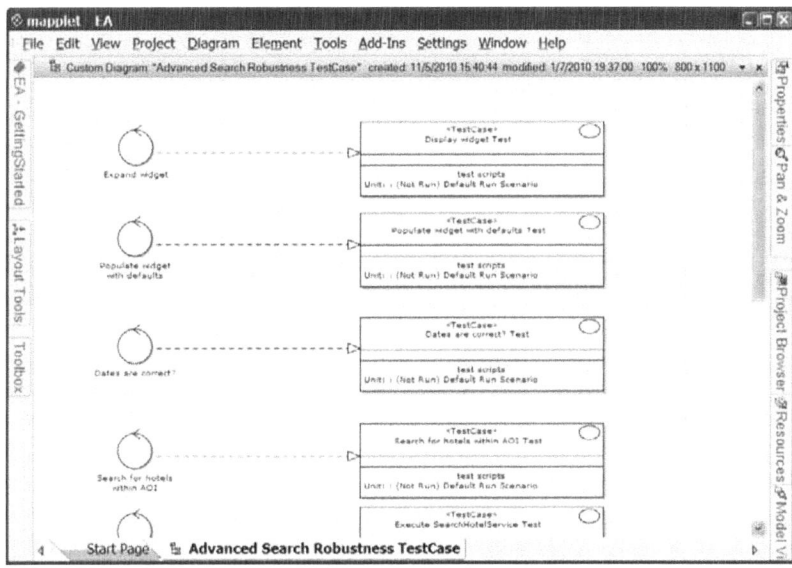

Figure 6–5. The test cases, one linked to each controller

Each test case has one scenario, "Default Run Scenario." You'll want to add something more interesting and specific to your application's behavior; so let's start to add some new test scenarios.

8. Define One or More Scenarios per Test Case

Take each test case that you have, and define one or more scenarios that exercise it. For the example in this chapter, we'll zero in on the "Dates are correct?" controller, and its associated "Dates are correct?" test case. Before we create the test scenarios for the Mapplet, let's pause for a moment to think about what a test scenario actually is, and the best way to go about identifying it.

Understanding Test Scenarios

Individual test scenarios are where you put one juncture in your code through a number of possible inputs. If you have a test case called "Test Validate Date Range," various test scenarios could be thrown at it, e.g., "Check-in date is in the past," "Check-out date is in the past," or "Check-out date is earlier than the check-in date."

Thinking up as many test scenarios as possible is a similar thought process to use-case modeling, when looking for alternate courses. Both are brainstorming activities in which you think: "What else could happen?" "Then what else?" "Anything else?" And you keep on going until the well is dry. The main differences between test scenarios and use-case scenarios (alternate courses) are the following:

- Test scenarios are limited to one software function, whereas alternate courses represent different routes through a use case.

- Test scenarios tend to vary by the input values being passed into a software function, whereas alternate courses are more about different user actions or system responses.

So with test scenarios you're often concerned with trying different sorts of boundary conditions.

■ **Note** Remember that controllers are *logical* software functions. Each logical function will map to *one or more* "real" code functions/methods.

Another way to view controller test scenarios is that they're a way of *specifying a contract for a software function*. In other words, given a set of inputs, you expect the function to return this specific value (assuming the inputs are valid), or to throw an exception if the inputs are invalid.

Identifying the Input Values for a Test Scenario

There tend to be a finite number of reasonable inputs into a software function, so the inputs can be readily identified by thinking along these lines:

- What are the legal (or valid, expected) input values?

- What are the boundaries (the minimum and maximum allowed values)?

- Will the function cope with "unexpected" values? (e.g., for a date range, what if the "to" date is before the "from" date?)

- What if I pass in some "curve ball" values (null, empty Strings, zero, -1, a super-long String)?

- If the function takes an array of values, should the ordering of the values make a difference?

■ **Tip** Remember to add test scenarios that also fall outside the basic path. If you're writing a high throughput, low latency table with thousands of rows of data, everyone will be focused on testing its scalability and responsiveness under heavy load. So remember to also test it with just one or two rows, or even zero rows of data. You'd be surprised how often such edge cases can trip up an otherwise well-tested system.

Naturally, you may well discover even more alternate paths while brainstorming test scenarios. When you discover them, add 'em into the use case… this process is all about comprehensively analyzing all the possible paths through a system. Discovering new scenarios now is far less costly than discovering them after you've completed the design and begun coding. That said, it makes sense to place a cap on this part of the process. It's to be expected that you won't discover every single possible eventuality or permutation of inputs and outputs. Gödel's incompleteness theorem suggests (more or less) that all possible eventualities cannot possibly be defined. So if it can't logically be done for a finite, internally consistent, formal system, then a team stands little chance of completely covering something as chaotic as real life. When you're identifying test scenarios, you'll recognize the law of diminishing returns when it hits, and realize that you've got plenty of scenarios and it's time to move on.[5]

When defining test scenarios, it's worth spending time making sure each "contract" is basically sound:

> *Soundness is much more important than completeness, in the sense that more harm is usually done if a wrong statement is considered correct, than if a valid statement cannot be shown.*[6]

It's worth clarifying exactly where we stand on this point:

- You should spend the time needed to thoroughly analyze use-case scenarios, identifying every alternate course or thing that can go wrong that you and the project stakeholders can possibly think of.

- You should spend *some* time analyzing test scenarios, identifying as many as you can think of within a set time frame. But put more effort into checking and making sure the test scenarios you have are actually correct, than in thinking up new and ever more creative ones.

---

[5] This is also an argument against the notion of 100% code coverage, which, in Chapter 5, we suggested to be a self-defeating exercise.

[6] Verification of Object-Oriented Software: The KeY Approach. ISBN: 978-3-540-68977-5

As there's a finite number of reasonable inputs into a software function, it makes sense to limit the time spent on this particular activity.

Now that we've discussed some of the theory about creating test scenarios, let's add some to the Mapplet's "Dates are correct?" test case.

WHAT'S AN INPUT?

An input value (or just "input") is most commonly a parameter passed directly into the function being tested, but not always. "Expected inputs" could also mean that an object is expected to be in a particular state when the function is called. In this case, there would be setup code called prior to the test method, to bring the object into the expected state. Here is an example:

```
private var reservation: ReservationDetail;

[Before]
public function setUp():void
{
    reservation = new ReservationDetail();
    reservation.setCheckInDate(checkInDate);
    reservation.setCheckOutDate(checkOutDate);
}
```

This code sets up a test fixture with some predefined date values, ready for a test to call a function and verify the expected output. In this case the "input" is the already-set software state, rather than the parameters being passed into the function. The same goes for the output: this may simply be the state that a function left the program in (which the test will need to be able to query) rather than the value returned from a function.

As you'll see later in this chapter, controller tests are sometimes chained together, so that the output from one function/controller forms the input for the next function/controller. To avoid relying on the tests being run in a specific order, the setUp() code for a controller later in the chain may be required to set up the complete controller state, as if all the previous controllers in the chain had been called. But if you're using a test framework that allows you to specify the tests' run order (e.g., JBehave), then the notion of inputs/outputs being the actual program state becomes important.

Using EA to Create Test Scenarios

If you bring up the Testing view (press Alt+3) and click the first test case, you can now begin to add individual scenarios to each test case (see Figure 6–6).

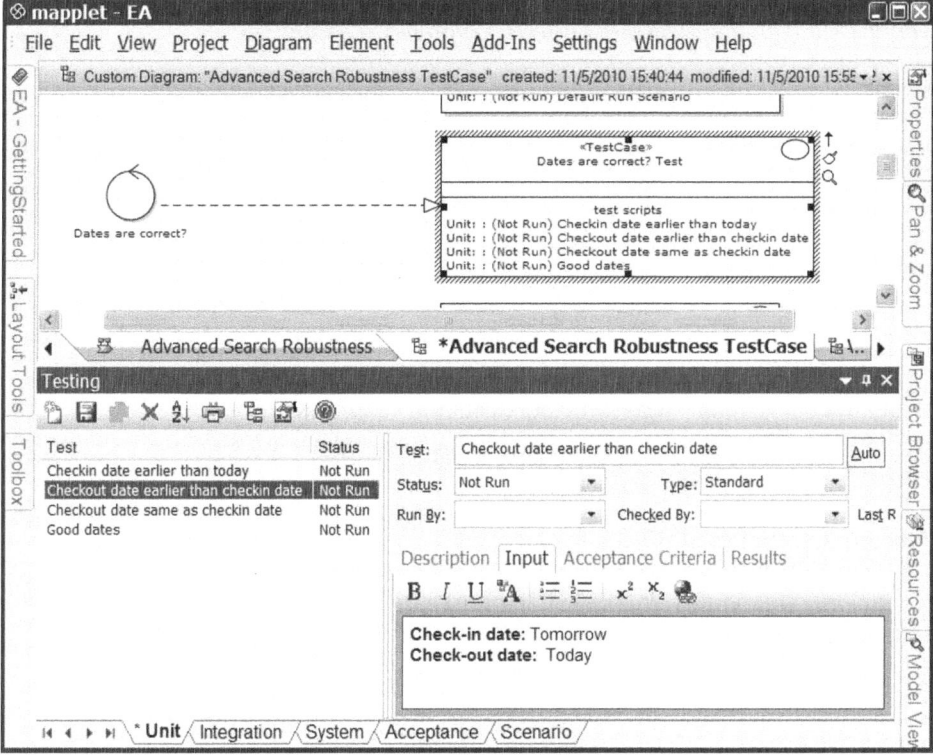

Figure 6–6. *Test scenarios for the "Dates are correct?" controller*

As you can see in Figure 6–6, we've replaced the Default Run scenario with four of our own scenarios. Each one represents a particular check that we'll want the code to perform, in order to validate that the dates are correct.

You may be wondering about the tabs running along the bottom of the screen in Figure 6–6: Unit, Integration, System, Acceptance, and Scenario. We've put the controller test scenarios on the Unit tab, as controller tests essentially are just big ol' unit tests. When it comes to writing the code for them and running them, most of the same rules apply (except for the white box/gray box stuff, which we'll discuss elsewhere in this chapter).

7. Fill in Description, Input, and Acceptance Criteria

If you look at Figure 6–6, each test scenario has its own Description, Input, and Acceptance Criteria fields. These define the inputs and the expected valid outputs (acceptance criteria) that we've been banging on about in this chapter. It's worth spending a little time filling in these details, as they are really the crux of each test scenario. In fact, the time spent doing this will pay back by the bucket-load later. When EA generates the test classes, the notes that you enter into the Description, Input, and Acceptance Criteria fields will be copied right into the test code as comments, making the perfect "test recipe" from which to implement the tests.

Table 6–1 shows the details that we entered into these fields for the "Dates are correct?" test case.

Table 6–1. *Test Scenario Details for the "Dates Are Correct?" Controller/Test Case*

Scenario	Description	Input	Acceptance Criteria
Check-in date earlier than today	Validation should fail on the dates passed in.	**Check-in date:** Yesterday **Check-out date:** Any	The dates are rejected as invalid.
Check-out date earlier than check-in date	Validation should fail on the dates passed in.	**Check-in date:** Tomorrow **Check-out date:** Today	The dates are rejected as invalid.
Check-out date same as checkin date	Validation should fail on the dates passed in.	**Check-in date:** Today **Check-out date:** Today	The dates are rejected as invalid.
Good dates	Validation should succeed for the dates passed in: Check-out date is later than the check-in date, and the check-in date is later than yesterday	**Check-in date:** Today **Check-out date:** Tomorrow	The dates are accepted.

6. Generate Test Classes

This is where the up-front effort really begins to pay off. You've driven your model and test scenarios from use cases, and you've disambiguated the use case text and gained sign-off from the customer and BAs. You can now make good use of the model and all your new test scenarios. Now is the time to generate classes. As we go to press, EA supports generating JUnit, FlexUnit, and NUnit test classes.

Before Generating Your Tests

If you're using EA to generate your FlexUnit tests, be sure to configure it to generate ActionScript 3.0 code instead of ActionScript 2.0 (which it is set to by default). Doing this is a simple case of going into Tools -> Options -> Source Code Engineering -> ActionScript. Then change the Default Version from 2.0 to 3.0—see Figure 6–7.

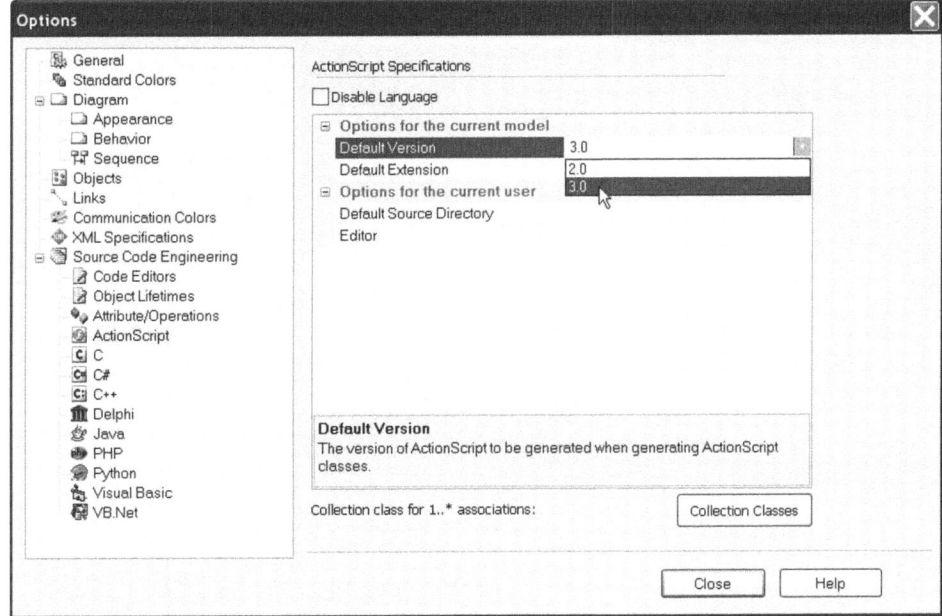

Figure 6–7. *Make sure EA targets ActionScript 3.0, not 2.0*

JUnit users also have a bit of setting up to do. Because EA generates `setUp()` and `tearDown()` methods, you won't need a default (empty) constructor in the test class. Also, you don't want a `finalize()` method, as relying on `finalize()` for tidying up is generally bad practice anyway, and definitely of no use in a unit test class. Luckily, EA can be told not to generate either of these. Just go into Tools **->** Options **->** Source Code Engineering **->** Object Lifetimes. Then deselect the Generate Constructor and Generate Destructor check boxes—see Figure 6–8.

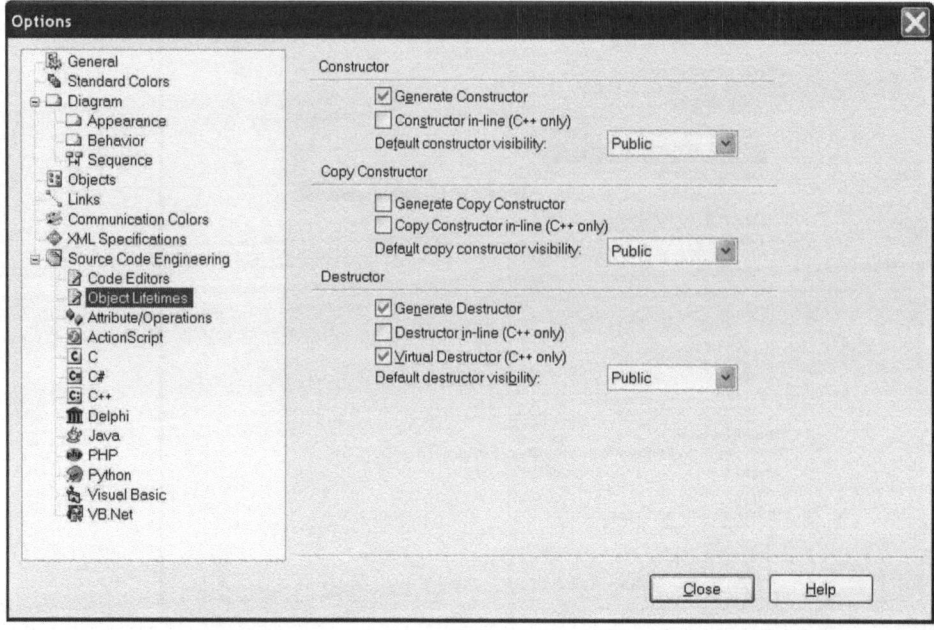

Figure 6–8. Make sure all the check boxes in this screen are unticked

Generating the Tests

Now that you've filled in the inputs, acceptance criteria, etc., and told EA exactly how you want the test classes to look, it's time to generate some code. There are really two steps to code generation, but there's no additional thought or "doing" in between running the two steps—in fact, EA can run the two steps combined—so we present them here as essentially one step. They are as follows:

1. Transform your test cases into UML test classes.

2. Use EA's usual code-generation templates to turn the UML test classes into Flex/Java/C# (etc) classes.

First, open up your test case diagram, right-click a test case, and choose Transform... You'll see the dialog shown in Figure 6–9. Choose the transformation type (Iconix_FlexUnit in this case) and the target package. The target package is where the new test classes will be placed in the model. EA replicates the whole package structure, so the target package should be a top-level package, separate from the main model.

■ **Tip** Create a top-level package called "Test Cases," and send all your test classes there.

Click the "Do Transform" button. To generate code at this stage, also select the "Generate Code on result" check box.

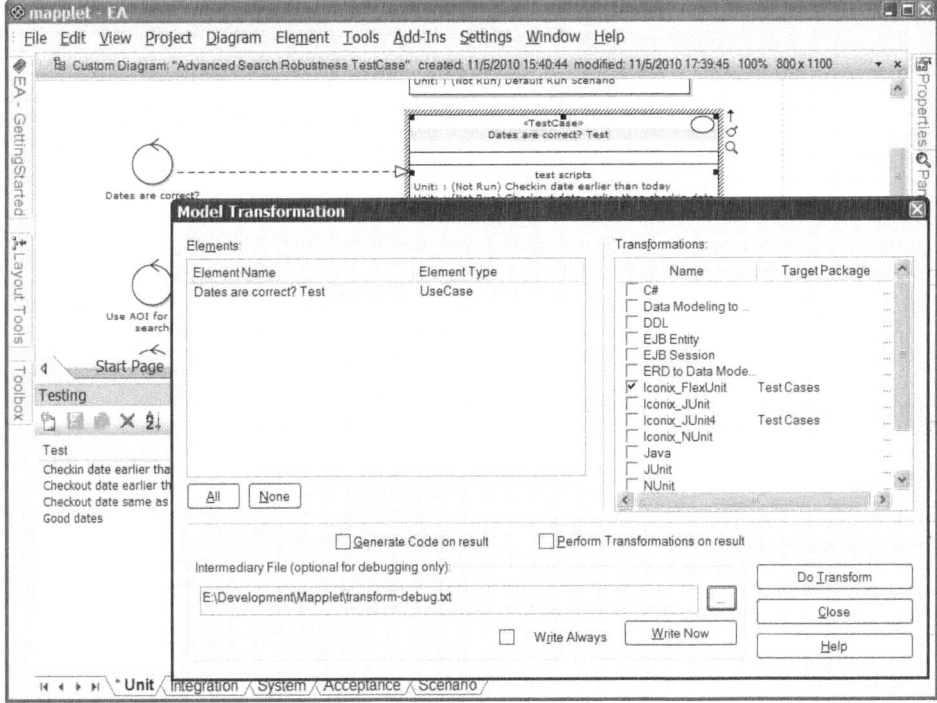

Figure 6–9. Transforming the test cases into test classes

Figure 6–10 shows the generated UML test class. As you can see, each test scenario has been "camel-cased." So "check-in date earlier than today" now has a test method called `checkInDateEarlierThanToday()`.

■ **Note** The original test case had a question mark in its name ("Dates are correct?"). We've manually removed the question mark from the test class, although we hope that a near-future release of EA will strip out non-compiling characters from class names automatically.

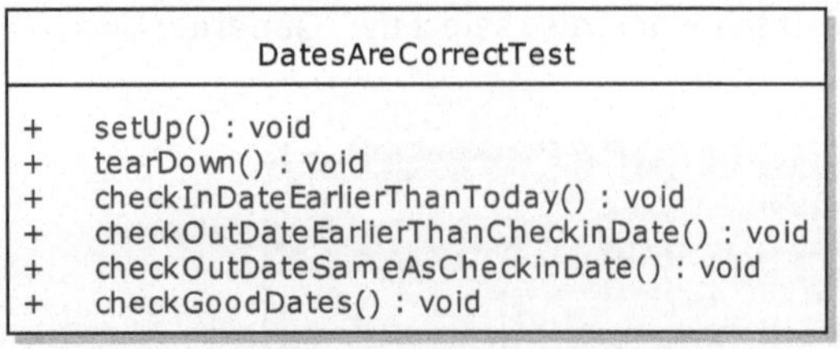

```
┌─────────────────────────────────────────────────────┐
│                  DatesAreCorrectTest                  │
├─────────────────────────────────────────────────────┤
│  +   setUp() : void                                   │
│  +   tearDown() : void                                │
│  +   checkInDateEarlierThanToday() : void             │
│  +   checkOutDateEarlierThanCheckinDate() : void      │
│  +   checkOutDateSameAsCheckinDate() : void           │
│  +   checkGoodDates() : void                          │
└─────────────────────────────────────────────────────┘
```

Figure 6–10. The generated test class

If you selected the "Generate Code on result" check box, you'll already be delving through the lovely auto-generated Flex code; if not, just right-click the new test class and choose Generate Code. (EA also has a Synchronize Code option if you've previously generated test code and modified the target class, but now want to re-generate it from the model.) For the Path, point EA directly to the folder containing your unit and controller tests, in the package where you want the tests to go.

Here's the ActionScript code that the ICONIX add-in for EA generates for the "Dates are correct?" test case:

```actionscript
import flexunit.framework.*;

class DatesAreCorrectTest
{
    [Before]
    public function setUp(): void
    {
        // set up test fixtures here...

    }

    [After]
    public function tearDown(): void
    {
        // destroy test fixtures here...

    }

    /**
     * Validation should fail on the dates passed in.
     * Input: Check-in date: Yesterday
     *              Check-out date: Any
     * Acceptance Criteria: The dates are rejected as invalid
     */
    [Test]
    public function checkInDateEarlierThanToday(): void
    {
    }

    /**
     * Validation should fail on the dates passed in.
     * Input: Check-in date: Tomorrow
     *              Check-out date: Today
     * Acceptance Criteria: The dates are rejected as invalid
```

```
 */
[Test]
public function checkOutDateEarlierThanCheckinDate(): void
{
}

/**
 * Validation should fail on the dates passed in.
 * Input: Check-in date: Today
 *         Check-out date:  Today
 * Acceptance Criteria: The dates are rejected as invalid
 */
[Test]
public function checkOutDateSameAsCheckinDate(): void
{
}

/**
 * Validation should succeed for the dates passed in:
 * Check-out date is later than the check-in date,
  * and the check-in date is later than yesterday
 * Input: Check-in date: Today
 *         Check-out date: Tomorrow
 * Acceptance Criteria: The dates are accepted
 */
[Test]
public function checkGoodDates(): void
{
}

}
```

Notice how each test method is headed-up with the test scenario details from the model. When you start to write each test, this information acts as a perfect reminder of what the test is intended to achieve, what the inputs should be, and the expected outcome that you'll need to test for. Because these tests have been driven comprehensively from the use cases themselves, you'll also have the confidence that these tests span a "complete enough" picture of the system behavior.

Now that the test classes are generated, you'll want to fill in the details—the actual test code. Let's do that next.

5. Implement the Tests

Having generated the classes, you can move on to implementing the tests. When doing that, use the test comments to help yourself stay on course.

Let's look at the first generated test function, checkInDateEarlierThanToday():

```
/**
 * Validation should fail on the dates passed in.
 *
 * Input: Check-in date:  Yesterday
 *         Check-out date: Any
 * Acceptance Criteria: The dates are rejected as invalid
 */
```

```
[Test]
public function checkInDateEarlierThanToday(): void
{
}
```

A programmer staring at this blank method might initially scratch his head and wonder what to do next. Faced with a whole ocean of possibilities, he may then grab a snack from the passing *Vol-au-vents* trolley and get to work writing some random test code. As long as there are tests and a green bar, then that's all that matters... Luckily, the test comments that you added into the test scenario earlier are right there above the test function, complete with the specific inputs and the expected valid output (acceptance criteria). So the programmer stays on track, and you end up with tightly coded controller tests that can be traced back to the discrete software behavior defined in the original use case.

4. Write Code That's Easy to Test

We have plenty to say on this subject in Part 3. However, for now, it's worth dipping into a quick example to illustrate the difference between an easily tested function and one that's virtually impossible to test.

When the user selects a new check-in or check-out date in the UI, the following ActionScript function (part of the MXML file) is called to validate the date range. If the validation fails, then an alert box is displayed with a message for the user. This is essentially what we need to write a controller test for:

```
private function checkValidDates () : void
{
    isDateRangeValid = true;
    var currentDate : Date = new Date();
    if ( compareDayMonthYear( checkinDate.selectedDate,currentDate ) < 0 )
    {
        Alert.show( "Invalid Checkin date. Please enter current or future date."
);
        isDateRangeValid = false;
    }
    else if ( compareDayMonthYear ( checkoutDate.selectedDate, currentDate ) < 1 )
    {
        Alert.show( "Invalid Checkout  date. Please enter future date." );
        isDateRangeValid = false;
    }
    else if ( compareDayMonthYear ( checkoutDate.selectedDate,
checkinDate.selectedDate  ) < 1 )
    {
        Alert.show( "Checkout date should be after Checkin date." );
        isDateRangeValid = false;
    }
}
```

As a quick exercise, grab a pencil and try writing the checkInDateEarlierThanToday() test function to test this code. There are two problems:

- Because this is part of the MXML file, you would need to instantiate the whole UI and then prime the checkinDate and checkoutDate date selector controls with the required input values. That's way outside the scope of this humble controller test.

- A test can't reasonably check that an Alert box has been displayed. (Plus, the test code would need a way of programmatically dismissing the Alert box—meaning added complication.)

In short, displaying an Alert box isn't an easily tested output of a function. That sort of code is a test writer's nightmare.

Code like this is typically seen when developers have abandoned OO design principles, and instead lumped the business logic directly into the presentation layer (the Flex MXML file, in this example). Luckily, the checkValidDates() function you just saw was really a bad dream, and, in reality, our intrepid coders followed a domain-driven design and created a ReservationDetail class. This class has its own checkValidDates() function, which returns a String containing the validation message to show the user, or null if validation passed.

Here's the relevant part of ReservationDetail, showing the function under test:

```
public class ReservationDetail
{

    private var checkinDate: Date;
    private var checkoutDate: Date;

    public function ReservationDetail(checkinDate: Date, checkoutDate: Date)
    {
        this.checkinDate = checkinDate;
        this.checkoutDate = checkoutDate;
    }

    public function checkValidDates(): String
    {
        var currentDate : Date = new Date();

        if ( compareDayMonthYear( checkinDate.selectedDate,currentDate ) < 0 )
        {
            return "Invalid Checkin date. Please enter today or a date in the future.";
        }

        if ( compareDayMonthYear ( checkoutDate.selectedDate, currentDate ) < 1 )
        {
            return "Invalid Checkout date. Please enter a date in the future.";
        }

        if ( compareDayMonthYear ( checkoutDate.selectedDate, checkinDate.selectedDate  ) < 1
)
        {
            return "Checkout date should be after Checkin date.";
        }

        isDateRangeValid = true;
        return null;
    }
}
```

Writing a test for this version is almost laughably easier. Here's our implementation of the checkInDateEarlierThanToday() test scenario:

```
/**
 * Validation should fail on the dates passed in.
 *
 * Input: Check-in date:  Yesterday
 *           Check-out date: Any
 * Acceptance Criteria: The dates are rejected as invalid
 */
[Test]
public function checkInDateEarlierThanToday(): void
{
    var yesterday: Date = new Date(); // now
    yesterday.hours = int (today.getHours)-24;
    var reservation: ReservationDetail = new ReservationDetail(yesterday, new Date());

    var result: String = reservation.checkValidDates();
    assertNotNull(result);
}
```

This test function simply creates a ReservationDetail with a check-in date of yesterday and a check-out date of today, then attempts to validate the reservation dates, and finally asserts that a non-null (i.e., validation failed) String is returned.

3. Write "Gray Box" Controller Tests

In the software testing world, tests are generally seen as black or white, but they're not often seen in shades of gray. Controller tests, however, are best thought of as "gray box" tests. The less that your tests know about the internals of the code, the more maintainable they'll be.

A "white box" test is one that sees inside the code under test, and knows about the code's internals. As you saw in Chapter 5, unit tests tend to be white box tests. Often the existence of mock objects passed into the method under test signifies that it's a white box test, because the test has to "know" about the calls that the code makes—meaning that if the method's implementation changes, the test will likely need to be updated as well.

At the other end of the scale, **scenario-level integration tests** (which you'll find out about in Part 3) tend to be black box tests, because they have no knowledge whatsoever of the internals of the code under test: they just set the ball rolling, and measure the result.

Controller tests are somewhere in between the two: a controller test is really a unit test, but it's most effective when it has limited or no knowledge of the code under test—aside from the method signature that it's calling. Because controller tests operate on groups of functions (rather than a single function like a unit test), they need to construct comparatively fewer "walled gardens" around the code under test; so they pass in fewer mock objects.

■ **Tip** Always set out to make your controller tests "black box." But if you find that you need to pass in a mock object to get the software function working in isolation, don't sweat it. We see mock objects as a practical means to "grease the skids" and keep the machine moving along, rather than a semi-religious means to strive for 100% code coverage.

---

2. String Controller Tests Together

String controller tests together, just like molecular chains. Then verify the results at each step in the chain.

You may have noticed from the robustness diagram in Figure 6–1 that controllers tend to form chains. Each controller is an action performed by the system. It'll change the program state in some way, or simply pass a value into the next controller in the chain.

■ **Note** This particular test pattern should be used with caution. There's the school of thought that says that groups of tests that are dependent on each other are fragile and a "test antipattern," because if something changes in one of the functions, all the tests from that point onwards in the chain will break—a sort of a domino effect. But there are sometimes clear benefits from "chained tests," in that each test doesn't need to set up its own set of simulated test fixtures: it can just use the output or program state from the previous test, like the baton in a relay race.

Think of it in terms of a bubblegum factory. Gum base, sugar, and corn syrup are passed into the mixing machine, and a giant slab of bubblegum rolls out. The next machine in the chain, the "slicer and dicer," expects the slab of bubblegum from the previous machine to be passed in, and we expect little slivers of gum to be the output. The next machine, the wrapping machine, expects slivers of gum, silver foil strips, and paper slips to be passed in… and so on. As you've probably guessed, each machine represents a controller (or "discrete" function), and a controller test could verify that the output is as expected given the inputs.

Figure 6–11 shows some examples of controllers that are linked to form a chain. The first example shows our (slightly contrived) bubblegum factory example; the second is an excerpt from the *Advanced Search* use case; the third, also from *Advanced Search*, shows a two-controller chain for the validation example that we're following. In the first two examples, the values being passed along are pretty clear: a tangible value returned from one function is passed along into the next function. At each stage your test could assert that the output value is as expected, given the value returned from the previous function.

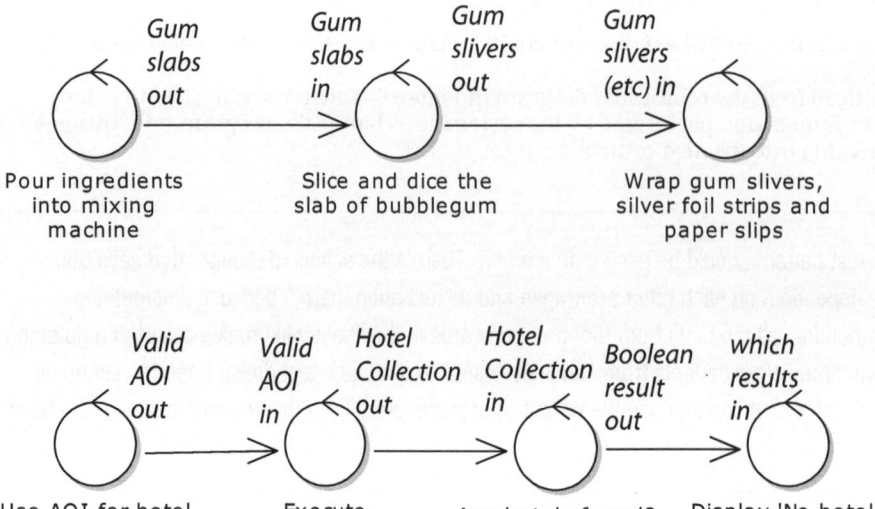

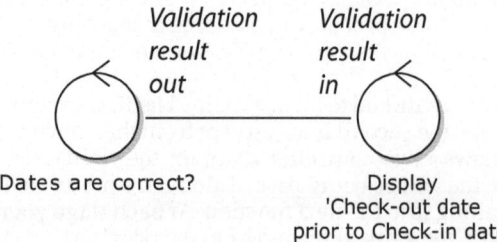

Figure 6–11. Controllers linked together like molecular chains

You'll normally want to create a test class for each one of these controllers (each test scenario is then a separate test method). Where controllers are linked together, because each controller will effectively have a separate test class, it would make sense to have a separate "program state tracking class," which survives across tests.

However—and this is a pretty major one—JUnit and its ilk don't provide a way of specifying the order in which tests should be run. There are test frameworks that do allow you to specify the run order. JBehave (itself based on JUnit) is one such framework. It has its roots firmly planted in Behavior-Driven Development (BDD), and allows you to specify a test scenario that consists of a series of steps that take place in the specified order.[7] For example, the Bubblegum Factory controller chain would look like this as a BDD scenario, where each line here is a step:

Given I have a bubblegum factory and lots of raw ingredients

When I pour the ingredients into a mixing machine

Then gum slabs should be returned

When I put the gum slabs into the dicing machine

Then gum slivers should be returned

When I put the gum slivers, silver foil strips, and paper slips into the wrapping machine

Then wrapped gum sticks should be returned

Let's go back to the Mapplet. The "Dates are correct?" controller would look like this as a BDD scenario:

Given the user entered a Reservation Detail with a check-in date of Tomorrow and a check-out date of Today

When the dates are validated

Then the system should display a user error dialog with "Check-out date prior to Check-in date"

Each step in these scenarios maps to a test method—so that's very close to the step-by-step execution of a controller chain.

If you're using "vanilla" JUnit, or any test framework that doesn't allow tests to run in a specific order, then you'll need to set up the expected state prior to each individual test method.

1. Write a Separate Suite of Integration Tests

Finally, write a separate suite of controller-level integration tests. Just as with unit tests, there are essentially two types of controller tests: isolated tests (the main topic of this chapter), and integration tests.[8] All the comments in "top ten" item #1 for unit tests (see Chapter 5) also apply to controller tests, so, rather than repeating them here, we'll point you straight to Chapter 11, where we show you how to write controller-level integration tests (that is, tests that validate a single logical software function and freely make calls out to remote services and databases).

Note that you may also find that, as you begin to master the technique, you'll write more controller tests as integration/external tests than as isolated tests. As soon as your project is set up to support integration tests, you'll probably find that you prefer to write integrated controller tests, as it's a more "complete" test of a logical software function. This is absolutely fine and won't cause an infection. But do remember to keep the integration tests separate from your main build.

---

[7] In Chapter 11 we discuss using BDD and JBehave to automatically test your use case scenarios "end-to-end."

[8] To reiterate, for the purposes of this book, "integration tests" are tests where the code calls out to external systems, while "controller tests" operate on a group of units or functions.

Another important caveat is that, while the integration tests may be run less often than the isolated tests, they *must* still be run automatically (e.g., on a nightly schedule). As soon as people forget to run the tests, they'll be run less and less often, until they become so out-of-sync with the code base that half of them don't pass anymore; the effort involved to fix them means they'll most likely just be abandoned. So it's really important to set up the integration tests to be run automatically!

MAKE YOUR ISOLATED CONTROLLER TESTS PART OF THE BUILD

In the previous chapter we established that it's a good idea to make your unit tests part of your automated build. So when new or modified code is committed into your version control system, an Ant or Maven script is triggered to build the whole project and run the tests. If the build fails, everyone in the team is emailed a build failure notification, and the tests failing count as a build failure. This way, the developers are forced to keep the tests up-to-date, and they may also find that the tests catch a genuine regression error.

The same goes for the controller tests, which are (when all's said and done) basically unit tests with a slightly different emphasis. This does mean that just like unit tests, you don't want your "run with every build" controller tests to call out to external systems (databases, REST services, CORBA, etc.), otherwise the build will become too fragile: a remote service being down shouldn't equal a build failure.

To a certain extent, this means that sometimes you'll need to use mock objects just as you would with unit tests. However, you should find that you need to do this less with controller tests because of their "gray box" nature: they're less prone to breaking because the code inside a function changed. Unit tests, on the other hand, are "white box" and, therefore, tend to depend more on the internal state of the function under test. You also need fewer controller tests, so there are fewer of them to break as a result of a code change!

Summary

In this chapter we walked through a behavioral unit testing technique that is in many ways the core of DDT. Controller tests bridge the gap between programmer-centric, code-level testing and business-centric testing. They cover the logical functions you identified in your conceptual design (during robustness analysis).

Controller tests are best thought of as broad-grained unit tests. They cover many of the functions of unit tests, meaning you can write far fewer tests; unit tests themselves are best kept for algorithmic logic where the test needs to track the internal state of a function.

We also inferred that, while starting out writing controller tests that "isolate" the code being tested, you might well end up writing more of them as integration tests, which is absolutely fine, and, in fact, provides a more thorough test of the logical software function. There will be more about this in Part 3.

So far we've covered "design-oriented" testing, with unit tests and controller tests. In the next couple of chapters we'll cover "analysis-oriented" testing, with acceptance tests that have a different audience—customers, business analysts, and QA testers.

CHAPTER 7

■ ■ ■

Acceptance Testing: Expanding Use Case Scenarios

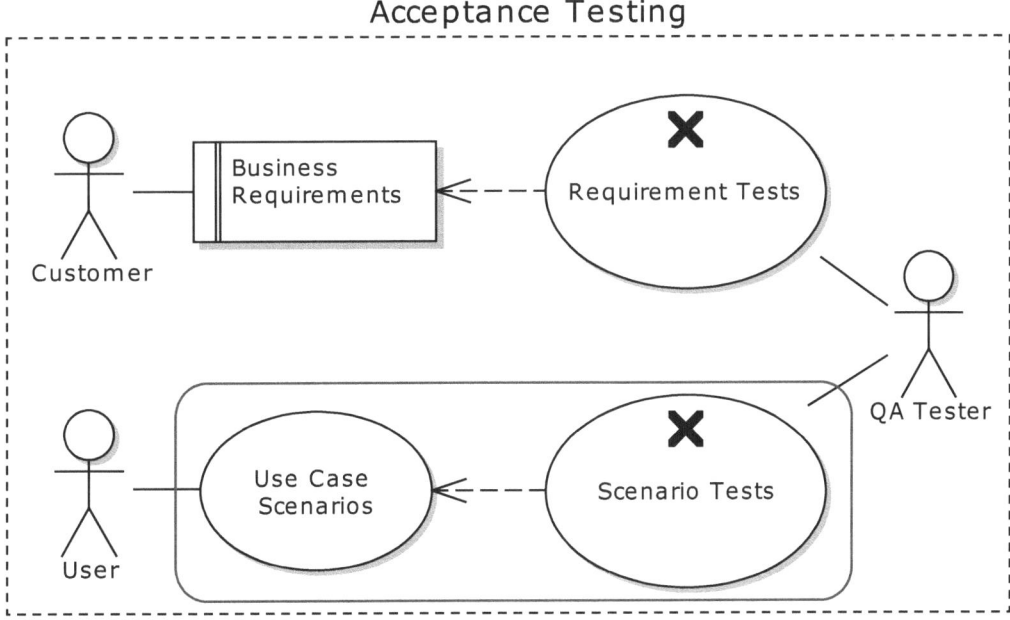

Acceptance Testing

This is the first chapter where we leave the realm of programmer tests. As we walk backwards from completion and a delivered product, through coding, design, and unit/controller tests, we reach the analysis stage that is covered by **acceptance tests** written from the perspective of users, customers, and business analysts.

Acceptance testing broadly covers two parts of your analysis model: the **business requirements** (functional and non-functional requirements), which we cover in Chapter 8, and the **behavioral requirements** (use cases), which we cover in this chapter.

When you write a use case, you're writing it in the form of scenarios ("sunny day" scenario and "rainy day" scenarios, aka basic course and alternate courses). So it stands to reason that the tests you'll write for these are called **scenario tests**. Scenario tests are "end-to-end" tests that verify that the system behaves as expected, when the user pushes the expected buttons—and also copes when some unexpected buttons are pushed too.

By "end-to-end," we mean that a scenario test verifies the complete scenario, from the initial screen being displayed, through each user step and system response, to the conclusion of the scenario. Sometimes scenario tests are automated, but they don't have to be. There's plenty of mileage in simply creating scenario test scripts that follow along the use case flow, and handing these test scripts to your QA team. In fact there's a lot to be said for human involvement in catching errors, and scenario tests provide a structured method for testers to follow. We'll illustrate this with a real-life example later in this chapter.

■ **Note** If you do have the time or the inclination to automate the scenario tests, there's benefit in doing so—the success or failure of the project won't depend on it, though (unlike with more "fragile over agile" processes such as XP). We consider automated scenario tests to be an advanced topic, so we cover that in Chapter 11.

In this chapter we'll show you how to identify and generate scenario tests from structured use case scenarios, as usual using the Mapplet as an example, and using Enterprise Architect (EA) for tools support. The chapter is structured around our top ten scenario testing "to-do" list.

REQUIREMENTS HANDED DOWN FROM THE MOUNTAINTOP

Use cases shouldn't be pure, technology-independent capsules of business thought (like pure air captured in an aerosol from the highest and snowiest Himalayan peaks[1]). However, we occasionally hear people disagree—their argument being that use cases shouldn't define anything that could be construed as being design (whether code/systems design or UI design). However, ICONIX-style use cases are more akin to interaction scenarios—concrete, specific, unambiguous, committing the hard questions and answers to paper. Meanwhile, business requirements (which we cover in Chapter 8) are where the pure business thought is captured. Business requirements should define the system's needed capabilities without regard to any particular user story.

Top Ten Scenario Testing "To-Do" List

When you're writing your scenario tests, be sure to follow our top ten "to-do" list. The first item (no. 10 in the list) involves preparing your analysis model so that writing scenario tests will be that much easier. Here's our list, which we expand upon later in the chapter:

---

[1] See Alice's encounter with a certain "abstract, essential, teleocentric" cat in Appendix A.

10. Start with a narrative use case.

9. Transform the narrative use case to a structured scenario.

8. Make sure all Alternate and Exception paths have steps.

7. Add pre-conditions and post-conditions, and joins for each Alternate/Exception path.

6. Check your structured scenario by generating an activity diagram.

5. Expand "threads" using "Create External Tests."

4. Put the test case on a test case diagram.

3. Drill into the EA testing view by clicking the scenarios.

2. Add detail to the scenarios as needed.

1. Generate a test plan document for the QA team.

Mapplet Use Cases

Before we dive headfirst into the top ten "to-do" list, Figure 7–1 shows a quick overview of the use cases for the Mapplet 2.0 project. As you can see, they're organized into two packages: Displaying and Searching. We'll focus on the *Use Address* use case (in Searching) in this chapter.

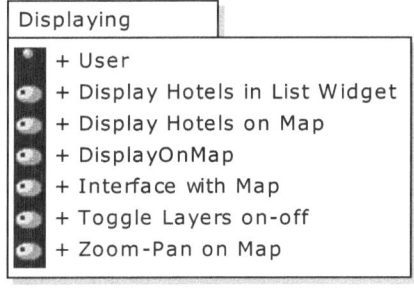

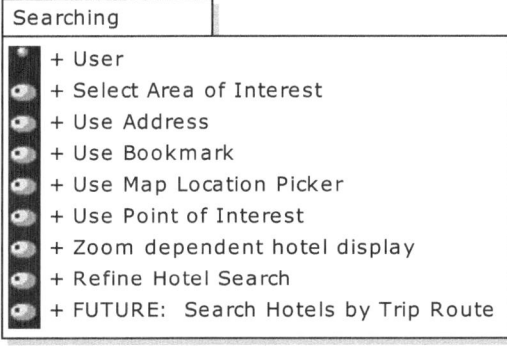

Figure 7–1. The Mapplet use cases, organized into two packages

10. Start with a Narrative Use Case

Begin your testing with a use case written in narrative form. If you've ever used software that's cumbersome, difficult to use, or doesn't seem to work quite right (and all of us have), you're almost certainly using software that didn't start out with somebody writing a good narrative "user manual style" use case. The easiest way to think about writing narrative style use cases is simply "write the user manual before you write the code." Writing the user manual (in use case form) forces developers to think through the user experience in detail before the code gets written. This is important because once the code is written, it's usually too late.

NARRATIVE USE CASES ARE STILL IMPORTANT

The thought processes of analysis/design and testing are inherently different. The analysis/design thought process involves thinking through the user experience, while the testing thought process involves comprehensively making sure that all paths have been exercised during an independent QA process. In addition to the thought process being different, there's a difference in the level of time investment people are willing to make in testing vs. analysis/design. While this varies from organization to organization and project to project, with "agile" approaches like TDD, the trend has been closer and closer to 100% time investment in testing and 0% investment in analysis/design. Without going too deeply into the debate about what an optimal percentage might be, it's safe to say that any delays introduced into the analysis/design phase of a project (i.e., analysis paralysis) run a risk of having the analysis/design effort aborted.

There's a lot of additional information required to prepare a use case for acceptance testing beyond the "user manual" view. Most notably, the use case's pre-conditions and post-conditions need to be specified so that an independent QA team can exercise the use case, and we need to specify where each alternate/exception path must rejoin the basic path in order to make sure we can generate all of the fully expanded "threads" for testing. Trying to specify this information during analysis/design while we're still trying to understand the user experience completely can be a major distraction, and can slow down the process of writing the use cases…in other words, we increase the risk of analysis paralysis. We also need to define one or more sets of data that will be used in the testing, and the choice of the data sets can determine how extensively the test covers the scenarios, especially the "rainy days." Conversely, the scenarios (sunny and rainy day) drive the need for test data.

So our process in this book is to use narrative use cases during analysis/design, and then transform them for the purposes of testing, using the techniques described in this chapter.

There's plenty of detail on how to write good "ICONIX style" narrative use cases in *Use Case Driven Object Modeling with UML: Theory and Practice,* but for now we'll just assume we have one—in this case, the Mapplet's *Use Address* use case:

BASIC COURSE:

The user types an address using all address fields on the Quick Search window. The system enables the "Locate" button as soon as an entry is made in either one of these fields: City, State, Postal, Country.
The user clicks "Locate." The system geocodes the location based on the level of detail provided by the user and stores any candidates in an Address Candidate Collection. If a single candidate is found or exactly one of the multiple candidates has a 100% match rate, the system sets the AOI based on this Address Candidate.

ALTERNATE COURSES:

The user clicks "Clear": *Entries in any fields will be cleared.*

Multiple valid candidates found: *The system displays an Address Candidate widget with a list of potential candidates to choose from. The user selects an Address Candidate.*

No candidates found: *The system displays a message "Location not found."*

Figure 7–2 shows the use case narrative in our EA model. We wrote the narrative text in the "General" tab of the use case specification dialog. To help visualize the use case, the development team at ESRI created the storyboards shown in Figures 7–3 (the basic course) and 7–4 (the alternate course, "Multiple valid candidates found").

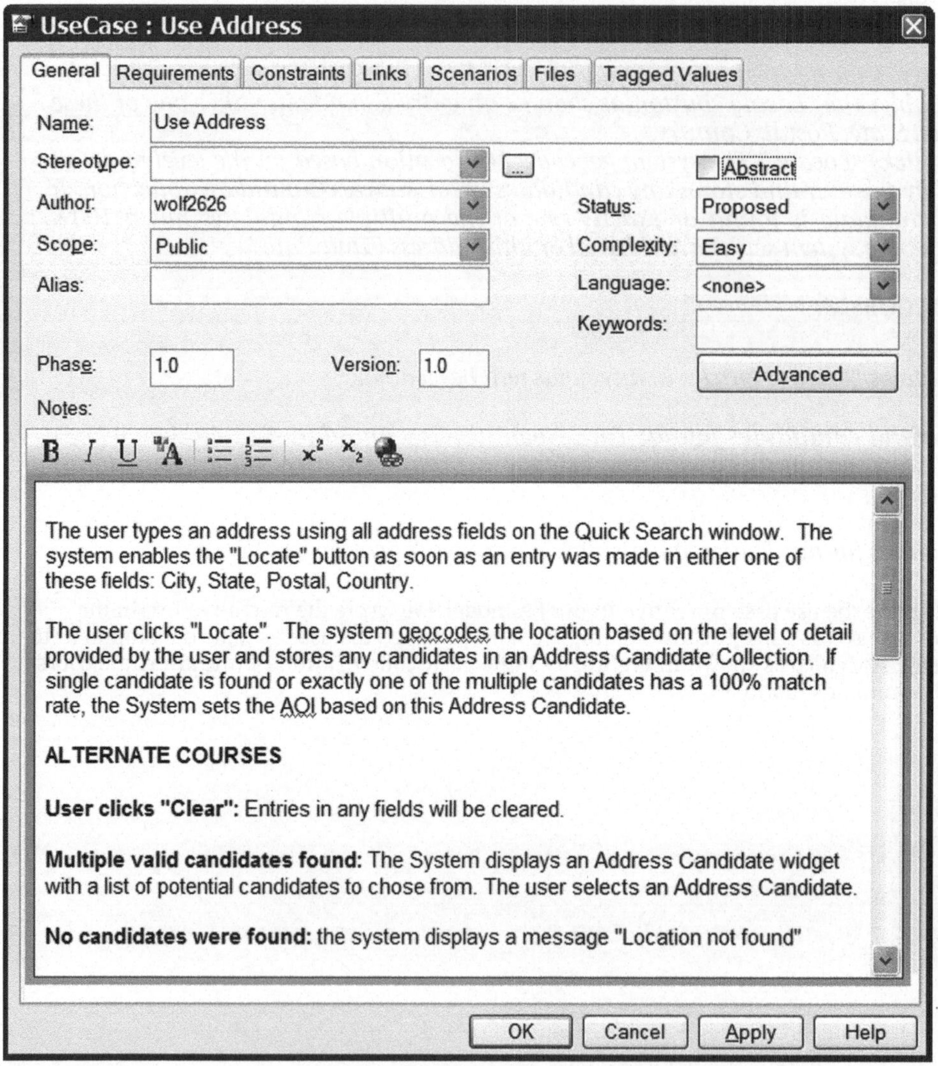

UseCase : Use Address

General | Requirements | Constraints | Links | Scenarios | Files | Tagged Values

Name: Use Address

Stereotype: [   ] [...] ☐ Abstract

Author: wolf2626   Status: Proposed

Scope: Public   Complexity: Easy

Alias: [   ]   Language: <none>

    Keywords: [   ]

Phase: 1.0   Version: 1.0   [Advanced]

Notes:

B *I* <u>U</u> ᴬA | ☰ ☰ | x² x₂ 🌐

The user types an address using all address fields on the Quick Search window. The system enables the "Locate" button as soon as an entry was made in either one of these fields: City, State, Postal, Country.

The user clicks "Locate". The system geocodes the location based on the level of detail provided by the user and stores any candidates in an Address Candidate Collection. If single candidate is found or exactly one of the multiple candidates has a 100% match rate, the System sets the AOI based on this Address Candidate.

ALTERNATE COURSES

User clicks "Clear": Entries in any fields will be cleared.

Multiple valid candidates found: The System displays an Address Candidate widget with a list of potential candidates to chose from. The user selects an Address Candidate.

No candidates were found: the system displays a message "Location not found"

[OK] [Cancel] [Apply] [Help]

Figure 7–2. The "Use Address" use case—this is the "full view," or narrative version.

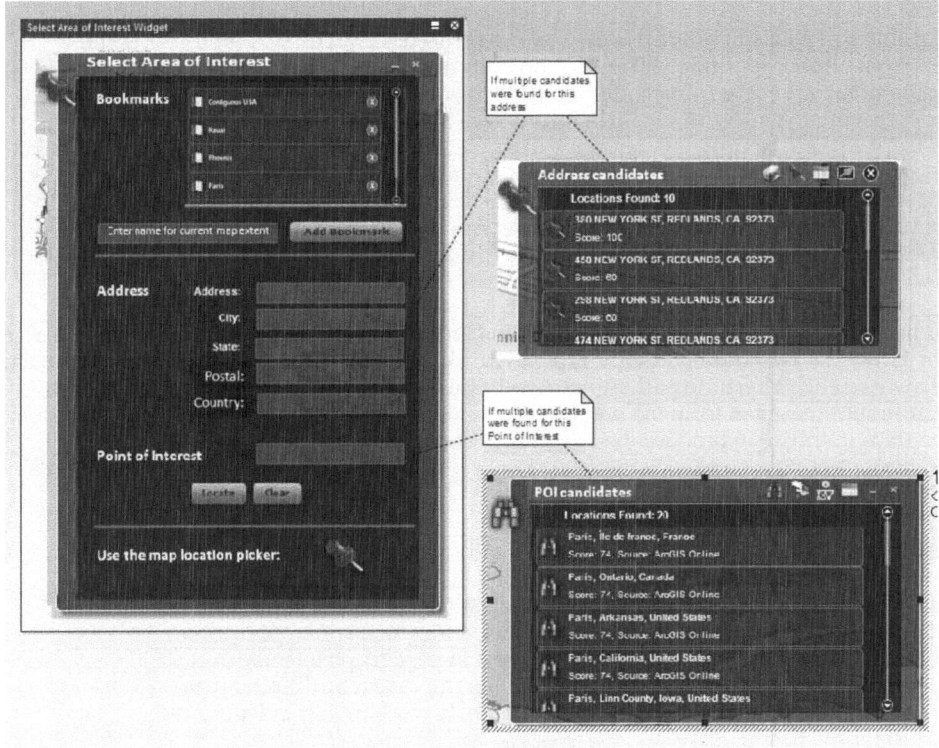

Figure 7–3. Mapplet storyboard for the "Use Address" use case

Figure 7–4. Mapplet storyboard for the "Multiple Candidates Found" alternate course

Now that the use case is written out in text form, that gives you the "whole view" of the use case—all of its scenarios (basic course and alternate courses) together in one place. But to drive tests from the scenarios, you'll need to create a more structured representation of the use case, which brings us to the next "to-do" item.

9. Transform to a Structured Scenario

Next you should transform your narrative use case to a structured scenario. Do that by using the "Create Structure from Clipboard" option. Think of this step, and the two that follow, as *preparing the use case for test generation*. All of the information you add to your use case in this step is useful and necessary when preparing to generate scenario tests. However, if you try to specify all of it immediately up-front without writing the narrative use case first, you might get bogged down during analysis and design, which is why it's so important to begin with the narrative version.

Let's start by looking at where we want to arrive with this step: Figure 7–5 shows *Use Address* converted into a structured scenario. EA has rather nicely separated the narrative into individual steps, and marked each one with an icon to show whether it's a System step ("The system does this or that," represented by a little computer icon) or a User step ("The user does something or other," represented by a stickman).

In the lower half of the screenshot, there's a tab called Entry Points, which shows more steps. These are the alternate paths. The alternate paths are explicitly linked to specific numbered steps in the basic path; they specify where each alternate path rejoins the basic path. Creating the alternate paths isn't automatic, though; to split these out from the narrative text takes a bit more work (but not much more).

Here are the steps involved to produce the structured scenario shown in Figure 7–5:

1. Go to the General tab, and copy just the basic course part of the use case narrative to the clipboard.

2. Switch over to the Scenarios tab, right-click inside the empty Steps area somewhere, choose "Create Structure from Clipboard Text," and then choose either "New Line Delimited" or "Sentence Delimited" from the pop-up menu. Use the first option if your narrative text has each step on a separate line, or the second option if you wrote the narrative text in paragraph form, with each step as a separate sentence. EA will parse the narrative text and split it into separate steps. You should now see something fairly close to that in Figure 7–5, so far just for the basic course.

3. Add in the alternate courses, and link each one to the relevant step in the basic course.

After these steps, you should see the final results shown in Figure 7–5.

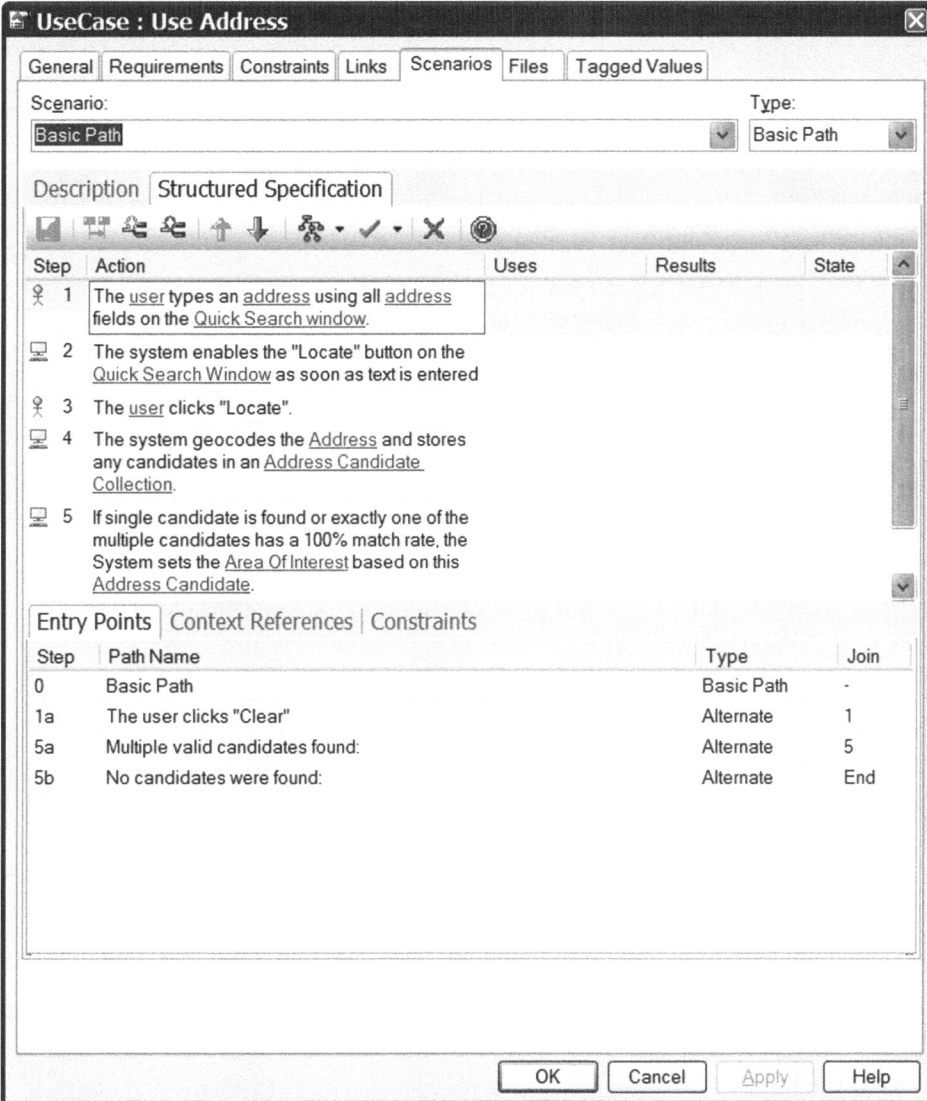

Figure 7–5. *"Use Address" converted into a structured scenario*

8. Make Sure All Paths Have Steps

Now you check your alternate and execution paths to ensure none of them are "blank." Each path should have some steps in it. Figure 7–5 shows that each step in the basic path is numbered sequentially. The alternate courses branch from the basic path at a particular step number, then rejoin at a step somewhere in the basic path; e.g., the alternate course "Multiple valid candidates found" branches at Step 5 (so it gets its own step number, 5a), and rejoins the basic path at the end of the same step (Step 5 again).

Another alternate course, "No candidates were found," also branches at Step 5, so it's numbered 5b. It rejoins the basic path at the end of the scenario, so its join point is simply "End" rather than a specific number.

It's possible to make mistakes when converting from a narrative use case to a structured scenario—and sometimes the process helps you to discover errors in the narrative use case.

Two common mistakes are

- Alternate paths with no step text

- Incorrect "join" information (we cover joins in the next "to-do" item)

EA makes it easy for you to detect these errors by automatically generating an activity diagram that shows the path logic, with branching. Generating an activity diagram verifies the logic of your structured scenario. We'll cover that in Step 6.

7. Add Pre-conditions and Post-conditions

Review each alternate and exception path. Write any pre- or post-conditions that you need. Also add any needed joins.

You're preparing the use case for an independent QA team to be able to run tests. Therefore, knowledge that developers have about the use case's pre- and post-conditions can't be assumed to exist in the heads of the QA team. While writing the narrative use case, you would be focusing purely on the narrative and not exhaustively specifying pre- and post-conditions, so as to avoid the dreaded analysis paralysis.

But we've now reached the stage in the process where pre- and post-conditions are important… so it's time to give them some thought.

In order to generate "threads" (paths through the sunny/rainy day scenarios), you need to know where each alternate/exception rejoins the basic path… hence the need for joins. This, again, is detail that can be skipped over when writing the narrative use case, enabling you to get through analysis/design without paralysis.

6. Generate an Activity Diagram

A good way to check your structured scenario for completeness is to generate an activity diagram. As we just alluded to, a structured scenario is really quite similar to an activity diagram: it has a flow of execution, and it branches and rejoins the main flow at specific points. It's possible to quickly generate an activity diagram from your structured scenario, to get a pictorial overview of your use case's logic flow.

To generate the diagram, click the button in the Scenarios tab that looks like the one circled in Figure 7–6.

Figure 7–6. *The button to generate an activity diagram*

Then choose *Activity* from the list. EA will create the diagram in the Model Explorer as a sub-node beneath the use case. Figure 7–7 shows the activity diagram generated for *Use Address* (we've reformatted the diagram slightly to fit it on the page).

■ **Tip** Checking your structured scenario with an activity diagram leads to better results in test case generation, as the test scenarios won't generate correctly if the path logic is wrong.

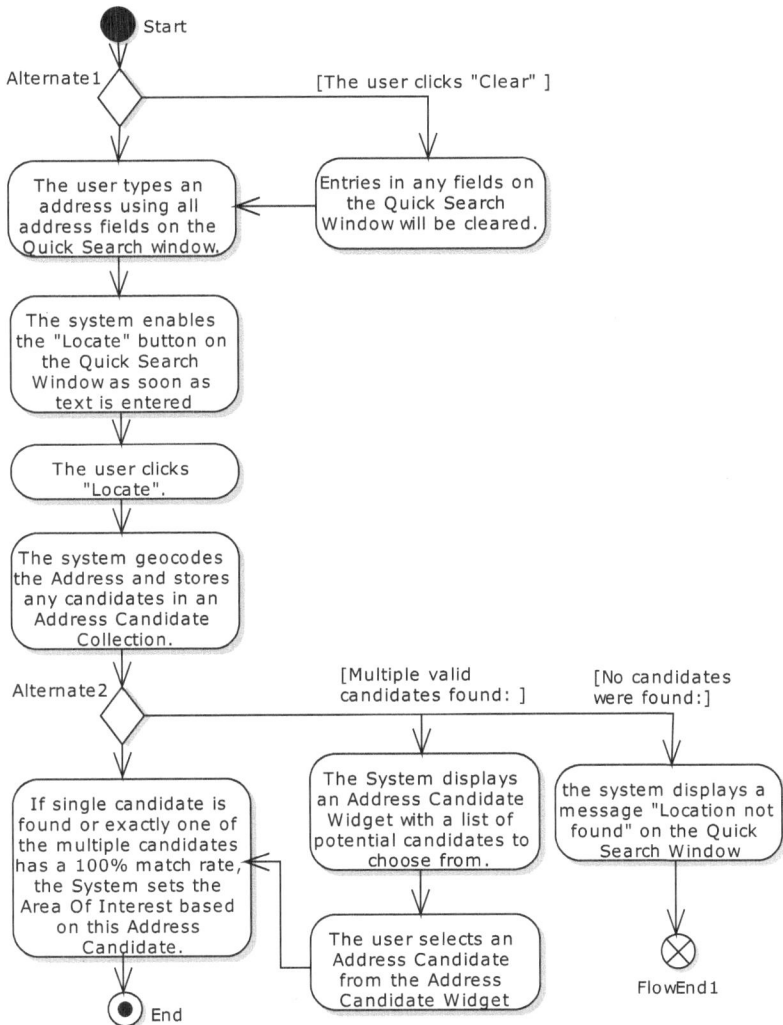

Figure 7–7. "Use Address" converted into an activity diagram

5. Expand "Threads" Using "Create External Tests"

A use case "thread" is an individual acceptance test scenario. Expand your use case "threads" using EA's Create External Tests option.

So, what's a use case thread expander, and why do you need one? Use cases generally have a sunny day scenario (the typical sequence of user actions and system responses) and several rainy day scenarios (eveything else that can happen: errors, exceptions, and less typical usage paths). When you're modeling systems with use cases, you make an up-front investment in "writing the user manual" one scenario at a time, with the expectation of recovering your investment later on in the project. If you do it right, you virtually always recover your investment multiple times over.

One of the places you can leverage the investment you've made in writing use cases is in scenario testing. If you have a use case with one sunny day scenario and three rainy day scenarios, you can expand that use case into at least four "threads," each of which defines a potential scenario test for some part of your system. There's one "thread" for the sunny day scenario and others for some portion of the sunny day combined with each of the rainy day scenarios, in turn. When you've covered all of the permutations, you've got a pretty good start on "black box" acceptance testing your use case from the user perspective.

To generate external tests, click the TestCase Generation toolbar button in the Scenarios tab, as shown in Figure 7–8.

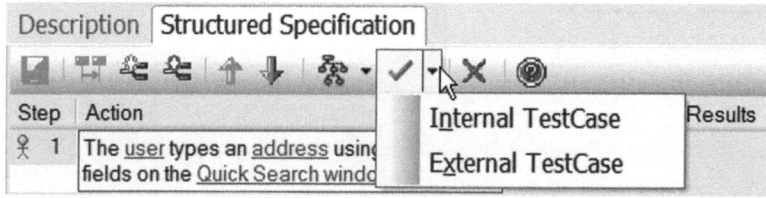

Figure 7–8. Creating an External TestCase

From the two options, choose External TestCase. The Test(s) can be viewed in the 'Scenario' tab of the Testing Window. With the initial release of this capability, you needed to hunt down the generated tests—as we're going to press, (after some intense lobbying by your faithful authors), we've just received word that EA now puts the test case on a diagram much as the ICONIX add-in does, so hunting around isn't necessary anymore. Our thanks to the folks at Sparx for being responsive to our concerns.

Once you've tracked down the Test Case element (in addition to being on an automatically opened test case diagram, it should be in the Project Browser, in the same package as the use case), press Alt+3 to activate the Testing view. Click the element once, and you should see it appear in the Testing view. *Do make sure that you're on the Scenario tab in the Testing view (see Figure 7–9), otherwise you won't see a thing.*

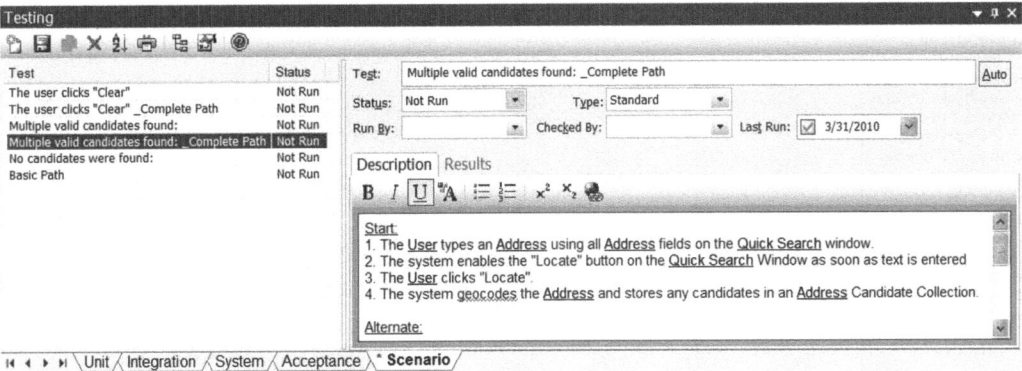

Figure 7–9. External test cases generated from "Use Address"

■ **Note** In Figure 7–9, notice that EA has recognized the domain objects, and shown them as hyperlinks. Linking the domain objects (which is done via Context References in the Scenarios tab) proves useful if you want to generate a robustness diagram from your use case. In fact, you can also link in screens (GUI widgets): if you import the storyboards into the model as screens, and give the screens the same names as used in the use case text, you can contextually link to them. Even cooler, if you generate a robustness diagram, EA creates the boundary classes for you.

---

4. Put the Test Case on a Test Case Diagram

As you may have gathered from the last step, it makes a great deal of sense to put your scenario tests on a test case diagram. Figure 7–10 shows the diagram we created for the *Use Address* test cases (as an added bonus, EA now performs this little housekeeping task for you automatically). We've added a note on there with the reconstituted "whole use case view" narrative text. Creating a diagram like this will make it easier to find your scenario tests when you return to the model later.

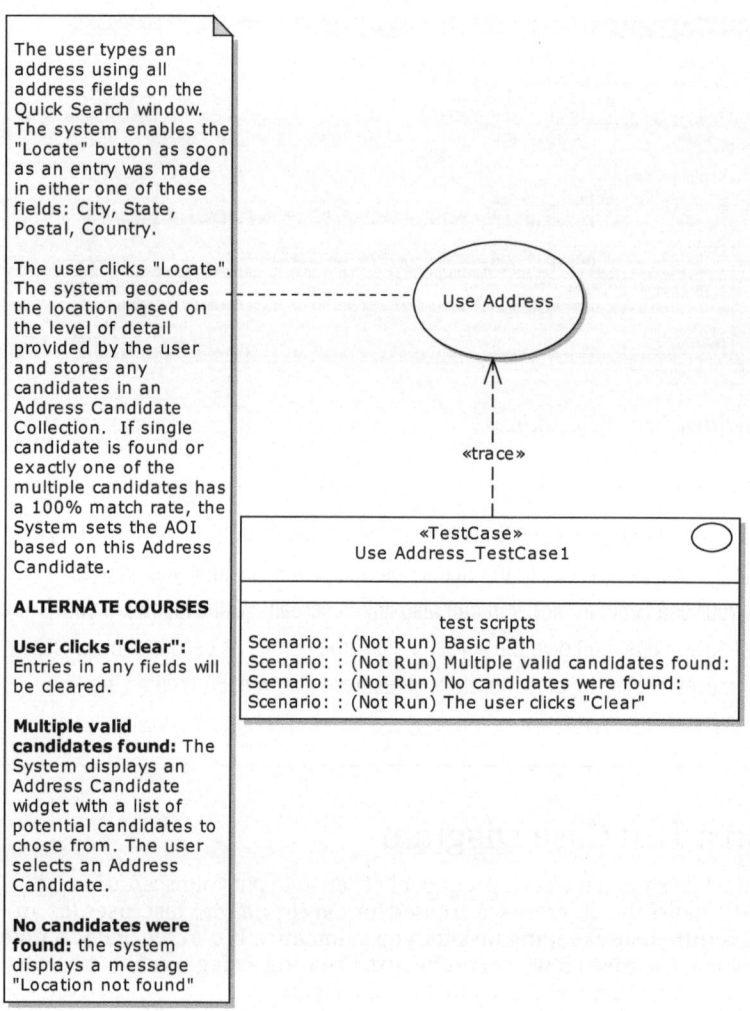

Figure 7–10. Test case diagram for "Use Address"

3. Drill into the EA Testing View

Once you've created the test case and placed it on the test case diagram, with EA's testing view open (just press Alt+3), you can simply click any of the scenarios within it to show the test details (see Figure 7–11). From here you can add additional detail that's useful for generating test plans for your QA department.

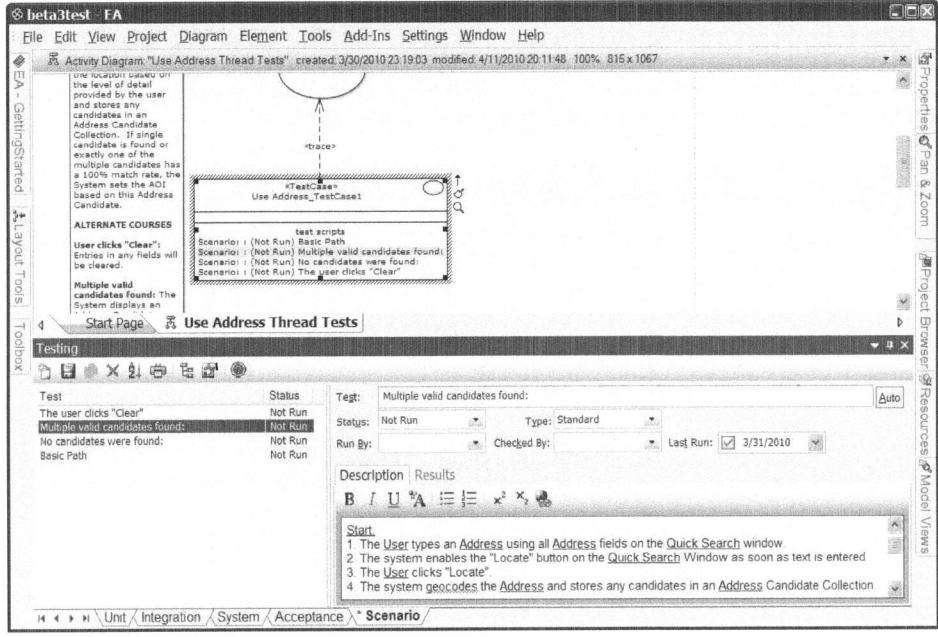

Figure 7–11. *Drilling into the EA Testing view from your test case diagram*

■ **Tip** When EA generates the test cases, it also creates some "_Complete Path" scenarios. These can safely be deleted as they're covered already by the other scenarios (we've already deleted them in Figures 7–10 and 7–11).

---

2. Add Detail to the Test Scenarios

EA generates the scenario threads automatically, but you'll still need to add information to the test case so that the QA department will know how to exercise the test scenario, and that's done using the EA testing view. Here's an example that actually found a bug in the Mapplet 2.0 project, "Multiple Candidates Found" scenario.

The "multiple candidates" condition can be caused by typing a city name of "Columbus" into the address field, with no state name. Since several states (Georgia, Ohio, etc.) have cities named Columbus, this should result in multiple candidates being displayed in the Address Candidate widget.

We'll talk more about the result of running this test at the end of the chapter.

1. Generate a Test Plan Document

If you hand a document to your QA team containing a structured, enumerated set of test steps all linked systematically back to the customer's behavioral requirements, we're pretty sure that their eyes will light up in pleasant surprise. Next time they'll probably want to get more involved in the process of creating these tests, which can only be a good thing.

To generate a test plan report from EA, first select a package in the Model Explorer, then go to the Project menu and choose Documentation -> Testing Report. A dialog appears (see Figure 7–12) from which you can then choose which tests to include. (EA can also generate a Test Details report, which, as you'd expect, contains more details.) The generated report is shown in Table 7–1.

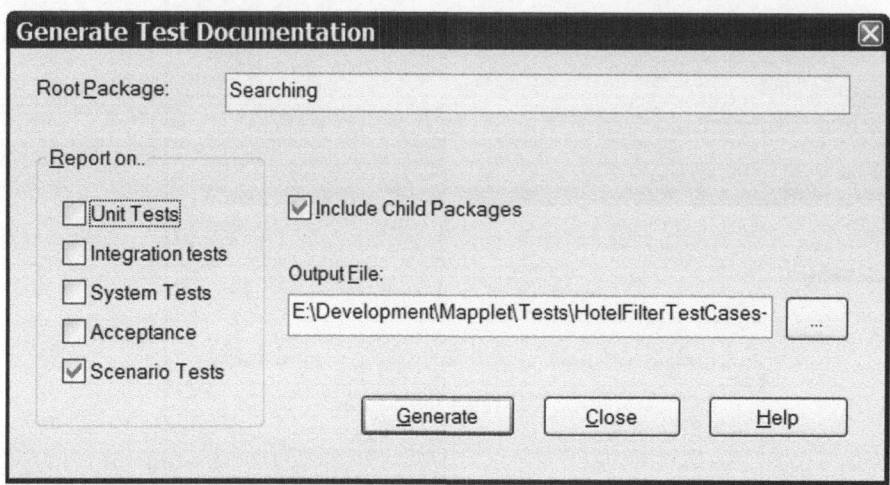

Figure 7–12. *Generating a test report*

Table 7–1. *The Work-in-Progress Generated Report for the "Use Address" Scenario Tests*

Name	Object	Description
Basic Path	Use Address_TestCase1	**Start:**
		1. The user types an address using all Address fields on the Quick Search window.
		2. The system enables the "Locate" button on the Quick Search Window as soon as text is entered.
		3. The user clicks "Locate."
		4. The system geocodes the address and stores any candidates in an Address Candidate Collection.
		5. If single candidate is found or exactly one of the multiple candidates has a 100% match rate, the system sets the Area of Interest based on this Address Candidate.
		Result:
		Basic path complete.
		Use case ends.

Name	Object	Description
No candidates were found:	Use Address_TestCase1	**Alternate:** When [No candidates were found:] 5b_1. The system displays a message "Location not found" on the Quick Search Window. **Result:** No candidates were found: complete. Use case ends.
Multiple valid candidates found:	Use Address_TestCase1	**Alternate:** When [Multiple valid candidates found:] 5a_1. The system displays an Address Candidate widget with a list of potential candidates to choose from. 5a_2. The user selects an Address Candidate from the Address Candidate widget. **Result:** Multiple valid candidates found: complete. Rejoin at 5.
The user clicks "Clear"	Use Address_TestCase1	**Alternate:** When [The user clicks "Clear"] 1a_1. Entries in any fields on the Quick Search Window will be cleared. **Result:** The user clicks "Clear" complete. Rejoin at 1.

And the Moral of the Story Is . . .

We thought it would be interesting to share with you how the theory presented in this chapter worked in practice on the Mapplet 2.0 project. As it happened, it was while we were writing this chapter that the first functional version of Mapplet 2.0 became available for testing. Since we had been writing about the *Multiple Candidates Found* alternate to the *Use Address* use case (Figure 7–12), Doug—wearing his QA department hat—decided to exercise this capability.

The first "live demo" was conducted over a web session, with the developers at ESRI driving the Mapplet, and Doug watching remotely, requesting demonstrations of various capabilities. Since "Multiple Candidates" was fresh in his mind, he immediately requested that Columbus be typed into the Address/City field, with no state name specified. The developers, having foreknowledge of how the code was built, proceeded to type Columbus into the Point of Interest locator field rather than the Address field (see Figure 7–13). They did this because they knew that the code used two different geocoding services: one that geocoded a "complete" address that required a state name to be specified for a city, and another that did a somewhat looser search that included landmarks and points of interest specified without a complete address. So they knew that typing Columbus with no state name in the Address field would fail, and return "No Matches Found" (see Figure 7–14), and thus they started typing it into the POI locator.

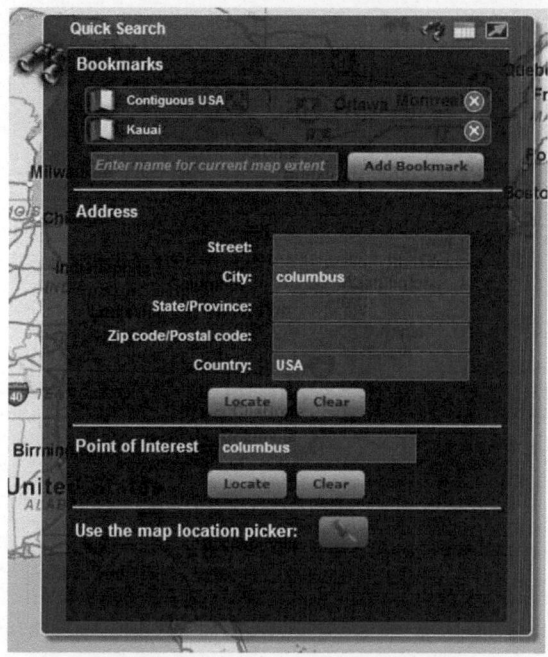

Figure 7–13. The Mapplet search dialog (prototype) where the user can type into either the Address or the Point of Interest fields

Figure 7–14. Caught on camera: the programmers naturally avoided this screen, but a tester walking the user's path (through a defined script based on the use cases) would discover this screen very quickly.

But our "independent QA department" said, "Not so fast. Your *Use Address* use case says that the locate button is enabled when anything is typed into the address field. It doesn't say anything about a state field being required."

After some discussion, the team resolved that if the first geocoding service returned no results, they could automatically try the second geocoding service. You can see the result in Figure 7–15. This resulted in an improved user experience, since now users can type a city name into the address field as they would expect, and properly get a list of candidate locations.

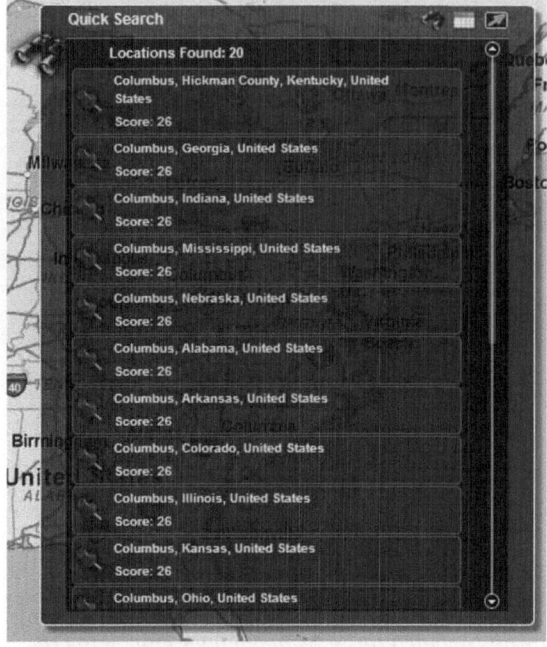

Figure 7–15. Caught and fixed: the user experience as the original use case specified

So what's the moral of the story? We hope you'll agree with the following points:

- It's important for someone other than the developers to perform independent acceptance testing.

- The acceptance testing activity should exercise all permutations of sunny/rainy day scenarios.

- Getting the user experience right (using narrative use cases) is still of paramount importance.

- Structured scenarios help us to rigorously test all paths of a use case.

We've tried to give you a step-by-step process in this chapter to put these points into practice.

Summary

In this chapter we took a complete narrative use case, structured it into specific scenarios and steps, and generated test cases that can then be handed over to the QA team, and, of course, be walked through with the customer or business analysts to gain their feedback.

Automating scenario tests is an advanced topic and not essential for your project's success, so we cover this in Chapter 11.

Testing use case scenarios, which we covered in this chapter, forms one half of acceptance testing. The other half—testing of business requirements—is covered in the next chapter.

CHAPTER 8

■■■

Acceptance Testing: Business Requirements

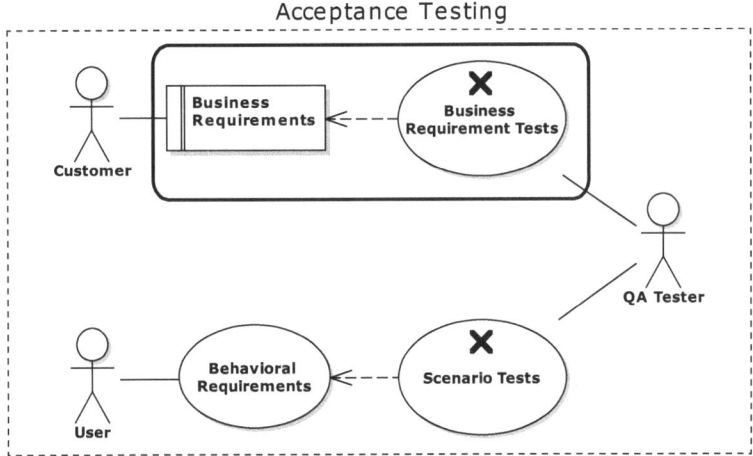

Acceptance Testing

In this chapter, you'll learn how to generate customer-facing **business requirement tests** from the requirements in your model, how to organize those tests, and how to generate a test plan document from them. To illustrate this, we'll once again make use of the "Agile/ICONIX add-in" for Enterprise Architect.

Have a look at the chapter-opening diagram, which should look familiar by now. In Chapter 7 we described the bottom half of this picture: you saw how use cases define the behavioral requirements of the system, and scenario tests are used as "end-to-end" automated tests to verify that the system behaves as expected. In this chapter, we'll describe the top half of the picture: you'll see how business requirements define what you want the system to do—and why.

Here's how business requirements differ from behavioral requirements (from Chapter 7):

- Business requirements define the system *from the customer's perspective*, without diving into details about how the system will be implemented.

- Behavioral requirements define how the system will work *from the end-user's perspective* (i.e. the "user manual" view).

Or, from a testing and feedback perspective:

- Requirement tests verify that the developers have implemented the system as specified by the business requirements.

- Scenario tests verify that the system behaves as specified by the behavioral requirements.

Requirement tests and scenario tests are really two sides of the same coin, i.e., they're both a form of acceptance tests.

SIGNED, SEALED, DELIVERED

While some proponents of agile methodologies proudly follow a philosophy of "software is never done,"[1] preferring to run the hamster wheel of an infinite loop of refactoring and unit testing while sprinting after a never-ending backlog, the authors believe there is still great merit (in some circumstances, at least) to be able to say to your customer: "OK, we've finished. Here are the acceptance test criteria that we mutually agreed upon, and test results showing that the system passes all of the tests we've agreed to." One of the chief merits of being able to say this is that it's often the determining criteria for getting paid by the customer. A second merit is the satisfaction of knowing you've completed a job well done, according to a concrete and objective set of criteria.

Instead of the XP notion that "software is never done," you'll be able to say: "Software is done, software gets signed off, and software gets released."

Top Ten Requirements Testing "To-Do" List

As usual, we'll begin the chapter with our top ten "to-do" list. The rest of the chapter is structured around this list, using the Mapplet 2.0 project as the example throughout. Here's the list:

10. *Start with a domain model.* Write everything—requirements, tests, use cases— in the business language that your domain model captures.

9. *Write business requirement tests.* While writing requirements, think about how each one will be tested. How will a test "prove" that a requirement has been fulfilled? Capture this thought within the EA Testing View as the Description of the test. Be sure to focus on the customer's perspective.

8. *Model and organize requirements.* Model your requirements in EA. Then organize them into packages.

7. *Create test cases from requirements.* You can use the Agile ICONIX add-in for EA for this step. That add-in makes it easy to create test cases from your requirements.

---

[1] See *Extreme Programming Refactored* – Part IV, "The Perpetual Coding Machine" and Chapter 11, starting on p. 249, for a satirical look at this philosophy. Then, if you'd like to know what we really think, just ask.

6. *Review your plan with the customer.* EA can be used to generate a test report based on the requirements. This makes an ideal "check-list" to walk through with the customer. With it, you're basically asking: "Given that these are our acceptance criteria, have we missed anything?"

5. *Write manual test scripts.* Write these test scripts as step-by-step recipes that a human can follow easily.

4. *Write automated requirement tests.* Automated tests won't always make sense. But when they do, write them. Just don't delay the project for the sake of automating the tests.

3. *Export the requirement test cases.* To help you track progress and schedule work, export your test cases to a task-tracking and scheduling tool such as Jira.

2. *Make the test cases visible.* Everyone involved in the project should have access to the test cases. Make them available. Keep them up-to-date.

1. *Involve your team!* Work closely with your testing team in the process of creating requirement tests. Give them *ownership* of the tests.

10. Start with a Domain Model

When the Mapplet 2.0 project was just getting underway, the ESRI project team and VResorts.com client met to define the project's scope, and to kickstart the project into its initial modeling phase: to define the requirements, and agree on a common set of business terms—the domain model—with which the "techies and the suits" (now there's a dual cliché!) would be able to communicate with each other. Figure 8–1 shows the resultant initial domain model.

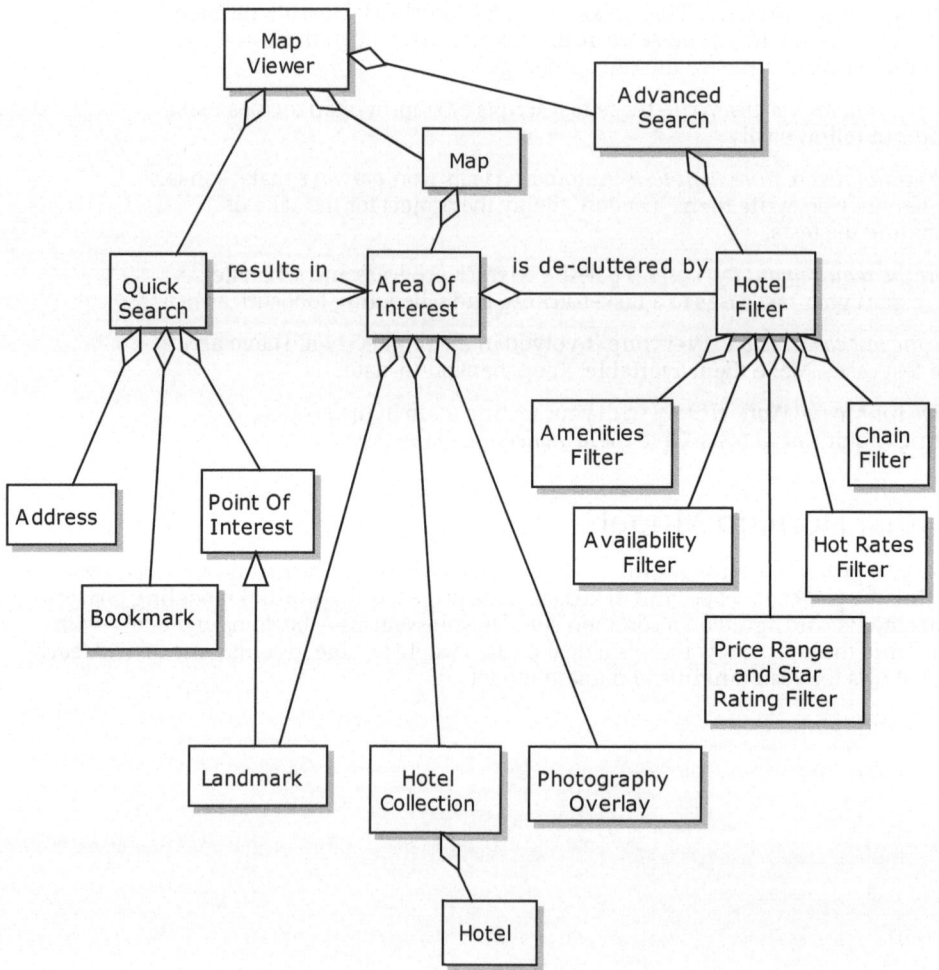

Figure 8–1. Initial Mapplet 2.0 domain model

■ **Note** The domain model in Figure 8–1 differs from the one we showed you in Chapter 4. The version shown here is from the start of the project, while the one in Chapter 4 evolved during conceptual design. You should find that the domain model evolves throughout the project, as the team's understanding of the business domain evolves.

As you can see in Figure 8–1, the Map Viewer supports a Quick Search and an Advanced Search. The result of a Quick Search is an Area of Interest that can display Hotels, Landmarks, and a Photography Overlay. A Quick Search specifies an Area of Interest via Bookmarks, an Address, or a Point of Interest (which might be a Landmark). An Advanced Search specifies a Hotel Filter that is used to declutter the map display. The Hotel Filter includes an Amenity Filter, an Availability Filter (based on check-in, check-out dates, number of rooms requested, etc.), a Price Range and Star Rating Filter, a Hot Rates Filter, and a Chain Filter.

Once you have a domain model in place, write everything—requirements, tests, use cases—in the business language that you've captured in the domain model. As the requirements are turned into use cases, and the use cases into design diagrams and code, the domain objects you defined should be used for class names, test names, and so forth.

■ **Tip** Don't stop at identifying the names of domain objects: also write a brief definition of each one—one or two sentences each. You'll be surprised how many additional domain objects you discover this way, as you dig into the nooks and crannies of the business domain.[2]

---

9. Write Business Requirement Tests

Business requirement tests should be written from the customer's perspective. But before "testing" a requirement, it makes sense to think about what you want to achieve from testing it. Requirements are the documented wants of the customer; so requirement tests are very much from the customer's point of view. To test that a requirement has been implemented, you'll need to put on your "customer hat," so when you're identifying and writing the business requirement tests, it's perfectly reasonable (essential, even) to have the customer in the room.

Here's an example of a business requirement:

17. map/photos -- photographic overlay links
The user can click a photographic overlay icon on the map in order to open a link to the destination web page and/or picture/movie.

And here are the sorts of acceptance criteria that a customer would be thinking about:

Does this work with photos, videos? Does the screen overlay display correctly?

---

[2] Doug recently had one ICONIX training client (with a very complex domain model) report that he identified an additional 30% more domain classes just by writing one sentence definitions for the ones he had. That's a pretty good "bang for the buck".

8. Model and Organize Requirements

Model your requirements using EA, and then organize them into packages.

With the Mapplet 2.0 domain model in place, it wasn't long before a comprehensive set of requirements was being captured. These were all modeled in EA (see Figures 8–2 through 8–6), inside these packages:

```
Functional Requirements
    |__ User Interface
    |__ Hotel Filter
    |__ Map

Non-Functional Requirements
```

The team also created a package called Optional Requirements (a euphemism for "Perhaps in the next release"), which we haven't shown here.

You'll often hear people talking about "functional" and "non-functional" requirements, but what exactly makes a requirement one or the other? To answer this question, it helps to think about the criteria often known as the "ilities": capability, maintainability, usability, reusability, reliability, and extendability.[3] Functional requirements represent the capabilities of the system; non-functional requirements represent all the other "ilities" that we just listed.

■ **Tip** There's a huge benefit to storing requirements in a modeling tool rather than a Word document, which is that the requirements model comes to life (in a manner of speaking). You can link use cases and design elements back to individual requirements; you can create test cases for each requirement, too.

---

[3] See Peter de Grace's insightful book *The Olduvai Imperative: CASE and the State of Software Engineering Practice* (Yourdon Press, 1993). It's unfortunately out of print, but the chapter "An Odyssey Through the Ilities" by itself makes the book well worth hunting down.

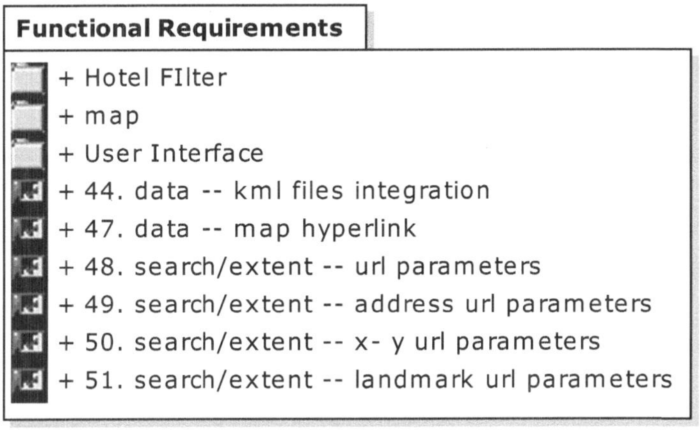

Functional Requirements

+ Hotel FIlter
+ map
+ User Interface
+ 44. data -- kml files integration
+ 47. data -- map hyperlink
+ 48. search/extent -- url parameters
+ 49. search/extent -- address url parameters
+ 50. search/extent -- x- y url parameters
+ 51. search/extent -- landmark url parameters

Figure 8–2. Mapplet 2.0 Functional Requirements (containing three sub-packages)

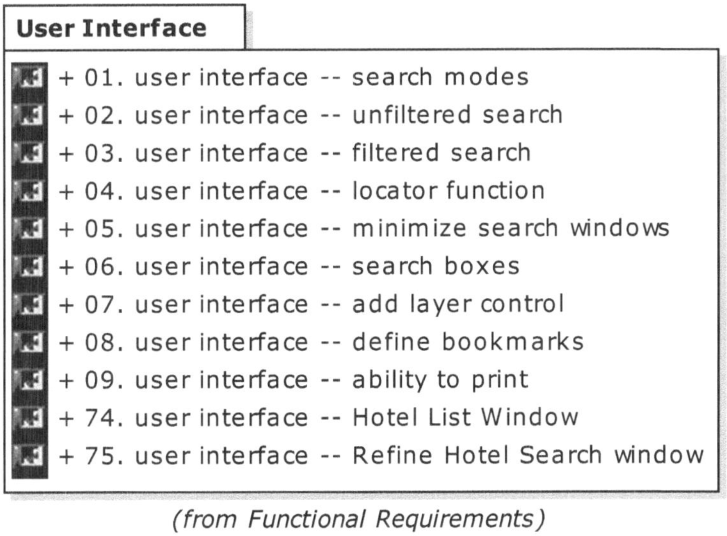

User Interface

+ 01. user interface -- search modes
+ 02. user interface -- unfiltered search
+ 03. user interface -- filtered search
+ 04. user interface -- locator function
+ 05. user interface -- minimize search windows
+ 06. user interface -- search boxes
+ 07. user interface -- add layer control
+ 08. user interface -- define bookmarks
+ 09. user interface -- ability to print
+ 74. user interface -- Hotel List Window
+ 75. user interface -- Refine Hotel Search window

(from Functional Requirements)

Figure 8–3. Mapplet 2.0 user interface requirements, nested inside the Functional Requirements package

189

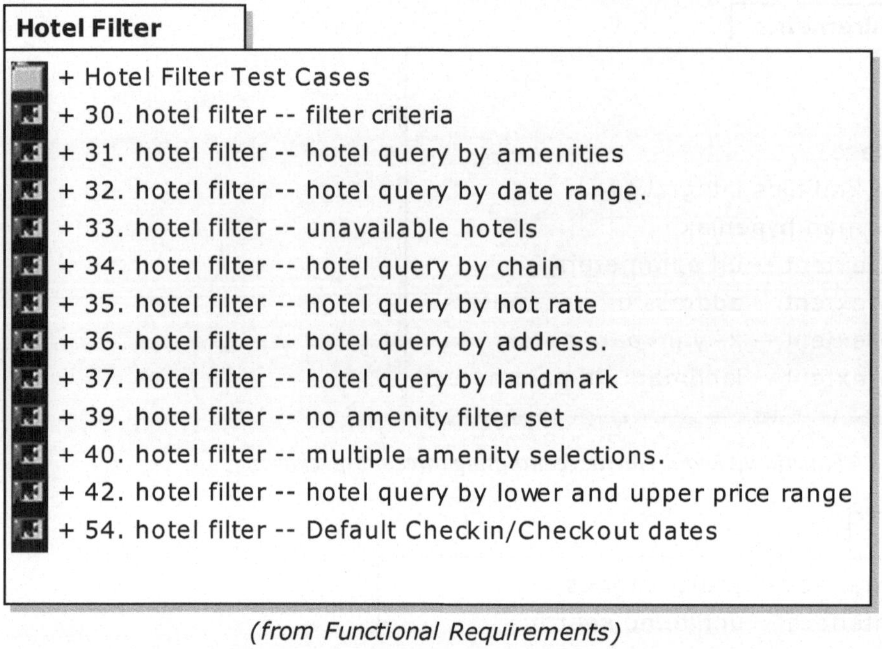

Hotel Filter

+ Hotel Filter Test Cases

+ 30. hotel filter -- filter criteria

+ 31. hotel filter -- hotel query by amenities

+ 32. hotel filter -- hotel query by date range.

+ 33. hotel filter -- unavailable hotels

+ 34. hotel filter -- hotel query by chain

+ 35. hotel filter -- hotel query by hot rate

+ 36. hotel filter -- hotel query by address.

+ 37. hotel filter -- hotel query by landmark

+ 39. hotel filter -- no amenity filter set

+ 40. hotel filter -- multiple amenity selections.

+ 42. hotel filter -- hotel query by lower and upper price range

+ 54. hotel filter -- Default Checkin/Checkout dates

(from Functional Requirements)

Figure 8–4. *Mapplet 2.0 hotel filter requirements, nested inside the Functional Requirements package*

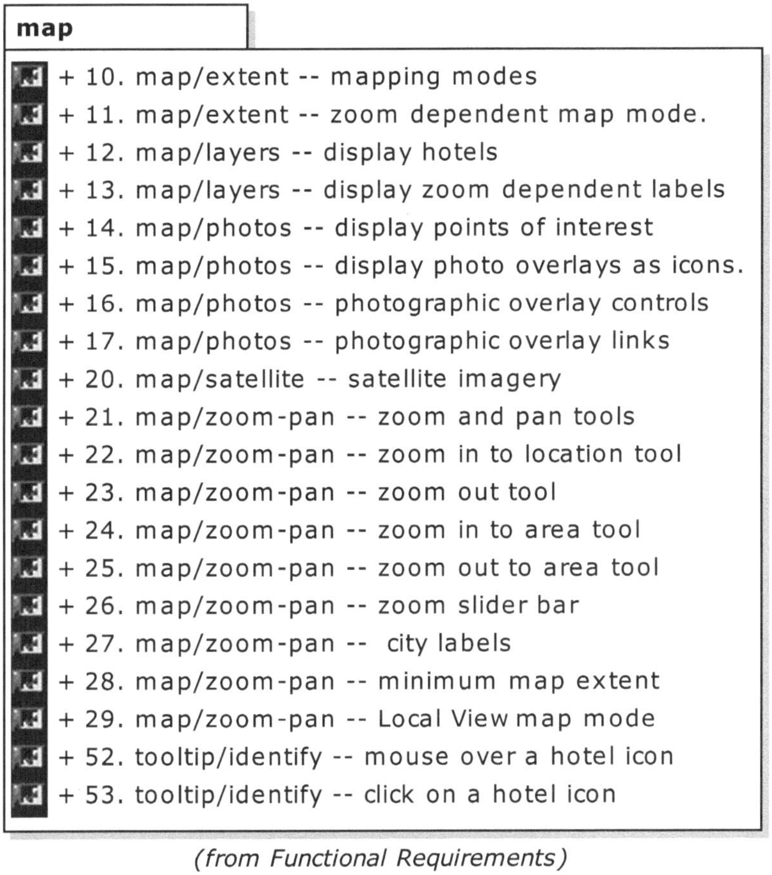

map

+ 10. map/extent -- mapping modes
+ 11. map/extent -- zoom dependent map mode.
+ 12. map/layers -- display hotels
+ 13. map/layers -- display zoom dependent labels
+ 14. map/photos -- display points of interest
+ 15. map/photos -- display photo overlays as icons.
+ 16. map/photos -- photographic overlay controls
+ 17. map/photos -- photographic overlay links
+ 20. map/satellite -- satellite imagery
+ 21. map/zoom-pan -- zoom and pan tools
+ 22. map/zoom-pan -- zoom in to location tool
+ 23. map/zoom-pan -- zoom out tool
+ 24. map/zoom-pan -- zoom in to area tool
+ 25. map/zoom-pan -- zoom out to area tool
+ 26. map/zoom-pan -- zoom slider bar
+ 27. map/zoom-pan -- city labels
+ 28. map/zoom-pan -- minimum map extent
+ 29. map/zoom-pan -- Local View map mode
+ 52. tooltip/identify -- mouse over a hotel icon
+ 53. tooltip/identify -- click on a hotel icon

(from Functional Requirements)

Figure 8–5. Mapplet 2.0 map requirements, nested inside the Functional Requirements package

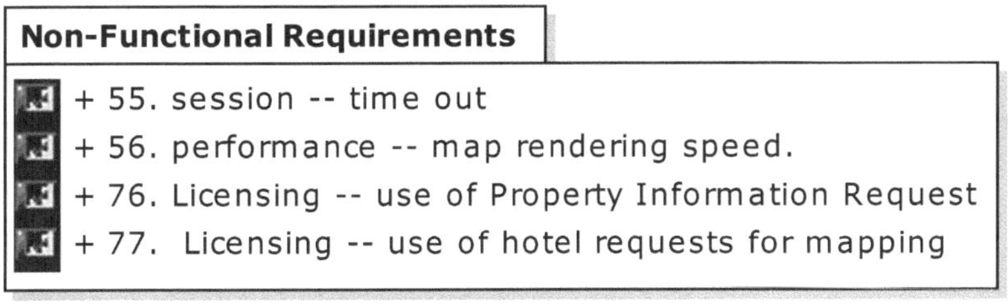

Non-Functional Requirements

+ 55. session -- time out
+ 56. performance -- map rendering speed.
+ 76. Licensing -- use of Property Information Request
+ 77. Licensing -- use of hotel requests for mapping

Figure 8–6. Mapplet 2.0 Non-functional Requirements

7. Create Test Cases from Requirements

You've probably gathered by now that we quite like EA. One reason is that you can easily use EA along with the Agile ICONIX add-in to create test cases from your requirements.

In EA, right-click either a single requirement, a package of requirements, or inside a requirements diagram. Then choose "Create Tests from Requirements"[4] (see Figure 8–7). This will produce something like the diagram shown in Figure 8–8.

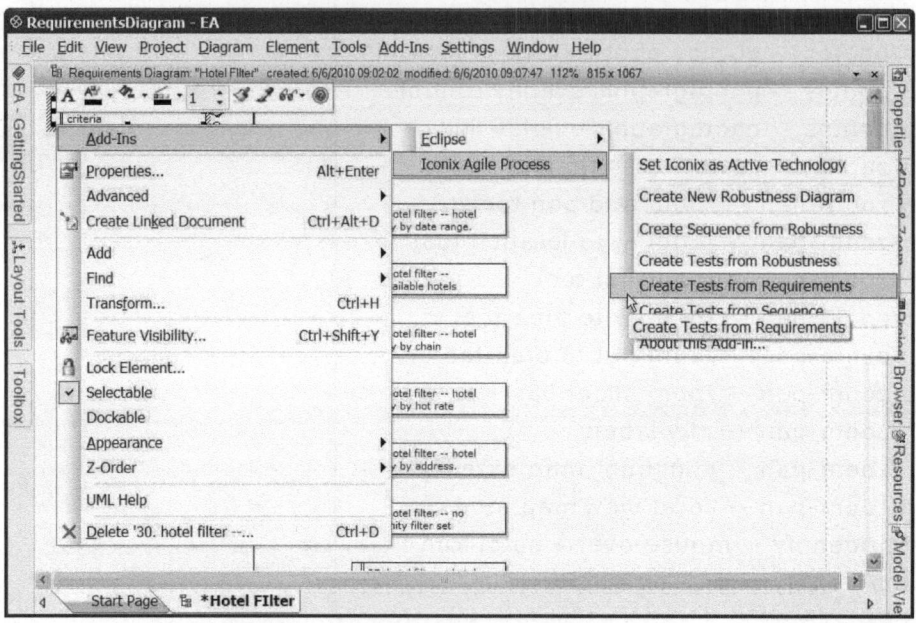

Figure 8–7. *Creating requirement test cases from requirements*

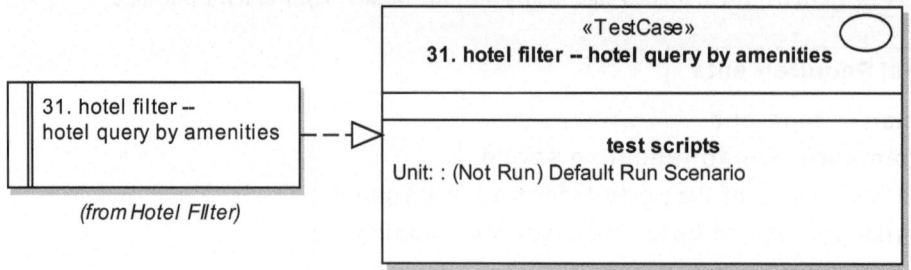

Figure 8–8. *A test case created from a requirement*

---

[4] At the time of writing, this is under the Add-In... ICONIX Agile Process sub-menu.

In Figure 8–8, the requirement on the left is linked to the test case on the right. The diagram also shows which package (Hotel Filter) the requirement is from. Initially, EA creates one default scenario for the test case. EA has created this as a "Unit" test scenario by default. This isn't what you want right now, though; you actually want to create Acceptance test scenarios (this does matter, as you'll see shortly when you create a Requirements test report). So let's delete the default unit test scenario, and create some Acceptance test scenarios instead—see Figure 8–8.

First switch on EA's Testing View: go to the View menu, and choose Testing—or press Alt+3. In the Testing View, you'll see some tabs at the bottom of the screen: Unit, Integration, System, Acceptance, and Scenario. (Recall from Chapter 7 that we spent most of our time on the Scenario tab, and in Chapter 5, on the Unit tab.) Click the "red X" toolbar button to delete the Default Run scenario from the Unit tab; then click over to the Acceptance tab (see Figure 8–9).

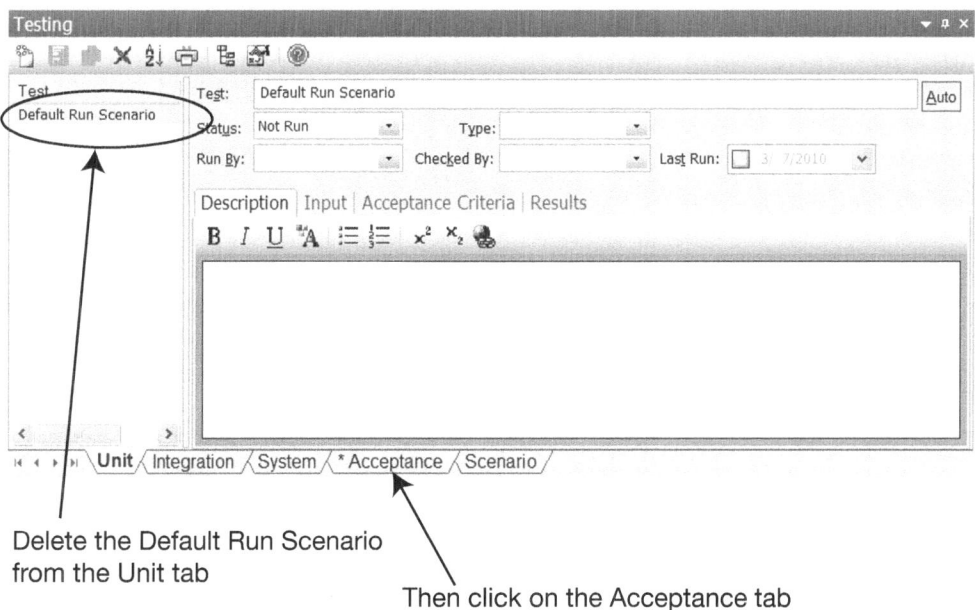

Figure 8–9. Make sure you're creating Acceptance test scenarios for requirements, not Unit test scenarios.

Higher level requirements will aggregate these tests with other "filter" tests; e.g., when testing the Filter Hotels requirement, the test plan should specify testing an "amenity filter set" concurrently with a date range:

> *Find a golf resort on Maui that's available on the last weekend in May (over Memorial Day weekend).*

Figure 8–10 shows the Test View with the Acceptance test scenarios added.

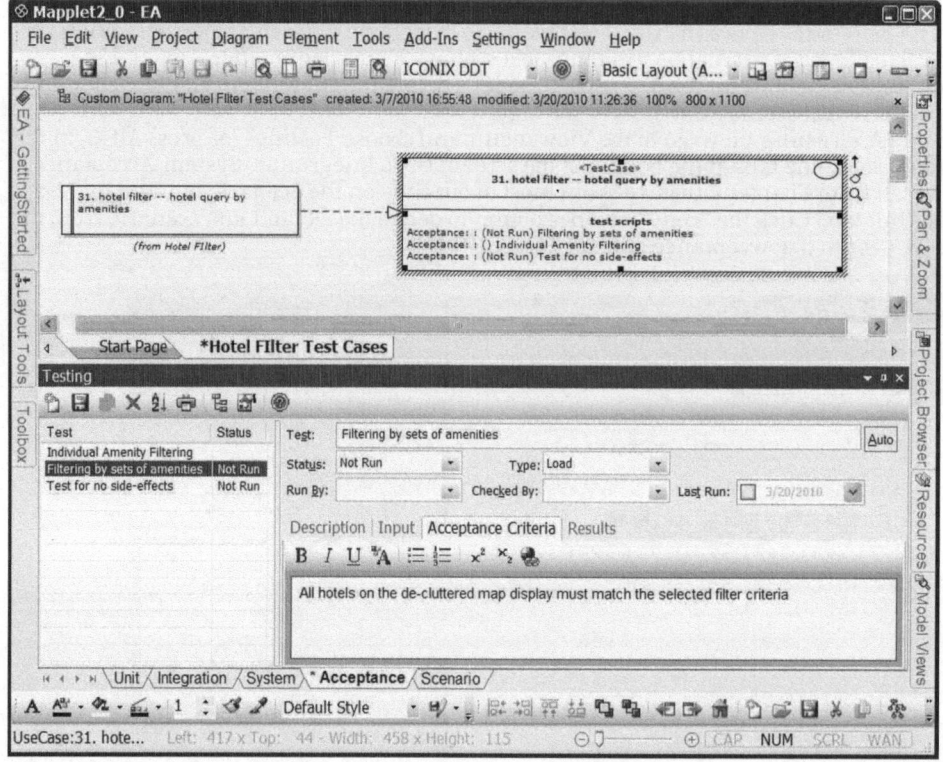

Figure 8–10. *Test View with the new Acceptance test scenarios*

With the requirements tests (or "acceptance tests" in EA nomenclature) added in, wouldn't it be nice if you could generate a clear, uncluttered test report that can be handed straight to the testers and the customer? Let's do that next...

6. Review Your Plan with the Customer

One of the key stages of specifying a business requirement involves asking why the requirement is needed. This question gets asked a second time while the tests are being written. If the customer is involved in either writing or reviewing the test plan, he will think of new things to be tested. Some of these will very likely lead to new requirements that were never thought about in the first place. Writing and reviewing the requirement tests can also help to pick holes in the requirements.

Another way to look at this process is the following:

- When you're writing and reviewing the requirement tests, you're validating the requirements themselves.

- When you're running (or executing) the requirement tests, you're validating that the finished software matches the requirements.

Because the tests play a key role in shaping and validating the requirements, it pays to write the requirement tests early in the project.

EA can be used to generate a test report based on the requirements. To do this, first select a package of requirements test cases, and then go to Project ➜ Documentation ➜ Testing Report. In the Generate Test Documentation dialog (see Figure 8–11), deselect all the test types except for Acceptance, and then click Generate. Table 8–1 shows the output from the test cases we created in the previous section.

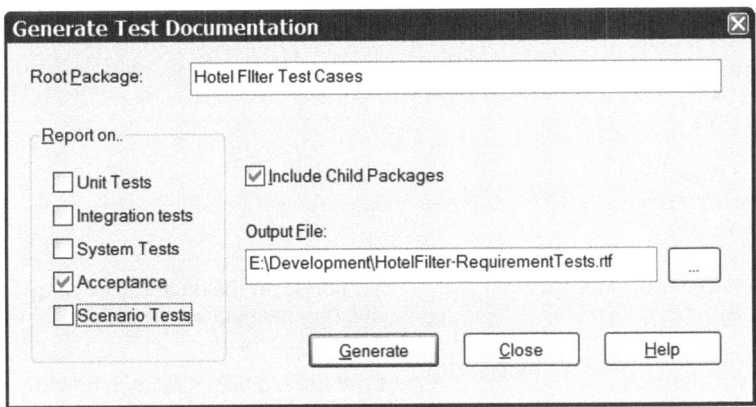

Figure 8–11. Generating a Requirements test report

Table 8–1. *The Work-in-Progress Generated Report for the Hotel Filter Test Cases*

Name	Requirement / Description	Input	Acceptance Criteria / Result Details
Test for no side-effects	31. hotel filter -- hotel query by amenities	Amenity Criteria Set Area of Interest (at a "local" map scale) Initial map display (showing hotels within AOI)	All hotels on the decluttered map display must match the selected filter criteria. Verify that amenity selection does not remove too many hotels from the map (i.e., filtering on "Room Service" shouldn't inadvertently affect other amenities).
Filtering by sets of amenities	31. hotel filter -- hotel query by amenities A series of "visual inspection" tests will be conducted to verify that amenity filtering is working properly. Each of these tests will involve checking various sets of amenities (for example "Pool, Room Service,	Amenity Criteria Set Area of Interest (at a "local" map scale) Initial map display (showing hotels within AOI)	All hotels on the decluttered map display must match the selected filter criteria. Decluttered map display (showing a filtered subset of Hotels on the map)

Name	Requirement / Description	Input	Acceptance Criteria / Result Details
	Bar," or "Pet-friendly, Restaurant, Babysitting," or "Golf Course, Tennis, Fitness Center"), and then inspecting all hotels that remain on the map after filtering to make sure the amenity filtering criteria are met correctly. Tests should be run in areas of interest that make sense for various "amenity sets"...e.g., Golf resorts in Tucson, AZ; Beachfront resorts in Waikiki; Hotels with bar and concierge in midtown Manhattan, etc.		
Individual Amenity Filtering	31. hotel filter -- hotel query by amenities A series of visual inspection tests exercising each individual amenity, one at a time	Amenity Area of Interest (at a "local" map scale) Initial map display (showing hotels within AOI)	All hotels on the decluttered map display must match the selected filter criteria. Decluttered map display (showing a filtered subset of Hotels on the map)
Test a combination of date range and price range filtering	30. hotel filter -- filter criteria Starting from a Quick Search result screen showing hotels on the map, filter the display using a combination of price and date ranges.		
Test a combination of amenity and price range filtering	30. hotel filter -- filter criteria Starting from a Quick Search result screen showing hotels on the map, filter the display using a combination of amenities and price ranges. For example, looking for hotels in midtown Manhattan with 24-hour room service and a concierge, for under $200/night, will likely declutter the map display by a great deal.		

Name	Requirement / Description	Input	Acceptance Criteria / Result Details
Test a combination of amenity and date range filtering	30. hotel filter -- filter criteria Starting from a Quick Search result screen showing hotels on the map, filter the display using a combination of amenities and date ranges. Some creativity may be needed to find a combination of location and date range that will result in "Sold Out" hotels. Examples might be New Orleans hotels during Mardi Gras, hotels in Rio de Janeiro during Carnival, Waikiki Beach on Memorial Day, Times Square at New Year's Eve, etc.		
Test with a date range where all hotels are available	32. hotel filter -- hotel query by date range.		
Test with a date range where some hotels are unavailable	32. hotel filter -- hotel query by date range.		Unavailable hotels should be grayed-out on the map.

The test report makes an ideal check-list to walk through with the customer. With it, you're basically asking: "Given that these are our acceptance criteria, have we missed anything?"[5] The customer may also use the test report to walk through the delivered product and test to his or her own satisfaction that it's all there. But whatever happens, don't rely on the customer to do this for you. There's nothing worse than having a customer say "Those tests you told me to run… they just confirmed that your software's broken!" In other words, make sure your own testers sign-off on the tests before the product is handed over. This will make for a happier customer.

---

[5] In practice, these tests indeed did catch several things on the Mapplet 2.0 project. Testing for no side-effects revealed that always filtering against a default date setting, even when the defaults were unmodified, resulted in too many hotels being removed from the map as "unavailable", and testing by date range where some hotels are unavailable discovered that the "unavailable hotels should be grayed-out" requirement had inadvertently been declared to be "Optional", with (pre-deployment) fixes underway as the book went to press. Are requirement tests important? We vote yes.

5. Write Manual Test Scripts

Given that you want your testers to be able to confirm that the finished software passes the requirement tests, you'll want to make sure that each test has a tangible, unambiguous pass/fail criterion. To that end, write test scripts that your testers can manually execute. Make each script a simple, step-by-step recipe. The test report in Table 8–1 shows some examples: it's easy to see from the Acceptance Criteria column what the tester will need to confirm for each test.

4. Write Automated Requirements Tests

As you identify and write the business requirements, you'll want to think about how the requirements are going to be tested. Some requirements tests can naturally be automated: non-functional requirements such as scalability will benefit from automation, e.g., you could write a script that generates a high volume of web site requests for "max throughput tests." Many business requirement tests, however, are more to do with observation from humans. When possible, write automated tests. However, don't delay the project in order to write the tests.

■ **Note** As with scenario tests, automated requirement tests are really *integration tests*, as they test the product end-to-end across connected systems. We explore integration testing in Chapter 11.

As we explored earlier in this chapter, the business requirement tests are a customer-facing document: a methodical way of demonstrating that the business requirements have been met. So automating these might defeat their purpose. Admittedly, we've seen great results from projects that have automated requirement tests. However, the use case testing already takes care of "end-to-end" testing for user scenarios. Non-functional requirements—such as scalability or performance requirements—are natural contenders for automated scripts, e.g., to generate thousands of deals per minute, or price updates per second, in an algorithmic trading system; but it wouldn't make sense to try to generate these from the requirements model.

3. Export the Test Cases

Export your requirement test cases to a task-tracking and scheduling tool. You'll want the test cases to be linked back to your requirements; during development, you'll want to track your requirements as tasks or features within a task-tracking tool such as Jira or Doors.[6] A "live link" back to the EA test cases is ideal, as you then don't need to maintain lists of requirement tests in two places. But failing that, exporting the test cases directly into your task-tracking tool—and then linking the development tasks to them—is an acceptable second-best. The goal is to make sure there's a tight coupling between the

---

[6] If you happen to be using both EA and JIRA, and want a nice way to integrate them, check out the *Enterprise Tester* product, available from: www.iconix.org. Enterprise Tester is a web-based test management solution that provides traceability between UML requirements and test cases.

requirement tests, the requirements themselves, and the development tasks that your team will use to track progress.

2. Make the Test Cases Visible

Communication is, as we all know, a vital factor in any project's success. The requirement tests, in particular, are the criteria for the project's completion, so everyone should be well aware of their existence. The requirements tests redefine the business specification in terms of "How do I know this is done?" With that in mind, it's important to make the requirement tests visible, easy for anyone in the project to access, and, of course, up-to-date. The best way to achieve this will vary depending on the project and even your organization's culture. But here are some possibilities, all of which work well in the right environment:

- Publish the generated test report to a project wiki.

- Email a link to the wiki page each time the test cases are updated (but don't email the test cases as an attachment, as people will just work off this version forever, no matter how out-of-date it's become).

- Print the test cases onto individual "story cards" (literally, little cards that can be shuffled and scribbled on) and pin them up on the office wall.

- Print the requirements onto individual story cards, with the requirement on one half and the test cases summarized on the other half.

1. Involve Your Team!

Make sure to involve your testing team closely in the process of creating requirement tests. We've seen many projects suffer from "over the fence syndrome"—that is, the business analysts put together a specification (if you're lucky) and throw it over the fence to the developers. The developers code up the system and throw it over the next fence along to the testers. The testers sign off on the developed system, maybe even referring back to the original requirements spec, and then the system gets released—thrown over the really big fence (with the barbed wire at the top) to the customer waiting outside. That's not the way to operate.

In theory, the sort of project we've just described ticks the boxes of "failsafe development." There are requirements specs, analysts, even a team of testers, and a release process. So what could possibly go wrong? The problem is that in this kind of setup, no one talks to each other. Each department regards itself as a separate entity, with delineated delivery gateways between them. Throw a document into the portal, and it emerges at some other point in the universe, like an alien tablet covered in arcane inscriptions that will take thousands of years for linguistic experts to decipher. Naturally, requirements are going to be misinterpreted. The "sign-off" from the testers will be pretty meaningless, as they were never closely involved in the requirements process: so their understanding of the true business requirements will be superficial at best.

Really effective testers will question the requirements and spot loopholes in business logic. And you'll be eternally grateful to them when they prevent a project from being released into production with faulty requirements. But the testers don't stand a chance of doing this if they're not closely involved with developing the requirement tests.

> ■ **Tip** Let the testers "own" the requirement tests (i.e., be responsible for their development and maintenance). The customer and your business analysts build the requirements up; the testers write tests to knock them down again.

Another way to think of the business tests suite is that it's an independent audit created by a testing organization to show that the system created by the developers does what the customer intended. If the developers are left to manage the testing themselves, then you end up with the "Green Bar of Shangri-La" that we discussed in Chapter 1: the system tells us there's a green bar, so everything's okay… This is why it's vital to have a separate team—the QA testers—verifying the software. And if the testers are involved early enough, they will also verify the requirements themselves.

Summary

In this chapter we looked at the "other half" of acceptance testing, business requirement tests (where the first half was scenario tests, in Chapter 7). We also looked at the business requirements for Mapplet 2.0, which brings us to the conclusion of the Mapplet 2.0 project. Once the requirements were verified, the software was ready for release. We invite you to view the final Mapplet on www.VResorts.com!

Our strategy for requirement testing, combined with the scenario testing we discussed in Chapter 7, supports an independent Quality Assurance organization that provides a level of assurance that the customer's requirements have been met, beyond the development team asserting that "all our unit tests light up green."

The capabilities of Enterprise Architect's testing view, combined with the Agile ICONIX add-in, supports requirement testing by allowing the following:

- Automated creation of tests from requirements

- Ability to create multiple test scenarios for each requirement test

- Ability to populate test scenarios with Description, Acceptance Criteria, etc.

- Ability to automatically generate test plan reports

This concludes Part 2 of the book, where we've illustrated both developer testing and acceptance testing for the Mapplet 2.0 project. Part 3 introduces some fairly technical "Advanced DDT" concepts that we hope the developers who are reading will find useful. Less technical folks might want to skip directly to Appendix "A for Alice", which we hope you'll enjoy as much as we do.

## PART 3

Advanced DDT

The Queen left off, quite out of breath, and said to Alice: "Have you seen the Mock Object yet?"

"No," said Alice. "I don't even know what a Mock Object is."

"It's the thing Mock Object soup is made from," said the Queen.

"I never saw one, or heard of one," said Alice. "And I hardly think we should need one whilst integration testing."

What we've covered up until now we would consider the minimum that a team should do in order to really benefit from DDT. As with any discipline, you'll find that you get better at it the more you do, and you may well reach the point where you want to do more with the process. This final part is for those people who want to take DDT to the "next level." These final chapters are also unashamedly technical: non-programmers beware!

If you stop here, you'll have learned most of what you need to use DDT in the real world. But you will miss out on the horrors of the Temple of Doom (aka un-testable codebase) and its thoroughly scrubbed-up, wiped-down, and redesigned, fully testable alternative. Testing experts who want to earn their peeling, sun-faded "I studied to become a DDT guru and all I got was this lousy sticker!" sticker should, of course, read on.

- **Chapter 9** looks at the world from a unit-testing developer's point of view, faced with a code base that must have been written by some "test-unconscious" colleagues.

- **Chapter 10** presents the flipside of the untestable codebase, re-approaching it with a proper design and an eye towards unit testing.

- **Chapter 11** explores integration testing—tests that involve calls to external systems. These are a vital part of DDT (and any other development process), but we've moved them to the "Advanced" section since integration tests involve a thorny set of issues, and it makes sense to master DDT first before being confronted by them.

- **Chapter 12** goes microcosmic—sub-atomic, in fact—and looks at how to use DDT for algorithmic unit testing.

## CHAPTER 9

Unit Testing Antipatterns
(The "Don'ts")

The majority of software projects are ongoing affairs. New screens and functions are released on (or around) specific, agreed dates, but a project itself keeps chugging along. So it's far more common for developers to join a project mid-flow, with its own dusty corners that no one dares to disturb, its homegrown object-relational mapping classes, crusted together with the foibles and wrinkles of a dozen long-since departed self-styled code gurus. Starting a brand new project from scratch is a rare joy: the opportunity to set the standards, consider the architecture, evaluate the available technologies given the business requirements, and produce clean, maintainable code that's easily unit-tested.

Code that's difficult to test tends to also be poorly designed code: difficult to maintain, a nightmare to debug, time-consuming, and obstinate, when all you want to do is add a new field, track down a particular database column reference, or figure out a calculation that snakes from an asynchronous listener object to a UI component and back.

Probably the best way to illustrate what's needed from a good design is to start by looking at a really bad design, and examine why it's bad—or in this case, why it's a nightmare to write tests for. That's what we'll do in this chapter. The idea of this chapter and the next is to provide a set of design criteria to think about while doing detailed design, and while turning the design into code and tests.

■ **Caution** All of the "testing antipatterns" described in this chapter are based on the point of view of improving testability. There may well be other concerns that trump this particular concern—e.g., in massively parallel, high-performance computing applications, factors such as execution efficiency and memory usage have to trump class-level encapsulation. As with most considerations in software design, it's a case of weighing up what's most important for this project, and producing a design to match.

The Temple of Doom (aka The Code)

We've built this entire chapter around a single code example. We refer to that example as *The Temple of Doom*, because in it we've consolidated what we believe to be the ten worst antipatterns (or suicidal practices) that make unit testing really difficult. We've marked each of our suicidal practices with an image of Ixtab, the Mayan goddess of suicide:

10. The complex constructor

9. The stratospheric class hierarchy

8. The static hair-trigger

7. Static methods and variables

6. The Singleton design pattern

5. The tightly bound dependency

4. Business logic in the UI code

3. Privates on parade

2. Service objects that are declared final

1. Half-baked features from the Good Deed Coder

All of these (very common) code constructs make your code difficult to unit-test. We're going to present a Java class implementing all ten at once, so brace yourselves for the big blob of bloated bleariness.

First we'll show you the code. Then we'll look at each antipattern in detail, explaining the problems it causes. Then, in Chapter 10, we'll introduce you to some design principles that facilitate good testing.

■ **Note** An honorable mention goes to the evil `equals()` method. You'll occasionally see an `equals()` method that has been hogged by a programmer and put into use as something that isn't really a test for equality. As well as breaking the Java contract for `equals()`, such a practice can make it difficult to do `assertEquals(..)` types of tests, as the results from those may be unpredictable.

The Big Picture

It's certainly not immediately obvious from looking at the code (which we'll get to very soon), but the rather dysfunctional example in this chapter is intended to be a price calculator that finds specific hotels in a database and then calculates how much it would cost to stay at that hotel for 'n' nights. The price may fluctuate (admittedly not as much as, say, a Forex price feed), but the coders saw fit to add in a live "hotel price streamer." This streamer listens to an external price streaming service, and feeds the results back into the hotel price calculator.

To map things out a little and provide a "big picture," Figure 9–1 shows a UML class diagram with all of the classes and their tangle of relationships. We're sure you've felt that moment of creeping dread when you know that you're about to dive into a particularly nasty area of legacy code, like plunging into a black tunnel, a deep crypt where untold horrors may lurk. It's because of this feeling that we refer to the code in this chapter as the "Temple of Doom."

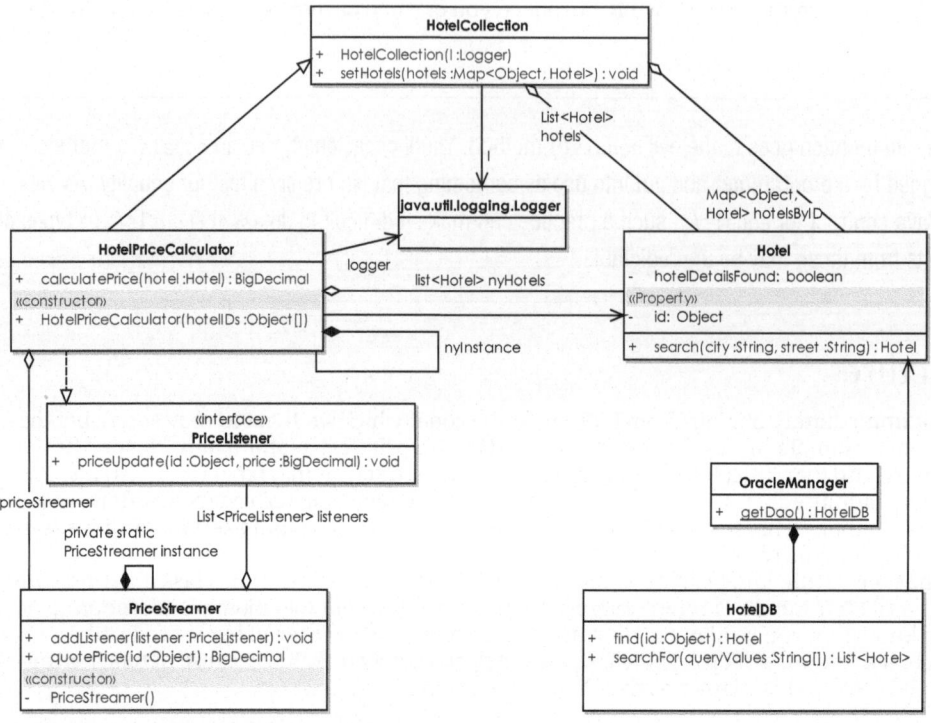

Figure 9–1. Dare you enter the Temple of Doom?

Over the next few pages we lay out all of the "Temple of Doom" in its inglorious horror. If you see code swimming before your eyes, feel free to skip this section—it's mainly just there for the "shock factor" anyway—as we'll present the relevant snippets of the code as we explore each antipattern.

So duck under your adventurer's fedora hat and take a swig from your authentic stitched-camelhide water bottle, as you enter the Temple of Doom (if you dare), where programmers were sacrificed to Quetzalcoatl, the ancient Mayan god of refactoring.

The HotelPriceCalculator Class

As you step trepidatiously into the outer crypt of this legacy hellhole, rays of sunlight from the crumbling doorway play across the main class, HotelPriceCalculator. Here's the code for the class:

```
package com.softwarereality.nottherealmapplet;

import java.math.BigDecimal;
import java.util.*;
import java.util.logging.*;

public class HotelPriceCalculator
    extends HotelCollection
```

```
implements PriceListener {

static Logger logger;
static final HotelPriceCalculator nyInstance =
    new HotelPriceCalculator(null);
final PriceStreamer priceStreamer = PriceStreamer.getInstance();
static List<Hotel> nyHotels;

static {
    try {
        logger = Logger.getLogger("not.the.real.mapplet");
        PriceStreamer.getInstance().addListener(nyInstance);
        nyHotels = ((HotelDB) OracleManager.getDao(HotelDB.class)).searchFor("New York");
    } catch (Exception e) {
        // fail silently
    }
}

public HotelPriceCalculator(Object ... hotelIDs) {
    super(logger);
    try {
        PriceStreamer.getInstance().addListener(this);

        // many lines of code to load up a list of Hotels from the DB:
        Map<Object, Hotel> hotelsByID = new HashMap<Object, Hotel>(hotelIDs.length);
        DAO db = OracleManager.getDao(HotelDB.class);
        for (Object id : hotelIDs) {
            Hotel hotel = (Hotel) db.find(id);
            hotelsByID.put(id, hotel);
        }
        super.setHotels(hotelsByID);

    } catch (Exception e) {
        logger.log(Level.SEVERE, "Error initialising", e);
    }
}

public BigDecimal calculatePrice(Hotel hotel, int numNights) {
    Object id = hotel.getId();
    BigDecimal pricePerNight = priceStreamer.quotePrice(id);
    return pricePerNight.multiply(new BigDecimal(numNights));
}

// "Just in case" code - why 5 nights? Uncompleted task?
// Programmer's thought in progress?[1] Bad dream?
public void priceUpdate(Object id, BigDecimal price) {
    try {
        DAO db = OracleManager.getDao(HotelDB.class);
```

---

[1] "Remember to bring chips and salsa to the standup meeting tomorrow..."

```
            Hotel hotel = (Hotel) db.find(id);
            calculatePrice(hotel, 5);
        } catch (Exception e) {
            logger.log(Level.SEVERE, "Error updating hotel price", e);
        }
    }
}
```

Supporting Classes

Going deeper into the mostly silent crypts, pausing only to wonder if that was the ghostly sound of a centuries-old sacrificial victim, or just the wind blowing through the oppressive tunnel, you peer through the flickering torchlight at HotelPriceCalculator's parent class, HotelCollection:

```
public class HotelCollection {

    private Logger l;
    private List<Hotel> hotels;
    Map<Object, Hotel> hotelsByID;

    public HotelCollection(Logger l) {
        this.l = l;
    }

    public void setHotels(Map<Object, Hotel> hotelsByID) {
        this.hotelsByID = hotelsByID;
        this.hotels = new ArrayList<Hotel>(hotelsByID.values());
    }
}
```

You'll see the next class, Hotel, used quite a bit throughout the code. It's rather central to the code's operations, though you wouldn't think so by looking at it. For such an important class, there's not very much to it, but here it is:

```
public class Hotel {

    private boolean hotelDetailsFound;
    private Object id;

    public Hotel() {}

    public Hotel(Object id) {
        this.id = id;
    }

    public void setId(Object id) { this.id = id; }
    public Object getId() { return id; }

    public static Hotel search(String city, String street) {
        try {
            List<Hotel> foundList = OracleManager.getDao().searchFor(city, street);
            if (foundList.size() == 0) {
                Hotel notFound = new Hotel();
                notFound.hotelDetailsFound = false;
```

```
                    return notFound;
                }
                Hotel found = foundList.get(0);
                found.hotelDetailsFound = true;
                return found;

        } catch (Exception e) {
            e.printStackTrace();
            return null;
        }
    }
}
```

Service Classes

You're now in the deeper tunnels, ancient crypts that stretch for miles beneath the ground. Everything down here is covered in thick layers of dust, where code has lain undisturbed for centuries. These dense, horrific classes are "services," non-glamorous plumbing code that nonetheless holds everything together and makes the "star performers," well, perform. It's strange, then, how often service classes like these are relegated to the darkest recesses of the project and given the least amount of design consideration—you'll often find a complete lack of object-orientation in them—thus they're extremely difficult to unit-test, even though there's a significant amount of functionality hidden away down here.

Following is the PriceStreamer class, which listens for price updates and notifies any interested listeners when an update arrives:

```
public final class PriceStreamer {

    private static PriceStreamer instance = null;

    private List<PriceListener> listeners =
                        new ArrayList<PriceListener>();
    private Map<Object, BigDecimal> livePricesByID =
                        new HashMap<Object, BigDecimal>();

    private PriceStreamer() {}

    static public synchronized PriceStreamer getInstance() {
        if (instance == null) {
            instance = new PriceStreamer();
        }
        return instance;
    }

    public void addListener(PriceListener listener) {
        listeners.add(listener);
    }

    /**
     * A price has come streaming in from outside.
     */
    public void update(Object id, BigDecimal price) {
        livePricesByID.put(id, price);
```

```
        // notify all listeners:
        for (PriceListener l : listeners) {
            l.priceUpdate(id, price);
        }
    }

    public BigDecimal quotePrice(Object id) {
        return livePricesByID.get(id);
    }
}
```

The OracleManager seems fairly generic from the name; but, as you can see, it's tightly bound to the business domain concept of hotels, with a HotelDB DAO (Data Access Object). Here's the code behind OracleManager:

```
public class OracleManager {

    static {
        // some trigger-happy code that
        // kick-starts a connection pool
        // with the database... (Omitted from this example)
    }

    // Tightly bound dependency:
    public static HotelDB getDao() throws Exception {
        return new HotelDB();
    }
}
```

HotelDB itself is intended to be a class that directly queries the database to return Hotel instances. In outline, it's like this (as with OracleManager before it, we've omitted the actual database access code to keep the example under control):

```
public class HotelDB {

    public Object find(Object id) throws Exception {
        return new Hotel();
    }

    public List<Hotel> searchFor(String ... queryValues) {
        // "Real" database access code
        // would be on or near this line…
        return new ArrayList<Hotel>();
    }
}
```

And that's the sum total of the code for this chapter. We'll now rewind a bit, and look at the brick walls (or sacrificial temple walls, rather) that we would hit, were we to try adding unit tests to this code.

The Antipatterns

The "anti" in our term "antipattern" refers to being "anti–unit test," as each pattern makes it difficult to cover the code with a unit test. As you'll see, all ten of our "top ten antipatterns" are to be found lurking in the example code. Let's step through them one by one, and examine why they're so problematic.

 ## 10. The Complex Constructor

The most common antipattern by far must surely be the complex constructor. The following code snippet should look familiar, but should also send shivers down your spine:

```
public HotelPriceCalculator(Object ... hotelIDs) {
    super(logger);
    try {
        PriceStreamer.getInstance().addListener(this);

        // many lines of code to load up a list of Hotels from the DB:
        Map<Object, Hotel> hotelsByID = new HashMap<Object, Hotel>(hotelIDs.length);
        DAO db = OracleManager.getDao(HotelDB.class);
        for (Object id : hotelIDs) {
            Hotel hotel = (Hotel) db.find(id);
            hotelsByID.put(id, hotel);
        }
        super.setHotels(hotelsByID);

    } catch (Exception e) {
        logger.log(Level.SEVERE, "Error initialising", e);
    }
}
```

Figure 9–2 shows the dependencies that HotelPriceCalculator has already built up, simply from its constructor code.

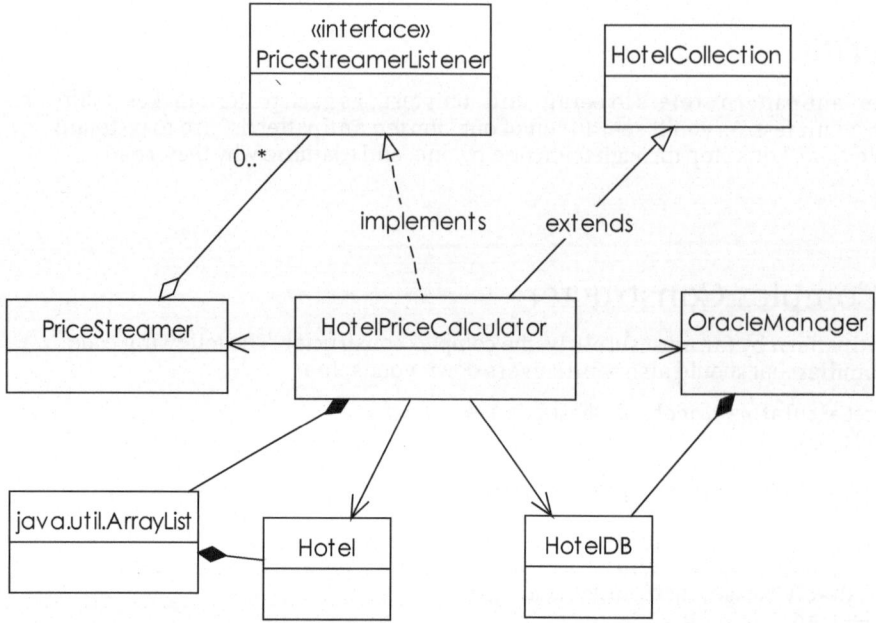

Figure 9–2. *All that baggage, and we haven't even used the new object yet...*

This code probably works fine for its originally intended purpose (although there may be issues, both insidious and not-so-subtle, as you'll see in a moment). But it's inherently rigid code: as soon as you want to do something even slightly different from the original purpose—like, hey, add some unit tests—things get *very* tricky *very* quickly.

As an example of the problem, let's start to write a JUnit test for the HotelPriceCalculator class:

```
HotelPriceCalculator priceCalc;
String[] hotelIDs = {"1234"};

@Before
public void setUp() {
    priceCalc = new HotelPriceCalculator(hotelIDs);
}
```

Before you even get to the test code, there are problems. Simply calling the constructor is going to result in the following:

- A listener being added to an external price streaming service

- A HashMap being created

- An external database connection being made, and a query run against the database

- A super() call being made to the parent constructor—the adventure continues. Who knows what additional initializing code might be run in the parent class, which might be completely irrelevant to this particular test?

This all-encompassing initialization work slows the test down, but it also makes the test suite brittle. What if neither the price streaming service nor the database is available? Or someone changes the test data? The data would be external to the build/test environment so probably not under the programmer's total control. This is a particular problem when the unit tests are run as part of the build (which you would generally want); "Service not available" should not count as a build error. Remember that unit tests are meant to be insular: they're testing a unit, a packet of functionality, rather than the outside world. (There are other, end-to-end integration tests for that purpose, but that's a different story.)[2]

We're sure you've seen constructor code that stretches on for screen after screen, hundreds of lines in length. As you probably noticed, this is not just bad for unit testing—it's also poor design generally: not at all OO. Where's the encapsulation? Where's the splitting out of functionality into separate methods and classes?

9. The Stratospheric Class Hierarchy

You've gone to all the effort of removing the complex initialization code from the constructor. But HotelPriceCalculator isn't just a nice, independent entity; it has an embarrassing parent who's decided to tag along to the party. And who knows what's going on in that parent constructor?

A subtle detail from the previous example was that HotelPriceCalculator extends HotelCollection (a collection of Hotels with added behavior)—see Figure 9–3.

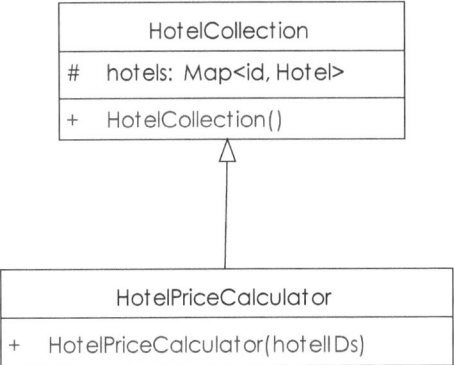

Figure 9–3. Based on true events—only the names have been changed to protect the giddy...

---

[2] One that we tell in Chapter 11...

■ **Note** A two-class hierarchy isn't quite stratospheric, but we've seen real-life class hierarchies six or seven classes deep… with proud comments from the original programmer as if his or her teetering complexity-magnet was a good idea!

Let's set aside for a moment the dubious design decision that might have led to a price calculator extending a HotelCollection, and peek ahead to the fixed-up HotelPriceCalculator constructor (see Chapter 10):

```
public HotelPriceCalculator(Object ... hotelIDs) {
    this.hotelIDs = hotelIDs;
}
```

The parent class, HotelCollection, has a no-arg constructor. In Java, no-arg constructors are called automatically if there are no other constructors available; so if there are subclasses, this sets off a chain reaction moving up the class hierarchy, with each parent constructor called in turn. In the case of HotelPriceCalculator, its parent's HotelCollection constructor will be called first—even though it isn't explicitly invoked in the code. So if there's further complex initialization code up there, then there's even more to potentially go wrong before we have a fully constructed object.

Of course, you can give the same treatment to the superclass as you did for HotelPriceCalculator earlier in this chapter: separate the complex initialization code into separate methods. But then things get complicated, as the order in which the methods are called might be important. Worse, there may be other child classes derived from the parent, which could break if you start messing with the constructor.

This is, of course, why legacy code can be a nightmare to unit-test: it's often impossible to simply change one piece of code, as there's always a hanger-on somewhere that's also affected.

It gets even worse when there's also a superclass above the superclass (and so on up, like fleas teetering on other fleas' backs). It could just be us, but it seems like the number of classes in an inheritance hierarchy is directly proportional to the turnover of programmers in a project. The more coders that have been let loose on a spaghetti plate of code, the taller the class structures will be, like some warped version of the Dubai skyline, or a demonic cluster of towering edifices from one of H. P. Lovecraft's most disturbing nightmares.

■ **Note** Occasionally a deep class hierarchy may be unavoidable, e.g., when using an off-the-shelf OO framework. In such cases, it's reasonable to make an exception and run with it, assuming the framework itself is robust and tested.

If you have the choice, don't even go there. Keep your class structures flat: use inheritance carefully and only where it makes sense. And (as we explore in the next chapter), *create a domain model* first. Keep it simple, and your code will be both easily unit-tested and easily modified.

8. The Static Hair-Trigger

One of the most common antipatterns—in fact, a whole nest of the little critters—tends to involve static code (that is, code at the class level rather than the object level... static methods and variables, static initializer blocks, the Singleton pattern...) These can all make unit testing a real nightmare—to the point where many programmers give up, declaring unit testing to be too difficult, more trouble than it's worth.

The static initializer block, or "static hair-trigger," is our favorite example of boneheadedness. In Java, the static initializer block is run automatically when a class is first loaded—this means when the class is first referenced, wherever (or by whomever) it's referenced. Here's an example from HotelPriceCalculator—the initializer block is the bit between the static { and } lines:

```
static Logger logger;
static final HotelPriceCalculator nyInstance =
    new HotelPriceCalculator(null);
final PriceStreamer priceStreamer = PriceStreamer.getInstance();
static List<Hotel> nyHotels;

static {
    try {
        logger = Logger.getLogger("not.the.real.mapplet");
        PriceStreamer.getInstance().addListener(nyInstance);
        nyHotels = ((HotelDB) OracleManager.getDao(HotelDB.class)).searchFor("New York");
    } catch (Exception e) {
        // fail silently
    }
}
```

So far, so scary. But let's start to write a unit test for HotelPriceCalculator. Remembering to keep our test-suite self-contained and quick-to-run by avoiding external calls and database connections, we write the following code:

```
public class HotelPriceCalculatorTest {

    HotelPriceCalculator calc;

    @Before
    public void setUp() throws Exception {
        Object[] hotelIDs = new Object[] {"123", "456"};
        calc = new HotelPriceCalculator(hotelIDs);
    }

    @After
    public void tearDown() throws Exception {
        calc = null;
    }
```

Before we even get as far as the first test method, there's a problem. Simply blinking or glancing at HotelPriceCalculator would cause the initializer code to run, creating external connections, loading database data, and so on. It causes something of a chain reaction: the HotelPriceCalculator static block refers to OracleManager, whose own static block is as follows (gory details omitted):

```
static {
    // some trigger-happy code that
```

```
        // kick-starts a connection pool
        // with the database...
}
```

This code in turn might reference another class, whose own complex static initialization code is thus triggered… and so on. It is, really, an even more vicious version of the complex constructor, and it massively limits the number of ways in which the class can be tested.

Figure 9–4 shows the chain reaction in graphical form. And all of that just because we wanted to get a copy of HotelPriceCalculator and test its price-calculating algorithm.

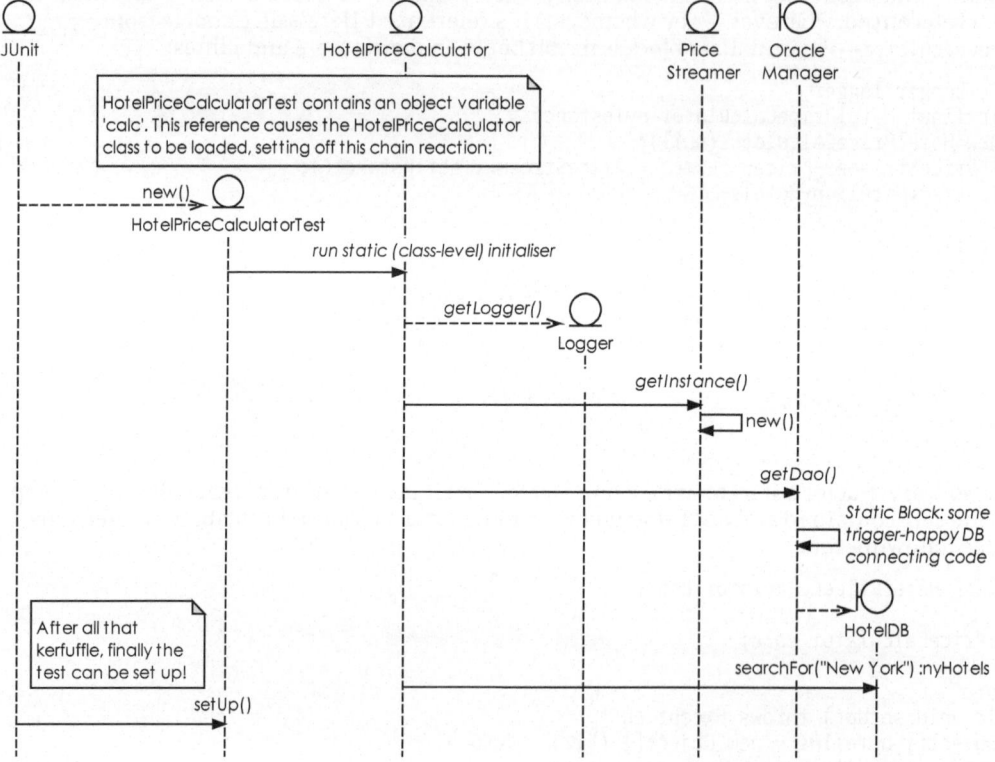

Figure 9–4. *A chain reaction (static method calls are shown in italics). And all we wanted to do was call* calc.calculatePrice()…

This antipattern is also bad form, stability-wise. Note the "fail silently" comment in the code fragment. That isn't fiction—we've seen examples of that many times in real code. But it also brings home a real problem with static initializer blocks: they are only ever run once, when the class is first loaded. If the initialization fails at run-time, the entire class is effectively "out of action" for the rest of the time the program runs. It would need a restart to get the class working again, even if the problem was just a momentary network glitch.

In Chapter 10 we present a better way of achieving what static initializer blocks tend to be trying to achieve, in the section "Avoid Using Static Initializer Blocks."

7. Static Methods and Variables

It's notable that Scala, a modern OO-functional hybrid that compiles to Java bytecode, has done away with static methods and members altogether. Instead, the closest it gets to static types is letting you define an entire class as a singleton. Scala is known for its pragmatic "take" on language design, effectively rebooting Java and throwing out all the bad bits. So it's significant that static members were among the parts that Martin Odersky, Scala's creator, chose to abandon.

Meanwhile, our HotelPriceCalculator has some static members:

```
static final HotelPriceCalculator nyInstance =
    new HotelPriceCalculator(null);
static List<Hotel> nyHotels;
```

(logger was also static, but we turned it into an object variable in the previous section.)

But why, you may ask, are static members such a problem when you're unit testing? Unit tests operate best when they're small and well-defined: lots of little test methods creating and destroying fixtures as needed, each test "proving" that one aspect of the implementation works as expected. For this to work well, the tests need the code under test to be self-contained, or encapsulated. Static members, if nothing else, break encapsulation across objects. You can see an example of this in the "Static Just Means Class-Level" sidebar earlier in this chapter.

Your small, self-contained unit tests also rely on being predictable: that is, each object under test beginning with the exact same state every time the test is run. However, if one of the variables under test happens to be static, then another test in the suite may get to it first and give it a different value, making the other test seem to break randomly.

Sure, you can get around this by remembering to set each static member with a specific value in the test's setup() method, but why leave it to chance? You end up setting different values to satisfy different tests, whereas the production system will be far less predictable, with different modules and threads going at it to restore the static member to a value it expects. This creates a situation where a passing test can't be trusted to mean "this code will also work in a production system."

Here is a summary of the problems with static members:

- They're not thread-safe.

- They break encapsulation.

- They're unpredictable.

For an example of how static members can be unpredictable, consider a unit test that passes with a "green bar." However, the same code may fail in production because some other class has set the static member to a different value.

To picture the problem, imagine a kitchen with 12 chefs. Over in one corner, a broth is boiling away in a shared saucepan. Chef 1 walks up and adds a dash of Tabasco sauce as he plans to pour the broth over his platter of devilled spare ribs, and returns satisfied to the meat station. Chef 2 wants the saucepan for his authentic Vietnamese eggplant, so he pours in a quart of mackerel sauce. Chef 3, whistling as he works, tips the contents away and replaces it with a pint of beef stock. Chef 4 turns the heat down because he wants the broth to be ready in sync with his entrée. Chef 5 turns up the heat because he needs the contents within the next 60 seconds. Chef 6 adds a turnip. And so on.

It's anyone's guess what will eventually come out of the saucepan. It's like Schrödinger's cat in 12 dimensions. And yet, for all of that, imagine if we ran a unit test for each chef. The tests would be along these lines:

1. Set up the test fixture: empty the saucepan and place it on a low flame.

2. Put the required ingredients in the saucepan.

3. Leave to simmer for the required time.

4. Let the chef pour out the result, and assert that the broth/beef stock/wild betel leaf garnish/turnip surprise tastes good.

All 12 tests, run individually and with pitch-perfect fixture setup, would pass just fine. But in the kitchen on a Saturday night, chaos ensues and the state of the finished dish is entirely non-deterministic. We return to this issue in Chapter 10, with a proposed solution.

The next antipattern continues the static theme, and should be familiar to just about every OO programmer on the planet.

 ## 6. The Singleton Design Pattern

Here's an example of a Singleton (capital S)[3]... pantomime fans should prepare to boo and hiss now:

```
public class PriceStreamer {
    private PriceStreamer instance = null;
    private PriceStreamer() {}
    static public synchronized PriceStreamer getInstance() {
        if (instance==null) {
            instance = new PriceStreamer();
        }
        return instance;
    }
}
```

This is possibly one of the most misused patterns in the history of both pantomimes and software design. Exactly why it's so popular escapes us. Perhaps it's because it's such a quick pattern to implement; yet it's rolled out automatically each time a "service" or "manager" type of class is needed. The role of a service or manager class is generally to be a central point of access for some function or other; but rarely does a service or manager genuinely need to be the only instance of its type in the whole system. There's a big difference between "need an object" and "must be the only object of this type in the whole system." In the first case, for the code's purposes it needs an instance of the class, so it creates one—fine and dandy. In the second case, the program would fail in some way if there were more than one instance. However, the second case is needed far less often than you might think.

■ **Note** More likely is that the code calls for a globally accessible object, one that it can go to without having to pass around and keep a reference to the object in every single other object that needs it.

---

[3] We distinguish between the Singleton design pattern, which closes off the constructor and uses a static getter method to restrict access to the one instance, and a "singleton," an object which has a genuine requirement to be the only one of its type.

When you're unit testing, you really want to just be able to create a throwaway instance of the object under test, test it, and then throw it away. The Singleton pattern makes this simple requirement impossible. To see why the Singleton is anathema to unit tests, let's look at an example:

```java
public class PriceStreamerTest {

    private PriceStreamer streamer;

    @Before
    public void setUp() throws Exception {
        streamer = PriceStreamer.getInstance();
    }

    @After
    public void tearDown() throws Exception {
        streamer = null;
    }
}
```

This should be a familiar pattern by now: we're setting up a test fixture—the PriceStreamer instance in this example. We can't get at the constructor because it's private, so we're forced to call the static PriceStreamer.getInstance() method. Then in tearDown(), which JUnit runs immediately after every test method, we clean up after the test. Unfortunately, simply setting our local copy of PriceStreamer to null doesn't achieve anything, as the instance still exists as a class member inside PriceStreamer itself. So the test is already pretty broken, before we've added any test code.

Let's go ahead and add a couple of test methods anyway, to see what happens.

```java
    @Test
    public void quotePrice_NoPriceYet() {
        BigDecimal noPriceYet = streamer.quotePrice("123");
        assertNull(noPriceYet);
    }

    @Test
    public void quotePrice_PriceAdded() {
        BigDecimal price = new BigDecimal(200.0);
        streamer.update("123", price);
        BigDecimal quote = streamer.quotePrice("123");
        assertEquals(price, quote);
    }
```

The first test checks that if no price has yet been sent to the PriceStreamer, then we get null if we ask for a quote. Then the second test adds a price (simulating an external price update being received), and attempts to get a quote. If we run this, we get a nice green bar... all good. However, something strange is going on behind the scenes. The first test (NoPriceYet) makes the assumption that we're starting with a clean test fixture—that is, an empty PriceStreamer with no tests added. Figure 9–5 shows what happens if these two test methods were to run in a different order.

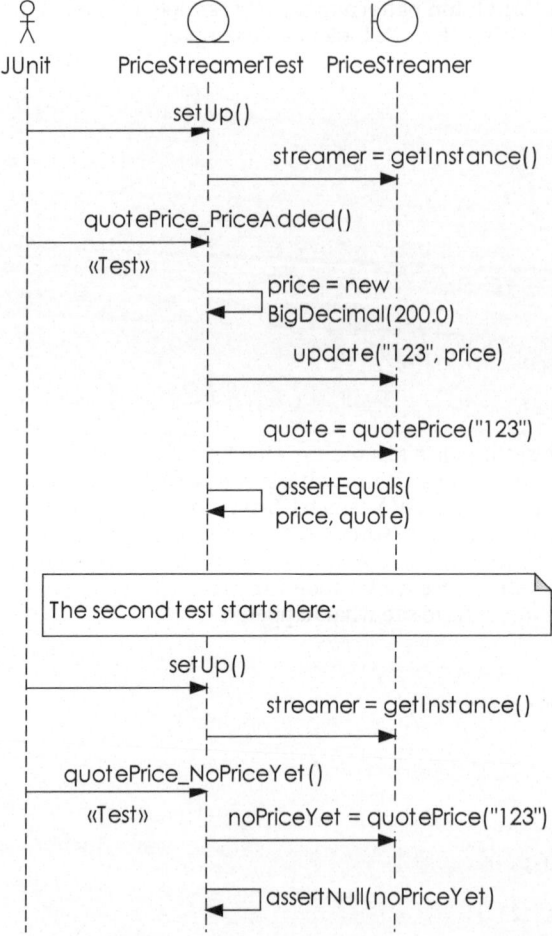

Figure 9–5. The first test spoils the fixture for the second test.

With PriceAdded being run first, we suddenly get an inexplicable test failure. This is simply because the same instance of PriceStreamer is being used for both tests. quotePrice_PriceAdded() adds a price to PriceStreamer, and then quotePrice_NoPriceYet() fails because it expects PriceStreamer to be empty.

Suddenly, we realize how fragile the test suite is, when simply rearranging the order that the tests are run can make them fail!

Given that you do sometimes want to ensure that a class is "single-instance only" when you're not unit testing, we present some better alternatives to the Singleton design pattern in Chapter 10.

5. The Tightly Bound Dependency

Often you'll see some code casually create (or fetch via a lookup) an instance of another class, and make use of it. There's nothing wrong with that, of course, as reusing other classes and objects is the "bread and butter" of object-oriented development. However, rampant use of this approach can sometimes lead to a tightly coupled design, where it's difficult or impossible to swap in a different instance, or even a new implementation. As well as making code difficult to extend, this also makes unit testing a bit of a chore.

The following code is really the heart of HotelPriceCalculator—it's the method that calculates the price to stay at a hotel for the specified number of nights:

```
public BigDecimal calculatePrice(Hotel hotel, int numNights) {
    Object id = hotel.getId();
    PriceStreamer streamer = (PriceStreamer)
SimpleRegistry.lookup.get(PriceStreamer.class);
    BigDecimal pricePerNight = streamer.quotePrice(id);
    return pricePerNight.multiply(new BigDecimal(numNights));
}
```

The code relies on a PriceStreamer having already received at least one price update for the hotel ID in question. Let's create a test for this important method and see what happens:

```
@Before
public void setUp() throws Exception {
    calc = new HotelPriceCalculator();
    calc.initPriceStreamer();
}

@Test
public void calculatePrice() throws Exception {
    Hotel hotel = new Hotel("123");

    // Give the PriceStreamer a price update:
    PriceStreamer streamer = new PriceStreamer();
    streamer.update("123", new BigDecimal(225.0));

    // Calculate the total price:
    BigDecimal price = calc.calculatePrice(hotel, 3);

    assertEquals(new BigDecimal(675.0), price);
}
```

By rights, this should be a perfect steal: an instant green bar, a ticket for home at 5 p.m. on the nose. But instead, running the test in Eclipse gives us the Red Bar of Grisly Stay-Late Misery (see Figure 9–6).

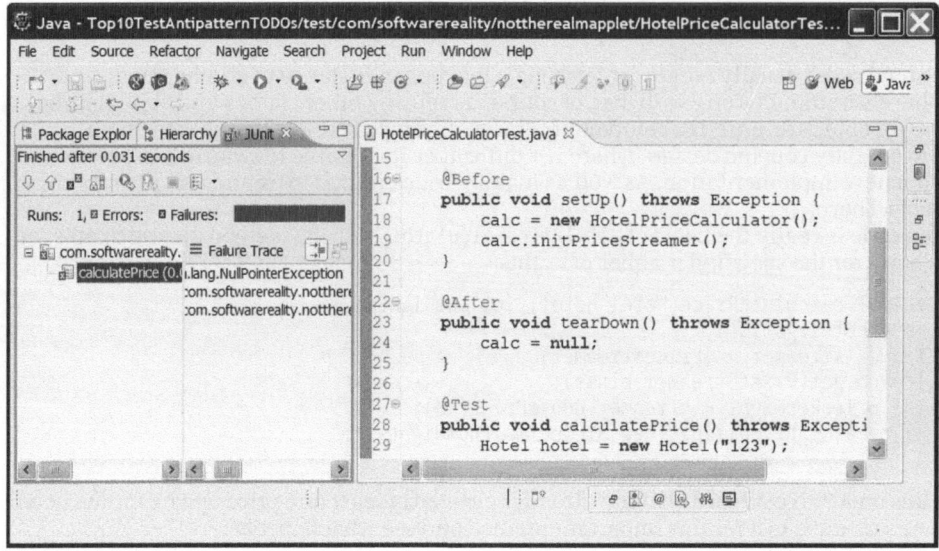

Figure 9–6. Red bar of "D'oh!"

As the screenshot shows, the red bar is due to a `NullPointerException`. Check the test method again… in that code we're creating our own `PriceStreamer` instance, but it isn't being passed in to `HotelPriceCalculator`. So we end up with two `PriceStreamers` (one in the test, one in `HotelPriceCalculator`), and the simulated price update that we send goes to the wrong one.

As you can see from the `calculatePrice()` method, the code looks up its copy of `PriceStreamer` from the `SimpleRegistry` that we created earlier in the chapter. A quick solution would be to make the test use `SimpleRegistry` itself… problem solved (kind of):

```
// Give the PriceStreamer a price update:
PriceStreamer streamer = (PriceStreamer)
        SimpleRegistry.lookup.get(PriceStreamer.class);
streamer.update("123", new BigDecimal(225.0));
```

Running this gives us a nice green bar, which, in a "Shangri-La" type of world, would indicate that all's well. But, for the same reasons that we discussed earlier, this isn't ideal. It's a fragile test, relying on a static (i.e., system-wide) field inside `SimpleRegistry`, which we hope (but can't guarantee) won't be modified elsewhere. The test passes today, but tomorrow it might fail because it's vulnerable to external changes.

Another issue—one that leads us neatly to the solution—is that the test we're writing is meant to be about `HotelPriceCalculator`, not about `PriceStreamer` (that gets its own set of tests). If the implementation of `PriceStreamer` changes, the `HotelPriceCalculator` tests might break in some way: so we're back to the issue of fragile tests. (Note that this isn't so much the case with behavioral tests and acceptance tests, as these types of tests are broader-grained and more about integration of classes and components.)

4. Business Logic in the UI Code

As the Mapplet UI code is all written using Flex, we'll switch to Adobe-land to illustrate the problem of business logic in the UI code. Figure 9–7 shows a screenshot of what we're trying to achieve: enter some search criteria such as hotel name and number of nights, and click Search. The Flex app will make a call to the server-side code, which will do its overly complex, under-designed, over-engineered, Temple of Doom thing, and finally return some prices.

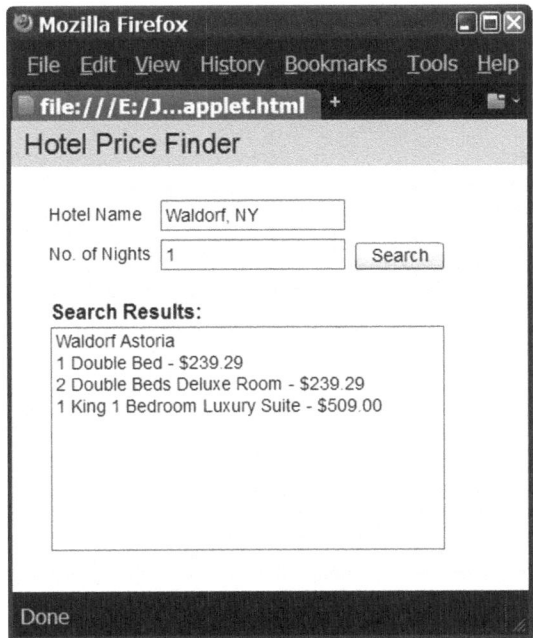

Figure 9–7. This front-end just wants to be loved… but there is ugliness behind the scenes.

Here's an excerpt from the Flex MXML mark-up:

```
<s:TextInput id="txtHotelName" />
<s:TextInput id="txtNights" />

<s:TextArea id="txtResults" text="{results}" editable="false" />
<s:Button label="Search" id="btnSearch" click="btnSearch_clickHandler(event)"/>

<fx:Script>
    <![CDATA[
        import mx.controls.Alert;

        [Bindable]
        private var results:String = "";

        protected function btnSearch_clickHandler(event:MouseEvent):void
```

```
            {
                // Perform validation before submitting the search:

                if (txtHotelName.text.length==0)
                {
                    Alert.show("Please enter a hotel name", "Hotel Name Required");
                }
                else if (txtNights.text.length==0)
                {
                    Alert.show("Please enter the number of nights", "Number of Nights
Required");
                }

                // Create a hotelSearch object and populate it from the input fields:

                var hotelSearch: Object = new Object();
                hotelSearch.hotelName = txtHotelName.text;
                hotelSearch.numNights = txtNights.text;

                // (code omitted) - call the Java PriceCalculator service,
                // and populate 'results' var with the result.

            }

        ]]>
    </fx:Script>
```

When the user clicks the "Search" button, the click handler method is called. This performs some validation on the input fields, then creates a hotelSearch object, and sends this along to the remote Java service. That all seems fine so far; but what if we want to create a unit test for the validation? Or, what if the customer wants something else to be done to the search fields before they're submitted—e.g., allow "number of nights" to be blank, in which case substitute the value 1 (i.e, default to a one-night search)? The additional code could go into the MXML mark-up shown here. However, the code is becoming less and less object-oriented. All that behavior, and no object to put it in.[4]

The validation really belongs in a HotelSearch class. We'll show how to fix this up in Chapter 10.

 ## 3. Privates on Parade

Private methods and members are the bane of a unit tester's life, as the test doesn't have access to them. This isn't as bad of a problem with DDT as it is with TDD, as DDT takes a more "gray box" approach, and doesn't assume a need to know the internals of every line and field within the class under test. However, it still can be an issue:

```
public class Hotel {
    private boolean hotelDetailsFound;
    . . .
```

---

[4] "Just stuff everything into the MXML" seems to be a pretty typical Flex design pattern, unfortunately.

}

Let's say you've written a hotel search test, and you want to assert that the object under test correctly flags that the hotel search was successful:

```
@Test
public void hotelFoundFlagIsSet() throws Exception {
    Hotel hotel = new Hotel();
    hotel.search("New York", "541 Madison Avenue");
    assertTrue("Hotel was found", hotel.hotelDetailsFound);
}
```

The code in bold text won't compile, because hotelDetailsFound is private, so the test can't gain access to it. There's more than one possible solution to this issue, with varying degrees of attractiveness. Like a page from www.AmIHotOrNot.com, vote on your favorite solution in Chapter 10, in the section "Use Black Box Testing So You Don't Have to Break Encapsulation."

2. Service Objects That Are Declared Final

With Java, fields that are declared final are immutable (note this doesn't mean that values inside the referenced object are immutable; just the reference to the object). Because they're final, it makes sense that they will be initialized as part of the declaration:

```
final String url = "http://articles.softwarereality.com";
final PriceStreamer priceStreamer = new PriceStreamer();
```

The first line is an example of a simple value that you want to remain constant, whereas the second line is an example of a complex object, or *service object*, that performs some task or other for the class under test.

"Simple value" fields that are declared final can generally be considered "a good thing" for the purposes of software quality. You know exactly what you're getting; you don't have to worry about multi-threading issues (e.g., one thread reading the field while another thread is modifying its value; or the race condition where two threads are updating a field, hence one value is lost). However, in the case of service objects, there are occasions when a final member can really put a dampener on a unit test's day.

1. Half-Baked Features from the Good Deed Coder

The just-in-case malady is the bane of developers everywhere, not just those wielding a JUnit test class. It's an insidious antipattern because it's born entirely of good intentions. "I'll make this class reusable *(read: "I'll make this class more complex than it needs to be")* just in case someone will need to use it later." The result, especially when this "good deed" happens at the coding stage and not at the design or analysis stage, is that the code can't be traced back to a particular business requirement. So when you're maintaining some mystery code—whether to apply unit tests to it, or extend it with new functionality, or refactor a crusty design—it can be difficult to determine whether the code even needs to be there. If the code is simply deleted, will something else in the system mysteriously stop working? It's impossible to say, as it isn't covered by a test or linked back to a requirement.

Summary

In this chapter we looked at a number of common "suicidally bad" antipatterns in software design, which make your code much harder to unit-test, and which, in some cases (e.g., static initializers and complex constructors), also happen to generally make software less stable and less maintainable. As we mentioned at the start, testability isn't the "be-all and end-all" of software design, and is just one (admittedly important) consideration to be weighed up among many. But from the point of view of a developer trying to write unit tests, the problems described in this chapter will make that developer's life *really* difficult.

In the next chapter, we'll transform the top ten antipatterns into a list of design guidelines, the top ten "to-do" items.

CHAPTER 10

■ ■ ■

Design for Easier Testing

In this chapter we emerge from the Temple of Doom to find the sun shining brightly and the water a lovely shade of turquoise...[1]

    If you've just finished reading Chapter 9, you should now be feeling utterly deflated and at a loss for the sanity of the programming world, to the point where even standing up to make a cup of tea feels like too much effort. So let us lift your spirits with the inverse of the Temple of Doom code base from Chapter 9. In this chapter we'll sweep away the difficult-to-test code and start over with a solid use case, a design, and a clear goal for the finished product. We hope you appreciate the difference, and

---

[1] You may have to take our word for the turquoise part... or, alternatively, check out the original image, along with more of Doug's photography from Tulum and Cancun (including 360-degree virtual tours), at www.vresorts.com/VRPages/Cancun/Cancun.html.

that within a few pages you'll feel sufficiently uplifted to make that cup of tea. (Whoever said that software development isn't an emotional rollercoaster ride?)

In a moment we'll present the top ten "Design For Testing" to-do list; the bulk of the chapter will be structured around these (just as Chapter 9 was structured around the "don'ts"). However—and this is really the key to easier testing—before we get started on the design, we'll start with a use case. By having a clear idea of what the finished product is meant to do, we'll know exactly what we want to achieve from the design. So if there's any doubt about whether a feature or design element should be included, we can ask: "Is it within the scope of our use case?"

Top Ten "Design for Testing" To-Do List

The following list is really the flipside of the top ten unit testing antipatterns (or "don'ts") from Chapter 9. If you keep the following design criteria in mind while creating a detailed design (see the next chapter), your design will be more amenable to unit testing (and also more pliant, easier to understand and maintain, and more likely to be picked up and used while the code is being cut):

10. **Keep initialization code out of the constructor.**
    Instead, create a separate initialize() method, to allow the object to be fully constructed before it starts strutting its stuff.

9. **Use inheritance sparingly.**
   Use inheritance sparingly, and only if it absolutely makes sense to use it. Instead, as a general guideline (but not an all-out rule) use aggregation instead. Use inheritance when you are adding behavior that directly manipulates private data and can do so with minimal dependence on other objects; use aggregation otherwise.

8. **Avoid using static initializer blocks.**
   A static initialization block is a block of code that gets run the moment a class is loaded into memory—so the code will be run the first time a class is referenced, even in an unassigned variable, by some other class. This is why we refer to these static initialization blocks as "static hair triggers."

7. **Use object-level methods and variables instead of static (class-level) methods and variables.**

   This rule holds true unless the variable in question is immutable and (if it's a complex object) has immutable data and little or no construction code.

6. **Use a Registry or some other pattern instead of the Singleton design pattern.**
   While singletons themselves are sometimes necessary, the Singleton design pattern itself has its problems, not least of which is that it makes unit testing difficult. Instead use a Registry class, or whatever mechanism fits your project, to access single instances. Also, question the need for a singleton: does the object in question really need to be the only instance in the system?

5. **Keep your classes as decoupled as the application permits.**
   Avoid tying your code too tightly to dependent implementations. Instead, allow callers to pass in their own implementation. In other words, "future-proof" your code (and make testing easier) by keeping it free of assumptions about how it'll be used. (That said, sometimes there are legitimate object collaborations driven by the application functionality, e.g., where a class delegates core functions that more properly belong to it.)

4. **Keep business logic out of the UI code.**

3. **Use "Black Box" and "Gray Box" testing so you don't have to break encapsulation.**
   Unit tests often need to know about the internals of a class or method in order to perform assertions. While this is sometimes unavoidable, it's a shame to have to break encapsulation in order for a class to be tested. Avoid the issue by writing controller tests first (which are "gray box" in nature), and use unit tests sparingly to fill in the gaps.

2. **With variable declarations, reserve the "final" modifier for constants. Generally avoid marking complex types such as service objects as final.**

1. **Always stick to what's been specified in the use cases and the design.**
   Don't be tempted to add complicating features such as extension frameworks "just in case" they'll be needed later… because the chances are that they won't.

There's also a "but above all else" list, which goes like this:

1. Start by understanding the requirements.

2. Create a domain model and keep on adding to it whenever you discover new domain objects.

3. Analyze the requirements by breaking them down into use cases.

4. Do a conceptual design (robustness analysis).

5. Know exactly which controller tests you're going to write—along with the inputs and acceptance criteria—before you do your detailed design (and definitely before you begin coding).

6. Spend time on the detailed design, preferably with more than one person involved, and definitely involving the people who will be writing the code.

The Temple of Doom—Thoroughly Expurgated

To render the Temple of Doom "design" (we hesitate to call it that) rigorously scrubbed-up, wiped down, demolished and rebuilt with reuse and testability in mind, we need to go back to basics… start with a use case, analyze it, create a design, and so forth. So, in "capsule summary" form, that's what we'll do in this chapter. Our effort actually forms a useful exercise in retrospectively looking at some legacy code and rethinking it so that unit tests can be added.

The Use Case—Figuring Out What We Want to Do

First, then, the use case. The core of the Temple of Doom code was unmistakably the `HotelPriceCalculator` class. So the use case should have to do with displaying the price for a hotel. This use case kicks into action immediately after the user has searched for a hotel. Here's a description of the use case in text form:

Use Case: Quote Hotel Price
BASIC COURSE:
The system displays the Hotel Details page. The user types in the number of nights he would like to stay for, and clicks the Calculate button. The system calculates the price based on the cost per night, and displays the result.

ALTERNATE COURSES:
(As this is just a quick capsule summary, we won't delve into the alternate courses. See Chapter 6 for a more complete example.)

Figure 10–1 shows the robustness diagram to accompany this use case.

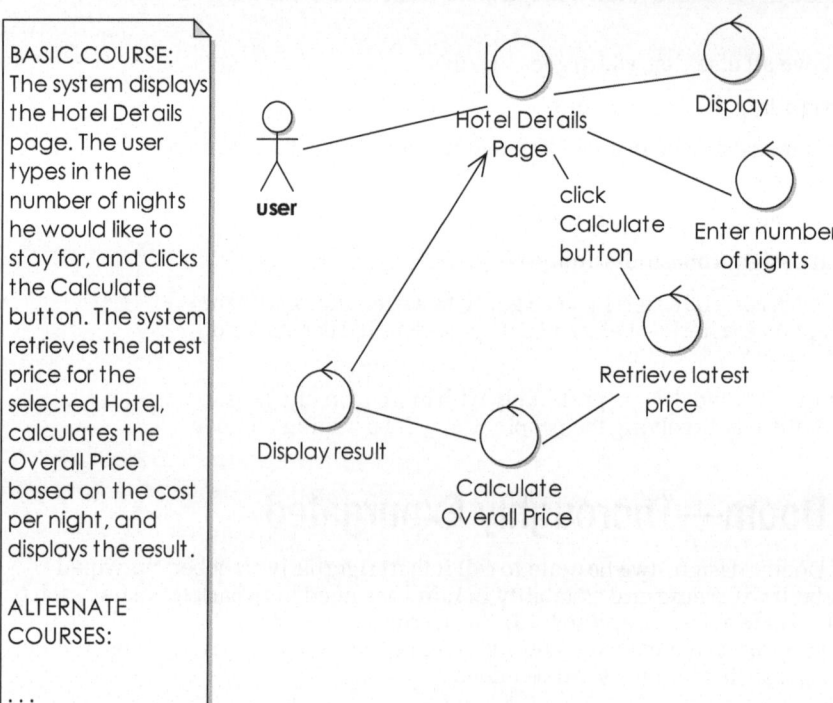

BASIC COURSE:
The system displays the Hotel Details page. The user types in the number of nights he would like to stay for, and clicks the Calculate button. The system retrieves the latest price for the selected Hotel, calculates the Overall Price based on the cost per night, and displays the result.

ALTERNATE COURSES:

...

***Figure 10–1.** Rethinking the Temple of Doom—robustness diagram, Part 1*

Here's where we immediately start to see a benefit of going back to the use case, and doing some simple analysis work. Looking at the diagram, the `Retrieve latest price` controller looks a bit lonely. That loneliness begs the question, "Where's the controller actually getting the latest price from?" In the legacy code[2] from the start of this chapter, there's the puzzling presence of a hotel price streamer. As we commented at the time, this would be more in place within a financial app. We kept it around "just in case" it really is needed. But now that we have a use case to refer to, it's obvious that there's no place for streaming price updates here. We simply need a way of querying and fetching a live price for the hotel in question.

Figure 10–2 shows the revised use case description and robustness diagram. Already, you just know the end result will be simpler and more focused, as we won't have to worry about unnecessary streaming price updates, and all the associated plumbing code.

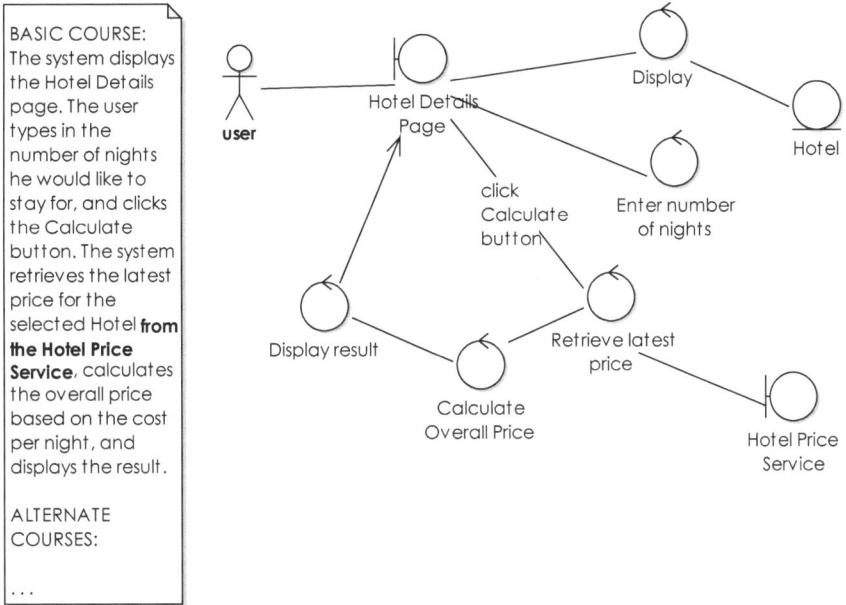

BASIC COURSE:
The system displays the Hotel Details page. The user types in the number of nights he would like to stay for, and clicks the Calculate button. The system retrieves the latest price for the selected Hotel **from the Hotel Price Service**, calculates the overall price based on the cost per night, and displays the result.

ALTERNATE COURSES:

. . .

Figure 10–2. Rethinking the Temple of Doom—robustness diagram, now magic-free

---

[2] When applying this technique to your own project, you can safely start to call the original code "legacy code," because it's being revisited with an eye towards refactoring it (even totally replacing parts of it). This change in stance has a remarkable psychological effect, producing a much-needed objectivity towards the code. Whereas you may have been wary of changing or ripping out old, established parts of the code base, suddenly you'll find that you're not wary of changing the code anymore. By creating use cases and talking to the business users, you know what the code is really meant to be doing, so there's less danger of accidentally removing needed functionality. The controller tests, when you add them, will make it safer still to go at the legacy code with a finely honed machete.

Identify the Controller Tests

We're now well positioned to identify the controller tests, based on the robustness diagram in Figure 10–2. As we stated earlier, ours is just a quick example, so we're not delving into alternate courses (which is really where you see some major benefits from controller testing). So with that in mind, let's next use EA to generate the test cases for our robustness diagram (see Figure 10–3). Remember that you want one test case per controller. Each test case starts out with a "Default Run Scenario," but you can add more scenarios as you think of them.

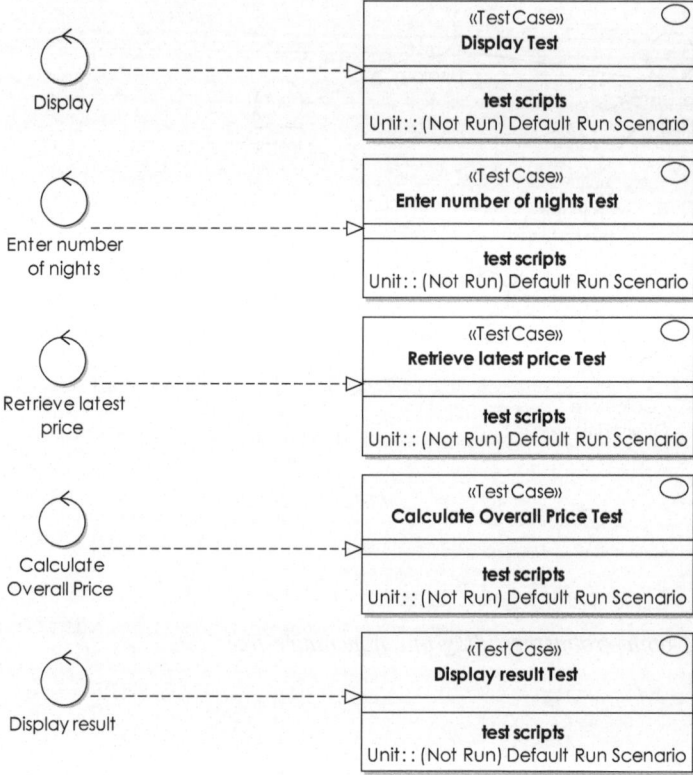

Figure 10–3. *Controller test cases for the Quote Hotel Price use case/robustness diagram*

You would expect to create tests for all of the controllers shown in Figure 10–3. However, for this chapter's example we'll focus on the *Calculate Overall Price* test case.

Calculate Overall Price Test

We construct a test to calculate the overall price. This test consists of just the one scenario, as shown in Table 10–1.

Table 10–1. Test Scenarios for the Calculate Overall Price Test Case

Test Scenario	Description	Input	Acceptance Criteria
Default run scenario	The system calculates the total price.	Price per night, Number of nights	The correctly calculated Overall Price should be returned.

We can now transform the test scenarios into a test class using the ICONIX/EA JUnit 4 transform, and generate the Java test class. We show this class in Figure 10–4.

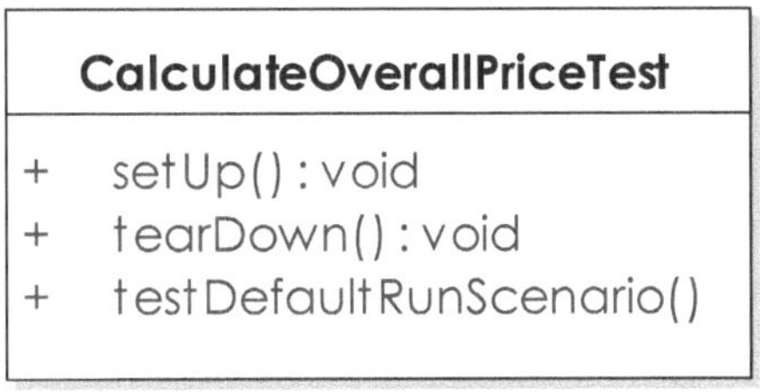

```
CalculateOverallPriceTest

+   setUp() : void
+   tearDown() : void
+   testDefaultRunScenario()
```

Figure 10–4. Our Java test class

The following is the code generated by EA, ready for us to fill in the gaps:

```java
public class CalculateOverallPriceTest {

    @Before
    public void setUp() throws Exception {
    }

    @After
    public void tearDown() throws Exception {
    }

    /**
     * The system calculates the total price.
     * @input Price per night, Number of nights
     * @AcceptanceCriteria The correctly calculated Overall Price should be returned.
     */
    @Test
    public void testDefaultRunScenario() throws Exception {
    }
}
```

This code gives us one test method (for this brief example). The method comments remind us that the test should provide two inputs (Price per night, and Number of nights), and then check that the returned Overall Price is correct.

Retrieve Latest Price Test

To recap (see the robustness diagram in Figure 10–2), the Retrieve Latest Price controller fetches the latest price for the current Hotel, then hands over to the Calculate Overall Price controller. Table 10–2 shows the one test scenario for Retrieve Latest Price.

Table 10–2. Test Scenarios for the Retrieve Latest Price Test Case

Test Scenario	Description	Input	Acceptance Criteria
Default run scenario	The system queries the Hotel Price Service for the current price per night.	The selected Hotel ID	The current price per night is returned.

As with CalculateOverallPriceTest, we can now transform this into a test class using the ICONIX/EA JUnit 4 transform, and generate the Java test class shown in Figure 10–5.

RetrieveLatestPriceTest
+   setUp() : void
+   tearDown() : void
+   testDefaultRunScenario()

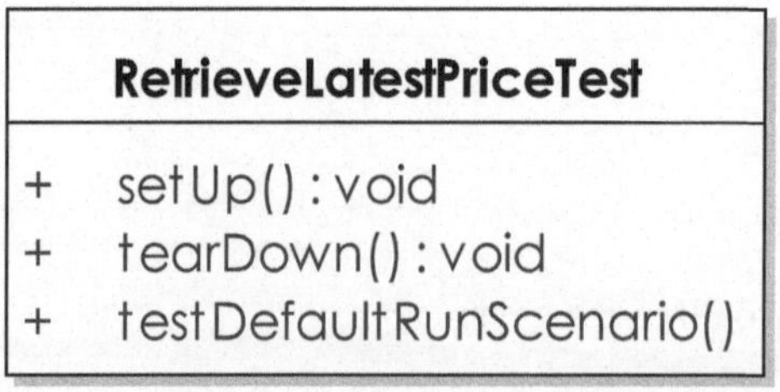

Figure 10–5. Test class to retrieve the latest price

The following is the test skeleton generated from the UML class shown in Figure 10–5:

```java
public class RetrieveLatestPriceTest {

    @Before
    public void setUp() throws Exception {
    }

    @After
    public void tearDown() throws Exception {
    }

    /**
     * The system queries the Hotel Price Service for the current price per night
     * @input The selected Hotel ID
     * @AcceptanceCriteria The current price per night is returned.
```

```
    */
    @Test
    public void testDefaultRunScenario() throws Exception {
    }
}
```

Design for Easier Testing

We've reached the detailed design stage, and the core of this chapter. So we'll now walk through the top ten "Design for Testing" to-do list. Each item in this list is really the flipside of the "don't" list in Chapter 9; therefore, each item is also a solution to a particular unit testing antipattern. So, **Don't #10**, "The Complex Constructor," is solved with **to-do item #10**, "Keep initialization code out of the constructor," and so on.

What you will find is that many of the problems solved here tend not to arise if you follow the ICONIX Process and DDT, e.g., allocating behavior to entity classes during sequence diagramming—essentially a domain-driven/responsibility-driven design approach. However, these coding problems are still well worth keeping in mind[3] (it's a case of "know your enemy").

10. Keep Initialization Code Out of the Constructor

Cast your mind back to the Complex Constructor antipattern described in Chapter 9. This antipattern led to all manner of problems, making HotelPriceCalculator difficult to test. So, what went wrong? Quite simply, the programmer confused object construction with object initialization. Constructing an object should be a simple case of setting any dependent objects that were passed in as arguments to the constructor. *Initializing* the object—doing further work to prepare it for use—is a different matter, and often involves complex code. This kind of code belongs in separate methods; lumping it all into the constructor isn't particularly OO.

In the case of HotelPriceCalculator, the perfect constructor, cutting out all of the initialization stuff, would be this:

```
public HotelPriceCalculator(Object ... hotelIDs) {
    this.hotelIDs = hotelIDs;
}
```

The only fly in the ointment here is that there's an implicit call to the superclass's no-arg constructor, so this constructor still may not be as straightforward as it looks—but more about that in the next section.

Of course, all of that object initialization that we've cut out still needs to take place. It might not have to take place for the particular test being run, but the product code will certainly need it to happen. You should end up seeing this sort of pattern:

```
HotelPriceCalculator priceCalc = new HotelPriceCalculator(hotelIDs);
priceCalc.initialize();
```

---

[3] It's shocking, we know, but we have actually heard of instances of programmers "going rogue" and deviating from the specified design.

Within initialize(), the very last thing it should do is hand out references to "this" (e.g., handing a reference to PriceStreamer). That way, you know the object's fully initialized before it starts advertising its existence to other objects. So the code, at this stage, should look something like this:

```
public void initialize() {
    // many lines of code to load up a list of items from the DB
    // many more lines of code to initialize some part of
    // HotelPriceCalculator that may or may not be needed
    PriceStreamer.getInstance().addListener(this);
}
```

From a unit testing perspective, the real benefit of separating construction from initialization is that it provides a breathing space, a chance to set mock services (e.g., a mock PriceStreamer or stubbed-out DB object), or even to choose not to call initialize() at all if it's not needed.

What if your test needs, say, the PriceStreamer listener to be added, but none of that other stuff? Easy, just split up the initialize() method:

```
public void initialize() {
    loadHotels();
    initOtherParts();
    theDreadedEtc();
    addExternalListeners();
}
```

Again, this is just good design: each method does one thing. But it also makes unit testing a whole lot easier, as your test's setUp() method can choose to avoid calling initialize() altogether, and instead simply call the init methods that it needs to—in this case, addExternalListeners().

9. Use Inheritance Sparingly

This to-do item solves antipattern #9, the Stratospheric Class Hierarchy. Whenever you encounter a teetering stack of inheriting classes, you'll almost always find that the reason for the inheritance is dubious at best. In the case of HotelPriceCalculator, it's highly questionable whether it needs to be a collection of Hotels at all. As you'll see later in this chapter, the reason for the class's existence—the calculatePrice() method—operates only on one Hotel at a time. In fact, it's only using the parent HotelCollection as a local cache of Hotel objects read in from the database. It's symptomatic of the kind of "design" that may have evolved without a clear picture of the overall system, or without any clear design thought whatsoever.

■ **Note** We should emphasize the ludicrousness of a HotelPriceCalculator being a type of HotelCollection. Of course, it doesn't make sense… and it's precisely the kind of error that's caught if you begin your project with some up-front domain modeling. In a collaborative activity, we're sure somebody in the group would have called out: "Hang on, how can a price calculator 'be' a collection of hotels?" Thus the error would have been caught early on, and a load of strife during design, coding, and testing would have been prevented. By now you've hopefully seen numerous discussions of domain modeling elsewhere in the book.

So a "quick fix" would be to make HotelPriceCalculator totally divorced from HotelCollection. But, as you might expect, the real answer is to return to the original use case—and if there wasn't one, write one now!—then do some conceptual design work based on the use case, write some controller tests, design the solution, fill in any remaining gaps with unit tests, and write the code. It's no surprise that the result will almost certainly be free of the majority of problems that we describe in this chapter.

We won't walk through this process right now (we're assuming you've digested Part 2 already), but let's say we arrived at the conclusion that HotelPriceCalculator is not a HotelCollection, but instead could simply have a HotelCollection (yes, it's that old "inheritance vs. aggregation" chestnut). Figure 10–6 shows an example of such a collection.

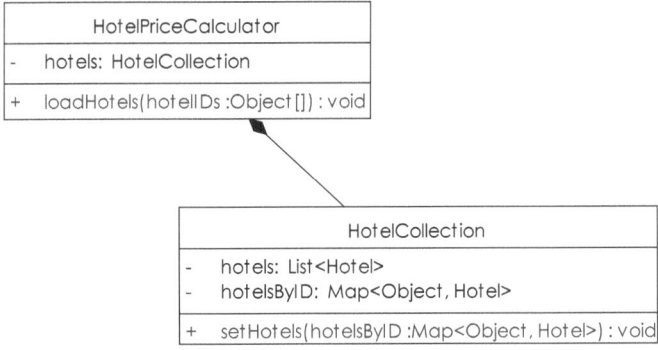

Figure 10–6. HotelPriceCalculator has a HotelCollection, but… why can't a Hotel calculate its own price?

There are some important changes in this class diagram: the most obvious one is, of course, that HotelPriceCalculator is no longer a type of HotelCollection, but instead contains one via its hotels attribute. Another change is that the array of hotel IDs is no longer passed into HotelPriceCalculator's constructor: instead, there's a loadHotels(hotelIDs) operation. The calling code can call this setup method if it needs HotelPriceCalculator to load some Hotels and populate its HotelCollection. But if (as is the case with our unit tests) it doesn't need that to happen, then the operation can be skipped altogether.

In fact, as you'll see later in this chapter when we get on to the detailed design for the "scrubbed-up" version, HotelPriceCalculator itself ends up not being needed at all. Instead, we put the behavior where the data lives—so the price calculating method ends up on Hotel.

8. Avoid Using Static Initializer Blocks

In Chapter 9 we talked about the perils of the static initializer block (or "static hair trigger"). Here is by far the best solution to this particular antipattern:

Just… don't do it!!

We could elaborate, but it really is as simple as that. Static hair triggers are evil incarnate, designed purely to give innocent programmers everywhere a hard time. Any code that's in the static block should just be moved to the initialize() method that we outlined earlier in this chapter. This simple action moves the static initialization to the object level, meaning it'll be run each time an object of that type is initialized. Most of the time, this is fine… e.g., our example has a static Logger. But does a logger really need to operate only at the class level?

Separating out the logger results in code that looks like this:

```
public class HotelPriceCalculator {
```

```
    Logger logger;

    public void initialize() {
        initLogger();
    }

    private void initLogger() {
        logger = Logger.getLogger("not.the.real.mapplet");
    }
}
```

There are, admittedly, rare cases when initialization code must be run only once in a program's lifetime. But in such cases, the static initializer block still isn't the answer, as we return to the question of error handling. In such cases, you'll need a more robust design that blocks during initialization, and throws an error if initialization failed.

7. Use Object-Level Methods and Variables

Remember the "too many chefs spoil the broth" problem from Chapter 9? The solution to the chef problem is, assuming that 11 of the chefs can't be fired, to give each one his or her own saucepan. Don't make use of static class-level methods and variables. Assign members to objects, not to classes.

Let's return to HotelPriceCalculator and its static members, nyInstance and nyHotels. These are both symptomatic of a dysfunctional design. Why on earth would a price calculator class need to contain a reference to a bunch of New York hotels? Some further digging suggests that this code was added in by a well-meaning programmer who wanted to test the price calculator with specific data, but hadn't heard of unit tests. So we have the remnants of test code mixed in with the product code, obfuscating the design. The code serves no other purpose, so—in this case at least—the answer's easy: delete it!

6. Avoid the Singleton Design Pattern

In Chapter 9 we donned our pantomime outfits and jumped around the stage encouraging you to boo and hiss at the Singleton design pattern; we also demonstrated why this particular pattern is so problematic. But for all of that, there is frequently a need for a class that has only one instance.

There are two solutions to the problem of creating a single-instance object. Which to use depends upon whether you genuinely need a single-instance-only object. Here are the two solutions:

Don't make your object a Singleton (capital S): Allow any class to create and dispose of instances of your one-object class.

Apply some other framework or pattern: Deem your class to be a singleton (lowercase S), but use some other framework or pattern to achieve that goal. For example, apply the *Spring/Inversion of Control* pattern, which maintains the object's lifecycle for you. Or apply a Registry class that your run-time code can use to get at a single instance of a class without preventing unit tests from instantiating their own limited-scope copy.[4]

Quite often, an object that must be a singleton in the deployed product doesn't have the same requirement when it's being unit-tested. In this case, Option 2 is the better option. In all other cases, give yourself a break and go for Option 1.

For PriceStreamer, we've gone with Option 2. This does mean that an extra Registry class is involved, but the improvements in stability, extensibility, testability, all those "ilities," make it worthwhile—especially as it can also be used to store any other "deemed-singleton" objects that you need. The registry class isn't used by the unit tests; they can simply create their own instance via the PriceStreamer's public constructor.

You don't need a big framework to do what's needed, though. Object registries are easy to implement. Here's a simple one in its entirety:

```
public class SimpleRegistry {

    public static final Map<Class, Object> lookup =
                new HashMap<Class, Object>();

}
```

To further simplify things, any object that uses the registry can do a static import at the top of the class. Here is an example:

```
import static com.softwarereality.nottherealmapplet.SimpleRegistry.*;
```

In the program's startup code, add this line to create your single instance:

```
lookup.put(PriceStreamer.class, new PriceStreamer());
```

■ **Tip** You can further decouple this design by defining an interface for PriceStreamer, and using the interface as the lookup key instead of the concrete class.

And then getting your single instance is as simple as doing this:

```
PriceStreamer streamer = (PriceStreamer) lookup.get(PriceStreamer.class);
```

This approach limits the use of static members to a single place in the code. Of course, it still violates the principle of encapsulation that we've discussed in this chapter. However, the reason it gets away with it is that *the sole purpose of the registry class's existence* is to create and keep a single instance

---

[4] A registry of objects is a single go-to place, a one-stop shop for all your single-instance needs. A "registry" is the basis for Cairngorm, Adobe's "official" application framework for Flex. Sometimes denigrated as being the reintroduction of global variables, it does at least solve the occasional case where you genuinely need a singleton object. Spring Framework takes a different approach, by allowing you to mark a Java bean as a singleton; the framework takes care of the lifecycle details without preventing unit tests from creating their own copies.

of PriceStreamer and other objects. If there were any further code in this class, or (shudder) actual business logic, then we would be thumbing through our Yellow Pages for a local Rent-a-Deity to smite the Registry class down from on high, leaving nothing but a couple of smoking boots where it once stood. (Or call on Ixtab the suicide goddess if she's available for parties).

The benefit of the keep-it-simple approach in this section can be seen straightaway in the more robust unit test setup. Remember that the tests don't need to use the Registry, as they want a fresh copy of PriceStreamer so that each test remains deterministic:

```
@Before
public void setUp() throws Exception {
    streamer = new PriceStreamer();
}
```

The two test methods—quotePrice_PriceAdded() and quotePrice_NoPriceYet()—remain unchanged, but the order in which they're run no longer matters. Result: more robust tests, which shouldn't randomly fail just because they're executed in a different order.

5. Keep Your Classes Decoupled

In Chapter 9 we illustrated the problem of code that is too tightly bound to its dependencies. In the example, HotelPriceCalculator was difficult to test because it assumed a particular implementation of PriceStreamer. The solution—if we definitely want the test to just be about HotelPriceCalculator, and not to be affected by the implementation of PriceStreamer—is to pass in a stubbed-out version, which will return a price for one night at hotel "123," which the method under test can then use in its calculation. Using the combined magic of Mockito and Java reflection, this is as simple as the following:

```
PriceStreamer streamer = mock(PriceStreamer.class);
when(streamer.quotePrice("123")).thenReturn(new BigDecimal(225.0));
```

The first line creates a mock instance of PriceStreamer. The second line configures the mock so that when its quotePrice() method is called with "123," it'll return 225.0.

We also need a way to tell HotelPriceCalculator to use this version, without going overboard on Inversion of Control frameworks or otherwise increasing the code's complexity. Luckily, we've already separated out the initialization code, so it's a simple case of the test *not* calling calc.initPriceStreamer(), and instead just assigning the mock streamer into the calc.streamer field.

Here's the complete test:

```
public class HotelPriceCalculatorTest {

    HotelPriceCalculator calc;
    PriceStreamer streamer;

    @Before
    public void setUp() throws Exception {
        streamer = mock(PriceStreamer.class);
        calc = new HotelPriceCalculator();
        calc.streamer = streamer;
    }

    @Test
    public void calculatePrice() throws Exception {
        Hotel hotel = new Hotel("123");
```

```
        when(streamer.quotePrice("123")).thenReturn(new BigDecimal(225.0));

        // Calculate the total price:
        BigDecimal price = calc.calculatePrice(hotel, 3);

        assertEquals(new BigDecimal(675.0), price);
    }
}
```

HotelPriceCalculator is also looking nice and straightforward now, far removed from the bamboozling mess that you saw in Chapter 9. Here's the relevant code for the calculatePrice() test (the complete class isn't much bigger than what you see here):

```
public class HotelPriceCalculator {

    PriceStreamer streamer;

    public void initialize() {
        initPriceStreamer();
    }

    private void initPriceStreamer() {
        this.streamer = new PriceStreamer();
        SimpleRegistry.lookup.put(PriceStreamer.class, streamer);
    }

    public BigDecimal calculatePrice(Hotel hotel, int numNights) {
        Object id = hotel.getId();
        BigDecimal pricePerNight = streamer.quotePrice(id);
        return pricePerNight.multiply(new BigDecimal(numNights));
    }
}
```

4. Keep Business Logic Out of the UI Code

If you recall from Chapter 9, we had a Flex/MXML-based Hotel Search screen. Now that the use case is better understood, it's obvious that this screen was just completely wrong. To match the use case, the user has already found the hotel, and wants to see prices for it. To recap, here's the basic course:

> *The system displays the Hotel Details page. The user types in the number of nights he would like to stay for, and clicks the Calculate button. The system calculates the price based on the cost per night, and displays the result.*

Figure 10–7 shows a screenshot of the component implementing the use case. The user sees a simple web page showing a photo of a nice hotel room, the price per night, and the total price for the user's planned stay.

Figure 10–7. A Flex UI matching the Quote Hotel Price use case. Compare with the "guessed-at" UI from Chapter 9.

Another problem with the Flex code from Chapter 9 was that the form validation logic was closely tied into the UI markup. There was little or no OO encapsulation going on. To fix this, we could create a PriceSearch class and give it properties matching the form. Here's the beginning of such a class, before any behavior is added:

```
public class PriceSearch
{
    private var numNights: int;
    private var hotelID: String;
}
```

But if you check the screenshot in Figure 10–7, it's obvious that this would have been created from a Hotel object... so why not simply add a quotePrice() method to Hotel? Here's how it could look:

```
public class Hotel
{
    private var id: String;
    public var pricePerNight: Number;

    // . . .
```

```
    public function quotePrice(numNights: int): Number
    {
        if (isNaN(Number(nights)))
        {
            throw new ValidationError("Please enter a valid number of nights.");
        }

        var numNights: int = parseInt(nights);
        if (numNights < 0)
        {
            throw new ValidationError("Please enter a positive integer.");
        }

        // Call the remote Java service:
        return PriceService.fetchQuote(this, numNights);
    }
}
```

Notice how the validation is now being done in this non-UI class, not in the UI mark-up. The quotePrice() function throws a ValidationError if the input fails validation. We ought to catch this in the UI button-click event handler, and show an appropriate dialog box.

Here are the relevant components from the UI mark-up:

```
<s:TextInput id="txtNights" />
<s:Button label="Calculate Price" click="btnCalculate_clickHandler(event)" id="btnCalculate"/>
<s:Label text="{totalCostOfStay}" />
<s:Label text="${hotel.pricePerNight}" />
```

And here's the ActionScript to go with it—notice how both hotel and totalCostOfStay are bindable:

```
import mx.controls.Alert;

[Bindable]
private var hotel: Hotel = new Hotel();

[Bindable]
private var totalCostOfStay: String;

protected function btnCalculate_clickHandler(event:MouseEvent):void
{
    try
    {
        totalCostOfStay = "$" + hotel.quotePrice(txtNights.text);
    }
    catch (error: ValidationError)
    {
        Alert.show(error.message, "Validation Error");
    }
}
```

> ■ **Note** If you look at the ActionScript code, the totalCostOfStay variable is tagged as "bindable." So when its value is changed, the Total Cost label will be automatically redrawn with the new value. The Hotel object is also bindable, because we're using its pricePerNight value in the "price per night" label.

In the button click handler, the hotel's quotePrice() function is called with the text value of txtNights. If any validation fails (non-numeric or negative value entered), the UI code catches the ValidationError and displays an alert dialog—see Figure 10–8.

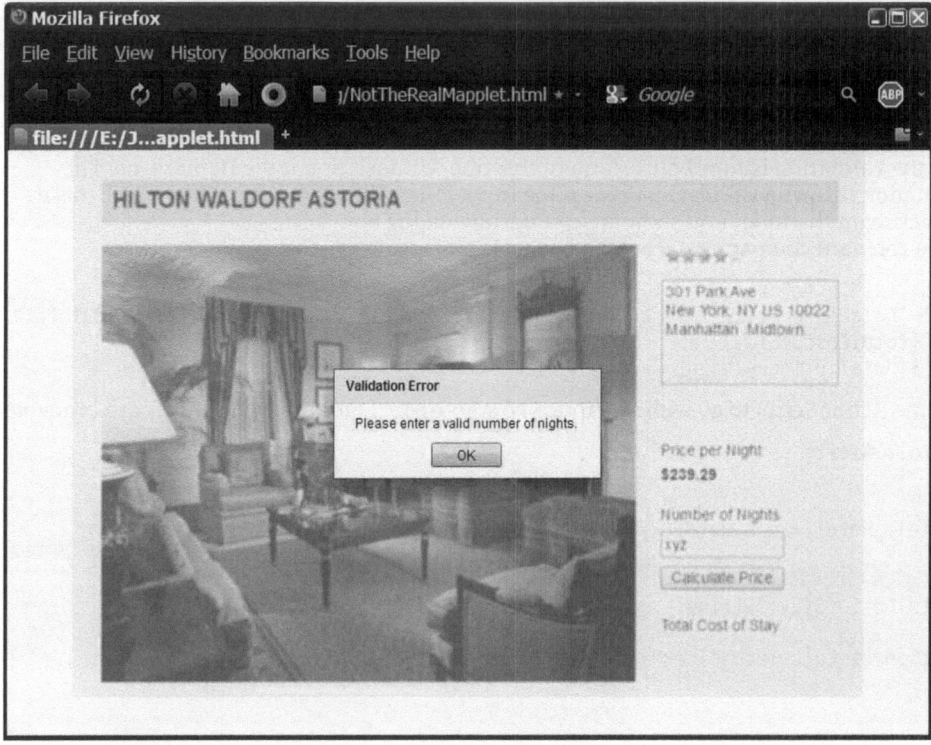

Figure 10–8. *Running a unit test is one thing, but good old visual inspection—seeing exactly what the user sees—is important, too.*

Adding a unit test for the validation code should now be pretty straightforward, as Hotel is a non-UI class. We can further split out the validation from the quotePrice() function to make it easier still. The two functions in Hotel are now the following:

```
public function quotePrice(nights: String): Number
{
    validateNumNights(nights);
    var numNights: int = parseInt(nights);
```

```
    return PriceService.fetchQuote(this, numNights);
}

public function validateNumNights(nights: String)
{
    if (isNaN(Number(nights)))
    {
        throw new ValidationError("Please enter a valid number of nights.");
    }

    var numNights: int = parseInt(nights);
    if (numNights < 0)
    {
        throw new ValidationError("Please enter a positive integer.");
    }
}
```

Here's the FlexUnit 4 unit test code for Hotel.validateNumNights():

```
public class HotelTest
{
    private var hotel : Hotel;

    [Before]
    public function setUp(): void
    {
        hotel = new Hotel();
    }

    [After]
    public function tearDown(): void
    {
        hotel = null;
    }

    [Test]
    public function testValidateNumNights():void
    {
        // Expect no ValidationError to be thrown:
        hotel.validateNumNights("1");
    }

    [Test(expects="ValidationError")]
    public function testValidateNumNights_Negative():void
    {
        hotel.validateNumNights("-1");
    }

    [Test(expects="ValidationError")]
    public function testValidateNumNights_NonNumeric():void
    {
        hotel.validateNumNights("xyz");
    }
}
```

The three test functions are pretty straightforward. The first test is the "basic course": a valid number is entered, so we don't expect a ValidationError to be thrown. The other two functions test for a negative number and a non-numeric number respectively: for both of these, we expect a ValidationError, and the test fails if we don't get one. Figure 10–9 shows the warm and snuggly green bar when we run the test class in Flash Builder.

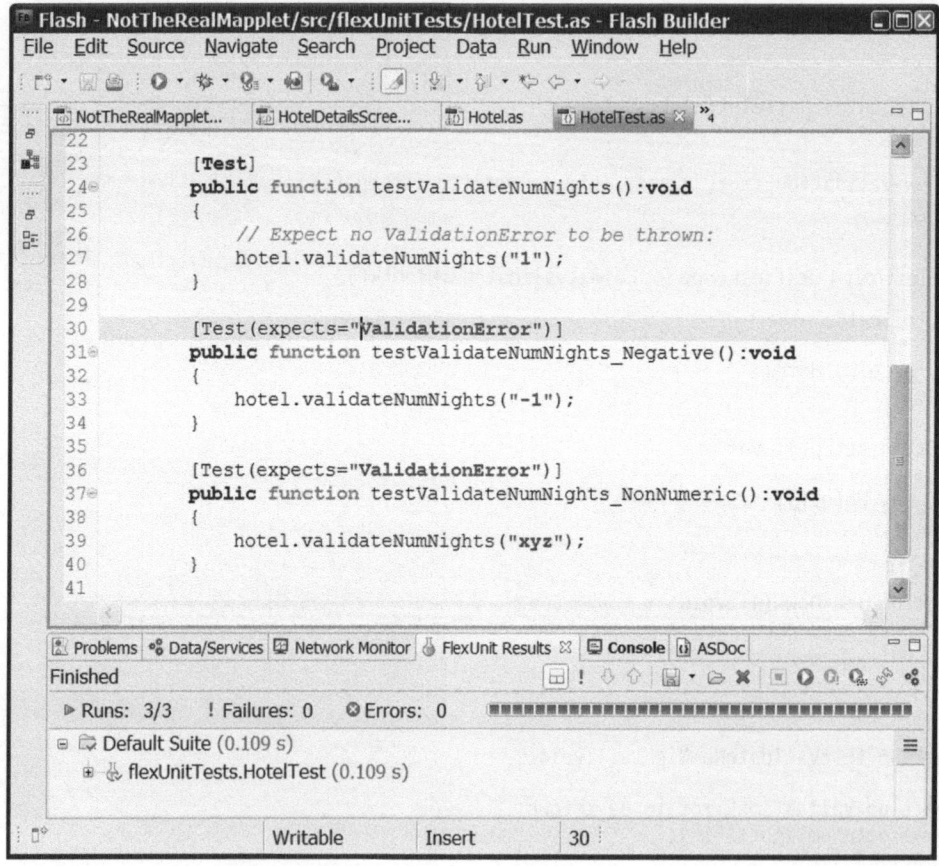

Figure 10–9. Green bar of Shangri—oh, you get the idea…

The main point here is to compare this code with the corresponding "antipattern #4" in Chapter 9: that version would have been impossible to unit-test, whereas with the validation code separated into a non-UI class, it's now very straightforward.

3. Use Black Box and Gray Box Testing

The reason to use black/gray box testing is to avoid breaking encapsulation. In Chapter 9, in the "Privates on Parade" antipattern, we illustrated the problem where a unit test needs to get inside an object to test its state, but it can't because the field in question is private. There are a couple of easy solutions to this problem:

- Make the field package-private instead of private
- Add a getter

These solutions both involve increasing the visibility of the field, either by making the field directly accessible to the unit test,[5] or by exposing the field in a "getter" method. Creating a public getXYZ method is the less desirable of the two, as it pollutes the class's interface, making a field public that is relevant only to the internal workings of the class. Conversely, simply making the field package-private (where only classes in the same package can access the field) does less damage to the class design. But it's still not ideal, and doesn't quite "ring true" as good design practice, as you're still exposing a field for the purpose of the unit test.

Luckily, there are also some more profound solutions—and this is another place where DDT and TDD differ in their approach:

- Don't test that specific field—checking the value of a "wannabe private" field makes the test know too much about the internals of the class under test.

- Test the result at a broader level—in other words, involve a controller test that relies on hotelDetailsFound being set in order to achieve a more business-level goal.

Our preferred solution out of all of these is the final one—testing the result at a broader level. If you find that you're considering increasing the scope of a field to test its value, then you should question the value of the test itself. Tests that "grub around" in the internals of a class are more brittle than tests that simply check the result of an operation using a class's published (or public) interface.

■ **Note** Chapter 6 illustrates in detail how to create controller tests that virtually eliminate the problem of unit tests needing to know too much about the code under test.

Thus armed with an essential set of design guidelines to make software easier to test, let's now return to our "rebooted" version of the hotel price calculator.

2. Reserve the "Final" Modifier for Constants—Generally Avoid Marking Complex Types Such as Service Objects as Final

This suggestion is purely from a testability perspective, and may not always be good advice when it comes to systems design, especially in a multi-threaded environment. It's a design decision, of course:

---

[5] In Java, package-private (or "default access") fields can be accessed by other classes as long as they're in the same package. Conventionally, unit tests are placed in a different root folder to the product code; but they can still be in the same package/namespace, giving them access to the package-private fields.

if you need to ensure that a reference is immutable, then mark the reference as final. However, this might make the code harder to test, as it means that the unit test code won't be able to substitute its own mock implementation.

One way around this is to assign the complex type on construction:

```
public class DBManager {

    private final DBConnectionManager dbManager;

    public DBManager(DBConnectionManager dbManager) {
        this.dbManager = dbManager;
    }
}
```

This will allow a test to still pass in its own mock implementation—assuming that it's instantiating this particular object directly.

1. Stick to the Use Cases and the Design

Of course, requirements do change and so does the design from time to time. But if it does, the worst approach is the "refactoring free-for-all," in which the code is swiftly pushed further and further away from any documented agreed-upon specification of what the customer's asking for, or from the design that the team collectively agreed on during design workshops. The time spent figuring out whether a unit test should be rewritten or abandoned after it breaks (because nothing ties back to the requirements or the design anymore) could have been saved by just a little time updating the use cases and the design model.

We illustrate some best practices for keeping the code and the design/use cases in-sync in our upcoming book, *ArcGIS Server Best Practices* (ESRI Press, 2010).

Detailed Design for the *Quote Hotel Price* Use Case

As you can see in Figure 10–10, the detailed design for the *Quote Hotel Price* use case is pretty straightforward. The design does exactly what it says on the tin (or in the use case text, in this case).[6]

---

[6] Having said that, we've omitted the first part of the use case—displaying the Hotel Details page—from the sequence diagram, as it isn't really within the scope of this refactoring example.

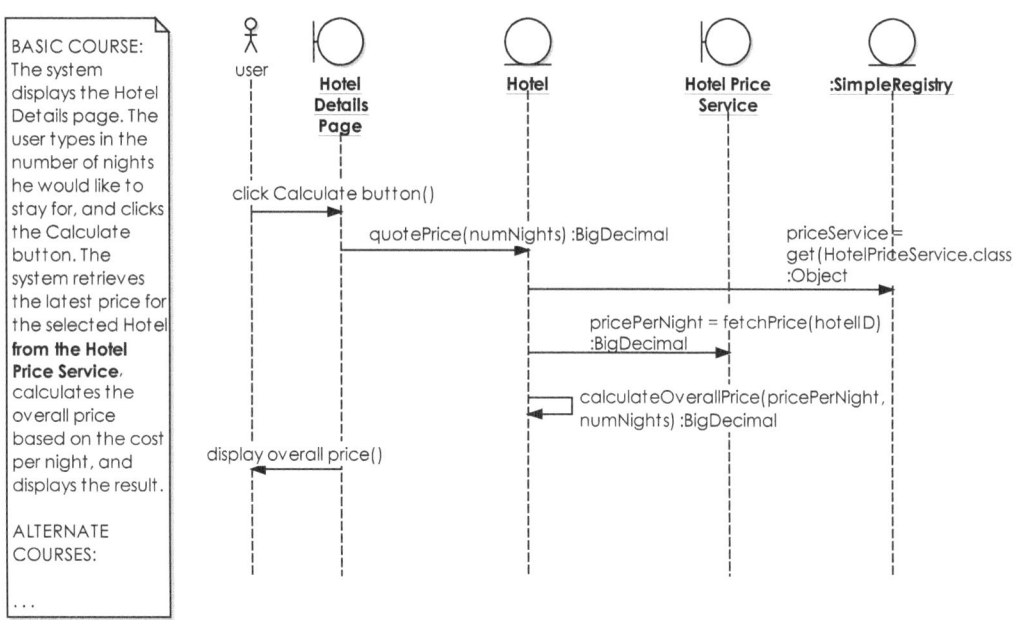

Figure 10–10. Detailed design for the Quote Hotel Price use case

You should already be seeing some big differences between this and the original design. The main change is that there isn't even a HotelPriceCalculator class anymore; the calculating behavior exists as a method on Hotel itself. This follows a key rule of OO design: put the behavior where the data lives.

We can now create an outline of our new Hotel class, following along with the design in Figure 10–10. Here's the result (the only bit that isn't shown in the diagram is retrieving the Hotel by its ID):

```java
public class Hotel {

    private String id;

    public Hotel(String id) {
        this.id = id;
    }

    public BigDecimal quotePrice(int numNights) throws Exception {
        HotelPriceService service = (HotelPriceService) lookup.get(HotelPriceService.class);
        BigDecimal pricePerNight = service.fetchPrice(id);
        return calculateOverallPrice(pricePerNight, numNights);
    }

    BigDecimal calculateOverallPrice(BigDecimal pricePerNight, int numNights) {
        return null;  // TODO (see next section)
    }
}
```

Controller Test: Calculate Overall Price

The quotePrice() method can be strung together just from the messages shown in the diagram. This leaves us with one method to complete: calculateOverallPrice(), which will do the actual calculation. To test calculateOverallPrice(), let's return to the CalculateOverallPriceTest class that EA generated for us, and complete the controller test method:

```
/**
 * The system calculates the total price.
 * @input Price per night, Number of nights
 * @AcceptanceCriteria The correctly calculated Overall Price should be returned.
 */
@Test
public void testDefaultRunScenario() {
    Hotel hotel = new Hotel("123");
    BigDecimal pricePerNight = new BigDecimal(220.0);
    int numNights = 5;
    BigDecimal quote = hotel.calculateOverallPrice(pricePerNight, numNights);
    assertEquals("The calculated price per night should be 220*5", new BigDecimal(1100),
quote);
}
```

This test code creates a Hotel object, then calls its calculateOverallPrice() method with a "predestined" pricePerNight value and number of nights. It then asserts that the value returned is the one expected. Running this straightaway gives us the Red Bar of Angry Marauding Goblins. So we can now fill in the product code to make the test pass:

```
BigDecimal calculateOverallPrice(BigDecimal pricePerNight, int numNights) {
    return pricePerNight.multiply(new BigDecimal(numNights));
}
```

Now, rerunning the test produces the Green Bar of Hazy Summer Days Spent Fishing by the River… altogether more preferable, we think.

As we're on a roll, let's also take a look at the other important test case here, Retrieve Latest Price Test.

Controller Test: Retrieve Latest Price Test

We're now faced with the problem that we want the code under test to call out to the remote Price Service, but we also want to keep the controller tests self-contained (see Chapter 11 for a discussion of "controller-level integration tests," which are possible and perfectly valid, but can be difficult to maintain). So… we *could* create a mock HotelPriceService here, and assert that when we tell Hotel to call it, then the mock object gets called. It would look something like this:

```
/**
 * The system queries the Hotel Price Service for the current price per night
 * @input The selected Hotel ID
 * @AcceptanceCriteria The current price per night is returned.
 */
@Test
public void testDefaultRunScenario() throws Exception {
    HotelPriceService service = mock(HotelPriceService.class);
    SimpleRegistry.lookup.put(HotelPriceService.class, service);
    when(service.fetchPrice("123")).thenReturn(new BigDecimal(225.0));
```

```
        verify(service).fetchPrice("123"); // asserts that the method under test was
definitely called
        Hotel hotel = new Hotel("123");
        hotel.quotePrice(5);
    }
```

But what do we actually gain from this test? (Hint: not an awful lot.) If there was some code that genuinely needed a mock object, in order to allow it to be tested, then we would add one. But this is one of those situations where the mock is simply satisfying the test[7], and we get the satisfaction of increasing the overall test count, which sounds good when related in the early morning stand-up meeting… but provides absolutely no business (or technical) value whatsoever. So we won't do that, then!

The Rebooted Design and Code

To finish up, here's the fully rebooted design and code. Figure 10–11 shows the (much simplified) class diagram, now completely tangle-free. Compare this with the original Temple of Doom class diagram in Figure 9-1 to get the full effect.

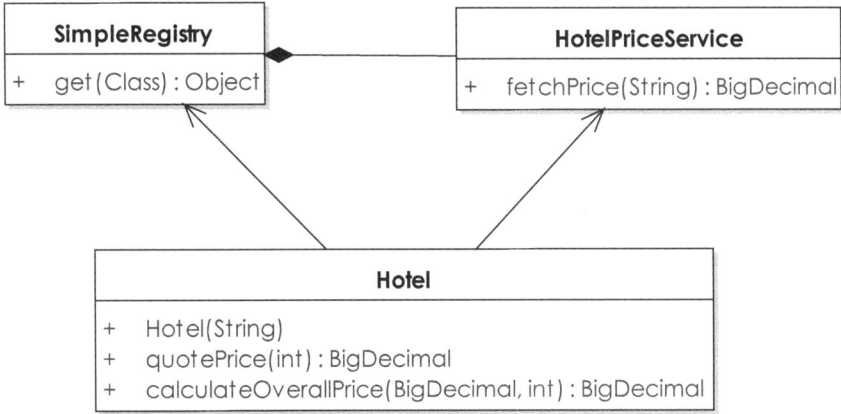

Figure 10–11.Class diagram for the Quote Hotel Price use case

Here's the complete Hotel class:

```
package com.softwarereality.nottherealmapplet;

import static com.softwarereality.nottherealmapplet.SimpleRegistry.lookup;
import java.math.BigDecimal;

public class Hotel {
```

---

[7] Or, as our good friend Alice might say: "Painting the unit test green."

```
    private String id;

    public Hotel(String id) {
        this.id = id;
    }

    public BigDecimal quotePrice(int numNights) throws Exception {
        HotelPriceService service = (HotelPriceService) lookup.get(HotelPriceService.class);
        BigDecimal pricePerNight = service.fetchPrice(id);
        return calculateOverallPrice(pricePerNight, numNights);
    }

    BigDecimal calculateOverallPrice(BigDecimal pricePerNight, int numNights) {
        return pricePerNight.multiply(new BigDecimal(numNights));
    }
}
```

HotelPriceService, in "real life," would implement a REST client (or similar HTTP/web service type of thing) to make calls to a remote service. For the example, we've used a simple, stubbed-out version:

```
public class HotelPriceService {
    public BigDecimal fetchPrice(String hotelID) {
        return new BigDecimal(300.0);
    }
}
```

Finally, SimpleRegistry—which allows us to maintain a single instance of HotelPriceService without adopting the problematic Singleton design pattern—is as simple as ever:

```
public class SimpleRegistry {
    public static final Map<Class, Object> lookup = new HashMap<Class, Object>();
}
```

We hope that gives you a good taste for the way in which going back to the use cases, talking to customers about what's really needed, doing some up-front design, and creating controller tests early on, all come together to make the code much easier to test... and also radically simplify the design. The example that we started the chapter with might seem like an extreme case, but we've seen production code like this way too often, where developers give up on unit testing because it's "Too Damn Difficult." Yet if they followed the process we've just described, the result would profoundly improve their code. Great swathes of code, boilerplate/plumbing classes, and so on, which might seem to be essential, suddenly turn out not to be.

Summary

This chapter presented the flipside to the antipatterns from Chapter 9. As you saw with the "expurgated" price calculator design, the introduction of a use case and controller testing resulted in a far simpler design, where the majority of design issues never even arose. There was no need to refactor them out of the code, as the antipatterns never even made it into the design.

In the next chapter we look at an advanced topic, but one that we wholeheartedly recommend that you introduce into your project once you're familiar with DDT (which hopefully you are by now!): automated integration testing.

## CHAPTER 11

Automated Integration Testing

Automated integration testing is a pig, but it's an important pig. And it's important for precisely the reasons it's so difficult.

The wider the scope of your automated test, the more problems you'll encounter; but these are also "real-world" problems that will be faced by your code, both during development and when it's released. So an integration test that breaks—and they will break frequently, e.g., when a dependent system has changed unexpectedly—isn't just a drag, it's providing an early warning that the system is about to break "for real." Think of an integration test as your network canary.

Integration tests are also important, and worth the pain of setting them up and keeping them working, because without them, you've just got unit tests. By themselves, unit tests are too myopic; they don't assert that a complete operation works, from the point when a user clicks "Go" through the complete operation, to the results displayed on the user's screen. An end-to-end test confirms that all the pieces fit together as expected. Integration is potentially problematic in any project, which is why it's so important to test.

Note The scope of an integration test can range from a simple controller test (testing a small group of functions working together) to a complete end-to-end scenario encompassing several tiers—middleware, database, etc.— in an enterprise system. In this chapter we'll focus on integration tests that involve linking remote systems together.

However, there's no getting around the fact that automated integration tests are also difficult and time-consuming to write and maintain. So we've put this chapter in the Advanced section of the book. This topic shouldn't be viewed as "optional," but you may find that it helps to have a clear adoption path while you're implementing DDT in your project.

Another reason we've separated out integration testing is that, depending on your organization, it might simply not be possible (at the current time) to implement meaningful integration tests there; e.g., the DBAs may not be prepared to set up a test database containing specific test data that can be reinstated at the run of a script. If this is the case, we hope you still get what you can from this chapter, and that when other teams start to see the results of your testing efforts, they might warm to the benefits of automated integration tests.

Top-Ten Integration Testing "To-Do" List

Keep in mind that we're using "integration testing" to refer to both "external system calls" and "end-to-end testing," i.e., "putting it all together tests." Here are our top ten integration testing guidelines:

10. Look for test patterns in your conceptual design.

9. Don't forget security tests.

8. Decide which "level" of integration test to write.

7. Drive unit/controller-level integration tests from your conceptual design.

6. Drive scenario tests from your use case scenarios.

5. Write end-to-end scenario tests, but don't stall the project if they're too difficult.

4. Use a "business-friendly" testing framework to house scenario tests.

3. Test GUI code as part of your scenario tests.

2. Don't underestimate how problematic integration tests are to write and maintain, but...

1. Don't underestimate their value.

The rest of this chapter is structured around this list…

10. Look for Test Patterns in Your Conceptual Design

Examine your conceptual design to find test patterns. These patterns will indicate when you might need a GUI test, an external system integration test, an algorithm test, etc. As Figure 11–1 shows, a robustness diagram (i.e., conceptual design) provides a handy way of determining what type of test to write.

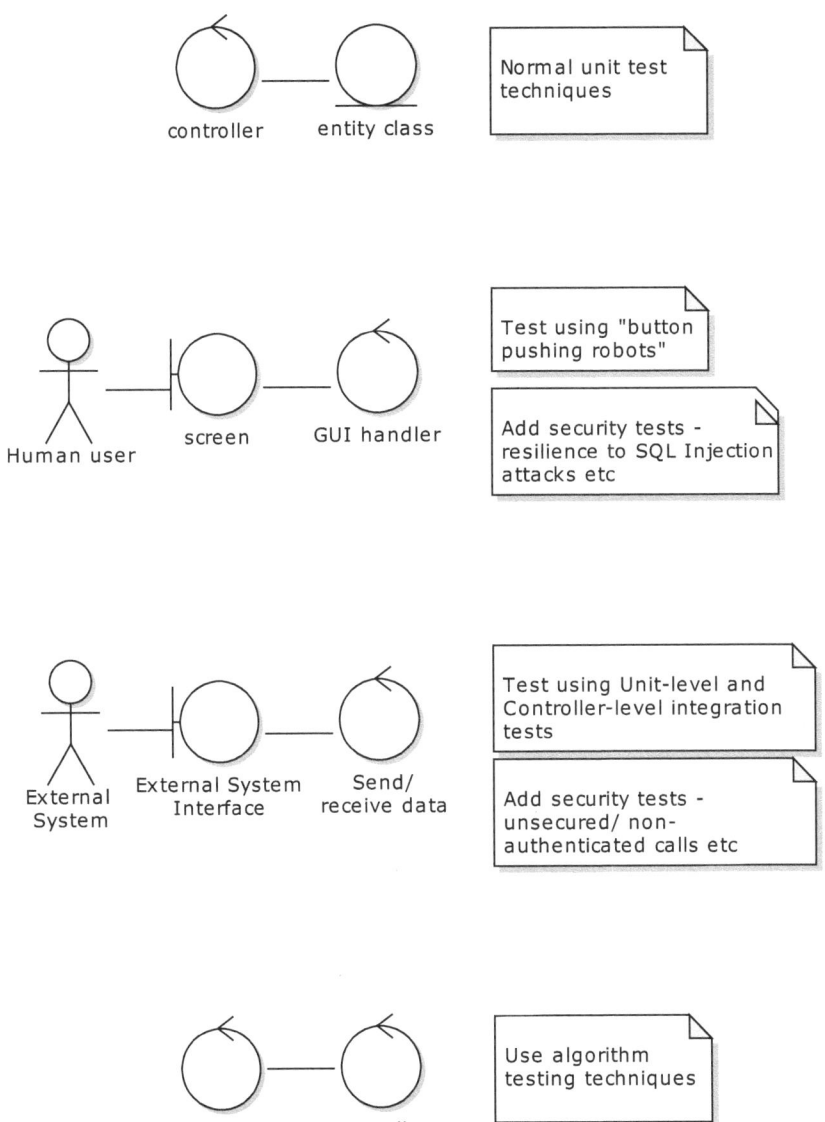

Figure 11–1. Spotting patterns in your conceptual design to figure out what type of test to write

If you have a controller talking to an entity class, then that's the easiest case: use an isolated unit or controller test (see Chapters 5 and 6).

If you have a controller that is handling a GUI event (e.g., the user clicked a button or pushed a slider), enlist the help of a GUI testing toolkit (more about these later in the chapter), aka button-

255

pushing robot, to simulate the user input. You would also want, as a standard sort of test, to be able to check for susceptibility to SQL Injection attacks, cross-site scripting, etc., at this level.

If you have a controller talking to an external system interface (usually remote, i.e., on a separate server somewhere), then it's time to write a unit-level integration test (more about these in the next section). Again, this would be a good opportunity to include security tests—this time from a client's point of view, but ensuring that the client can't make unsecured calls, or calls to an external service without the correct (or any) credentials. If you're also developing the server-side module that the client converses with, then it also makes sense to implement the server-side corollary to these security tests.

Finally, a controller talking to another controller suggests that this is some algorithmic code, and potentially could do with some "zoomed-in" tests that are finer-grained even than normal unit tests (i.e., sub-atomic). We cover design-driven algorithm testing in Chapter 12.

As you can see, none of these are really "end-to-end" tests: they're integration tests, but focusing only on the objects immediately on either side of the interface. Keeping the tests focused in this way— keeping everything scoped down to manageable, bite-sized chunks—can reduce many of the headaches we described earlier in this chapter.

However, automated end-to-end testing does also have its uses—more about this level of testing later.

9. Don't Forget Security Tests

Remember to test security (it's really important, and it's not that difficult to do). It seems like a week doesn't go by without a report of an SQL injection attack or cross-site scripting exploit impacting a high-profile web site. It's bamboozling, since SQL injection attacks, in particular, are so simple to avoid.

While lack of security is an ever-present issue that your tests must be designed to expose, the flipside—security that works—can also pose a problem for your tests. We'll talk about that in a moment, but first let's take a look at one of the more common—and easily prevented—security holes.

Security Testing: SQL Injection Attacks

SQL injection isn't the only type of exploit, of course, but it's worth a brief description as it's such an outrageously common—and easily avoided—form of attack. The attack, in a nutshell, is made possible when a search form is inserted directly into an SQL query; e.g., searching for hotels in Blackpool, the SQL query, constructed in your server code, would look something like this:

```
SELECT * FROM hotels WHERE city = 'Blackpool';
```

In the search form, the user would enter a town/city; the server component extracts this value from the submitted form, and places it directly into the query. The Java code would look something like this:

```
String city = form.getValue("city");
String query = "SELECT * FROM hotels WHERE city = '" + city + "';";
```

Giving effectively free access to the database opens up all sorts of potential for sneaky shenanigans from unscrupulous exploiters. All the user has to do is add his or her own closing single-quote in the search form, as in the following:

```
Blackpool'
```

Then the constructed query passed to the database will look like this:

```
SELECT * FROM hotels WHERE city = 'Blackpool'';
```

The database would, of course, reject this with a syntax error. How this is shown in the front-end is down to how you code the error handling—another "rainy day scenario" that must be accounted for, and have its own controller in the conceptual design and, therefore, its own test case.

But it's a simple task for the user to turn this into a valid query, by way of an SQL comment:

```
Blackpool'; --
```

This will be passed directly to the database as the following:

```
SELECT * FROM hotels WHERE city = 'Blackpool'; --';
```

Everything after the -- is treated as a comment, so the door to your data is now wide open. How about if the user types into the search form the following?

```
Blackpool'; DROP TABLE hotels; --
```

Your server-side code will faithfully construct this into the following SQL, and pass it straight to the database, which, in turn, will chug away without question, just following orders:

```
SELECT * FROM hotels WHERE city = 'Blackpool'; DROP TABLE hotels; --
```

Depending on how malicious the attacker is, he or she could wreak all sorts of havoc, or (worse, in a way) build on the "base exploit" to extract other users' passwords from the database. There's a good list of SQL Injection examples on http://unixwiz.net.[1]

Protecting against this type of attack isn't simply a case of "sanitizing" the single-quotes, as this excludes valid names such as "Brer O'Hare," in which a quote is a perfectly valid character. Depending on which language/platform/database you're using, there are plenty of libraries whose creators have thought through all the possible combinations of "problem characters." The library function will escape these characters for you—e.g., MySQL has a built-in function, mysql_read_escape_string(). You just have to make sure you call one. Or even better, use bind variables and avoid the problem altogether.

But either way, make sure you write tests that confirm your application is immune from SQL injection attacks. For example, use Selenium (or directly use HttpClient in your JUnit test) to post a "malicious" form to the webserver, and then query the test database directly to make sure the attack didn't work.

Also keep an eye on the SANS "top cyber security risks" page,[2] and keep thinking about tests you can write—which can usually be shared among projects or components—to verify that your system isn't vulnerable to these kinds of attacks.

Security Testing: Set Up Secure Sessions

Setting up a secure session for automated tests can be a bit of a drag, but usually you only have to do it once. It's worth doing, because it brings the test system much closer to being a realistic environment—meaning the tests stand a better chance of catching "real-life" problems before the system's released into the wild.

However, one issue with security is that of passwords. Depending how integrated your system is with Microsoft Exchange, LDAP, Single Sign-On (SSO), Windows (or Unix) logins, etc., there may be an issue with storing a "real" password so that the test code can log in as a user and run its tests. The answer is, of course, to set up a test account where the password is commonly known, and the test account has

---

[1] http://unixwiz.net/techtips/sql-injection.html

[2] www.sans.org/top-cyber-security-risks

restricted access just to the test environment. The ability to do this will depend on just how co-operative your organization's network services team happens to be.

8. Decide the "Level" of Integration Test to Write

As ever, we want to make your life easier by recommending that you write tests that give you as much leverage as possible, and to avoid duplicated effort. So, with that in mind, here are the three levels of DDT integration testing, starting from the most "macroscopic," zoomed-out level, down to the microscopic, zoomed-in world of unit tests:

1. Scenario-level integration tests

2. Controller-level integration tests

3. Unit-level integration tests

How the Three Levels Differ

Table 11–1 describes the properties of each level of integration test.

Table 11–1. How the Three Levels of Integration Test Differ

Level	Scope	What it covers
Scenario	A "broadly scoped" end-to-end test	A whole use case scenario
Controller	A "medium-sized" test	A logical software function
Unit	A "small" test	One function or method

They key characteristic of all three is that you don't use mock objects or stunt services to isolate the code. Instead, let the code run wild (so to speak), calling out to whatever services or databases it needs to. Naturally, these will need to be in a test environment, and the test data will need to be strictly controlled, otherwise you'll have no end of problems with tests breaking because someone's been messing with the test data.

These tests will need to be run separately from the main build: because they're so easily broken by other teams, you definitely don't want your build to be dependent on them working. You *do* want the tests to be run automatically, just not as often as the isolated tests. Setting them up to run once an hour, or even just nightly, would be perfectly fine.

Knowing Which Level of Integration Test to Write

Start by identifying and writing integration tests at the scenario level. These are "end-to-end" tests, as they involve the entire system running, from one end of a use case scenario to the other. ("Start-to-finish" might be a more apt description than "end-to-end"!) They also involve simulating a user operating the GUI—clicking buttons, selecting rows in a table, etc.; most importantly, they involve the code sending actual requests to actual remote systems. These are true integration tests, as they involve every part of all the finished components working together as one fully integrated system.

Usually, scenario-level integration tests are quite straightforward to write, once you know how. But on occasion they can be difficult to write, due to some technical quirks or limitations in the system or framework you're utilizing. In this case, don't "bust a gut" or grind progress to a halt while trying to implement them. Instead, move to the next level down.

Controller-level integration tests are exactly like the controller tests in Chapter 6: they're there to validate that the logical software functions identified during conceptual design have been implemented correctly—and remain implemented correctly. However, there's one key difference: the integration tests don't isolate the software functions inside a walled garden; they call out to external services, and other classes within the same system. This makes them susceptible to the problems we described at the start of this chapter, so you'd normally only write an integration test at the controller level if the software function in question is solely focused on making a remote call.

If there are any gaps in the fence left over, plug them up with unit-level integration tests. These are the most "zoomed-in" and the most focused of the tests.

■ **Note** You could feasibly cover all the integration points with unit tests, but if you're also writing scenario-level tests then there wouldn't be any point duplicating the integration points already covered.

Let's walk through the three levels, from the narrowest in scope up to the broadest.

7. Drive Unit/Controller-Level Tests from Conceptual Design

We cover unit-level and controller-level integration tests together as, when they're making external calls, in reality, there's very little to separate them. It sometimes just helps to think of them as distinct concepts when determining how much code an individual test should cover.

As Figure 11–2 shows, each external system call is a potential point of failure, and should be covered by a test. You want to line the "seams" of your remote interface with tests. So each controller (software function) on the left potentially gets its own unit/controller test. (We say "potentially" because some of these control-points may already be covered by a broader-scoped integration test.)

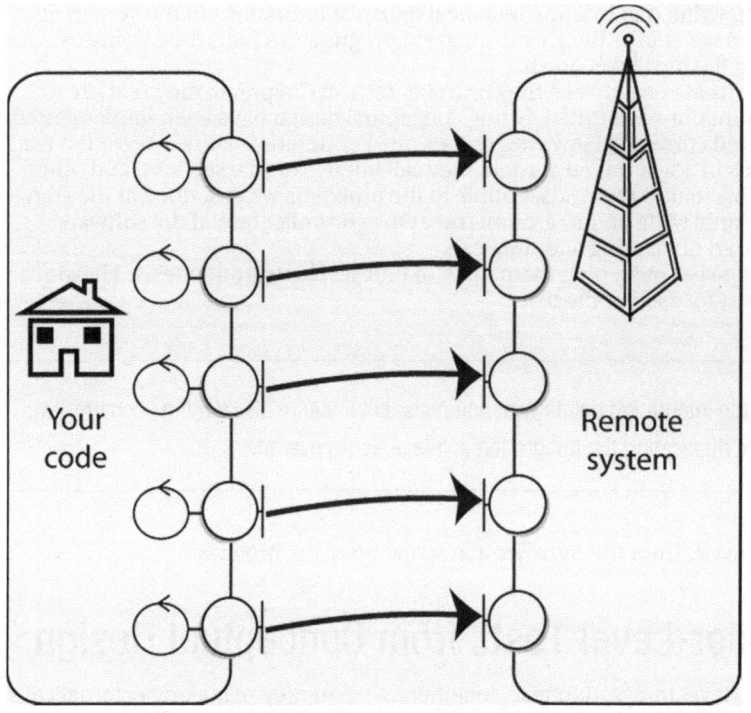

Figure 11–2. Line up your external system calls with unit-level integration tests

It's well worth writing unit-level integration tests if each call can be isolated as in Figure 11–2. However, you'll sometimes find that your code makes a series of remote system calls, and it's difficult to isolate one aspect of the behavior to test. This is one time when broader-scoped, scenario-level tests can actually be easier to write. Deciding which level of test to write is simply a judgment call, depending on a) how straightforward it is to isolate the software behavior, and b) how detailed or complex the code is, and whether you feel that it would benefit from a finer-grained integration test.

Later in the chapter we talk about the complexities, barriers, and wrinkles you'll face while writing integration tests. But for now, it's worth comparing the sort of "walled garden" isolated controller tests we showed in Chapter 6 with an equivalent controller-level integration test.

Chapter 6 dealt with the *Advanced Search* use case, in which the user enters search criteria and gets back a collection of matching hotels on a map, and listed in the search widget for further whittling-down. Here's a sample test that initiates a sequence in which a call is made to an HTTP service, the XML response is parsed, and a HotelCollection containing the matching hotels is returned. The test then confirms that the number of hotels returned is as expected. Here's the test method:

```
@Test
public void searchForHotels() throws Exception {
    HotelSearchClient searchClient = new HotelSearchClient();

    Object[] params = {
        "city", "New York"
        ,"coordinates", new String[] {
```

```
                    "latitude", "123"
                    ,"longitude", "456"
                    ,"maximumDistance", "7"
        }
    };

    HotelCollection hotels = searchClient.runQuery(params);
    assertEquals(4, hotels.size());
}
```

The runQuery() method encapsulates the work of querying the HTTP service and parsing the XML response into a HotelCollection object; i.e., there are several methods being called "behind the scenes" in the search code.

So this is both a controller test and, essentially, an integration test, as the code is calling out to an external service. The point here is that the result-set isn't really under our control. There may be four matching hotels returned today, but tomorrow one of the hotels could close down, or more hotels may be added to the database. So the test would fail, even though the service hasn't really changed and still technically works. Add to this all of the problems you'll face with integration tests, which we describe later in this chapter, and it quickly becomes obvious that there's a trade-off in terms of time spent dealing with these issues vs. the value you get from integration tests.

If you just want to test the part of the code that parses the XML response and constructs the HotelCollection, then you'd use an isolated controller test—use a "mock service" so that HotelSearchClient returns a consistent XML response.

Here's the same test method, with additional code to transform it from an integration test into an isolated controller test—the four new lines are shown in bold:

```
@Test
public void searchForHotels() throws Exception {
    HotelSearchClient searchClient = new HotelSearchClient();

    Object[] params = {
        "city", "New York"
        ,"coordinates", new String[] {
                "latitude", "123"
                ,"longitude", "456"
                ,"maximumDistance", "7"
        }
    };

    String xmlResponse = load("AdvancedSearch.xml");
    HttpClient mockClient = mock(HttpClient.class);
    when(mockClient.execute(params)).thenReturn(xmlResponse);
    searchClient.setHttpClient(mockClient);

    HotelCollection hotels = searchClient.runQuery(params);
    assertEquals(4, hotels.size());
}
```

This version loads up the simulated XML response from a file, and then inserts the mock `HttpClient` into the code being tested. We've fenced the code in so that it *thinks* it's making an external call, but is really being fed a simulated response.

It really is that simple to pass in a mock object—a minute's work—and it makes life much easier in terms of testing.[3]

However—and that should really be a big "however" in a 50-point bold+italic font—hiding the live interface loses a major benefit of integration testing: the whole point of integration testing is that we *are* testing the live interface. The number of hotels may change, but what if the format of the XML was randomly changed by the service vendor? Our system would break, and we might not find out until end-users report that they're seeing errors. A controller-level integration test like the one we just showed would catch this change straightaway.

You could, of course, reduce the integration test's dependence on specific data by changing the nature of the assertion; e.g., instead of checking for a range of hotels returned, check that one particular expected hotel is in the result-set, and that its fields are in the right place (the hotel name is in the Name field, city is in the City field, etc.). There'll still be cases where the test has to check data that's likely to change; in this case, you'll just have to grit your teeth and update the test each time.

■ **Note** Both of the tests we just showed are valid: they're achieving different things. The integration test is checking that the live interface hasn't inexplicably changed; the isolated test is focused on the XML parsing and HotelCollection construction. While there appears to be an overlap between them, they both need to exist in separate test suites (one run during the build, the other on a regular basis but independently of the build).

So the "pain" of integration testing is worth enduring, as it's quite minor compared with the pain of producing a system *without* integration tests.

6. Drive Scenario Tests from Use Case Scenarios

Scenario-level integration tests are "end-to-end" tests. By this, we mean that the test verifies the complete scenario, from the initial screen being displayed, through each user step and system response, to the conclusion of the scenario. If you're thinking that scenario-level tests sound just like automated versions of the "use case thread expansion" scenario test scripts from Chapter 7, you'd be right: that's exactly what they are. So, however you go about automating them, the first stage in automating scenario-level tests is to follow the steps described in Chapter 7, to identify the individual use case threads and define test cases and test scenarios for each one.

---

[3] One side-effect that we should point out is that we've just transformed the test from a "black box" test to a "white box" (or "clear box") test—because the test code now "knows" that HotelSearchClient uses an HttpClient instance internally. As we discussed in Chapters 5 and 6, this is sometimes a necessary trade-off in order to isolate the code under test, but it does mean that your code is that bit less maintainable—because a change inside the code, e.g., replacing HttpClient with some other toolkit, or even just an upgraded version of HttpClient with its own API change, means that the test must also be updated.

> ■ **Tip** There's a lot to be said for being able to run a full suite of end-to-end integration tests through a repeatable suite of user scenarios, just by clicking "Run". And there's even more to be said for making these end-to-end tests run automatically, either once per hour or once per night, so you don't have to worry about people forgetting to run them.

There are many, many options regarding how to write scenario-level tests. In the next section we'll suggest a few, and give some pointers for further reading, though none of these is really DDT-specific or counts as "the DDT way." The main thing to keep in mind is that an automated scenario-level test needs to follow a specific use case scenario as closely as possible, and should have the same pass/fail conditions as the acceptance criteria you identified for your "manual" scenario tests (again, see Chapter 7).

Another thing to keep in mind is that scenario-level integration tests are simply unit tests with a much broader scope: so they can be written just like JUnit tests, with `setUp()`, `tearDown()`, and test methods, and with an "assert" statement at the end to confirm that the test passed. The language or the test framework might differ, but the principle is essentially the same.

5. Write End-to-End Scenario Tests

It'll always be important to have real-life humans running your scenario tests (see Chapter 7), using initiative, patience and intuition to spot errors; but there's also value in automating these same scenario tests so that they can be run repeatedly, rather like a Mechanical Turk on steroids.

That said, automated scenario tests do have their own set of unique challenges. If the project hasn't been designed from the ground up to make testing easy, then automating these tests might be more trouble than it's worth. If you find that the project is in danger of stalling because everyone's struggling to automate scenario/acceptance tests, just stick to manual testing using the test cases discussed in Chapter 7, and fall back on unit- and controller-level integration tests.

The challenges when automating scenario tests are these:

- Simulating a user interacting with the UI

- Running the tests in a specific sequence, to emulate the steps in a scenario

- Sharing a test database with other developers and teams

- Connecting to a "real" test environment (databases, services, etc.)

We've already discussed the last item, and the first item has its own "top ten items" (which we'll get to shortly); so let's look at the other two, and then show an example based on the Mapplet's *Advanced Search* use case from Chapter 6.

Emulating the Steps in a Scenario

You'll want to run tests in a specific sequence. Do that as a way of emulating the steps in a scenario.

Scenario-level tests have a lot in common with behavior-driven development (BDD), which also operates at the scenario level. In fact, BDD uses "scenario files," each of which describes a series of steps: the user does this, then the user does that… BDD scenarios are very close to use case scenarios, so close that it's possible to use BDD test frameworks such as JBehave or NBehave to implement DDT scenario-level integration tests.

Another possibility is to use a customer/business-oriented acceptance testing framework such as Fitnesse—essentially a collaborative wiki in which BAs and testers can define test scenarios (really, inputs and expected outputs on existing functions), which are then linked to code-level tests.

One final possibility, which xUnit purists will shoot us for suggesting, is—given JUnit and FlexUnit don't provide a mechanism for specifying the order that their test methods/functions are executed in—to write a single test function in your scenario test case, which then makes a series of function calls, each function mapping to one step in your use case scenario.

ABOUT FITNESSE

Fitnesse[4] is an acceptance testing framework that complements agile testing processes with a customer focus. It's essentially a webserver whose pages can be edited "wiki-style" to create test definitions in the form of tables of input data and expected output data. The idea is that BAs and testers can edit these tables directly and create new ones, while programmers link these tables up to actual test code in the background.

Sharing a Test Database

Databases are possibly the most problematic aspect of integration testing. If your test searches for a collection of hotels balanced on a sandy island in the Maldives, the expectation that the same set of hotels will always be returned might not remain correct over time. It's a reasonable expectation: a test needs consistent, predictable data to check against its expected results. However, who's to say that another team won't update the same test database with a new set of hotels? Your test will break, due to something outside your team's control.

A list of hotels should be fairly static, but the problem can be exacerbated when the data is more dynamic, e.g., client account balance. Your test might perform an operation that updates the balance; the next step will be to query the database to return the correct balance, but in that moment someone else's test runs, which changes the balance to something else—pulling the rug out from beneath the feet of your own test. Data contention with multiple tests running against a shared database is, as you'd expect, unpredictable: not good for a repeatable test.

One particularly tempting answer is to isolate a copy of the database for your own tests. This may or may not be practicable, depending on the size of the database, and how often it's updated. Each time someone adds a new column to a table, or inserts a new foreign key, every test instance of the database, on each developer's PC and the testers' virtual desktops, would need to be updated.

A simple answer is to run the integration tests less often, and only run them from one location—a test server that's scheduled to run the integration tests each night at 1 a.m., say. In fact, this is a fairly vital setup for integration tests. They just can't be run in the same "free-for-all" way that unit tests are run.

But there's still the problem that the database may not be in a consistent state at the start of each test.

From a data perspective, think of each integration test as a very large unit test: self-contained, affecting a limited/bounded portion of the overall database. Just as a unit test initially sets up its test fixtures (in the setUp() method), so an integration test can prepare the database with just the data it needs to run the test: a restricted set of hotels and their expected amenities, for example.

---

[4] See http://fitnesse.org.

■ **Tip** Identify a partial dataset for each integration test, and set it up when the test case is run.

For example, the following method (part of the Hotel class) calculates the overall cost of staying at a hotel over a number of nights (ignoring complications like different prices for different nights during the stay):

```
public double calculateCostOfStay(int numberOfNights, String discountCode) {
    double price = getPricePerNight(new Date());
    double discount = getDiscount(discountCode);
    return (price * numberOfNights) - discount;
}
```

We could test this method of Hotel with the following JUnit code:

```
@Test
public void calculateCostOfStay() throws Exception {
    Hotel hotel = HotelsDB.find("Hilton", "Dusseldorf");
    double cost = hotel.calculateCostOfStay(7, "VRESORTS SUPERSAVER");
    assertEquals(1300, cost, 1e-8);
}
```

This code attempts to find a hotel from a live connection to the test database, and then calls the method we want to test. There's a pretty big assumption here: that the rooms will cost $200 per night, and that there's an applicable discount code that will produce a $100 discount (resulting in a total cost of stay for seven consecutive nights of $1300). That might have been correct when the test was written; however, you'd expect the database to be updated at random times, e.g., the QA team might from time to time re-inject it with a fresh set of data from the production environment, with a totally different set of costs per night, discount codes, and so on.

To get around this problem, your integration test's setup code could prepare the test data by actually writing what it needs to the database. In the following example, JUnit's @BeforeClass annotation is used so that this setup code is run once for the whole test case (and not repeatedly for each individual test method):

```
@BeforeClass
public static void prepareTestData() throws Exception {
    Hotel hotel = HotelsDB.findOrCreate("Hilton", "Dusseldorf");
    hotel.setPricePerNight(200.00);
    hotel.addDiscount(100.00, "VRESORTS SUPERSAVER");
    hotel.save();
}
```

As long as it's a fair bet that other people won't be updating the test database simultaneously (e.g., run your integration tests overnight), this is an easy, low-impact way of ensuring that the test data is exactly what that precise test needs, updated "just-in-time" before the test is run.

This approach keeps the amount of setup work needed to a minimum, and, in fact, makes the overall task much less daunting than having to keep an entire database in a consistent and repeatable state for the tests.

Mapplet Example: The "Advanced Search" Use Case

We'll run through a quick example using one of the scenarios (or "use case threads") from the Mapplet—specifically, the basic course for *Advanced Search*. Here it is as a quick reminder:

> *The system enables the Advanced Search widget when an AOI exists of "local" size. The user clicks the Advanced Search icon; the system expands the Advanced Search widget and populates Check-in/Check-out fields with defaults.*

> *The user specifies their Reservation Detail including Check-in and Check-out dates, number of adults and number of rooms; the system checks that the dates are valid.*

> *The user selects additional Hotel Filter criteria including desired amenities, price range, star rating, hotel chain, and the "hot rates only" check box.*

> *The user clicks FIND. The system searches for hotels within the current AOI, and filters the results according to the Hotel Filter Criteria, producing a Hotel Collection.*

> *Invoke Display Hotels on Map and Display Hotels on List Widget.*

■ **Tip** We were asked whether the first sentence of this use case should be changed to something like "The advanced search widget is enabled when an AOI of 'local' size exists." The simple answer is: Nooooooooooo. Your use case should always be written in active voice, so that it translates well into an object-oriented design. You can find (lots) more information about the subject of use case narrative style in *Use Case Driven Object Modeling with UML: Theory and Practice*.

We want to write an automated scenario test that will step through each step in the use case, manipulating the GUI and validating the results as it goes along. Ultimately we're interested in the end-result displayed on the screen, based on the initial input; but a few additional checks along the way (without going overboard, and as long as they don't cause the test to delve too deeply inside the product code) are worth doing.

A Vanilla xUnit Scenario Test

An xUnit test class is the simplest way to implement a scenario test, being closest to the code—therefore, the test won't involve any additional files or setup. However, using a unit test is also the least satisfactory way, as it offers zero visibility to the customer, testers, and Business Analysts (BAs), all of whom we assume aren't programmers or don't want to be asked to roll their sleeves up and get programming.

The Mapplet scenario tests are implemented in FlexUnit, because the Flex client is where the UI action happens. So even though the system being tested does traverse the network onto a Java server, the actual interaction—and thus the scenario tests—are all Flex-based.

The scenario test for the *Advanced Search* basic course looks like this:

```
[Test]
```

```
public function useAddress_BasicCourse(): void {
    findLocalAOI();
    enableAdvancedSearchWidget();
    clickAdvancedSearchIcon();
    confirmAdvancedSearchWidgetExpanded();
    confirmFieldsPopulatedWithDefaults();

    enterReservationDetail();
    confirmValidationPassed();

    selectHotelFilterCriteria();
    clickFIND();
    confirmMatchingHotelsOnMap();
    confirmMatchingHotelsOnListWidget();
}
```

Notice how this covers each *user-triggered* step in the use case. For example, the clickAdvancedSearchIcon() function will programmatically click the Advanced Search icon, triggering the same event that would happen if the user clicked the icon.

We don't add additional steps for events that happen after the user has clicked a button, say, as these additional steps will happen as a natural consequence of the user clicking the button. However, we do include "confirm" functions, in which we assert that the UI is being shown as expected; e.g., confirmAdvancedSearchWidgetExpanded() does exactly that— it confirms that, in the UI, the "state" of the Advanced Search Widget is that it's expanded.

As we mentioned, this style of scenario test is the easiest for a developer to write and maintain, but you'll never get a customer or business analyst to pore over your test code and sign off on it—at least, not meaningfully. So (depending on the needs of your project) you might prefer to use a more "business-friendly" test framework, such as Fitnesse or one of the BDD frameworks.

4. Use a "Business-Friendly" Testing Framework

House your scenario tests in a business-friendly testing framework such as the Behavior-Driven Development (BDD) framework.[5] BDD is an approach to agile testing that encourages the developers, QA, and customer/BAs to work more closely together. To use the BDD framework for your scenario tests, you'll need to map each use case scenario to a BDD-style scenario—not as difficult as it sounds, as they're already pretty similar.

MORE ABOUT BDD

BDD builds on unit testing approaches to include a more customer-centric view of testing—with acceptance test scenarios that are pretty close to use cases.

BDD's creator Dan North described it as follows:

---

[5] See http://behaviour-driven.org/Introduction.

"BDD is a second-generation, outside-in, pull-based, multiple-stakeholder, multiple-scale, high-automation, agile methodology. It describes a cycle of interactions with well-defined outputs, resulting in the delivery of working, tested software that matters."

But despite that first sentence, we still kind of like it.

BDD can serve as either a "drop-in replacement" for the acceptance testing parts of DDT, or the BDD frameworks such as JBehave and NBehave can be used to execute the DDT use case scenario steps in the correct order.

A BDD version of the *Advanced Search* use case scenario would look like this:

Given an AOI exists of "local" size

When the system enables the Advanced Search widget

And the user clicks the Advanced Search icon

And the user specifies Reservation Details of check-in today and check-out next week, 2 adults and 1 room

And the user selects Hotel Filter criteria

And the user clicks FIND

Then the system displays the Hotels on the map and List Widget

(In this context at least, And is syntactically equivalent to When.)[6]
Depending on your BDD framework, the framework will text-match each line with a particular Step method, and then run the Step methods in the sequence specified by the scenario, passing in the appropriate value ("check-in," "check-out," number of adults and rooms, etc.) as an argument to the relevant Step methods.

■ **Note** One similarity is that the "Given" step at the start of the BDD scenario is usually equivalent to the initial "Display" step in an ICONIX use case: "The system displays the Quick Search window" translates to "Given the system is displaying the Quick Search window."

You may have noticed already that only about half of the original use case is described here. That's because BDD scenarios tend to focus on the user steps, finishing up with a "Then" step that is the system's eventual response, the condition to test for. However, with ICONIX/DDT use case scenarios, pretty much every user step has a system response: click a button, the system responds. Type something in, the system responds. And so on. So to match this closer to an ICONIX-style use case scenario, almost

---

[6] "And being equivalent to when is very curious, indeed," said Alice. "It's almost as if 'and are they equivalent?' is the same as 'when are they equivalent'? And how do I say 'and when are they equivalent?'"

every line should be followed by a "Then" that shows how the system responded, and allows the test to confirm that this actually happened.

To generate a DDT-equivalent BDD scenario, each "When" step would be immediately followed by a counterpart "Then" system response. So the example BDD scenario, written in a more DDT-like style, would read as follows:

Given the system displays the Map Viewer

And an AOI exists of "local" size

Then the system enables the Advanced Search widget

When the user clicks the Advanced Search icon

Then the system expands the Advanced Search widget and populates fields with defaults

When the user specifies Reservation Details of check-in today and check-out next week, 2 adults and 1 room

Then the system checks that the dates are valid

When the user selects Hotel Filter criteria

And the user clicks FIND

Then the system displays the Hotels on the map and List Widget

It should then be a relatively straightforward task to map each test case to a specific BDD step.

At the time of writing, there's a paucity of BDD support for Flex developers. So we'll show the example here using the Java-based JBehave (which also happens to leverage JUnit, meaning that your JBehave-based scenario tests can be run on any build/test server that supports running JUnit tests).

■ **Note** ICONIX-style "active voice" use cases often start with a screen being displayed. So we changed the opening part of the scenario to begin with displaying the Map Viewer. This results in a check being performed to verify that the system properly displays the Advanced Search widget.

---

3. Test GUI Code as Part of Your Scenario Tests

Testing GUI code is often shied away from as the most apparently difficult part of automated testing. In the past, it certainly used to be, with heavyweight "robot"-style frameworks simulating mouse clicks at rigid X,Y screen co-ordinates. Naturally such frameworks were ridiculously fragile, as even a change in screen resolution or window decoration (anything that even slightly offsets the X, Y co-ordinates) would break the entire suite of tests and require every single test to be redone.

GUI testing has come a long way in recent times, though. Swing developers have it easy with toolkits such as Abbot,[7] UISpec4J,[8] and FEST.[9] Swing testing is actually pretty straightforward even without an additional toolkit, as everything's accessible via the code, and with built-in methods already available such as `button.doClick()`.

.NET developers may like to check out NunitForms,[10] an NUnit extension for windows.forms testing. Flex developers also have plenty of options, e.g., FlexMonkey[11] and RIATest.[12]

And finally, web developers are probably already familiar with the deservedly popular Selenium web testing framework.[13] The ever-changing nature of web development—where the "delivery platform of the month" is usually specific versions of half a dozen different web browsers, and IE 6, but next month could involve a whole new set of browser versions—means that automated scenario testing is more important than ever for web developers. Swapping a different browser version into your tests provides a good early indication of whether a browser update will cause problems for your application.

2. Don't Underestimate the Difficulty of Integration Testing

Integration tests can be problematic. Don't underestimate by how much.

Unit testing—"testing in the small"—is really about matching up the interface between the calling code and the function being tested. Interfaces are inherently tricky, because they can change. So what happens if you "zoom out" from this close-in picture, and start to look at remote interfaces? It's easy (and rather common) to picture a remote systems environment like the one in Figure 11–3. Client code makes a call out over the network to a remote interface, retrieves the result, and (in the case of a test) asserts that the result is as expected.

Unfortunately, the reality is more like Figure 11–4.

---

[7] http://abbot.sourceforge.net/doc/overview.shtml

[8] www.uispec4j.org

[9] http://fest.easytesting.org/swing/wiki/pmwiki.php

[10] http://nunitforms.sourceforge.net/

[11] www.gorillalogic.com/flexmonkey

[12] www.riatest.com

[13] http://seleniumhq.org/

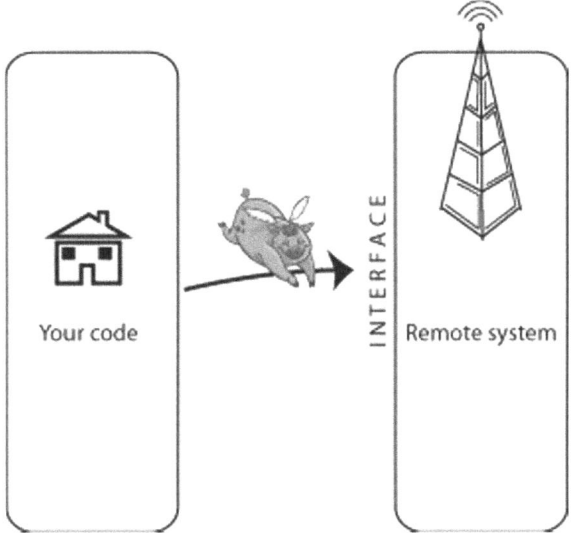

Figure 11–3. A naïve view of remote systems testing

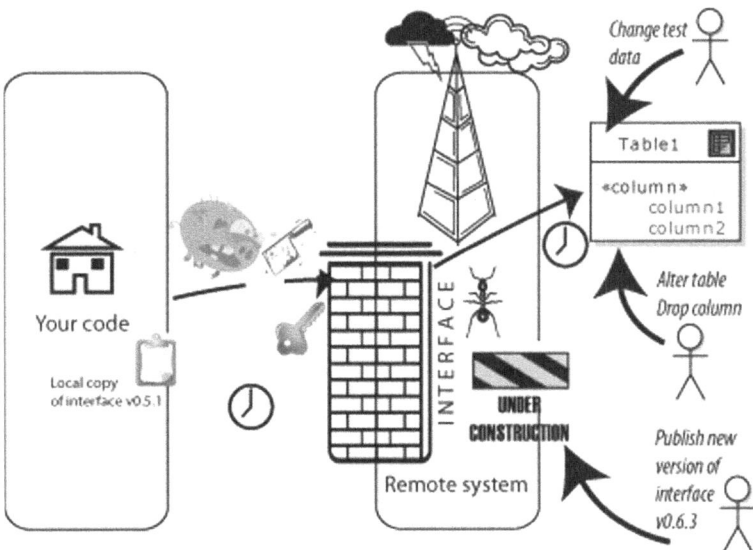

Figure 11–4. *The reality of remote systems testing*

The same problems that take place between code interfaces during unit or controller testing become much bigger, and a whole new breed of problems is also introduced. Here are some of the typical issues that you may well encounter when writing remote integration tests in a shared environment:

- Network latency
- Data contention (where two or more remote systems may be competing to read or update the same data simultaneously)
- Database metadata changes
- Randomly Mutating Interfaces
- Bugs in the remote system
- Security—firewalls, secure sessions, expired keys, etc.
- Cloudy days

We've been looking at some of these issues in the course of this chapter, presenting ways to mitigate each one. Let's have a quick run-through of the remaining issues here.

■ **Note** We hope that, by the end of the chapter, you'll agree with us that the problems we've just described aren't just limited to integration tests—they're typical of systems development in general, and integration tests actually highlight these problems earlier, saving you time overall.

Network Latency

Socket code that works perfectly on one PC with local loopback might fail unexpectedly when connecting over a network, simply because communication takes longer. The programmer might not have thought to include a "retry" function, because the code never timed out while running it locally. Similarly, he may not have included buffering, simply reading data until no more bytes are available (when more could still be on the way), because locally the data would always all arrive at once.

This is a good example of where struggling to create an integration test (and the test environment, with network-deployed middleware, etc.) can actually save time in the long run. Encountering these real issues in an end-to-end test means they'll be addressed during development, rather than later when the allegedly "finished" system is deployed, and discovered not to be working.

Database Metadata Changes

We touched on this in the previous section, but the problem of a database changing (tables being dropped or renamed, new columns added/renamed/removed, or their type being changed, foreign keys randomly removed, and so on) seems to have a particularly harsh effect on automated tests. Each time the database is changed, it's not just the product code that needs to be updated, but the tests that assume the previous structure as well.

Keeping your tests "black box" can help a lot here. In fact, as you'll see later, the only real way for integration tests to be viable is to keep them as "black box" as possible. Because their scope is much broader than myopic unit tests, they're susceptible to more changes at each juncture in the system they pass over. So the fewer assumptions about the system under test that are placed in the test code, the more resilient your integration tests will be to changes. In the case of database changes, this means not putting any "knowledge" of the database at all (column names, table names, etc.) in the tests, but making sure everything goes through a business domain-level interface.

Randomly Mutating (aka "Agile") Interfaces

Evolutionary development (as "agile" used to be known) has become rather popular, because it gives teams the excuse to design the system as they go along, refactoring services, interfaces, and data structures on the way.[14] While the opposite antipattern (the rigid refusal to change anything once done) is also bad, being *too* fluid or agile can be highly problematic in a multi-team project. Team A publishes an interface that is consumed by team B's client module. Then team A suddenly changes their interface, breaking team B's client module because team B had somehow forgotten that other teams were using their public interface. It happens all the time, and it slows development to a crawl because teams only find out that their (previously working) system has broken at the most inopportune moments.

Again, this will break an automated test before it breaks the "real" deployed product code. This may be regarded as an example of why automated integration tests are so fragile, but, in fact, it's another example of the automated tests providing an early warning that the real system will break if it's deployed in its current state.

Bugs in the Remote System

It's to be expected that the remote system is under construction just as your client system is. So the team developing the other system is bound to have their fair share of teething troubles and minor meltdowns. A set of automated integration tests will find a problem straightaway, causing the tests to break—when, otherwise, the other team may have quietly fixed the problem before anyone even noticed. So automated tests can amplify integration issues, forcing teams to address a disproportionately higher number of problems. This can be viewed as a good or a bad thing depending on how full or empty your cup happens to be on that day. On the positive side, bugs will probably be fixed a lot quicker if they're discovered and raised much sooner—i.e., as soon as one of your tests breaks.

Cloudy Days

A "cloudy day" isn't a tangible problem—in fact, perhaps we're just feeling a bit negative after listing all these other problems! But there are definitely days when nothing on an agile project seems to fit together quite right—you know, those days when the emergent architecture emerges into a Dali-like dreamscape. Whole days can be wasted trying to get client module A to connect with and talk to middleware module B, Figure 11–5 being a case in point! If client module A happens to be test code, it's tempting to give up, deeming the test effort "not worth it," and return to the product code—storing up the integration issues for later.

With these problems in mind, it could be easy to dismiss integration tests as just too difficult to be worth bothering with. But that would be to miss their point—and their intrinsic value—entirely.

---

[14] Our favorite example of this is Scott Ambler's epic work on "Agile Database Techniques" (Wiley, October 2003) much beloved by DBAs everywhere. And our favorite line: "Therefore if data professionals wish to remain relevant they must embrace evolutionary development." Riiiiight…

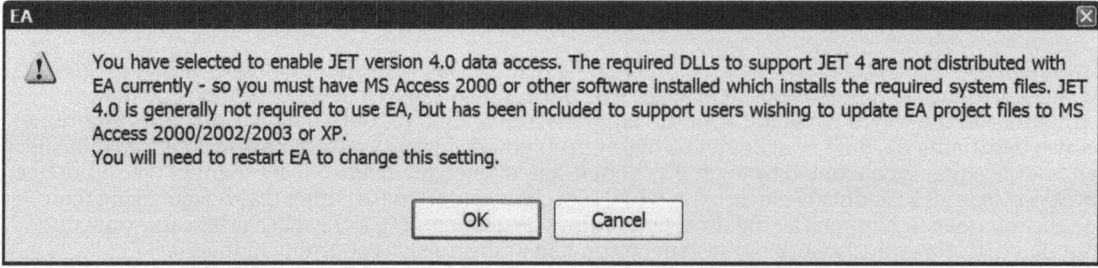

Figure 11–5. When it comes to integration, even the best software can have a cloudy day.

1. Don't Underestimate the Value of Integration Tests

Integrating two systems is one of the most problematic areas of software development. Because it's so difficult, automated integration tests are also difficult to write and maintain—not least because they keep breaking, for exactly the same reasons remote code keeps breaking. So many teams simply avoid writing integration tests, pointing out their problematic nature as the reason. Kind of ironic, huh?

As we demonstrated earlier in this chapter with the Hotel Search controller-level test, the real value of integration tests is in providing a consistent, relentless checking of how your code matches up with live, external interfaces. External interfaces are, by their nature, outside your team's control; so there's value in an ever-present "breaker switch" that trips whenever an interface has been updated with a change that breaks your code.

A breaking integration test also immediately pinpoints the cause of a problem. Otherwise, the error might manifest with a seemingly unrelated front-end error or oddity—a strange message or garbled data appearing in your web application—which would take time to trace back to some random change made by one of your service vendors, or by another team that you're working with. The integration test, conversely, will break precisely because the external interface has done something unexpected.

Key Points When Writing Integration Tests

We'll round off the chapter by summing up some of the key points (and adding a couple of new ones) to think about while writing integration tests. Here is our list:

- Create a test environment (test database, etc.) to run the tests in. This should be as close as possible to the live release environment. A frequent data refresh from the live system will keep the test database fresh and realistic. Multiple test environments may be necessary, but try not to go crazy as they all need to be maintained. However, you might want one database that can be torn down and reinstated regularly to provide a clean environment every time, plus a database with a dataset similar to the live system, to allow system, load, and performance testing.

- Start each test scenario with a script that creates a "test sandbox" containing just the data needed for that test. A common reason given for not running integration tests against a real database is that it would take too much effort to "reset" the database prior to each run of the test suite. In fact, it's *much* easier to simply have each test scenario set up just the data it needs to run the scenario.

- Don't run a tear-down script after the test. That might sound odd, but if a test has to clean up the database after itself so that it can run successfully next time, then it totally relies on its cleanup script having run successfully the previous time. If the cleanup failed last time, then the test can never run again (albeit not without some cursing and hunting for the problem and figuring out which cleanup script to manually run, to get the tests up and running again). It's much easier if you consistently just run a "setup script" at the *start* of each test scenario.

- Don't run the scenario tests as part of your regular build, or you'll end up with a very fragile build process. The tests will be making calls to external systems, and will be highly dependent on test data being in a specific state, not to mention other unpredictable factors such as two people running the same tests at the same time, against the same test database. It's great for unit and controller tests to be part of your automated build because their output is always deterministic, but the scenario tests, not so much. That said, you still want the scenario tests to be run regularly. If they're not set up to run automatically, chances are they'll be forgotten about, and left to gradually decay until it would take too much effort to get them all passing again. So a good "middle ground" is to schedule them to run automatically on a server, either hourly or (at a minimum) once per night. Make sure the test results are automatically emailed to the whole team.

- Think of scenario tests as "black box" tests, because they don't "know" about the internals of the code under test. Conversely, unit tests are almost always "white box" because they often need to set internal parameters in the code under test, or substitute services with mock objects. Controller tests, meanwhile, are "gray box" tests because it's preferable for them to be white box, but occasionally they do need to delve into the code under test.

Summary

Alice was just beginning to think to herself, "Now, what am I to do with this creature when I get it home?" when the baby grunted again, so violently, that she looked down into its face in some alarm. This time there could be no mistake about it: it was neither more nor less than a pig, and she felt that it would be quite absurd for her to carry it further.[15]

In this chapter we've illustrated some of the main issues you'll encounter while writing integration tests, but countered these with the point that it's those same issues that actually make integration testing so darned important. While integration testing is a pig, it's an important pig that should be put on a pedestal (preferably a reinforced one).

By "forcing the issue" and addressing integration issues as soon as they arise—i.e., as soon as an integration test breaks, pinpointing the issue—you can prevent the problems from piling up until they're all discovered later in the project (or worse, discovered by irate end-users).

We also demonstrated some key techniques for writing integration tests, DDT-style: first, by identifying the type of test to write by looking for patterns in your conceptual design diagrams, and then by writing the tests at varying levels of granularity. Unit-level and controller-level integration tests help to line the seams between your code and external interfaces, while scenario-level integration tests provide "end-to-end" testing, automating the "use case scenario thread" test scripts that we described in Chapter 7.

In the next chapter, we swap the "integration testing telescope" with an "algorithm testing microscope," and change the scope entirely to look at finely detailed, sub-atomic unit tests.

---

[15] *Alice's Adventures in Wonderland*, Chapter 6 (Lewis Carroll, 1865).

## CHAPTER 12

Unit Testing Algorithms

*"What a curious feeling!" said Alice. "I must be shutting up like a telescope!"
And so it was indeed: she was now only 10 inches high, and her face brightened at the thought that she was now the right size for going through the little door into that lovely garden.[1]*

One of the main messages in this book has been "test smarter, not harder"—that is, write fewer tests that each cover more code. If done using the techniques we've described, you can actually improve your effective test coverage while having fewer test cases (but comparatively more test scenarios, or "inputs" and their "expected outputs," for each test case).

---

[1] Lewis Carroll, *Alice's Adventures in Wonderland* (1865), Chapter 1.

This approach should work well for the majority of business code out there. However, almost every project has a "core" element: an engine or state machine that's central to the rest of the system; core business logic that would potentially cost the company millions of dollars if it went wrong; "mission critical" code; intricate algorithms; and so on.

For this type of code, it makes sense to apply a more comprehensive set of tests, which don't just test the outputs of a function, but zoom in to a sub-atomic level and examine the function's internal operations, not leaving any code flow or state transition to chance or assumption. Thankfully, DDT can help here too: you can draw out a design diagram (or set of diagrams) and then use the "standard" DDT pattern to identify test cases and test scenarios.

■ **Caution** Algorithmic unit tests are even finer-grained than "normal" unit tests—i.e., they go sub-atomic. Though algorithmic unit tests are well suited to the types of code we've just described, we wouldn't recommend them for "everyday" code—you'd be there for most of this decade and the next, writing intricate tests for code that almost certainly doesn't require that level of testing.

In this chapter we'll demonstrate how to apply DDT to create algorithmic unit tests. We'll illustrate the process with UML activity diagrams, but the same principles should hold true for other types of "dynamic" diagrams (that is, diagrams that describe a sequence of events or state changes rather than a static model such as a class diagram).

The unit testing techniques described in this chapter build on the "ICONIX Process for Algorithms" roadmap, which originated with Doug's work with the Large Synoptic Survey Telescope image processing pipelines, and is described in the upcoming book *ICONIX Process Roadmaps* (Fingerpress, September 2010).

Top Ten Algorithm Testing "To-Do"s

Following is a list of the top ten "to-do" items for algorithm testing:

10. Start with a controller from the conceptual design.

9. Expand the controller into an algorithm design using activity diagrams, state-chart diagrams, etc.

8. Tie the diagram loosely to your domain model.

7. Split up decision nodes that look like they're doing more than one check.

6. Create a test case for each node (Activity and Decision nodes).

5. Define test scenarios for each test case, specifying a range of inputs and expected outputs.

4. Create input data from a variety of sources, depending on the algorithm; e.g., use "fuzzing" techniques.

3. Assign the logic flow into individual methods and assign them to classes.

2. Write "white box" unit tests.

1. Apply DDT to other types of design diagrams.

We'll structure the remainder of the chapter around this top-ten list.

10. Start with a Controller from the Conceptual Design

Think back to Part 2 for a moment... you've created a slightly higher-level conceptual design (see Chapter 6), and then evolved this into a low-level detailed design (Chapter 5), with a "gritty" real-world sequence diagram drawn out for each use case, exploring all the ins and outs, the sunny day and rainy day scenarios. From this you've identified unit tests that weren't already covered by controller tests, or which looked like they would benefit from a more "zoomed-in" form of test, operating on an individual function instead of a group of functions.

In this chapter we'll create an algorithmic design for a single controller from the *Use Address* use case from Chapter 7. To recap, here's the full narrative use case. We've shown the part of the Basic Course that we'll focus on in this chapter in bold:

> *BASIC COURSE:*
> *The user types an address using all address fields on the Quick Search window. The system enables the "Locate" button as soon as an entry was made in either one of these fields: City, State, Postal, Country.*
> *The user clicks "Locate".* **The system geocodes the location based on the level of detail provided by the user and stores any candidates in an Address Candidate Collection. If a single candidate is found or exactly one of the multiple candidates has a 100% match rate, the System sets the AOI based on this Address Candidate.**
>
> *ALTERNATE COURSES:*
> *The user clicks "Clear": Entries in any fields will be cleared.*
> *Multiple valid candidates found: The System displays an Address Candidate widget with a list of potential candidates to choose from. The user selects an Address Candidate.*
> *No candidates were found: The system displays a message: "Location not found".*

Figure 12–1 shows the robustness diagram (i.e., conceptual design) for this use case—we've circled the part that we'll turn into an activity diagram.

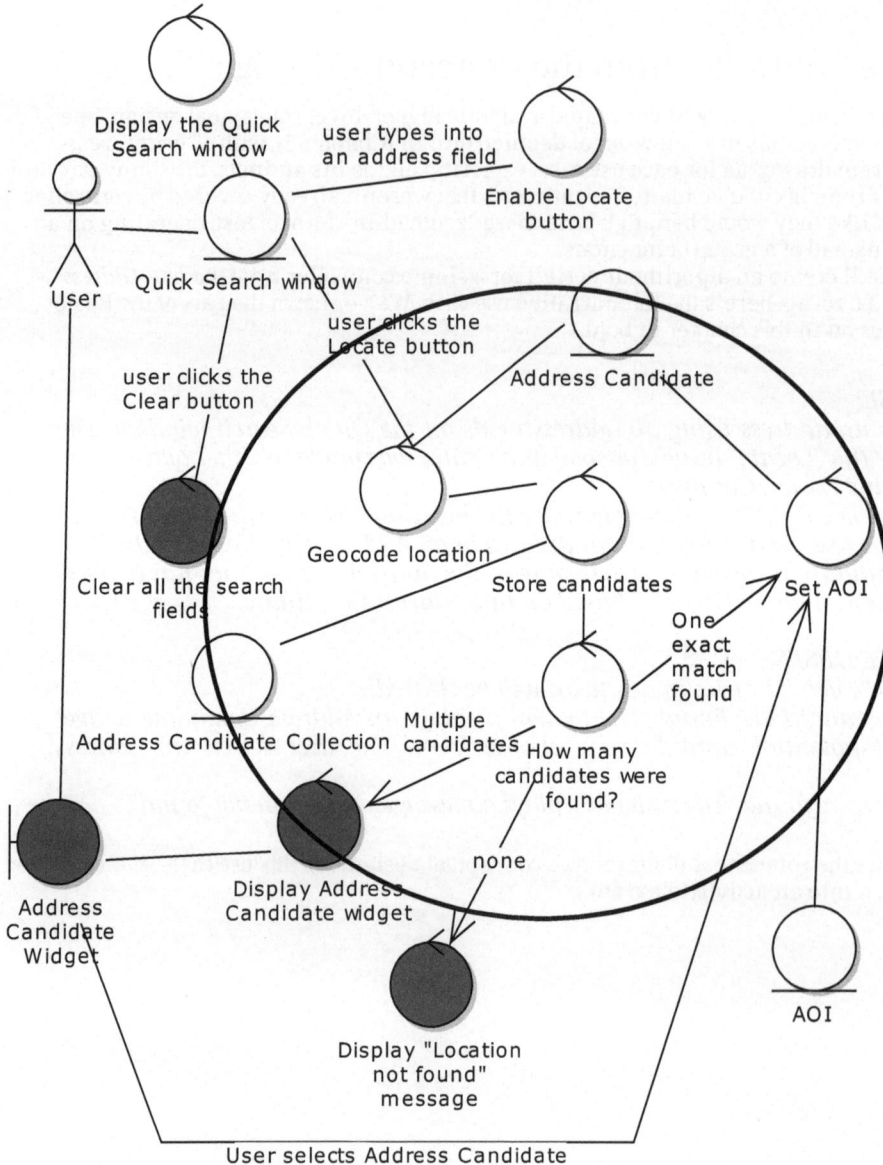

Figure 12–1. Robustness diagram for "Use Address"

We'll zero in on one of the controllers shortly, but the activity diagram actually covers four of the controllers: *Geocode location, How many candidates were found?, Set AOI,* and *Display Address Candidate widget.*

The system geocodes the address using ESRI's Geocoding Service, then checks to see how many candidate hotels were returned. If none, then a separate service—the POI Locator Service—is given a try. If any hotels were found, the AOI ("Area Of Interest") is set around the address candidate; if more than one hotel was found, the address candidates are listed in the Search Widget.

Collectively, this small group of controllers is a subsystem that should get more attention in the detailed design. Much of this design detail could be added to the original sequence diagram, as it falls outside the remit of an "algorithm test." However, we'll focus on the *How many candidates were found?* controller (in which there's some deceptively complex logic going on) to see how more in-depth testing will benefit the code.

■ **Note** You might well find that one software function covers a single algorithm; e.g., a controller called "Sort Results" would imply that some sorting code will need to be written (assuming there's no suitable sorting algorithm built in to the language or its collections API). So "going sub-atomic" in that case would involve diving inside a single controller and designing the internal logic in fine detail; i.e., you'd draw one activity diagram for a single controller.

---

9. Expand the Controllers into an Algorithm Design

The "Geocode location" and related controllers can be expanded out into the following logic:

```
geocode the address using the geocoding service
if the geocoding service returns at least one candidate then
  if there is exactly one candidate or one of the candidates is a 100% match then
    set the AOI around that candidate
  else
    display the candidates in the candidate widget
else (no candidates found)
  try the POI locator service
  if there is exactly one candidate or one of the candidates is a 100% match then
    set the AOI around that candidate
  else
    display the candidates in the candidate widget
```

Figure 12–2 shows the same pseudocode transcribed into an activity diagram.

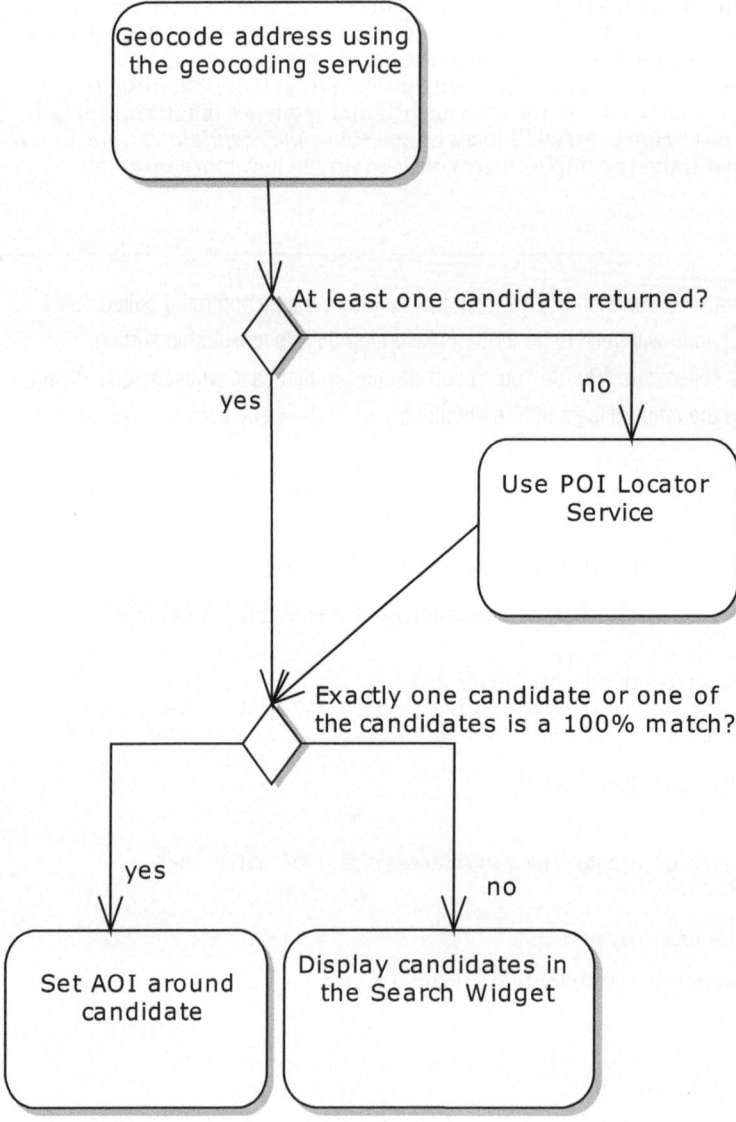

Figure 12–2. Initial activity diagram for "Geocode Address"

With a more complex algorithm you may also want to create additional diagrams, or use different diagram types, to describe the logic. The diagram doesn't necessarily need to be UML, as long as the format allows you to describe individual steps and state changes as discrete operations.

8. Tie the Diagram Loosely to Your Domain Model

Using the ICONIX Process, you create a domain model, then use this during conceptual design—identifying further domain classes in the process—and then allocate behavior to each domain class during the detailed design. Normally you allocate behavior using sequence diagrams, which allow you to draw lines between objects to allocate operations/methods. But when designing algorithms, you're more likely to be using an activity or state chart diagram.

You'll probably already have a pretty good idea which class or classes your algorithm will be implemented in. So at this stage, all that's needed is to drag the relevant domain classes onto the diagram, and place each one down the right-hand side, next to the relevant node—see Figure 12–3.

Think about not just the names mentioned in the activity, but what the output function is—e.g., "Geocode address using the geocoding service" points to "At least one candidate returned?" So from this it's fairly obvious that a collection of Candidates is returned... so we'll add a CandidateCollection class to the model.

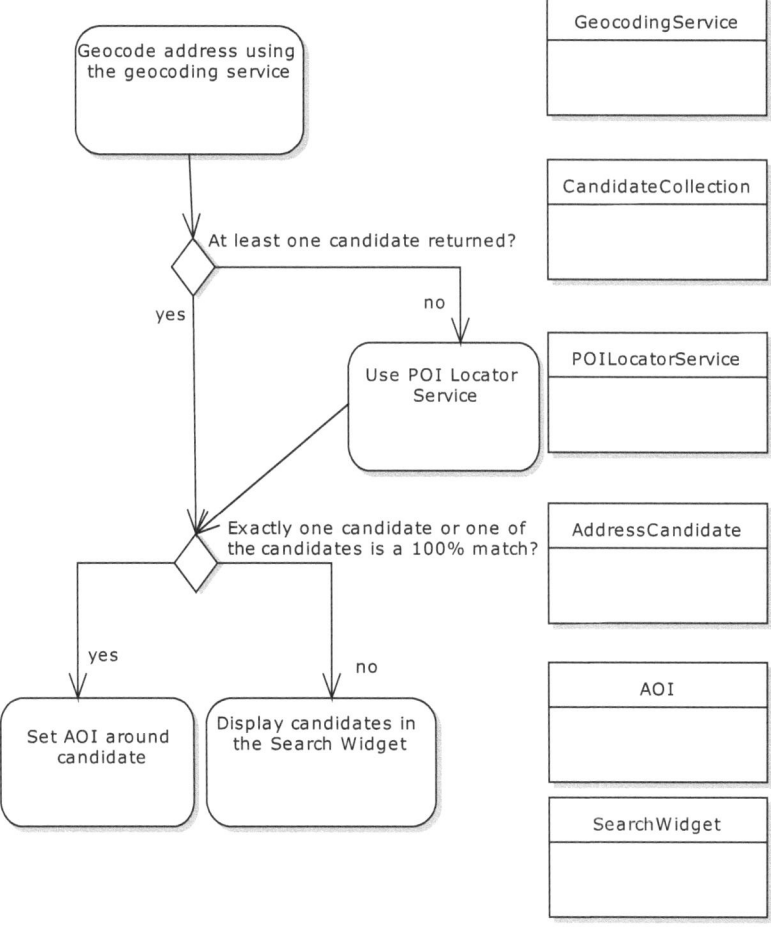

Figure 12–3. *"Geocode Address" algorithm with domain classes dragged onto the diagram*

Each of the objects on the right in Figure 12–3 is essentially a "helper object," but the flow of the algorithm itself takes place on whatever class is central to the main operation. In this case it's a server-side Java class called SearchService. (This part of the behavior allocation—linking the main operation to SearchService—would already have been done on a sequence diagram during detailed design.) So each activity in Figure 12–3 will be part of a method on SearchService, and may (or may not, depending how the design turns out) call out to one of the (currently loosely associated) domain classes on the right.

7. Split Up Decision Nodes Involving More Than One Check

Review decision nodes and identify those that appear to involve more than one check. In Figure 12–3, one of the decision nodes is called "Exactly one candidate or one of the candidates is a 100% match?" That node represents, of course, two checks, so it could be a candidate for being split into two separate decision nodes.

There's no hard and fast rule for this, though. If splitting them up makes the design simpler, and you want to test them as two separate decisions, then split them up. But if you find that it just makes the code or the design more obtuse (with code having to work around the fact that they're separate), then keep them together. But do keep a lookout for such choices while you're designing. (In the example in this chapter, we're keeping it as one check, as it befits the design.)

6. Create a Test Case for Each Node

Create a test case for each activity and decision node. This step is not at all dissimilar from how you'd create behavioral test cases and use case scenario test cases: just identify a control point at the relevant level of granularity (very large-grained, "scenario-sized" for scenario tests; medium-grained, "controller-sized" for controller tests; fine-grained or "function-size" for unit tests, and, of course, "pico-grained"/sub-atomic for algorithm tests).

First create a new diagram beneath the activity diagram's package, to hold the test cases. (In EA, create a "Custom" diagram that is in its "Extended" group of diagram types.) For each node on the activity diagram, create a new test case with the same name (see Figure 12–4).

■ **Note** At the time of writing, EA doesn't yet auto-create test cases from activity diagrams, as it does with other diagram types such as sequence diagrams. Luckily, it takes only a couple of minutes to create the test cases manually, but it's certainly high up on our "wish list" of time-saving new features!

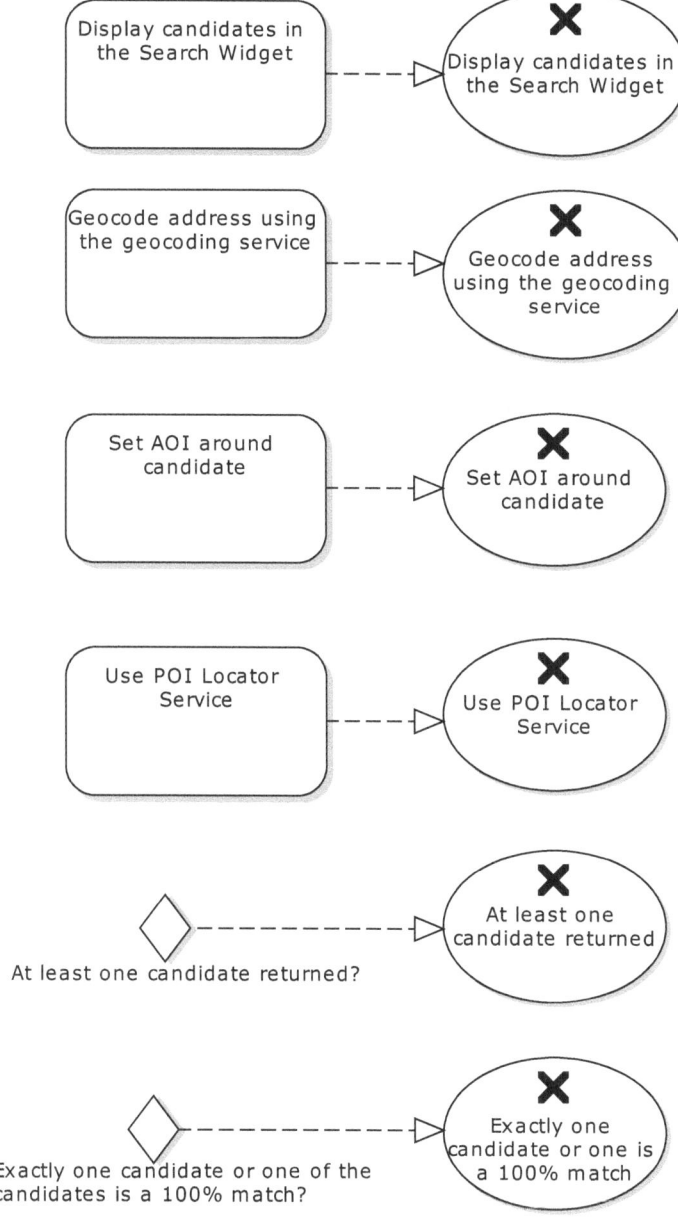

Figure 12–4. *Test case diagram showing individual activity nodes each linked to its own test case*

For the example in this chapter, we'll implement and test the two decision point nodes, "At least one candidate returned?" and the snappily titled "Exactly one candidate or one of the candidates is a 100% match?"

5. Define Test Scenarios for Each Test Case

Define your test scenarios, as many as you need for each test case. Be sure to specify the range of inputs and outputs for each scenario.

With a normal unit test case, you'd test a function with a variety of inputs, and define the acceptance criteria/expected results for each one. Algorithm test cases are no different.

The "At least one candidate returned" test case, for example, could have test scenarios added, as shown in Table 12–1.

Table 12–1. *Test Scenario Details for the "At least one candidate returned" Test Case*

Name	Input	Acceptance Criteria
No candidates	an empty CandidateCollection	false returned
One candidate	CandidateCollection containing one address	true returned
Two or more candidates	A CandidateCollection containing a random number (>1) of addresses	true returned

The three test scenarios in Table 12–1 give us the "classic" testing cardinality of "zero," "one," or "more than one," where any value greater than one is essentially treated the same: two will be subject to the same issues, limitations, and effects as 1,000. Our test scenario could use a random value each time.[2] Some tests will benefit from a range of random numbers being used each time; there will be more about sourcing of test data in the next section.

Table 12–2 shows the test scenarios we've added for the second decision node test case, "Exactly one candidate or one is a 100% match."

---

[2] Also see this page for a discussion of useful values to test for:
www.testingreflections.com/node/view/4828.

Table 12–2. *Test Scenario Details for the "Exactly one candidate or one is a 100% match" Test Case*

Name	Input	Acceptance Criteria
No candidates	an empty CandidateCollection	false returned
One candidate	CandidateCollection containing one address	true returned
Two inexact candidates	CandidateCollection with two addresses, neither of which is a 100% match	false returned
One exact and some inexact candidates	CandidateCollection with several addresses, one of which is a 100% match	true returned
Several exact candidates	CandidateCollection containing several addresses, all of which are exact candidates	false returned

That last test scenario in Table 12–2—"Several exact candidates"—is a crucial one, as you'll see shortly, since (at the risk of revealing the plot too early in the story) it will highlight a bug in the code.

Now that we've added test scenarios, we'll quickly transform our two test cases into UML test classes (Ctrl+H in EA) using the ICONIX_JUnit4 transformation—see Figure 12–5—and turn them straight into JUnit 4 test code.[3]

---

[3] If you're not sure how to do these bits, read through Chapters 5 and 6 first, and then come straight back here…

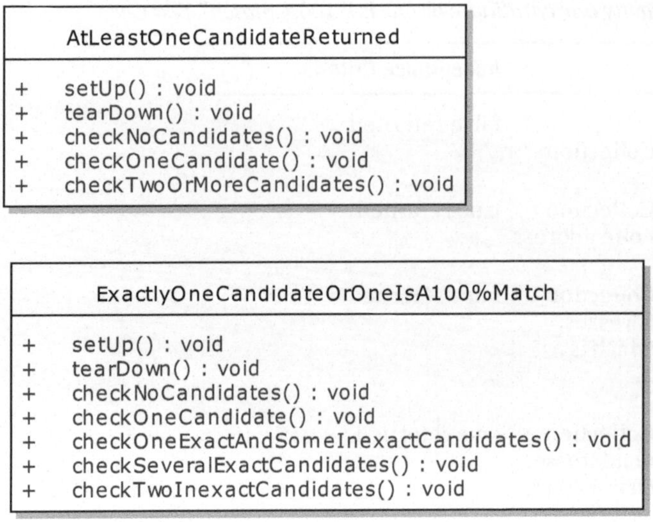

```
┌─────────────────────────────────────────────────┐
│          AtLeastOneCandidateReturned            │
├─────────────────────────────────────────────────┤
│  +    setUp() : void                            │
│  +    tearDown() : void                         │
│  +    checkNoCandidates() : void                │
│  +    checkOneCandidate() : void                │
│  +    checkTwoOrMoreCandidates() : void         │
└─────────────────────────────────────────────────┘
```

```
┌─────────────────────────────────────────────────────────┐
│        ExactlyOneCandidateOrOneIsA100%Match             │
├─────────────────────────────────────────────────────────┤
│  +    setUp() : void                                    │
│  +    tearDown() : void                                 │
│  +    checkNoCandidates() : void                        │
│  +    checkOneCandidate() : void                        │
│  +    checkOneExactAndSomeInexactCandidates() : void    │
│  +    checkSeveralExactCandidates() : void              │
│  +    checkTwoInexactCandidates() : void                │
└─────────────────────────────────────────────────────────┘
```

Figure 12–5. The new unit test classes ready to be turned into code

Here's the generated test code for the first test class—the pattern of which should be starting to look pretty familiar by now:

```java
import org.junit.*;
import static org.junit.Assert.*;

/**
 * 'At least one candidate returned' - controller tests.
 */
public class AtLeastOneCandidateReturned {

    @Before
    public void setUp() throws Exception{
        // set up test fixtures here...

    }

    @After
    public void tearDown() throws Exception{
        // destroy test fixtures here...

    }

    /**
     * Input: an empty CandidateCollection
     * Acceptance Criteria: false returned
     */
    @Test
    public final void checkNoCandidates() throws Exception{
```

```
    }

    /**
     * Input: CandidateCollection containing one address
     * Acceptance Criteria: true
     * returned
     */
    @Test
    public final void checkOneCandidate() throws Exception{

    }

    /**
     * Input: A CandidateCollection containing a random number (>1) of addresses
     * Acceptance Criteria: true returned
     */
    @Test
    public final void checkTwoOrMoreCandidates() throws Exception{

    }
}
```

The second test class is more of the same generated "skeleton" code, so we'll skip it for now. You'll see the fully implemented test code later in the chapter, though.

4. Create Input Data from a Variety of Sources

Two is an impossible number, and can't exist... [4]

Admittedly Asimov was referring to absolute singletons like universes and deities when he wrote this. When you're testing, it would be dangerous to assume that certain input values or mid-transition states can never exist: testing outside the expected bounds—adding "rainy day scenarios"—is a key part of DDT.

The test data you use will need to be a mix of "realistic" day-to-day test data, and erroneous data that potentially trips the system up with unexpected input values. You're really testing for two different things here: that the system works as expected, and that it reports errors correctly.

Sourcing useful test data can be a problem. For example, if you happen to be developing a credit risk system (which would use hoards of historical data to predict the likelihood that counterparties will default on their loan repayments), randomly generated data won't be much use: you'll need accurate, real, and, above all, meaningful data.

The data can be loaded into your test from a number of sources, e.g., CSV files or spreadsheets, or via a database (a local DB could be set up to keep the data free from outside interference or ghost reads). A lot depends on the type of algorithm, how much data it needs for effective testing, who needs

---

[4] Isaac Asimov, *The Gods Themselves* (Doubleday, 1972).

to create the data (BAs, "quants" or a customer), and whether it needs to be kept up to date once created.

If the purpose of your test is to chase down the "rainy day scenarios" and test the code's resilience to erroneous data, a technique known as **fuzzing** might be useful.[5] Fuzzing (or **fuzz testing**) involves finding bugs using malformed or semi-malformed data, randomly generating input values that fall outside the expected range.

Just generating random values may not be especially effective, as hitting the particular value that exposes a bug can become too much like a game of chance with infinitesimally low odds. Another technique, known as **constrained random testing** (sometimes used in chip design), constrains the inputs in some way so that the potential source isn't infinite; e.g., instead of "any non-zero natural number," restrict the number to the number of known available address candidates in the database.

3. Assign the Logic Flow to Individual Methods and Classes

Think of an algorithm test as more finely grained than a "normal" unit test. In fact, it may help to think of algorithm tests as being sub-atomic.

Like operating a string puppet, the idea behind algorithm tests is (figuratively speaking) to throw a line around each step in the process, and give it a little tug. It's micro-control, as you want to monitor each state change within the algorithm to ensure that it did what you expected based on the design. As individual functions tend to involve more than one state change, this means that your unit test needs to monitor something smaller than a single function.

ELECTRON BUBBLES

Another way to think of micro-controlling tests is in terms of the bubblegum factory example from Chapter 6 (see Figure 6-11). In that example, controllers (software functions) included things like "Slice and dice the bubblegum," with gum slabs in and slivers out. An algorithmic design of this picture would set up a slicing loop, with an initial slab size and desired sliver width/number of slivers. The test would then track each individual slicing operation in the loop, in addition to the loop construction, preparation, and "finishing up" of the output. It turns out that, even though each function in theory just does one thing, that "one thing" is composed of many, smaller operations.

An algorithm test confirms that each of these smaller operations does what it's meant to.

You may wonder how a unit test can test something smaller than a single function call. Generally a function consists of "Input value → process → Expected result." The test sets up the input value via a test fixture, starts the process by calling the function, and then validates the expected result. The "process" itself is atomic; so how do you get inside it?

---

[5] Proving that there's a book available on every subject, see *Fuzzing: Brute Force Vulnerability Discovery*, and the accompanying web page: http://fuzzing.org/. OWASP also has a page about fuzz testing: www.owasp.org/index.php/Fuzzing.

There are essentially two ways to get inside an atomic process:

- Inject a "spy object" into the object under test
- Divide the function into yet-smaller functions, and write individual unit tests for each one

Which method you choose depends on what you want to achieve from the test, of course. If you use a "spy object" to monitor state changes and report on them afterwards, you're effectively monitoring the overall process from start to end; it's an integration test on a pico scale. Conversely, subdividing the function into smaller functions (like blasting the rocks in a game of *Asteroids*) means you'll be testing each function separately; each one becomes an isolated unit with its own input value, process, and expected result.

A SEEMINGLY SIMPLE METHOD MAY NOT BE PROVABLY CORRECT

Here's a Java method that sums together all the values in an array of integers:

```java
public int sumArray(int... values) {
    int count = 0;
    for (int value : values) {
        count += value;
    }
    return count;
}
```

The code's pretty simple: it just loops through the values array, adds each value in turn to a running total, and then returns the result. A "normal" unit test would pass in an array of values and assert that the result is correct—like this:

```java
@Test
public void sumArray() {
    LoopingExample looper = new LoopingExample();
    int result = looper.sumArray(2,2);
    assertEquals(4, result);
}
```

However, how many different sets of arrays would you need to pass in—i.e., how many different test case scenarios—before you could state with confidence that the function is "proven" to be mathematically correct?

At the risk of going all contrived, if the programmer had accidentally made the function multiply each array element with the previous sub-total instead of adding them, passing in {2, 2} would, of course, return 4 in either case; so the previous test would pass either way. A more complex function could have all kinds of traps and special cases that would be missed by a simple set of input scenarios.

To be absolutely sure that each part of the algorithm is working as expected, you'd need to delve deeper into the function and ensure that each step matches up with the design—i.e., that the initialization of "count" is done as expected; every value in the array is "hit" during the loop; the addition is done correctly; and the correct variable is returned. In other words, if the overall unit isn't provably correct, then "proving" that each *step* in the unit works is another way to exhaustively test it—assuming that you trust the overarching algorithm, of course.

Back to the Mapplet example, we need to create a method for each activity node and assign them to classes. Not all of the activity nodes will turn into a whole method; some will go inside a single method. Deciding whether to create a new method is partially based on the choice of how you're planning to test the activity—i.e., whether you'll pass in a spy object or just test the outputs of individual methods. We'll compare both approaches for the "At least one candidate returned" test case.

■ **Note** EA has a behavioral code generation feature with which you can drag methods from classes onto an activity diagram, and then generate algorithmic code from the diagram. It genuinely creates working source code from your design.[6] We anticipate that it's just a matter of time before it'll also generate the matching algorithm test code. Be sure to keep an eye on the Sparx web site, as well as www.designdriventesting.com, for new developments.

Assigning the methods to classes here creates a "stronger" association than when you earlier placed the domain classes next to nodes on the activity diagram. In fact, much of the behavior allocation should already have been done during detailed design using sequence diagrams, so there should be very little left to do here: any straggling operations should now be allocated to the class that most closely matches their domain.

The domain objects you placed on the diagram should be a pretty strong hint as to which class you allocate each method to; e.g., "At least one candidate returned?" is next to CandidateCollection, and it also seems like CandidateCollection would be a suitable place to put such a check.

Figure 12–6 shows the class diagram with our new methods allocated. The decision node "At least one candidate returned?" has turned into the method hasAtLeastOneCandidate() on CandidateCollection. Also, the Candidate domain class has evolved into AddressCandidate.

---

[6] For more about this feature, see *ICONIX Process Roadmaps* by Doug Rosenberg (Fingerpress, 2010) and its chapters about SysML and SOA.

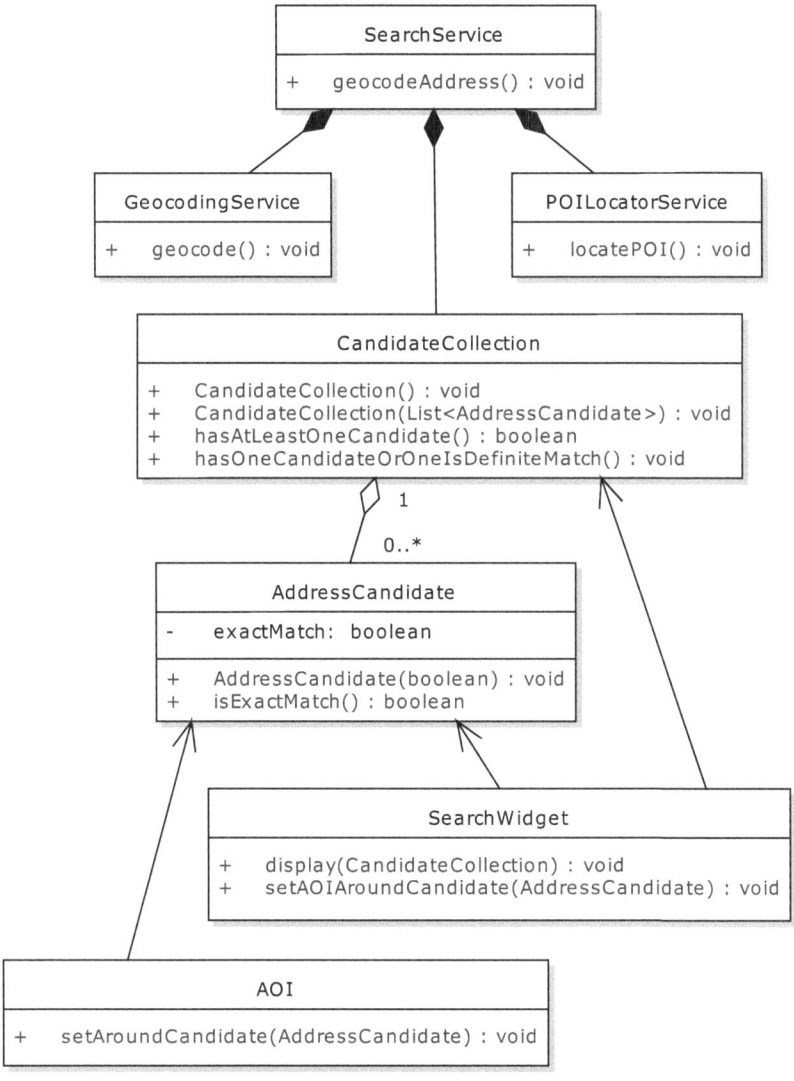

Figure 12–6. The new unit test class ready to be turned into code

The AddressCandidate objects are the ingredients, the slivers of gum, being passed through the algorithm's machinery. The SearchService would call out to GeocodingService and POILocatorService, and in each case receive back a CandidateCollection, which will contain zero or more AddressCandidates. For the test, we'll just create input data consisting of CandidateCollections with varying numbers of AddressCandidates, and pass these into the code under test.

Here's the (currently quite minimal) code for AddressCandidate:

```java
public class AddressCandidate {

    private boolean exactMatch;

    public AddressCandidate(boolean exactMatch) {
        this.exactMatch = exactMatch;
    }

    public boolean isExactMatch() {
        return exactMatch;
    }
}
```

In the finished implementation, this will also contain identifying data such as a name and lat/long co-ordinates; but for the algorithm in this chapter we need only the exactMatch flag.

We'll dissect the main class that we want to test, CandidateCollection, over the next couple of pages. But to start off, here it is in its entirety:

```java
package com.vresorts.mapplet.geocoding;

import java.util.*;

public class CandidateCollection {

    private List<AddressCandidate> candidates;

    public CandidateCollection() {
        this(new ArrayList<AddressCandidate>());
    }

    public CandidateCollection(List<AddressCandidate> candidates) {
        this.candidates = candidates;
    }

    public boolean hasAtLeastOneCandidate() {
        return candidates.size() > 0;
    }

    public boolean hasOneCandidateOrOneIsDefiniteMatch() {
        if (candidates.size()==1) {
            return true;
        }
        for (AddressCandidate candidate : candidates) {
            if (candidate.isExactMatch()) {
                return true;
            }
        }
        return false;
    }
}
```

■ **Note** Remember that we mentioned that one of the test scenarios would highlight a bug in the code. If you can spot the bug in CandidateCollection based on the test scenarios in Table 12–2, you win a massive pork pie with lashings of Worcester sauce (just present cash at your nearest grocery store to redeem prize). If not, running the JUnit tests that we're about to implement will also highlight the bug. But no pork pie in that case...

As you can see from the code, CandidateCollection is primarily a wrapper around a java.util.ArrayList (a type of Collection), with added behavior that's relevant to a grouping of address candidates. CandidateCollection has two constructors: one's zero-arg, which will initialize the object with an empty list of AddressCandidates, and the other one takes a pre-prepared list of AddressCandidates. This second constructor is how the collection is initially populated. It will also prove useful shortly, when we inject a "spy object" into the class.

Now that we have the actual code that we want to test, let's go back to the "skeleton" test class that EA generated, and fill in the gaps with the interesting stuff.

2. Write "White Box" Unit Tests

Just as a quick recap, Figure 12–7 shows the two decision nodes in the activity diagram that we're going to test here.

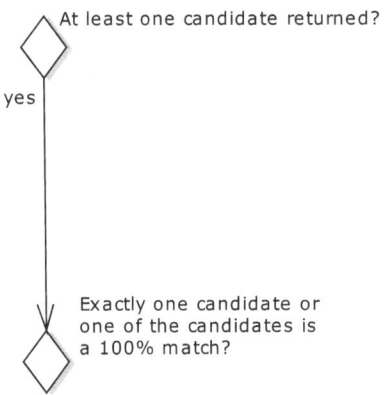

Figure 12–7. Excerpt from the activity diagram showing the decision nodes we're about to test

We'll now write the test code to validate both these decision nodes.

■ **Tip** Reserve this level of test detail for algorithm tests; avoid going "sub-atomic" for normal unit tests.

Testing the "At least one candidate returned" Decision Node

Remember that each activity or decision node on the activity diagram has its own test case, and each test case has several test scenarios (i.e., varying input data for the same test case).

So here's the first test scenario, for the "At least one candidate returned" case:

```
/**
 * Input: an empty CandidateCollection
 * Acceptance Criteria: false returned
 */
@Test
public final void checkNoCandidates() throws Exception{
    CandidateCollection addresses = new CandidateCollection();
    assertFalse( addresses.hasAtLeastOneCandidate() );
}
```

As we mentioned earlier when looking at the class diagram, CandidateCollection has a no-arg constructor, which initializes the object with an empty list of address candidates. A quick run of the JUnit test runner in Eclipse produces a green bar, so we're golden (or green, depending how you look at it).

On to the next two test scenarios, to complete the first test case. Remember each of these is testing the hasAtLeastOneCandidate method:

```
/**
 * Input: CandidateCollection containing one address
 * Acceptance Criteria: true returned
 */
@Test
public final void checkOneCandidate() throws Exception{
    List<AddressCandidate> testData = new ArrayList<AddressCandidate>(1);
    testData.add(new AddressCandidate(false));
    CandidateCollection addresses = new CandidateCollection(testData);
    assertTrue( addresses.hasAtLeastOneCandidate() );
}
```

```
/**
 * Input: A CandidateCollection containing a random number (>1) of addresses
 * Acceptance Criteria: true returned
 */
@Test
public final void checkTwoOrMoreCandidates() throws Exception{
    int numCandidates = new Random().nextInt(100)+1;
    List<AddressCandidate> testData = new ArrayList<AddressCandidate>(numCandidates);
    for (int num=0; num<numCandidates; num++) {
        testData.add(new AddressCandidate(false));
    }
    CandidateCollection addresses = new CandidateCollection(testData);
    assertTrue( addresses.hasAtLeastOneCandidate() );
}
```

■ **Note** checkTwoOrMoreCandidates() uses a random function to pass in a varying number of address candidates. Test purists might find this worrying, as it means the test could potentially pass or fail randomly each time it's run. This *would* be worrying if the random input potentially crossed the range between "correct" and "incorrect" data. However, as long as the random values can fall only within a "correct" (sunny day) range or an "incorrect" (rainy day) range, it's a valid way to eke out unexpected test failures. Also see the section previously on fuzzing, and constrained random testing.

Another quick run of the test runner produces a green bar—as you'd expect really, since the code under test (so far) is just a one-liner. The next test case is a little more complicated, though.

Testing the "Exactly one candidate or one is a 100% match" Decision Node

The first test scenario in this case is very similar to the first one for the previous test case. We're calling a different method, but ultimately the input data and expected result are identical. Here's the first scenario, then, for our second test class:

```
/**
 * 'Exactly one candidate or one is a 100% match' - controller tests.
 */
public class ExactlyOneCandidateOrOneIsAnExactMatch {
    /**
     * Input: an empty CandidateCollection
     * Acceptance Criteria: false returned
     */
    @Test
    public final void checkNoCandidates() throws Exception{
        CandidateCollection addresses = new CandidateCollection();
        assertFalse( addresses.hasOneCandidateOrOneIsDefiniteMatch() );
    }
```

The second test scenario is also largely identical to the previous test case, so we'll skip that.

In the third test scenario, our test data consists of a CandidateCollection with several AddressCandidates; one is an exact match and the others aren't. Here's the test code:

```
/**
 * Input: CandidateCollection with several addresses, one of which is a 100% match
 * Acceptance Criteria: true returned
 */
@Test
public final void checkOneExactAndSomeInexactCandidates() throws Exception {
    List<AddressCandidate> testData = new ArrayList<AddressCandidate>(5);
    testData.add(new AddressCandidate(true));
    testData.add(new AddressCandidate(false));
    testData.add(new AddressCandidate(false));
    testData.add(new AddressCandidate(false));
    testData.add(new AddressCandidate(false));

    CandidateCollection addresses = new CandidateCollection(testData);
```

```
    assertTrue( addresses.hasOneCandidateOrOneIsDefiniteMatch() );
}
```

Running this gives us another green bar... so we're very nearly home and dry. There's just one more test scenario to go. This is the test method for the "CandidateCollection containing several addresses, all of which are exact candidates" scenario:

```
/**
 * Input: CandidateCollection containing several addresses, all of which are exact
 * candidates
 * Acceptance Criteria: false returned
 */
@Test
public final void checkSeveralExactCandidates() throws Exception {
    List<AddressCandidate> testData = new ArrayList<AddressCandidate>(3);
    testData.add(new AddressCandidate(true));
    testData.add(new AddressCandidate(true));
    testData.add(new AddressCandidate(true));

    CandidateCollection addresses = new CandidateCollection(testData);
    assertFalse( addresses.hasOneCandidateOrOneIsDefiniteMatch() );
}
```

This one should return false, even though all the address candidates are exact matches. The business rule requires that exactly one of them be an exact match.

However, the result of running the test is shown in Figure 12–8.

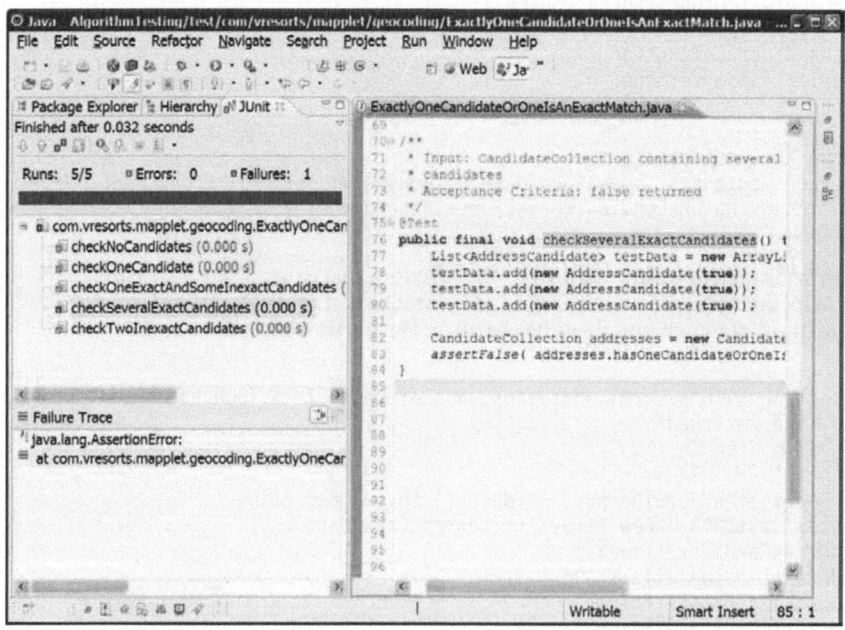

Figure 12–8. checkSeveralExactCandidates() produces a test failure.

To examine why this test failed, let's revisit the method under test—here it is from earlier:

```
public boolean hasOneCandidateOrOneIsDefiniteMatch() {
    if (candidates.size()==1) {
        return true;
    }
    for (AddressCandidate candidate : candidates) {
        if (candidate.isExactMatch()) {
            return true;
        }
    }
    return false;
}
```

As you can see, there's a quite blatant bug in there: there's an assumption that any address candidate with an exact match should result in true being returned. However, the test caught this wrong assumption. The rewritten code is as follows:

```
public boolean hasOneCandidateOrOneIsDefiniteMatch() {
    if (candidates.size()==1) {
        return true;
    }
    boolean foundExactMatch = false;
    for (AddressCandidate candidate : candidates) {
        if (candidate.isExactMatch()) {
            if (foundExactMatch) {
                return false;
            }
            foundExactMatch = true;
        }
    }
    return foundExactMatch;
}
```

The idea behind this version is that if the first exact match is found, that's good, but if another exact match is found, the code immediately returns with false. Re-running the tests produces a pass. But seeing as this code caused us a bit of a problem, let's focus on it and see if there are further test techniques we can use to zoom in and peek inside the (supposedly atomic) function.

Send in the Spy Object

"Never imagine yourself not to be otherwise than what it might appear to others that what you were or might have been was not otherwise than what you had been would have appeared to them to be otherwise," said the Duchess.[7]

One way to keep an eye on the code's internals and check that they're working as expected is to pass in a "spy object." This is a bit like a mock object, but it's a "tracking" implementation of an object used by the code under test, to record various diagnostics, such as whether a particular method was called, how many times it was called, the order that the methods were called in, and the mid-algorithm, or "transition state" values that were passed around.

■ **Tip** Use spy objects to test for correct state transitions within functions.

---

[7] Lewis Carroll, Alice's Adventures in Wonderland (1865), Chapter 9 "The Mock Turtle's Story".

Looking at the fixed version of hasOneCandidateOrOneIsDefiniteMatch(), and the checkSeveralExactCandidates() test scenario—which is passing in a collection of three exact matches—we expect the overall size of the collection to be checked once (to see if it has exactly one match), and we expect candidate.isExactMatch() to be called twice. (That should be the case whether three exact matches are passed in or 300, as the code will exit as soon as a second exact match is found.)

So we'll create two spy objects—one for the java.util.ArrayList collection (the "backing store" behind CandidateCollection), and the other for AddressCandidate. In other words, see Figure 12–9.

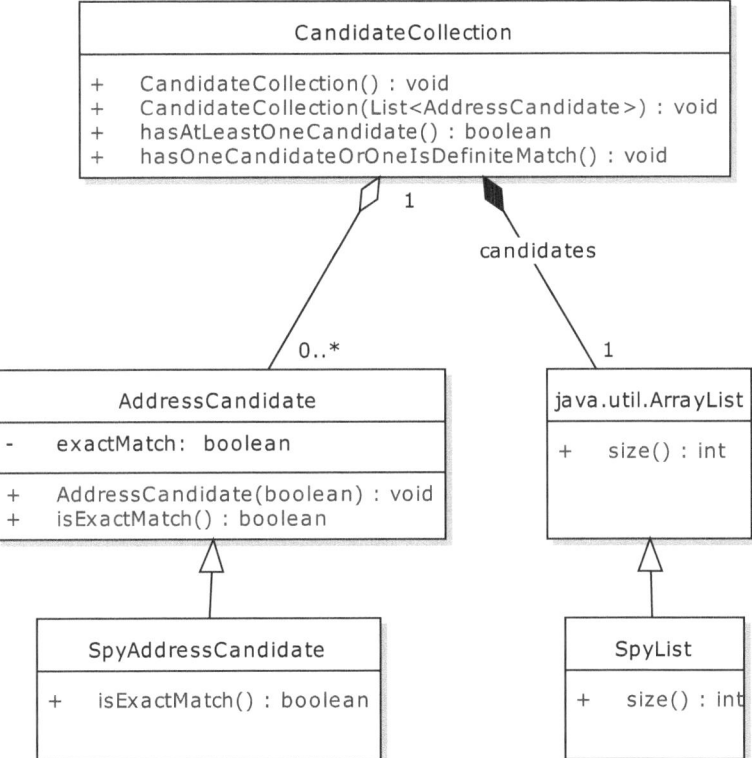

Figure 12–9. Our new "spy" classes pretending to be the real ones while taking notes

We'll create both as static inner classes inside the test class. Let's start with SpyList.

Spy Object 001: SpyList

Referring back to Figure 12–9, SpyList extends java.util.ArrayList with additional "spy" functionality. Here's our new SpyList inner class:

```
static class SpyList<E> extends ArrayList<E> {
    public int size() {
        sizeCalled++;
        return super.size();
```

```
    }
    private int sizeCalled = 0;
}
```

Each time the size() method is called, the spy object first increments its internal count, and then calls up to the "proper" method in the parent class. We'll now modify the test scenario to use the SpyList:

```
/**
 * Input: CandidateCollection containing several addresses, all of which are exact
 * candidates
 * Acceptance Criteria: false returned
 */
@Test
public final void checkSeveralExactCandidates() throws Exception {
    SpyList<AddressCandidate> spyData = new SpyList<AddressCandidate>();
    spyData.add(new AddressCandidate(true));
    spyData.add(new AddressCandidate(true));
    spyData.add(new AddressCandidate(true));

    CandidateCollection addresses = new CandidateCollection(spyData);
    boolean result = addresses.hasOneCandidateOrOneIsDefiniteMatch();

    assertEquals(1, spyData.sizeCalled);
    assertFalse(result);
}
```

Running this version produces a test failure, though:

```
java.lang.AssertionError: expected:<1> but was:<3>
```

You may already have spotted the reason: in CandidateCollection. hasOneCandidateOrOneIsDefiniteMatch(), there's one *explicit* call to candidates.size(), but there's also an implicit call in the loop header:

```
for (AddressCandidate candidate : candidates) {
. . .
```

That's Java's new-ish sugary syntax for you—candidates.size() is called "behind the scenes" by Java each time the loop iterates. In this case, the code iterates twice, so that's an additional two calls.

As this is valid calling of size(), we can modify the expected test result to get our green bar:

```
assertEquals(3, spyData.sizeCalled);
```

Now let's move on to the second spy object, SpyAddressCandidate.

Spy Object 002: SpyAddressCandidate

The purpose of this spy object is to ensure that AddressCandidate.exactMatch() is being called the expected number of times. Here's our new SpyAddressCandidate inner class:

```
static class SpyAddressCandidate extends AddressCandidate {
    public SpyAddressCandidate(boolean exactMatch) {
        super(exactMatch);
    }
    public boolean isExactMatch() {
        exactMatchCalled++;
        return super.isExactMatch();
    }
    private int exactMatchCalled = 0;
}
```

The pattern is exactly the same as with SpyList: we've overridden one of the methods to increment a count each time it's called, and then defer control up to the real method in the parent class. Aside from that (and the matching constructor to satisfy Java's grammar requirements), absolutely none of the functionality of the real AddressCandidate is modified.

Here's the updated test scenario method in full:

```
/**
 * Input: CandidateCollection containing several addresses, all of which are exact
 * candidates
 * Acceptance Criteria: false returned
 */
@Test
public final void checkSeveralExactCandidates() throws Exception {
    SpyList<AddressCandidate> spyData = new SpyList<AddressCandidate>();
    spyData.add(new SpyAddressCandidate(true));
    spyData.add(new SpyAddressCandidate(true));
    spyData.add(new SpyAddressCandidate(true));

    CandidateCollection addresses = new CandidateCollection(spyData);
    boolean result = addresses.hasOneCandidateOrOneIsDefiniteMatch();

    SpyAddressCandidate spy0 = (SpyAddressCandidate) spyData.get(0);
    assertEquals(1, spy0.exactMatchCalled);

    SpyAddressCandidate spy1 = (SpyAddressCandidate) spyData.get(1);
    assertEquals(1, spy1.exactMatchCalled);

    SpyAddressCandidate spy2 = (SpyAddressCandidate) spyData.get(2);
    assertEquals(0, spy2.exactMatchCalled);

    assertEquals(3, spyData.sizeCalled);
    assertFalse(result);
}
```

There's noticeably quite a bit more to this test method now. It's not just trusting that the return value was *false* by design; it's reaching into the code under test and making flipping well sure that the return value was calculated in the expected and correct way.

■ **Note** Of course, developing a whole project at this "zoomed-in" level would be torturously slow; going into this level of detail on the tests is only worth doing for "core" code that large portions of the project depend on. But in those few rare cases, where every aspect of a section of code needs to work 100% well and the slightest flaw could prove extremely costly, it's well worth doing.

Let's get one more green bar for the road (or gray bar as it'll appear in print, of course), the final one in the book, in fact—see Figure 12–10.

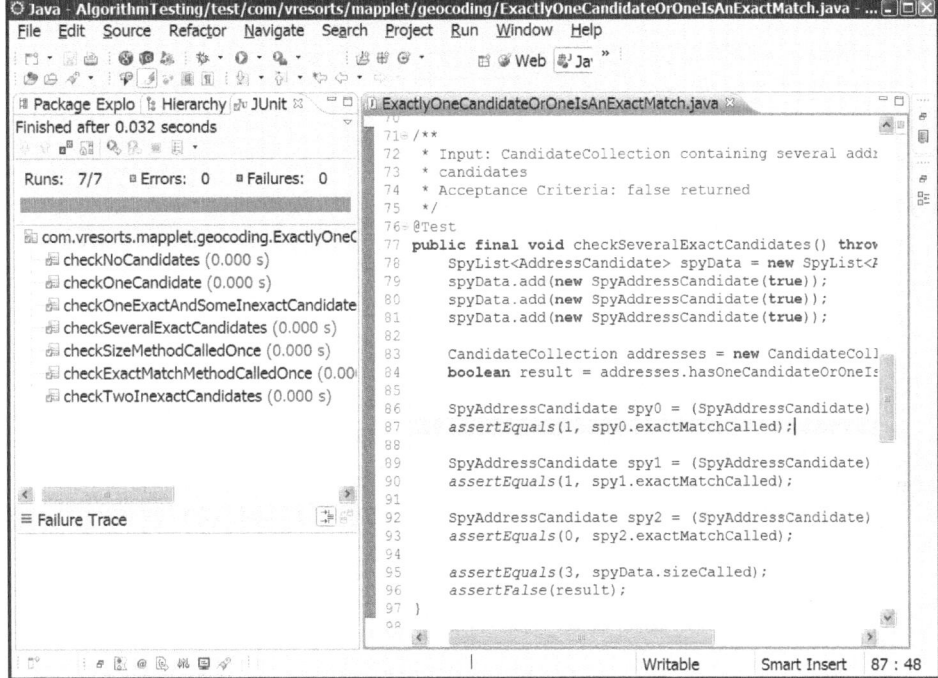

Figure 12–10. One green bar for the road…

To finish off, we'll briefly look at another way to delve into the code under test.

Break the Code into Smaller Methods

An algorithm test covers many control points/state shifts within one or more methods/functions. If each of these points is within the same method, then you'd need to pass in a spy object to track what's going on. However, that's assuming that you specifically want to confirm that certain methods are being called.

If, on the other hand, you want to confirm that each portion of code is working, then you'll need to divide the code into smaller methods, so that each one can be tested individually, with its own inputs and expected output.

With hasOneCandidateOrOneIsDefiniteMatch(), we could make a start on doing this by separating out the bulk of the code into a separate method, as follows:

```
public boolean hasOneCandidateOrOneIsDefiniteMatch() {
    return checkCandidateHasOneMatch()
        && checkForOneExactMatch();
}

boolean checkCandidateHasOneMatch() {
    return candidates.size() == 1;
```

305

```
}

boolean checkForOneExactMatch() {
    boolean foundExactMatch = false;
    for (AddressCandidate candidate : candidates) {
        if (candidate.isExactMatch()) {
            if (foundExactMatch) {
                return false;
            }
            foundExactMatch = true;
        }
    }
    return foundExactMatch;
}
```

The code does exactly the same thing, but the two main checks have been separated out so that your unit test code can now call them individually.

checkForOneExactMatch() could be split out further. To do this effectively, and keep the code understandable, you would really need to introduce a new class so that you're not passing state data back and forth between methods, which could get ugly.

Whether you want to go the "whole hog" and do this depends on how deep into the code you feel the algorithm tests need to go. It becomes a case of code readability (and time spent on the tests) versus adding in more tests, and the diminishing returns that increased code coverage may provide.

1. Apply DDT to Other Design Diagrams

One of the reasons we wanted to include this chapter was to demonstrate that it's possible to apply DDT to all sorts of design diagrams and models, by applying the same basic DDT formula. As long as you can get from the design model to an "intermediate" point—the intermediate point in this case being test cases and their respective test scenarios—then you should be good to systematically drive test code from your design.

If you're using EA to transform your model elements into test cases, it is possible to write your own transformations. This is generally easiest if you're adapting one of their transformations to go from an existing source (e.g., robustness diagrams) to a new target (e.g., a new version of FlexUnit, TestNG, or whatever). Creating a whole new transform from a new diagram type may be a little trickier, but it's certainly possible.

**WE'LL LEAVE YOU WITH AN ALGORITHM-LEVEL DDT
EXERCISE FOR THE READER . . .**

The maths programming web site Project Euler[8] presents some interesting, self-contained programming conundrums based around mathematical problems. If you want to practice writing unit tests for algorithmic logic, solving those conundrums is a great way to do it. For example, the particular one we've linked to in the footnote goes as follows:

If we list all the natural numbers below 10 that are multiples of 3 or 5, we get 3, 5, 6, and 9. The sum of these multiples is 23.

Find the sum of all the multiples of 3 or 5 below 1000.

As an exercise, try designing an algorithm for this problem as an activity diagram. Then write the code and unit tests using the design-driven technique we describe in this chapter.

Summary

In this chapter we walked through a Mapplet example to create a design-driven–tested algorithm.

Algorithm unit tests end up being very, very "white box": their knowledge of the code's activities would make an inner-city priest blush. This means that, while you can be confident enough that design-driven–tested algorithms are bug-free, they're not especially maintainable. But they tend to be for "core code," which gets changed only rarely, if at all; so this shouldn't be a problem, as long as algorithm tests are used sparingly.

It's worth noting that the in-depth, "leave no stone unturned" approach described in this chapter is similar to the "push for 100% code coverage" attitude that has grown out of TDD culture, where any line of code that isn't being tested makes the TDDer feel uncomfortable. However, 100% code coverage—even for a small amount of code like an algorithm—is an advanced form of unit testing; taking this approach for the entire code base really would be Too Damn Difficult.

---

[8] See http://projecteuler.net/index.php?section=problems&id=1

Alice in Use-Case Land

It's Not as Surreal as You Might Think . . .

The following talk was given by Doug Rosenberg, as keynote speaker at UML World in 2001, and again by request at the Rational User Conference a couple of years later. Doug provides some uncanny prescience on how surreal the industry has since become, as the agile ethos renders it "okay" to start coding without a clear idea of where the team's headed.

Here's the full transcript of Doug's talk.

Introduction

This talk is probably going to be different from most of the talks you've attended before. Before I get started I'd like to make everybody is aware that this talk is going to contain some satire, by its nature, being based on *Alice in Wonderland*, which is one of the great satirical works of all time. So, if you're easily offended by satirical humor, this talk might not be for you.

I'm using satire in this talk to point out a few things about current software development practices that seem like, while they may have started off from good ideas and may still contain some good ideas, they have acquired a significant amount of momentum in some directions that might be counterproductive. At least, they seem that way to me.

In fact, having been involved with software development in one form or another for the better part of the last 30 years, and having spent most of the last 10 of those years teaching OO analysis and design, there's some stuff going on these days that seems downright strange to me. Hence the subtitle "it's not as surreal as you might think." We're going to be talking about things like "code smells" and "designs that figure themselves out from the code" a little later on, and I'd like to make sure everybody knows…I'm not making most of this stuff up. I read a posting on a newsgroup awhile ago that said, "a little forethought can add a lot of work because forethought uses imaginary feedback to keep it on track." This is the first time I've ever heard someone postulate that thinking was harmful in software development.

So, Alice and I are attempting to use humor to point out what we perceive to be the risks of some of these practices, and, at the same time, we're also making some serious points.

So, here goes….The presentation is in 3 parts.

In Part 1, Alice, intrigued by the benefits of use-case–driven development, enters use-case land, and encounters the dangers of analysis paralysis.

In Part 2, seeking to avoid analysis paralysis, Alice meets some XtremelyCuriousCharacters and encounters the dangers of skipping analysis.

Finally, in Part 3, Alice wakes up and finds a minimal yet sufficient approach to development that avoids analysis paralysis without skipping analysis.

Part 1

Use case driven development as a paradigm of software engineering was pioneered in Sweden during the late 1980s at Ericsson Corporation and was introduced to the world in Ivar Jacobson's book on object-oriented software engineering around 1991. From that moment forward, nearly every development approach began to claim the attribute of being "use case driven," because the benefits of driving software designs from well-understood user requirements seemed so obvious.

As the use case buzzword spread, many variants appeared, and much debate ensued over how best to approach use case driven development. Many of those who claimed to be use case driven were not doing anything remotely similar to what Jacobson and his team had proposed (and already used in practice on an extremely large project), but, instead, they just tacked use cases on to the front end of whatever they were already doing.

Still others made use cases an end goal in themselves, rather than a means towards the end goal of driving software designs from user requirements.

As a result, many so-called "use case driven" approaches led projects into analysis paralysis, and to the common phenomenon of "thrashing" with use cases.

So now, let's join Alice as she enters use-case land…

Alice Falls Asleep While Reading

Oh, how sleepy she was getting. And before long, she nodded off.

Alice was beginning to get very tired while sitting in the big chair reading. The book she was reading was good, and it certainly had an interesting premise…that intriguing notion that software designs could be driven from detailed descriptions of usage scenarios.

But the book was over 500 pages long, and didn't contain many pictures, at that… and oh, how sleepy she was getting. And before long, she nodded off.

The Promise of Use Case Driven Development

As she slept, Alice dreamed of a simple yet elegant development process where first, everyone made their best effort to make sure the requirements were complete and well understood, a design was constructed to meet those requirements, and then the system was built, and tested against those very same, written, behavioral requirements to make sure the customers got what they wanted.

"Goodness," said Alice. "A simple, straightforward, step-by-step development process that actually makes sense! I wonder why nobody thought of this before?"

"It's really such a clever idea!" said Alice to herself. "It's like writing the user manual first, with a few extra details, and then designing the software to match the user's requirements."

An Analysis Model Links Use-Case Text with Objects

Right at the center of the use-case–driven development process was a clever little technique called robustness analysis that seemed to link everything else together and make the whole use-case–driven modeling process work. But Alice, who had been spending lots of time reading books about UML, had mysteriously never encountered this technique before.

Alice saw how software structure and user interface design could all be linked to a simple and clear expression of the behavioral requirements of the system.

"It all seems so intuitive and obvious," she said. "But I'm certain that I read all 32 chapters and 482 pages of the UML User Guide, and it's never mentioned, not even in the chapter on stereotypes. Whatever could have possessed them to leave this out? And how can they claim to be use-case–driven without it?"

Simple and Straightforward

"So, let's see. Use cases describe a dynamic view of system behavior, while classes and objects are about static structure," she said. "And this robustness diagram links the dynamic behavioral requirements directly to the software structure by forcing the analysts to reference objects by name right in the use-case text. I wonder if that's what 'use-case–driven' really means, because the software structure can be directly driven from the behavioral requirements," said the clever little Alice.

"It certainly seems to make sense to link the static and dynamic parts of the object model together—much more sense than to keep the software structure isolated from the behavior descriptions," she mused, "but it doesn't seem very close to code, yet."

She followed the path deeper into use-case land.

<<includes>> or <<extends>>

As Alice walked down the path, she came upon two men who kept hitting each other over the head with sticks, arguing violently over something. Alice stopped and stared at the fat little men until they noticed her and stopped fighting. Everyone was quiet for a while. Then Alice asked, "What were you fighting about?" But Tweedledum and Tweedledee just looked at each other and grinned.

With great politeness, Alice said, "Would you kindly tell me the best way to get from use cases to code? It's getting late, and soon everyone will want to start coding." But Tweedledum and Tweedledee started arguing and fighting again, and soon they were going round and round about nothing at all.

One of them cried out, "The *extending* use case overrides sections of the *extended* use case, so when the *extended* use case changes... all of the *extending* use cases can inherit the changes without modification!"

The other yelled, "*Extends* informs the developer that the integration between use cases is one to one, but *includes* informs the developer that integration is one to many !"

On and on they went, jumping and shouting and hitting each other, and ignoring poor Alice completely. After a time, she gave up, shook her head in puzzlement, and started down the path again to try to find out how to get from use cases to code.

We're Late! We Have to Start Coding!

Alice kept walking until suddenly a large white rabbit rushed past, stopped suddenly in front of her, turned in a circle three times, and shouted, "We're late! We're late! We have to start coding *immediately! The Duchess will be furious!*"

"Whatever are you doing?" Alice asked.

"*Iterating!*" The rabbit began to spin around again.

"Stop!" said Alice. "Doesn't all that iterating make you dizzy? And can you please tell me how to get from use cases to code?"

"Use cases?" shouted the rabbit. "There's no time for use cases, it's *late* and we have to start coding." And off he rushed.

"No use cases?" said Alice. "I wonder how they know what they're supposed to code, without any requirements about how the system is supposed to behave?"

She continued down the path, muttering, "Curiouser and curiouser..."

Alice Wonders How to Get from Use Cases to Code

"Oh, how I wish I could find a straightforward way to get from use cases to code," thought Alice, who didn't quite know what to make of the rabbit. "It all makes sense up through the analysis model, but it still seems quite a trick to turn behavioral requirements into software designs. It's all very well to identify some objects and identify some behavior, but how do you figure out which objects perform which bits of behavior? Maybe the answer is waiting down the path," she said to herself, hopefully.

Abstract... Essential

Alice kept walking down the path and soon came upon a Cheshire cat sitting in a tree.

"Excuse me," Alice said with a cough. "Can you tell me how to get from use cases to code?"

The cat grinned, and repeated the words, "Essential, abstract, technology-free, and implementation-independent..."

But as it did so, it began to fade slowly away.

A Little Too Abstract?

Alice watched the cat turn first translucent and then to barely an outline, until nothing was left but the grin. But the cat's mouth continued to repeat the words, "Essential, abstract, technology-free, and implementation-independent," even as it disappeared.

Alice was rather startled by the cat's disappearance. "I've seen a cat without a grin, but I've never seen a grin without a cat before," she said, shaking her head slowly. "But I can't possibly see how this is going to help me get from use cases to code. This is just so abstract that there doesn't seem to be enough detail there to build a design from."

She walked on.

Teleocentricity...

Alice soon came upon an enormous caterpillar, sitting on a giant mushroom, and smoking a hookah.

"Hello," said Alice to the caterpillar. "You look very wise indeed, sir. Do you think you could possibly help me find out how to get from use cases to code?"

"Who are you?" the caterpillar drawled sleepily. "And why do you want to get to code?"

"My name is Alice, thank you very much for asking, sir. And I want to get to code because if I don't, someone is likely to come along and cancel my project, and whatever will I do then, don't you see?"

"I do *not* see," said the caterpillar. "We define an essential use case as: a single, discrete, complete, meaningful, and well-defined task of interest to an external user in some specific role or roles in relationship to a system, comprising the user intentions and system responsibilities in the course of accomplishing that task, described in abstract, technology-free, implementation-independent terms using the language of the application domain and of external users in role." He inhaled an enormous quantity of smoke from the hookah.

After a time, he added, "We were not alone in recognizing the need for such a teleocentric, that is to say *purpose-centered*, approach to use-case modeling and for a move toward abstraction in use-case construction."

"Oh, but all these five-syllable words do make my head spin, I wish you could put it more clearly," said Alice.

The caterpillar just sat there, smoking, and after a time, Alice began to feel quite vexed.

"Shouldn't use cases be easy to understand?" she asked the caterpillar. "Doesn't it make more sense to just say 'the user does this and the system does that,' instead of rambling on about 'abstract, essential, teleocentricity' and so on? All these buzzwords make me feel very small, indeed."

"Keep your temper," said the caterpillar, "You'll get used to it, in time." He put the hookah back into his mouth and puffed away. Alice waited, not sure exactly what she should do. In a minute or two the caterpillar took the hookah out and yawned once or twice. He shook himself. Then he slid down off the mushroom and crawled away into the grass, remarking, as he went, "Taste the mushroom if you're feeling small."

Are We Really Supposed to Specify *All* This for *Every* Use Case?

Alice wondered whether it would be a very good idea to taste the mushroom as the caterpillar had suggested, but she was feeling quite small, and, as she thought about it, she realized that, not having eaten since breakfast, she was quite hungry indeed.

"I'll just try a small taste," she said, and broke off a piece. "Not bad at all," she said appreciatively. "In fact, it's really quite tasty."

After eating the mushroom, she continued down the path and soon saw a sign marked "This Way to the Template Forest." Not being sure which way to go, she walked in, and soon was surrounded by enormous signs with use-case templates written on them.

Alice stretched her neck trying to see to the top, and soon she found herself 10 feet tall! She began reading one of the templates.

Use Case Name, Actors, Priority, Status, Pre-Conditions, Flow of Events, Basic Path, Alternative Paths, Post-Conditions.....

"Goodness!" exclaimed Alice. "Are we really supposed to specify *all* this for *every* use case?" she asked, and continued reading.

"Oh, dear me!" said Alice. "Where will it ever end?"

Included Use Cases, Extended Use Cases,

"Oh *no*," groaned Alice. "Not *those* again!" and she kept going.

Generalized Use Cases, Activity Diagram, User Interface, Database Mapping, Scenarios, Sequence Diagrams…

"I'm afraid this is worse than my uncle's income tax forms," she said. "But I'm sure I heard him mention something about using a shorter form next year—maybe there should be a short-form for use cases, too."

Alice kept reading the gigantic use-case template.

Subordinate Use Cases, View of Participating Classes, Other Artifacts, <Anything else you might want to include. Possibly an analysis model, a design model, or test plans.>

"Well, I don't like *that* very much," said the wise little Alice. "Putting 'anything else you might want to include' into a use-case template seems like a sure guarantee of never getting to code," she said. "I wonder if this one is any better?" Looking at another template, she began to read.

CHARACTERISTIC INFORMATION, Goal in Context, Scope, Level, Success End Condition. Failed End Condition, Primary Actor Trigger, MAIN SUCCESS SCENARIO, EXTENSIONS, SUB-VARIATIONS, RELATED INFORMATION, Priority….

"Oh, dear me," said Alice. "Where will it ever end?" She continued on...

Performance Target, Frequency, Superordinate Use Case, Subordinate Use Cases, Channel to Primary Actor, Secondary Actors, Channel to Secondary Actors

"Channel to secondary actors?" said Alice, startled. "I can't even think what that might mean, much less specify it for all my use cases. I guess this is what they mean by analysis paralysis. Specifying lots of useless information without ever getting to code. I'd better keep looking," and down the path she went.

Part 2

OK, this brings us to the end of Part 1, and I hope I was able to shed some light on why use cases became popular, on just what it means to be use-case–driven, and on how some of the conventional wisdom about use cases is responsible for the all-too-common phenomenon of "thrashing" with use cases that we see across industry today.

In the next section of our talk, Alice meets up with some XtremelyCuriousCharacters, who, like Alice, are determined to avoid falling into analysis paralysis. But Alice finds that some of their methods and philosophies, which include (and I'm *not* making this stuff up, folks) oral documentation, code smells, "The code is the design" and so on, are just a little bit extreme... so let's rejoin her now as her journey through use-case land gets curiouser and curiouser.

Alice Gets Thirsty

Alice, who had been walking for some time now, had become quite thirsty. After she walked for a time, she came upon a little clearing, where she saw a table with a little bottle on it.

Around the neck of the bottle was tied a paper label with the words DRINK ME beautifully printed on it in large letters, along with the phrase "Guaranteed to avoid analysis paralysis," which was printed in smaller letters.

"It's all very well to say DRINK ME," she thought, "and I certainly would like to avoid analysis paralysis—my neck is still stiff from those giant templates." she said. But the wise little Alice was not going to just pick up a strange bottle and drink it in a hurry. "No, I'll look first," she said, "and see whether it's marked 'poison' or not."

However, this bottle was not marked "poison," so Alice ventured to taste it, and finding it very nice, she soon finished it off.

"It's all very well to say DRINK ME," she thought,
"and I certainly would like to avoid analysis paralysis..."

Alice Feels Faint

Alice became very dizzy, and started to see many swirling colors. "What a queer feeling!" she said. "I wonder if that was such a good idea. Perhaps I'd better sit down for a while," she said. As she sat, she heard someone singing a curious song, and didn't quite know what to make of it.....

Imagine... (with Apologies to John Lennon)

Imagine there's no requirements. It's easy if you try
Just a bunch of coders, reachin' for the sky
Imagine all the people, coding for today

Imagine there's no schedules. It isn't hard to do
No silly project deadlines, no one supervising you
Imagine all the people, coding hand in hand

You may say I'm an extremer but I'm not the only one
I hope someday you'll join us and make coding lots more fun.

Imagine oral documentation. I wonder if you can
No need for UML diagrams. Just words passed, man to man
Imagine just refactoring, playing in the sand

You may say I'm an extremer, but I'm not the only one
I hope someday you'll join us and make coding lots more fun.[1]

---

[1] You can find more "Songs of the Extremos" on the web at
www.SoftwareReality.com/lifecycle/xp/extremers.jsp.

Alice got up, rubbed her eyes, and shook her head vigorously. "I do wonder what can have happened to me," she said. "I knew something interesting was sure to happen. It does anytime I eat or drink something around here. But it was much pleasanter at home, really, when everything wasn't upside down all the time. Perhaps I'd better try to find my way back."

Pair Programming Means Never Writing Down Requirements

Alice, still somewhat dizzy, walked unsteadily down the path until she came to a clearing, where she saw a bunch of programmers, coding in pairs, and singing softly while they worked. An atmosphere of peace and tranquility prevailed in the clearing.

Alice paused near a sign that said, "The concept of schedule depends on the notion of done-ness, and since software is never done, it's all about developing at a constant velocity." Another sign nearby read, "Written requirements are for cowards—don't be afraid of oral documentation."

"You might as well say 'I code what I want' is the same as 'They want what I code'."

"Goodness," said Alice. "I never felt afraid when I was writing those requirements down… I was just trying to make sure I understood what the client wanted. All these people seem so happy and sure of what they're doing, programming in pairs and all. But I wonder if they're not blinded by their own faith? Without requirements, how can they be sure they're building the right system? Why, you might as well say 'I code what I want' is the same as 'They want what I code.'"

And Alice, who was feeling a bit stronger by this time, continued down the path.

There's No *Time* to Write Down Requirements

Suddenly the white rabbit, whom Alice had encountered earlier, dashed up, and began shouting at her, "There's no *time* to write down *requirements*," iterating furiously. "And what's more, users never know what they want!" he added, continuing to spin around.

"Just have them tell you a story, and *code it*," he said. "They change their minds several times each morning anyway—the only way to keep up is to refactor the code faster than they can change their mind. Why, we can go through five iterations in the time it takes a typical user to change his mind, you see if we can't!" he said.

"Refactoring?" asked Alice. "I think I've heard of that, somewhere."

"It's the latest thing," said the rabbit. "Everybody's doing it! Design's dead, you know. With enough refactoring, you don't need design. The design figures itself out from the code. Ask the Hatter!" And off he rushed again.

You Might As Well Say, "The Code Is the Design"

Alice, not knowing what else to do, and feeling somewhat shaky again after hearing about designs figuring themselves out from code, decided to follow the rabbit for a while. On they went, the rabbit pausing every few feet to iterate around in a circle a few times. Eventually the rabbit, rushing ahead at top speed, pulled far enough ahead that Alice couldn't see him anymore.

Alice kept walking, and after a time she came to a clearing where she saw the rabbit, along with a large mouse and a little man wearing a big hat, all working furiously over a table and some chairs. When Alice walked up, all the legs from the table and chairs were sitting in a big pile on the ground. Alice watched as the Hatter, the rabbit, and the dormouse each grabbed four legs from the pile and screwed them into a chair. The problem was that the legs were of different lengths, and Alice watched in fascination as they each finished assembling their chair, turned it over, and sat down. The chairs often tipped over, what with the legs being of different lengths and all, and when this happened they all yelled out, in unison, "Failed the unit test," flipped the chairs back over, and began unscrewing the legs and tossing them back onto the pile.

"How can designs figure themselves
out from code?" asked Alice.

"What kind of game are you playing?" asked Alice.

"It's not a game, we're refactoring the furniture," replied the Hatter.

"Why don't you read the documentation for assembling the chairs?" asked Alice. "It's sure to specify which legs should go on which chairs."

"It's oral documentation," said the Hatter.

"Oh. You mean you don't have any."

"No. Written documentation is for cowards! We can refactor very quickly, so we can be brave enough to let the design figure itself out."

"Oh, yes. The rabbit said I should ask you about that," said Alice. "How can designs figure themselves out from code?"

"You poor, ignorant child," said the Hatter, in quite a condescending tone. "The code IS the design, don't you see? Perhaps you'd better let the Duchess explain it to you." He resumed refactoring the chairs.

Who Cares for Use Cases?

Alice remembered some reading she had done as she continued to walk down the path.

"I remember reading about refactoring, pair programming, and oral documentation on the Internet," she said to herself as she walked. "What was that web site again—oh, yes, it was called the Wiki Web. I remember reading about some kind of payroll project. It was called C3 or something like that, I think… but… didn't that project get cancelled? It seems like they did an awful lot of bragging about it, considering that it wasn't really that much of a success." [2]

By this time Alice had come suddenly upon an open place with a little house in the middle of it. She walked timidly up to the door, and knocked, but no one answered. She could hear a most extraordinary noise going on within—a constant howling and sneezing, and every now and then a great crash, as if a dish or kettle had been broken to pieces.

"Well, there's no use in waiting out here," said Alice, and she opened the door and went in.

The door led right into a large kitchen, which was full of smoke from one end to the other. The Duchess was sitting on a three-legged stool in the middle, nursing a baby. The cook was leaning over the fire, stirring a large cauldron, which seemed to be full of soup.

"There's certainly too much pepper in that soup!" Alice said to herself, as well as she could for sneezing.

The Duchess looked at Alice and said, "Can you smell the code?"

"Code?" said Alice. "I thought it was soup."

"That," said the Duchess, "is a code smell, and our Goal Donor over there is refactoring the code so it smells better."

"What is your code supposed to do?" asked Alice. "Do you have any requirements, or use cases?"

"Who cares for use cases? We don't *like* written requirements," said the Duchess. "We keep a customer in the room with us, and make him code up acceptance tests. We call him the Goal Donor. That way, we're free to add whatever features we want without any interference from those jerks over in marketing. *They* don't know anything anyway," she sneered.

Alice remembered reading about Goal Donors on the Wiki Web site, where there was some kind of disagreement between them and management, who were referred to as Gold Owners.

"But, what if the Goal Donor and the Gold Owner disagree?" she asked the Duchess. "The Gold Owner might inexplicably cancel the project. And anyway, if customers could code acceptance tests, why would they need programmers?" she added, quite perplexed.

C3 Project Terminated

The Duchess became very angry with Alice. "How *dare* you talk such nonsense!" she stormed.

But Alice did not back down. She had remembered that she was carrying her new Palm Pilot, which had wireless Internet access, and that she had bookmarked a page on the Wiki Web site.

---

[2] Don't take Alice's word for it! Read it yourself at http://c2.com/cgi/wiki?CthreeProjectTerminated.

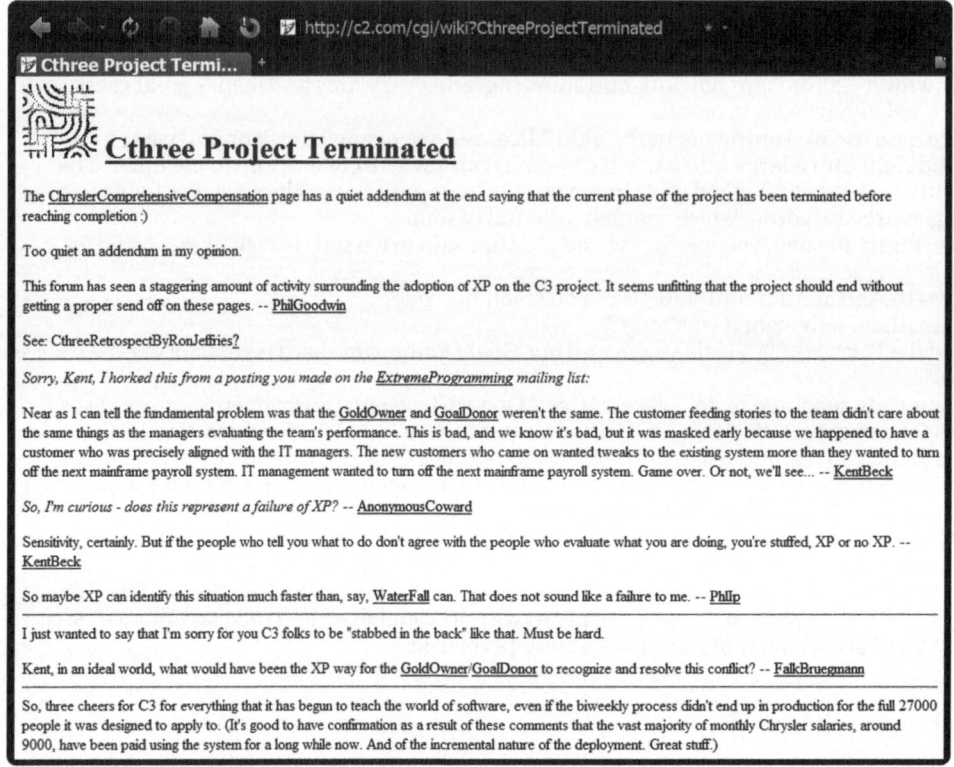

Cthree Project Terminated

The ChryslerComprehensiveCompensation page has a quiet addendum at the end saying that the current phase of the project has been terminated before reaching completion :)

Too quiet an addendum in my opinion.

This forum has seen a staggering amount of activity surrounding the adoption of XP on the C3 project. It seems unfitting that the project should end without getting a proper send off on these pages. -- PhilGoodwin

See: CthreeRetrospectByRonJeffries?

Sorry, Kent, I horked this from a posting you made on the ExtremeProgramming mailing list:

Near as I can tell the fundamental problem was that the GoldOwner and GoalDonor weren't the same. The customer feeding stories to the team didn't care about the same things as the managers evaluating the team's performance. This is bad, and we know it's bad, but it was masked early because we happened to have a customer who was precisely aligned with the IT managers. The new customers who came on wanted tweaks to the existing system more than they wanted to turn off the next mainframe payroll system. IT management wanted to turn off the next mainframe payroll system. Game over. Or not, we'll see... -- KentBeck

So, I'm curious - does this represent a failure of XP? -- AnonymousCoward

Sensitivity, certainly. But if the people who tell you what to do don't agree with the people who evaluate what you are doing, you're stuffed, XP or no XP. -- KentBeck

So maybe XP can identify this situation much faster than, say, WaterFall can. That does not sound like a failure to me. -- PhiIp

I just wanted to say that I'm sorry for you C3 folks to be "stabbed in the back" like that. Must be hard.

Kent, in an ideal world, what would have been the XP way for the GoldOwner/GoalDonor to recognize and resolve this conflict? -- FalkBruegmann

So, three cheers for C3 for everything that it has begun to teach the world of software, even if the biweekly process didn't end up in production for the full 27000 people it was designed to apply to. (It's good to have confirmation as a result of these comments that the vast majority of monthly Chrysler salaries, around 9000, have been paid using the system for a long while now. And of the incremental nature of the deployment. Great stuff.)

What Alice saw on her Palm Pilot . . .

"It's not nonsense," she protested. "Look at what it says, right here, on this web page called C3ProjectTerminated. It says that the Goal Donor didn't want the same thing as the Gold Owners. That the programmers kept adding features to the code, while management wanted to turn off the mainframe computers because C3 was a Y2K replacement project. Why, that's nothing but good, old-fashioned featuritis, and quite a nasty case of it, too. What would have happened, do you think, if the mainframe payroll programs had actually broken in January 2000?"

The Duchess was livid. "You _fool_," she howled. "You just don't get it, do you? How much code have _you_ written recently?"

But the plucky little Alice still refused to back down. "Featuritis," she said calmly, "is why it's important to write down requirements. So the programmers don't build lots of cool stuff that's not what the client is paying for."

"_Get out!_" screamed the Duchess. "You'll have to answer to the Queen!"

OnceAndOnlyOnce?

Alice was not quite ready to leave, however, and by this time she was feeling seriously annoyed by the Duchess's belligerent attitude. She continued scrolling down the web page on her Palm Pilot.

"It's a pity," said Alice, "that you didn't base all of your lofty claims on a project that was actually a success. It says here that this C3 project was a Y2K replacement project started in 1996. It was terminated in February 2000 when it was still only paying 1/3 of the people that it was originally intended to pay. And look what it says over here… not only will the client never try this approach again, but it even made the term object-oriented 'unutterable by anyone wishing management to take them seriously…' Keep in mind," Alice continued, "this Wiki Web site isn't *my* web site, it's *yours*! This reminds me of that story about the emperor who had no clothes on. Don't you have any other large project success stories to brag about?"

The Duchess was speechless. "Get out!" she sputtered. "The Queen will have your head." This piece of rudeness was more than Alice could bear. She turned, in great disgust, and walked off.

Alice Refuses to Start Coding Without Written Requirements

Alice continued walking for a time, and was just in the midst of wondering whether she could use her Palm Pilot to get a map home from wherever this curious place she was lost in was, when two soldiers, who looked strangely like index cards, approached her. "Excuse me, Miss," said the first soldier, "but the Queen of Hearts demands to see how much code you have written."

Alice, who was still quite vexed after her unpleasant encounter with the Duchess, replied, "Please tell Her Majesty that nobody has given me any requirements yet, so I don't have any code."

The two soldiers looked at each other. "No code," said the first, shaking his head. "The Queen's not going to like that."

"No," said the second. "It will be a beheading for sure," he said under his breath to the first soldier, so that Alice couldn't hear him. Out loud, he said, "You'd better come with us, Miss!"

Alice, who, after all, had nowhere else to go, followed the soldiers until they came to a big lawn, where people were playing croquet. Alice could see a castle off in the distance. There was a sound of trumpets, whereupon the two soldiers exclaimed, "The Queen, The Queen!" and immediately threw themselves face down on the ground.

Alice looked up, and there stood the Queen in front of her, with her arms folded, frowning like a thunderstorm.

"Well?" said the Queen to Alice. "Where is it? Where's the code?"

"May it please Your Majesty," said Alice, in a very humble tone, going down on one knee as she spoke, "I haven't written any code yet, because nobody has told me what the requirements are."

"I'm NOT going to start coding without requirements!" said Alice.

The Queen turned crimson with fury, and after glaring at her for a moment like a wild beast, began screaming, "Off with her head! Off with—"

"Nonsense," said Alice, very loudly and decidedly, and the Queen went silent.

The King laid his hand upon her arm, and timidly said, "Consider, my dear, she is only a child!"

The Queen turned angrily away from him, and said to Alice, "I demand you start coding this minute."

"I won't do it!" said Alice, surprised by her own courage. "There's no accountability without written requirements, and my project will get a bad case of feature-itis. I'm *not* going to start coding without requirements."

The Queen began to shout again, but the King spoke first. "Before we can behead the child, we'll have to have a trial." And then in a louder voice, he proclaimed, "Trial of Alice to commence immediately!"

With that, the soldiers, who had gotten up off the ground, grabbed Alice by the arms and the whole procession marched off to the courtroom.

You Are Guilty of BDUF...

The King and Queen were seated on their thrones, with a great crowd assembled about them. Near the King was the white rabbit, with a trumpet in one hand, and a scroll of parchment in the other. In the very middle of the court was a table, with a large dish of cookies on it: they looked so good that it made Alice quite hungry to look at them.

"I wish they'd get the trial done," she thought, "and hand round the refreshments." But there seemed to be no chance of this; so she began looking at everything around her to pass away the time.

Alice had never been in a court of justice before, but had read about them in books. She was pleased to find that she knew the name of nearly everything there. "That's the judge," she said to herself, "because of his great wig." The judge, by the way, was the King; as he wore his crown over the wig, he did not look at all comfortable, and it was certainly not becoming.

"Herald, read the accusation!" said the King.

On this, the white rabbit blew three blasts on the trumpet, unrolled the parchment scroll, and read as follows:

> *The child named Alice we do confront*
> *In these proceedings today*
> *For insisting on Big Design Up Front*
> *And not coding right away.*

"Consider your verdict," the King said to the jury.

"Not yet, not yet!" the rabbit hastily interrupted. "There's a great deal to come before that!"

"Call the first witness," said the King; the white rabbit blew three blasts on the trumpet, and called out, "First witness!"

Alice took the stand, nervously.

"Give your evidence," said the King.

"Beg pardon, Your Majesty, but I just wanted to write the requirements down before I started coding," said Alice, "because, I think I should understand them better, you see, if I have them written down, and I can't always follow them as they're spoken."

"Requirements," said the King, "are *not* one of the four important things about software. Those are coding, testing, listening, and design. That's all there is to software. Anyone who tells you something different is selling something. Designs are only to be recorded on index cards, and these are to be immediately thrown away as they'll be obsolete when the architecture changes in the morning."

"Let the jury consider their verdict," the King said, for about the twentieth time that day.

"No, no!" said the Queen. "Sentence first—verdict afterwards."

"Stuff and nonsense!" said Alice loudly. "The idea of having the sentence first!"

"Hold your tongue!" said the Queen, turning purple.

"I won't," said Alice.

"Off with her head!" shouted the Queen, at the top of her voice.

CMM's Dead! Off with Her Head!

The crowd immediately began chanting: "Enough of BDUF... CMM's dead... Off with her head... Off with her head!" Alice was surrounded by dozens of index-card soldiers, all beating drums.

Alice, who had heard of the Capabilities Maturity Model, but was not personally involved in any effort to reach CMM Level 5—she just wanted a simple and straightforward approach that involved a reasonable amount of forethought and provided a reasonable amount of documentation—didn't understand all the drum-beating about CMM.

"What's so bad about trying to find a repeatable development process?" she wondered.

All the drum beating and chanting scared little Alice quite badly. She was sure that she would be executed soon, although she didn't understand why. She covered her ears and cowered in fear.

Some Serious Refactoring of the Design

As the pack of soldiers descended upon Alice, she gave a little scream, half of fright and half of anger, and tried to beat them off.

"Who cares for you?" shouted Alice. "You're nothing but a pack of cards!"

Suddenly a big gust of wind blew up, refactoring the entire stack of cards, and the design that was scribbled upon them. Alice woke up and found herself back in the big chair in her living room. The window was open, and a strong breeze had sprung up.

"Oh, I've had such a curious dream!" she said. "I'm not sure which was worse—getting stuck in analysis paralysis, or jumping straight to code without understanding the requirements. How I do wish there was some straightforward approach that was somewhere in between."

Part 3

Alice picked up another book, this one much thinner than the first, that claimed to talk about use-case–driven object modeling, for the first book had convinced her that use cases were a good idea.

"Thinner books," she remarked, "are much more appealing than the big fat ones."

"Thinner books," she remarked, "are much more appealing than the big fat ones. Goodness knows I don't want to fall asleep and have another dream like that again. Who knows what I'd dream up next time, probably 'just-in-time-architecture' or something."

Alice Wakes Up

"Hmm," said Alice. "It says on the back cover that this book has analysis paralysis alerts to help steer clear of common modeling pitfalls, and also an extensive discussion of requirements and how to design in a traceable manner. And look, it doesn't try to teach everything in the UML User Guide, but focuses on a minimal subset of diagrams. Look, there are only four different kinds of diagrams in the core subset that they use… I guess this is what they were talking about in the UML User Guide where they said you can do 80% of your modeling with 20% of the UML." She glanced upwards and mused, "Only this book actually tells you which 20% that is."[3]

Closing the Gap Between "What" and "How"

"Aha," said Alice. "It's that missing link diagram again. Now I can see how important it is. Getting from *what* to *how* seems to be one of the most difficult things to do in software development. That caterpillar and the Cheshire cat never got past talking about what the system was supposed to do, and the rabbit, Hatter, and that horrible duchess and queen couldn't think of anything except code… although it was pretty funny how afraid they all were of written requirements, wasn't it? I think they just didn't want anybody telling them anything, so they could build whatever they wanted," said the wise little Alice.

Static and Dynamic Models Are Linked Together

"It's really quite fascinating," said Alice, "how many things go on during preliminary design. Both the use-case model and the object model get updated during robustness analysis. The use-case text is made less ambiguous and more precise, at the same time as new objects are discovered. The static and dynamic parts of the model are linked together, and forced to be consistent with one another, and the behavior descriptions are double-checked, to make sure they're correct, they're complete, and they're feasible to build. What an incredibly useful little technique!" exclaimed Alice. "It sure beats trying to jump from requirement-level use-case descriptions to design-level sequence diagrams," she added.

Behavior Allocation Happens on Sequence Diagrams

"And this looks like the big payoff," said Alice. "A straightforward process for building sequence diagrams where the first three steps can be automated in a script, and the fourth step is simply to focus in on making behavior allocation decisions. Why, this takes a lot of the mystery out of object-oriented design."

"There's certainly no analysis paralysis here," Alice observed. "Everything starts with the use cases; there's a requirements review with the client, then the behavior descriptions get refined during preliminary design, and there's a preliminary design review, which the clients can also attend. After that comes the detailed design, and then there's a critical design review, but the clients don't go to that one—it's just an internal review by the development team. And the quality assurance folks test what the developers built against the use-case text.

"So, it's 'here's what we think you want, please correct us if we're wrong.' Then, after those corrections, it's 'OK, we made the changes you suggested, and added a bunch more detail, please tell us

---

[3] See www.iconixsw.com/UMLbook.html.

if we got it right.' And then, after that, it's 'we're going to go ahead and build what you told us you wanted now, then you can verify that we built what we all agreed on.' And you can do it for whatever size of iteration you choose, just for those use cases that you're planning to implement.

"It works for both small projects and large ones, and for large and small chunks of functionality within an iteration. There's no confusion about the requirements because everything is written down, and the design traces directly back to the behavior requirements, which can then be used to generate acceptance test plans.

"What a relief to find a simple and straightforward process that is both minimal and sufficient," said Alice. "Avoiding analysis paralysis without skipping analysis is possible after all. You can learn a lot in dreams, sometimes," she reflected thoughtfully. "Now if only someone would build a plug-in to RUP that would let my entire project follow this process..." Alice mused.

And the Moral of That Is...

"I quite agree with you," said the Duchess. "And the moral of that is, 'Be what you would seem to be'— or, if you'd like it put more simply, 'Never imagine yourself not to be otherwise than what it might appear to others that what you were or might have been was not otherwise than what you had been would have appeared to them to be otherwise.'"

"I think I should understand that better," Alice said very politely, "if I had it written down; but I can't quite follow it as you say it."

"That's nothing to what I could say if I chose," the Duchess replied, in a pleased tone.

"Pray don't trouble yourself to say it any longer than that," said Alice.

'Twas Brillig and the Slithy Tests...

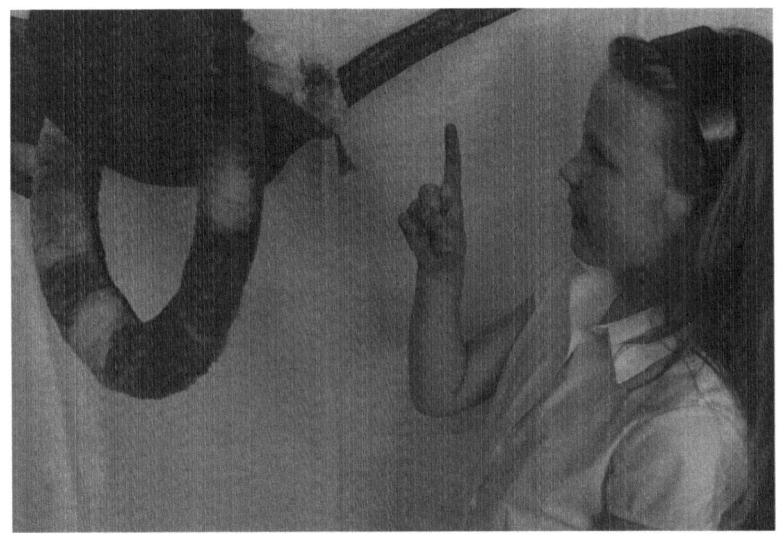

Suddenly Alice, who was puzzling over the meaning of strange words like "YAGNI" and "refactoring", and trying very hard to imagine what a wooden timebox might look like, found herself on the edge of a very slippery slope, and completely lost her footing. And before she knew it she had slid halfway down the hill! When she sat up, she found herself face to face with a large (but rather cute and friendly looking) snake.

"Have a nice trip?" said Fangs. "The footing is sometimes a bit manxome around here, especially around brillig when the ssssun gets in your eyes. But I'm frabjously glad that you seem to be uninjured." he said. "Perhapsss you should consssider increasing your coefficient of agility.", he mused, darting out his bifurcated tongue.

"You seem very clever at using words, Sir" said Alice. "Would you tell me the meaning of the poem called 'Beware the Agile Hype'?"

"Let'sss hear it", said Fangs. "I can explain all the agile poemsss that ever were invented -- and a good many that haven't been invented jussst yet."

This sounded very hopeful, so Alice repeated the first verse:

T'was brillig when the YAGNI'd code
did build itself ten times a day.
All flimsy were the index cards,
designs refactored clear away.

"That'sss enough to begin with," Fangs interrupted. "There are plenty of hard words there. Brillig means four o clock in the afternoon -- the time you begin broiling things for dinner."

"That'll do very well," said Alice. "And YAGNI? What's YAGNI'd code?"

"You Aren't Going To Need It", said Fangs.

"How do I know I won't need it if I don't know what it is?"

Fangs screwed his eyes shut. "No… YAGNI! YAGNI! YAGNI!"

"What are you doing?" Alice asked, concerned. "Are you quite alright?"

"Oh, it'sss perfectly okay," the slippery-slope serpent replied, opening his eyes to narrow slits. "You sssee, YAGNI is what I repeat when I want to avoid thinking."

"You mean YAGNI is an excuse for developers not to think?" asked Alice, surprised by her own insight.

"I shouldn't have thought to sssay it like that," he said, giving her a venomous look.

"And what about code building itself ten times a day? Whyever should it want to do such a thing?"

"You can't do consssstant rrrefactoring without an automated build processsss," the snake hissed, getting into its (legs-free) stride.

Alice remembered that refactoring means to rewrite code that's already finished. "So the code has to rebuild itself in order to be rewritten?"

"How else could the code be rewritten, if not rebuilt after refactoring?"

"I see," said Alice, not wanting to be rude - though she really didn't see. "And anyway, wouldn't all that rewriting of finished code introduce vexatious problems?"

"We guard againsst vexatiousss problemsss with regressssion testsss," the snake hissed, its tongue tying into a knot of circular logic.

"So for every line of code you rewrite, you have to write a test?" asked Alice, who thought the idea more absurd than the idea of unemployment checks creating jobs.[1] "But surely the code actually does things? How can you keep re-running the tests without breaking something?"

"For continuousss tesssting we have mock objectsss. They keep the code from actually doing anything usssseful. And of course you can't tell the mock objectsss without an index card."

"Wouldn't that require a mock index card?" Alice retorted. "And how does that work, anyway?"

"I can't go into detail now, but I promise to tell you later."

"What do you mean?" asked Alice, whose brain was beginning to hurt.

"Now it's later so I can tell you. You write a ssstory on an index card, but unlike a real story it has no details. It isss just a promise for a future conversssation with the cussstomer."

"But what if the customer isn't around then? Why not write down the details while he's there?"

The serpent shook its head. "You poor, ignorant child, that would involve asking the customer to make up his mind, and we cannot demand such commitmentsss from our cussstomersss, or we would be deemed impertinent. Not only that but if the cussstomer made up his mind then the project might

---

[1] Special thanks to House Speaker Nancy Pelosi for providing us with a notion just as ridiculous as the idea of writing a test for every line of code so that you can rewrite the code (and rewrite each test, of course): www.foxnews.com/politics/2010/07/01/pelosi-unemployment-checks-best-way-create-jobs

actually get done, and we can't be having that, can we? Don't you know that software is never done? Otherwise, we would all be out of work!"

On and on hissed the snake (who had by now contorted his python-like form into a complete circle), explaining the circular "agile hype" logic to the little girl. Alice's attention wandered a bit during the explanation of snack food as a development methodology, and she noticed that a large unit test tree stood a short distance away from where she sat with the circular logic snake. The tree was covered with red unit tests.

As she looked, she noticed that a pair of programmers were working at it, busily painting the tests green, then cutting them from the tree and carrying them over to a large pile, which steadily grew towards the sky. The tree seemed to re-grow new red unit tests almost instantly, budding out from a single line of code. Alice thought this a very curious thing, and began to watch them as Fangs continued with his circular story.

After a time, she heard one of them say "Look out now, JoJo! Don't go splashing paint all over me like that."

"Sorry," said JoJo to Loretta.[2] "You keep bumping my elbow while I'm trying to code. We really need a two-keyboard workstation. But then who would drive and who would snooze?"

"That's right, JoJo. Always lay the blame on others!"

---

[2] For more on the adventures of JoJo, Loretta, Fangs, Uncle Joe and his regression testing gulag "Camp Regretestskiy", we heartily recommend *Extreme Programming Refactored: The Case Against XP.*

"You'd better not talk at the stand-up meeting!" said JoJo. "I heard Uncle Joe say yesterday that you deserved to go to the regression testing gulag, for not beheading the tests before running them on a headless server."

"Why are those index cards" (for that's what the pair of programmers looked like) "painting those red unit tests green?" asked Alice.

"Yessss," said Fangs. "It's the sssimplest thing that can posssibly work. We paintssss them green, we does, with mock objectsss. We just asssssssert that everything's perfectly preciousss."

Alice, who was by now beginning to become very angry indeed, replied; "Why that's the most mind numbingly stupid idea I've ever heard. How are your regression tests going to help you avoid vexatious problems if you just paint the red tests green?"

"Painting the regresssion testsss green helps us avoid vexatiousss problemsss with managementss", replied the snake. "Since they don't really know what'sss going on anyhow, it's easy to convince them that all of our code is working by showing them the pretty green testsss. When the pile of green testsss reaches the sssky, it takes us to Sssshangri-La, where we can reach tesssting nirvana. Care for a bisscuit?"[3]

Just then, the rabbit sprinted past, wearing a tracksuit, and carrying a wooden box under his arm. "We're late, we're late" shouted the rabbit, "my timebox just went off! That's the end of the sprint!" He slowed his velocity enough to iterate in a circle, then opened the box, rummaged around and finally checked his watch as he shouted "So many tests, so little time, it will be a beheading for sure if the Queen finds out. Better start cloning mock objects. Oh dear, oh, dear."

"So that's what they call a timebox?" asked Alice.

"Sssshhhhh" said Fangs. "Not while he's gyrating. Anyhow cussstomers aren't allowed to ssspeak in ssstandup meetingsss, and you are quite unsssureptitiousssly ssstanding."

But before Alice could answer him, the Agility drum-beating began. The noise, like a raging torrent of hype, came from all directions. The air seemed full of it, and it rang through and through her head, louder even than an XP development shop, till she felt quite deafened.

From beyond the clearing a full pack of index-card soldiers ran through the trees towards them, their paper drums pounding as they chanted: "Smell the code! Smell the code!" The rabbit let out a frightened squeak and pitter-pattered from the clearing, muttering "Mary-Ann! Mary-Ann! Time to find a new customer, the burndown chart's gone through the roof and the house is burning down!" as the soldiers gave chase with a great clattering and drumming.

"If that doesn't drum them out of town," Alice thought to herself, "nothing ever will!"

---

[3] See "Green Bar of Shangri-La": www.theregister.co.uk/2007/04/25/unit_test_code_coverage

Index